Recreating Amsterdam

Recreating Amsterdam

Fred Feddes (essay)
Sonia Mangiapane (photography)

Architectura & Natura

Contents

- 6 **Images of urban decay**
- 25 **Stadsherstel: restoring order in the city**
  Fred Feddes
- 65 **Landscape**
- 129 Romantic city portrait
- 137 **Churches**
- 233 Windows and doors
- 241 **Living**
- 337 Stairs and winding staircase
- 345 **Interior**
  Sonia Mangiapane
- 417 Gables
- 425 **Relocation**
- 481 Colour
- 489 **Industrial**
- 561 New gable stones
- 569 **Abroad**

Images of urban decay

An awareness of the history of the city's decay will go a long way to understanding Stadsherstel's true value. Take one location as an example, the corner of Vijzelgracht and Prinsengracht.
In 1918 there was a billiards café here; next to it you can make out a cigar shop and a perfumery, and a lamppost with no lamp. Twenty years later, in 1938, the corner building's characteristic gable was torn down and replaced by a provisional roof. The café made way for a cobbler called De Adelaar, while the perfumery became an ice cream parlour.
Shortly thereafter, the three buildings were decapitated, which can be seen in a photo from 1942. The upper stories were in such disrepair that they had to be torn down, but the owners could not afford to rebuild them. And, as the Algemeen Dagblad wrote on 9 March 1940: 'Given the times we are living in, the sale of this land would represent a major financial setback, even more so as the municipality cannot lend a helping hand.' The city council therefore gave permission for the lower stories to be left standing for the time being. 'This meant that three respectable businesses could continue to exist, so that the owners of the buildings could at least generate some kind of income. Until the day comes when the land can be sold for a good price again, we will continue to enjoy the curiosity of three half-houses on the old canal corner!'

After the war, the corner building was given a fresh coat of paint, but it had to be shored up to stay upright. The cars parked next to the sidewalk and the new shops, including one for model trains, shows that the country was on the mend. The Netherlands finally has money and time for hobbies.
In the 1960s, there was an increasingly stark contrast between the run-down city corner and the prosperous society, which, as the advertising posters reveal, was unfolding elsewhere. In 1962, the corner building was demolished, and the other two buildings followed suit in 1965. As a result, there was plenty more space for hoarding to advertise camping holidays, vacuum cleaners, James Bond films and other pleasures of life.
The corner seems to come to life again in 1967: we see signs and vans from construction companies, a temporary pharmacy. What is in the making here? Plans for new buildings were already on the drawing board then, with tidy redevelopment flats and a photo shop on the ground floor. They were never built.
Then, in 1969, half a century after the first photo, Stadsherstel's construction sign appeared bearing the slogan: 'Stadsherstel is restoring the city here too.'
Two years later, in 1971, the new version of the old building was completed. Cleanly designed and sturdier than before, it had more storeys than previously, but it had also regained its air of inevitability.

1918

1938

Dames
85
35
70

1.15
50
90

1942

BROCHES

AUTOMATIEK

BUFFET

1950

MEUBELEN · JOH. BLOM

BRANDKASTEN SPECIALIST
SLEUTELKLUIS

1962

joh. blom SINDS 1870

meubelen

VIJZELGRACHT, 7

BRANDKAST SPECIALIST
DE "SLEUTELHUIS"

MEUBELEN

1965

blom
meubelen
toonkamers
TUSCHINSKI
AMES BOND OPNIEUW IN ACTIE!
U KLAAR MET HET
ook voor
rmuizen
MIXERS
KOFFIEMOLENS
VENTILATORKACHELS
VLOERWRIJVERS
CENTRIFUGES
WASAUTOMATEN

1967

London House
KENTGRAN TRADING CO. LTD LONDON
H.R. SHALSON ASSOCIATES LONDON
SCHERPENHUYSEN
PURMEREND
HOUT en
STAALBOUW
Elisabeth
BAS
10 Basjes 1.10

1969

STADSHERSTEL
RESTAUREERT OOK HIER DE STAD
G.PRINS ARCHITEKT h.b.o
Verwacht in PARISIËN
RADIO

1971

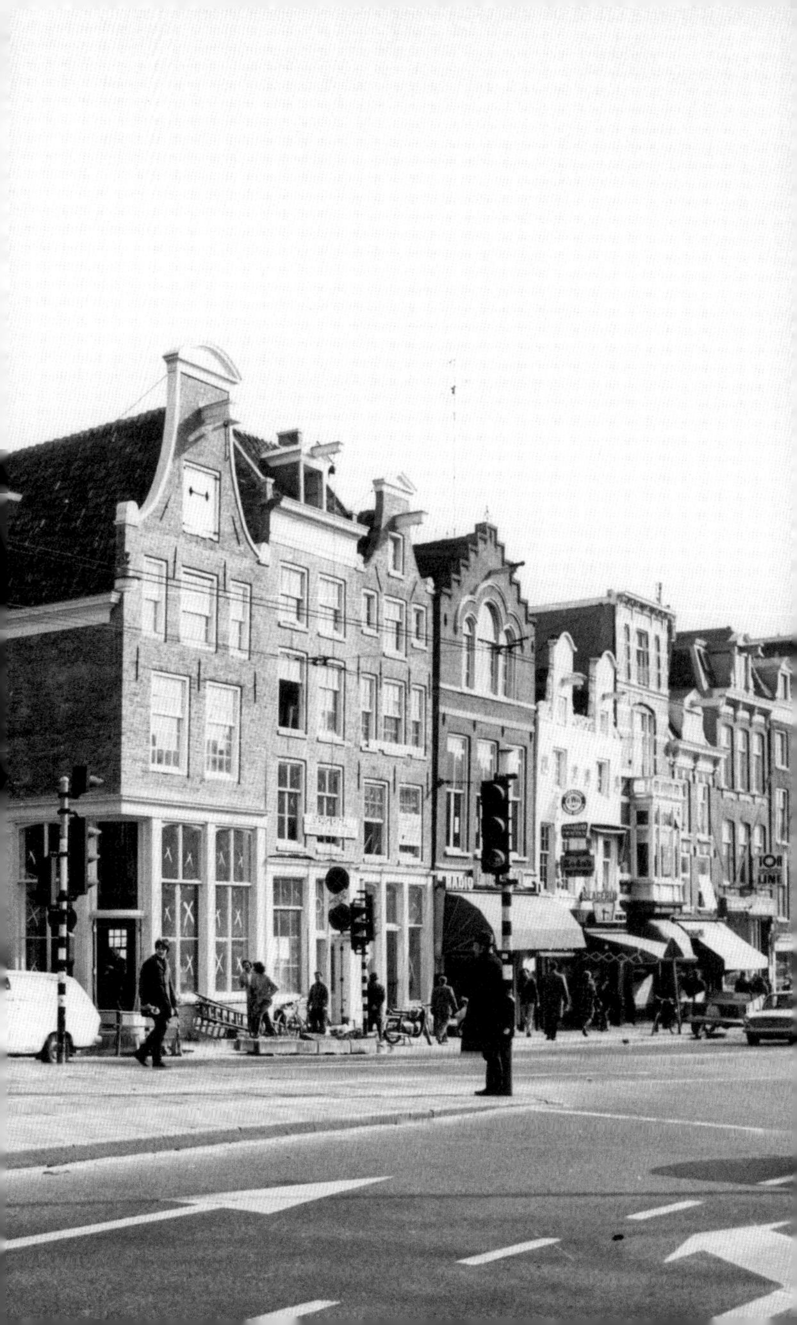

Stadsherstel: restoring order in the city

Fred Feddes

Stadsherstel: restoring order in the city

The Amsterdamse Maatschappij tot Stadsherstel – the 'society for city restoration' – was founded on 30 August 1956 as a calm in the storm during a tumultuous period for the Amsterdam city centre, meant to focus on urban recovery in a manner that was both practical and idealistic.

Two years earlier, the journalist Fred Thomas had written that war was in the air, a war for the future of Amsterdam's city centre. In March 1954 he interviewed the directors of the Department of Public Works and the Building and Housing Inspection Authority, who formed, together with their colleague from Urban Development, the 'triumvirate', 'which many believed was the most powerful *and* dangerous institution in Amsterdam'. They were non-committal about their plans for the old city centre, but according to Thomas the conversation could 'certainly be viewed as a skirmish, one of the armed reconnaissance missions that are going on right now in anticipation of the impending struggle, the major battle for Amsterdam's city centre'. He went on to add that 'both parties are on high alert. They have assumed and consolidated their positions and are devising their tactics'.[1]

Indeed, the 'battle for Amsterdam' did break out in the ensuing years, and it lasted a long time. But, much like when there is a real threat of war, there was diplomacy behind the scenes too: cautious strategic discussions that introduced new ideas, in an attempt to make diverging interests converge in a more peaceful manner. The result of these diplomatic efforts was Stadsherstel, the 'company for city restoration'.

---

1 *De Tijd*, 20.03.1954
2 Ida Jager, *Hoofdstad in gebreke*, Rotterdam 2002, p. 23

Century-old problems

There was a great deal at stake in the battle for the city centre anticipated by Fred Thomas. Amsterdam had a powerful and assertive planning machine, specialised in urban expansion. Many inhabitants of Amsterdam, along with Fred Thomas, were even frightened of this machine's power and 'mysterious elusiveness', especially now that the focus had shifted to the old city centre, which was dilapidated and in dire need of revival. The city centre was plagued by an accumulation of problems, many of which had dragged on for as long as a century. Twenty years of neglect through times of crisis, war and post-war stagnation had exacerbated matters. Considering the Public Works Department's power, perhaps now it would finally be possible to rigorously tackle these questions. That is why the stakes were high.

At the bottom of the pile of problems, still there, was an inheritance from the nineteenth century. Amsterdam was neglected and impoverished around 1850. Everything suffered from a lack of maintenance: the canals, the quays, the streets, the buildings, the ports and the utilities, not to mention the economy, the elite and the city council. A contemporary commentator colourfully described Amsterdam as on the verge of 'falling ever deeper into a pool of humiliation and decay, and before long will sink in it altogether'.[2]

There certainly were efforts to restore and modernise the city. Some came from enterprising and idealistic citizens, such as the industrialist Paul van Vlissingen and the physician Samuel Sarphati; others came from the state, which built railways and canals and forced municipalities to become more professional following the 1851 Municipality Act. Over time, efforts were also made by the city council, which overcame its initial apathy and became gradually more active and efficient. Amsterdam began to enjoy renewed prosperity, which is referred to today, with some exaggeration, as its 'second golden age'.

Nonetheless, the long-overdue problems were not completely

Stadsherstel: restoring order in the city

solved after 1850, and meanwhile the new prosperity was creating new problems or exacerbating old ones. The population continued to grow for a century, from 220,000 inhabitants in 1850 to 840,000 in 1950, and all of these people had, for a start, to live somewhere. Housing construction tried to keep up with the speed of growth, but it remained chronically behind demand. And so even the worst slums and hovels in the Jordaan, the Jodenbuurt and the Eilanden were still needed, no matter how much the city yearned to be healed or have its 'slums cleared'. The effects of modernising and scaling up the economy also permeated the old city centre. Small buildings were replaced by large ones. Canal houses, no longer affordable as residences, were turned into offices. The historic city, now a 'city centre', increasingly became a business district, at the expense of residential use. This process was called 'cityfication', named after London, the city where it first occurred. By 1915 the term had become common usage in Amsterdam. 'Cityfication is an economic phenomenon, which we must accept as it arises,' the chairman of the Healthcare Commission said in 1914, for example. The main canals were in for it too. 'Not only can we not stop the modernisation of the canals,' said alderman Willem Vliegen in 1916, 'but it actually is necessary.'[3]
And then there was the increasingly serious problem of traffic. The city was not built to absorb this traffic increase, nor the shift from water to land traffic or the explosive growth of motorisation. One option for the city to gain space for traffic was to fill up canals or engage in large-scale demolition to make way for roads, much like Eugène Haussmann's Paris. Both interventions were used several times, but more often

---

3 *Algemeen Handelsblad*, 17.11.1914. *Het Volk*, 06.11.1916
4 *De Gooi- en Eemlander*, 02.07.1935
5 *Leeuwarder Courant*, 28.02.1931

than not the plans failed due to a lack of funding or frugality. Or, and that happened increasingly often, they failed as a result of protests by outraged citizens.

Resistance to change that would harm the beauty of the city, became a progressively powerful political bargaining chip after 1900. This focus on the unique heritage enriched the discussion, but it further complicated the conundrum that was the city centre. The disputes dragged on endlessly, for example about whether or not to fill in Rokin in the heart of the city. A petition signed by dignitaries in 1935 shows that those opposed to filling had no answers of their own to solve the traffic problem: as far as they were concerned, people could cram their cars onto every piece of every street and square from Vischpleintje near Brakke Grond to the market for stamp collectors on Nieuwezijds, as long as no one dried up Rokin.[4]

'Amsterdam, as everyone knows, has a city centre, but no one knows where it's heading,' remarked a correspondent in 1931, regarding the Rokin question: 'The divisions among the citizenry and the battle between the two parties have been raging for decades now. One half of the citizenry is not interested in sparing the old city centre and wants to remove every obstacle, once and for all. The other half believes that we cannot sacrifice the city's historical past and architecture to traffic.' These words could have been written a quarter of a century later.[5]

Demolition for traffic, cityfication, slum clearance: all of this could already be found in the design for a 'Broad Fashionable High Street' presented by the architect Cornelis Outshoorn and his partner J.L. Kuinders in 1866. They envisaged extending Plantage Middenlaan from the east straight through to Dam Square and demolishing everything in its way. Their street was to become Amsterdam's Rue de Rivoli, with distinguished buildings to boost the quality of cityfication; and the dilapidated Jewish Quarter that skirted the high street along the way would be cleared and transformed into a 'central residential area'. The plan typified the search for ways of modernising the city

– and its failure: Outshoorn and Kuinders were unable to find financial backing.[6]
Geurt Brinkgreve, who we will encounter again below, summarised what he considered to be the threats to Amsterdam's old city centre in a lecture he gave in early October 1954: 'These dangers are threefold: architectural deterioration, the continuous concentration of companies in the centre and traffic congestion.' After almost a hundred years, it was still the same three key issues in the city centre. The only thing that had changed was their intensity and appreciation.[7]

Warning shot for both parties

The post-war urban expansion efforts were based on the ambitious General Expansion Plan (GEP) from 1935 and was implemented by a powerful municipal apparatus. But would this machine be able to shift from its major interventions in the western garden cities of Amsterdam to the subtle approach needed in the historic city centre area?
Not everyone was convinced. The GEP treated the city centre mainly in relation to the larger city as a whole, into which the centre was woven by a network of main roads. The city centre, which had limited space and a central function, was extremely sensitive to traffic congestion and that is precisely what was causing great uncertainty. Traffic forecast studies from the

6   *De Tijd*, 21.07.1866. *Utrechtsch Provinciaal en Stedelijk Dagblad*, 06.08.1866. Michiel Wagenaar, *Stedebouw en burgerlijke vrijheid*, Bussum 1998, p. 151-153
7   'Brief summary of a lecture by Mister Geurt Brinkgreve' on October 1954 in "the Amsterdamsche Kring"', 27.09.1954 (Archives Stadsherstel)
8   H. Hellinga (e.a.), *Algemeen Uitbreidingsplan 50 Jaar*, Amsterdam 1985, p. 68, 213. *Algemeen Handelsblad*, 11.12.1931
9   Hillary Ballon and Kenneth T. Jackson (ed.), *Robert Moses and the Modern City*, New York & London 2007. Jane Jacobs, *The Death and Life of Great American Cities*, New York 1961

1930s – which argued that the Netherlands would never exceed forty cars per thousand inhabitants – were outdated, and all formulas for traffic improvement could be thrown in the bin. Also, the corporate culture of urban planners regarded light, air and space more highly than the old city centre's narrow streets, steep staircases and irregularity.[8]

There are similarities with the situation in New York, where 'master builder' Robert Moses dynamically directed the expansion of the metropolis, building hundreds of kilometres of motorway and countless parks, swimming pools and public beaches in the process. It failed when Moses tried to apply methods from the suburbs to the existing city, in which he had plans for mass demolition and the construction of motorways straight through Lower Manhattan. He faced opposition from 'a bunch of mothers' and eventually had to yield to their gentle but influential, highly educated and eloquent vigour. One of them was Jane Jacobs, who would make this struggle famous worldwide in her 1961 book *The Death and Life of Great American Cities*. It was a struggle between different interests and different views of what a modern city is, but it was also a question of scale. The priority for Moses was the metropolis, and he considered individual neighbourhoods mere details, whereas Jacobs focused on the smaller elements of the city, such as streets, sidewalks and diversity.[9]

Amsterdam was embroiled in a similar cultural battle and was several years ahead of New York in that respect. Amsterdam's battle entailed the same clash of value systems, and a similar tension between top-down planning and bottom-up civilian initiatives. Though Amsterdam lacked a colourful emissary like Robert Moses, in October 1954 an outsider arrived on the scene and turned the city onto its head with a single wild plan à la Moses, which immortalised him in the process. He was not a professional architect but the chief commissioner of police, Hero Kaasjager. As a remedy for the increasing daily traffic chaos, he suggested building two ring roads in the old city by filling in stretches of historic canals totalling 15 kilometres long, including the Singel, Kloveniersburgwal, Lijnbaansgracht and part of the Amstel River. Half of the city was outraged, and suddenly the future of the city centre was the talk of the town. It never became clear whether his plan was totally serious, or whether he had set the cat among the pigeons to at least provoke some kind of reaction to solve the traffic problem. The response from the mayor and the aldermen made it instantly clear that this plan would never be carried out, but the problem was etched in everyone's memories now.[10]

'Rarely has a response been so unanimously dismissive,' wrote Fred Thomas again. But the provocation was profoundly effective. Both parties used the extreme plan to raise their profile. The city council promised that it would never surrender the historical city centre so completely to traffic as stipulated in this plan, and said that it would continue to seek a compromise between modern demands and historical values. The conservationists, meanwhile, realised that the reprehensible plan was actually a godsend that gave their cry for help a larger audience. Kaasjager thus helped to shape the battleground. 'The Kaasjager project,' wrote Thomas, 'is like a bolt out of the blue, and at the same time a warning shot for both parties, (…) It has double merit: first it is honest and blunt about what other institutions actually desire secretly but do not dare speak out about publicly. And subsequently it accentuates the need to, at least in the short term, find a solution to the traffic problem in the city of Amsterdam.'[11]

---

10 For instance: *De Telegraaf*, 21.10.1954. *Algemeen Dagblad*, 21.10.1954; 29.10.1954; 30.10.1954. *De Tijd*, 23.10.1954. Cordula Rooijendijk, *That City is Mine!*, Amsterdam 2005, p. 101-132
11 *De Tijd*, 06.11.1954
12 Geurt Brinkgreve, *Mozaïek van mijn leven*, Apeldoorn/Antwerpen 2006, p. 80-81

Geist und Macht

Much has been written about the battle for Amsterdam that raged in the following decades. The outcome was a mixture of preservation and new build, with on balance more preservation than in many other cities. Some large-scale interventions proceeded, especially on the east side of the city, while others failed to materialise or were toned down. The construction of the underground inflicted a wound on the Nieuwmarkt area, which was eventually healed in an acceptable manner. The battle mostly took place in complete openness, but the direction the city would take was also determined by diplomatic activity behind the scenes. Some of the key figures have remained all but unknown. A striking example is Pieter Joseph Hendrik Marie van der Does de Willebois, otherwise known as 'Uncle Joost'. Van der Does was president of the Court of Justice and therefore a prominent citizen of Amsterdam without any business interests in the city. He was interested in nature conservation and cultural heritage, and by chance was indirectly related to Geurt Brinkgreve, a young sculptor and author who created a stir with a series of articles that began to appear in the weekly *Elsevier* in late 1953 about the fate of historical city centres. Van der Does and Brinkgreve discussed the issue during a family dinner, and Van der Does suggested that it was time for a citizens' initiative 'in favour of *herstel*' instead of demolition'. Two things were needed for an effective campaign: a solid and convincing story, and the support of an influential network. Van der Does arranged both. He gave Brinkgreve a monthly allowance so he could dedicate himself, as an unhampered theoretician, and he arranged a talk with a key figure in the business world, Daniël Delprat. Delprat, apart from running a shipping company, was chairman of the Chamber of Commerce and would later become a senator for the conservative-liberal VVD party. Van der Does believed that Delprat had a moral obligation to the city centre, because his 'father-in-law was Jan Veth, saviour of Reguliersgracht, and should serve as an example to him'.[12]

In May 1954, Van der Does wrote a short letter to Delprat in which he left little room for dissent:

> 'The battle for the preservation of Amsterdam will only succeed if the prominent members of trade and industry in Amsterdam are prepared to positively and unambiguously choose for the preservation and *herstel* of the city centre and against the short-sighted politics of large-scale demolition to make way for roads and clear slums.
> And you should be able to act as a major impetus for improvement by virtue of the fortunate combination of your prominent position in business and the strong feeling that you undoubtedly have for the unique beauty of 17th-century Amsterdam and for the significance of the city centre as a place to live.
> We will need conservationists, business people and potentially the Municipal Authority to collectively join forces in a modest body or organ, or however you wish to call it, for one common goal, saving the city centre.'[13]

Van der Does and Brinkgreve visited Delprat together. The judge thus forged an alliance between what the Germans call *Geist und Macht*, intellect and power. It became a memorable talk, especially for young Brinkgreve: 'Two highly prominent men listening attentively to a young man who was a novice in the subject, who thought he knew more than

---

13 Letter Van der Does to mr. D.A. Delprat, 03.05.1954 (Archives Stadsherstel)
14 Geurt Brinkgreve, *Mozaïek van mijn leven*, Apeldoorn/Antwerpen 2006, p. 81
15 Quoted in: Geurt Brinkgreve (e.a.), *Phoenix; verdwijnend of herrijzend Amsterdam*, Amsterdam 2004, p. 38. Juliet Oldenburger, 'Hoe het allemaal begon. Interview met mevrouw Brinkgreve-Kunst', in: *Binnenstad* 250, March 2012

the city's distinguished urban development specialists.' Van der Does and Delprat got down to business. For the short term: 'You have to tell that story to the Amsterdamsche Kring.' And for the long term: 'A highly representative, non-political citizens' committee, that's what we need, with a chairman that no one dares say "no" to,' said Van der Does. Delprat immediately knew someone: 'That can only be Jan Six.'[14]

Brinkgreve held a lecture at the Amsterdamsche Kring on 8 October 1954, which meant he could now promote his mission to the city's upper class. This select society, founded in 1945 for 'the reconstruction of Amsterdam in all its facets,' consisted of one hundred members from the economic, cultural and administrative elite. Six and Delprat belonged to it, as did the mayor, the director of the Rijksmuseum, dozens of prominent businesspeople, and also the chief commissioner of police.

Brinkgreve wrote, studied and talked with his contemporary Ruud Meischke, head of the recently established municipal office for the preservation of cultural heritage monuments, Bureau Monumentenzorg. Brinkgreve and Meischke were looking for a new way to approach the old city: 'To no longer focus on the interesting building itself, but rather the house as an element of a block, a neighbourhood, and yes, of the old city with its own structure and proportions. This meant that the ultimate goal would shift from occasional house *herstel* to city *herstel*.' They also got inspiration from their personal lives, according to Brinkgreve's wife Sjuwke: 'Meischke regularly visited us at our house on Lijnbaansgracht, and we became friends. He said; "You live in such an incredibly pleasant place", and that's how the idea arose to refurbish run-down houses and make them habitable again.'[15]

Brinkgreve outlined in his lecture to the Amsterdamsche Kring, which bore the concise title 'Amsterdam's city centre', the threats facing the city centre, but also an alternative: 'Does the old city centre have a future other than more cityfication, and is there a future for more cityfication outside the old city centre?' Thanks to its great variety of buildings, the city centre could become an attractive residential area for anyone not interested in the standard housing in the new-build areas. He pointed out 'the unique significance of the old city centres for the spiritual climate of our time,' and the next passage could have been inspired by the lecture 'Building Dwelling Thinking' by the German philosopher Martin Heidegger from 1951: 'Dwelling, after all, aside from being a physical and a social need, is also a spiritual one. And one does not merely dwell in an apartment with umpteen electrical appliances, but also in a house with a certain atmosphere, in a street with a certain character, in a neighbourhood with its own identity. Precisely these characteristics were (…) lost in post-war housing construction.' Brinkgreve thus turned what seemed to be the disadvantages of the old city into advantages, and to a certain degree he was an early theoretician of gentrification. He argued that it would be better to continue cityfication outside the centre, for example by tearing down the low-value nineteenth-century district De Pijp, as the cultural heritage society Bond Heemschut had also suggested. De Pijp is still standing today, but with a little imagination one could argue that this proposal foreshadowed today's Zuidas business quarter further south, also known as the 'financial mile'.[16]

16 Geurt Brinkgreve, 'De binnenstad van Amsterdam', typescript (Archives Stadsherstel)
17 *Trouw*, 11.05.1995
18 Geurt Brinkgreve, *Gevecht om Amsterdam; Lezing gehouden voor het Genootschap Amstelodamum op 30 november 1954*, Amsterdam 1954. *Algemeen Handelsblad*, 01.12.1954. Geurt Brinkgreve, 'Hoe Stadsherstel ter wereld kwam', undated typescript (Archives Stadsherstel)
19 See also: Richter Roegholt (ed.), *Levend Amsterdam*, Amsterdam 1987. Geurt Brinkgreve (e.a.), *Phoenix; verdwijnend of herrijzend Amsterdam*, Amsterdam 2004

Brinkgreve remembered getting a 'lengthy, approving applause' after his lecture, but at least one listener was seething, alderman Goos van 't Hull. He asked whether he could respond, and the members of the Kring thought it was a good idea to hear both sides. Van 't Hull chose a telling moment to present his arguments, on 22 October, because just a day earlier someone had leaked the Kaasjager plan.[17]

The Kaasjager commotion gave Brinkgreve's alarmist argument a massive boost. The Genootschap Amstelodamum – a society fighting for the preservation of the city of Amsterdam – asked him to hold his lecture again, this time in front of an audience of hundreds of people in the Stedelijk Museum's auditorium. There was no mistaking the new title: 'The battle for Amsterdam'. Thus in a short time Geurt Brinkgreve became the voice for a new vision of the city, with a well-founded story and an urgent message: 'The decision will be made in the coming years whether the beauty of Amsterdam will be preserved and *hersteld* or permanently perish.'[18]

Then we'll just have to do it ourselves

The concern for the old city centre had been aroused; the key thing now was to consolidate the momentum. To start with, by making the argument stronger, more appealing, more concrete and completely inevitable, and involving more people in it. This steady growth of a network of knowledge and support took shape in a long series of lectures and articles, exhibitions such as 'Levend Amsterdam' (Amsterdam Alive) in 1955, the book *Alarm in Amsterdam* in 1956, and many other initiatives, foundations and societies in the following decades.[19]
But from the perspective of people like Van der Does it was also important to ensure that the controversies did not get out of hand. The differences in views had to remain professional, because personal vendettas and prestige battles could backfire. This required a balancing act between activism and reconciliation.

The reconciliation was reflected in the thoughtful words of Herman de la Fontaine Verwey, chairman of Genootschap Amstelodamum, to interpret the word 'battle' in the title 'The battle for Amsterdam'. The soft-spoken book historian was all too happy to point out to his opponents their common love for Amsterdam:

> 'It is a battle, but it is not a battle about power, not a political battle, nor a battle between the government and its citizens. In fact, it is not even a battle between two parties. (…) The conflict resides (…) in ourselves to be honest, in all of the citizens of Amsterdam that love their city. One can only fight for what one loves, and one can only love what lives. The fact that Amsterdam never died, never became a relic of the past, like Venice, but a living city – that is what has made this battle so difficult. We are all struggling, in our own way, with the problem of how to live, work and flourish in our living, working, flourishing city, which our ancestors built (…).'[20]

And the activism was initiated by the establishment, in early January 1955, of the Comité De Stad Amsterdam. The Comité was meant to be a broad civil society platform for discussion and research that simultaneously attempted to influence the municipality. It consisted of twelve prominent citizens, including (indeed) esquire Jan Six van Hillegom as chairman. He took over the leading role from Van der Does. In his sixties, Six was

---

20 *Maandblad Amstelodamum*, January 1955, p. 1
21 *Persoonlijkheden in het Koninkrijk der Nederlanden in Woord en Beeld*, Amsterdam 1938, p. 1356. Geurt Brinkgreve, 'Hoe Stadsherstel ter wereld kwam', undated typescript (Archives Stadsherstel)
22 *De Telegraaf*, 26.01.1955. *Algemeen Handelsblad*, 22.01.1955

director of the Amstel Brewery and also chairman of Theater Carré, the Artis zoo and the VVV, the Amsterdam Tourist Association. As a businessman he had a direct, sometimes abrasive style, and as a networker he harboured warm feelings for his city. In 1935 he signed the petition against filling the Rokin, and after travelling extensively he 'came to the conclusion that no city surpassed Amsterdam's beauty in terms of urban planning'. Six was 'an old-school ruler of Amsterdam: authoritarian, energetic, curt, and brimming with love for his city,' as Brinkgreve phrased it; with him the committee gained a chairman 'that totally personified Amsterdam both in terms of its history and commerce'.[21]

As far as the Comité was concerned, there was a precarious balance between harmony and activism. Six must have felt content about the commentary in the daily paper *De Telegraaf*, and may well have whispered in their ears: 'There was a danger that this large-scale initiative would exacerbate the divide between the P.W. camp and the conservationist camp. It is to the great credit of the Comité that the gap will not deepen nor widen, but instead will be bridged. (…) Political motives were ignored. It was decided that prestige would have no influence on process. Personal considerations were brushed aside. The issue, the main concern, was too important to give pettiness or over-sensitivity any kind of opportunity.' Six also received congratulatory messages from people in the tourism sector, who he knew well as chairman of the VVV. Because, as one person commented in a letter, the city centre of Amsterdam was 'a jewel for any idealist, and for any materialist a goose that will lay more and more golden eggs.'[22]

The Comité couldn't afford to be soft. 'The Comité would like to share its insights with the municipal authorities,' stated the press release, 'regarding the development of measures that will protect the historical beauty of old Amsterdam from irresponsible mutilation and also meet the demands of traffic and trade in a modern and progressive manner.' That was a harsh message, albeit in diplomatic language, because it suggested that the municipal authorities had been leaning towards mutilating the city were it not for the Comité's insights. It was repeated in talks with the municipal council, when the Comité proposed to have the city and traffic issue examined 'by several of the most competent urban planners in our country.' It was a thinly veiled vote of no-confidence against the city's own urban planners, and for that reason alone, the municipal authorities couldn't accept it. It is said that Six left this meeting saying the following words: 'Then we'll just have to do it ourselves.'[23]

Chairman Six, meanwhile, realised that the public performance of Comité member Geurt Brinkgreve posed a risk to deliberations with the municipality. During the inaugural meeting on 14 January 1955, Six announced that he would prefer not to make Brinkgreve's involvement public knowledge for the time being, 'in order to avoid unnecessary friction'. Indeed, Brinkgreve was missing from the list of initiators in the first newspaper report, but within a few weeks his name was leaked after all, much to Six's dismay. And that wasn't the end of the affair.[24]

'Then we'll just have to do it ourselves' – but how? Brinkgreve and Meischke had already been playing with the idea of establishing a new society or company, and now was the time to do it. Brinkgreve and new Comité member Huibert van Saane worked together in June 1955 on the details of setting up a society for the restoration of the city: Maatschappij Stadsherstel. Van Saane was a successful and innovative building contractor,

---

23   *De Tijd*, 06.01.1955
24   Geurt Brinkgreve (e.a.), *Phoenix; verdwijnend of herrijzend Amsterdam*, Amsterdam 2004, p. 37. *De Tijd*, 06.01.1955. *De Telegraaf*, 26.01.1955
25   M. Burkunk, '40 jaar behoud en beheer van de Amsterdamse binnenstad; 1956 – 1966', in: Vereniging Vrienden van de Amsterdamse Maatschappij tot Stadsherstel, *Nieuwsbrief*, nr. 30, January 1996, p. 19

having done a great deal of work in the western extensions of Amsterdam. He introduced prefab building systems such as Airey and Maycrete in the Netherlands and commissioned the well-known Sloterhof ensemble, designed by architect J.F. Berghoef. What's especially relevant is that he was the only private individual in the Netherlands to own a public limited company with the same privileged status of 'authorised institution' as a housing cooperative. His NEMAVO, the Dutch Society for Public Housing, served as a model for the business-like structure that Stadsherstel would soon take on.[25]

Anyone exploring the prehistory of Stadsherstel is likely to encounter another puzzling document. It is an undated memorandum about a page and half long by J.H.W. Veenstra, entitled 'Conservation plan for the Amsterdam city centre'. Veenstra was an author, journalist and literary critic for *Vrij Nederland* weekly, and lived on Reguliersgracht near Amstelveld. Since it contains no references whatsoever to the Kaasjager plan, this memorandum about an organisation similar to Stadsherstel may well have been written *before* October 1954. 'Preserving the heart of Amsterdam as a living and highly characteristic city centre with essentially unique aesthetic value is only possible if a good and realistically conceived plan is implemented,' Veenstra began. 'We are therefore considering an independent body – in the form of a society, foundation or association – that operates based on an ideal goal but also professionally.' The 'body', in Veenstra's proposal, would buy up housing in the city centre, restore and develop it, and pay out 'reasonable interest' for investors, including banks and insurance companies. It could also perform other tasks, such as relocating polluting companies and supporting individual owners. It could increase the body's recognition with annual competitions for the best-maintained facade, the most tastefully decorated interior or the most praiseworthy restoration. 'The purchased and refurbished houses could also be made instantly recognised as such by means of a coat of arms on the facade'. Many of these ideas dovetail with

the memorandum by Brinkgreve and Van Saane, though crucial
ingredients are lacking. Veenstra and Brinkgreve probably knew
each other, or at least thought in similar ways.[26]
Brinkgreve and Van Saane presented their 'Memorandum in
preparation of a Society for City Restoration' on 6 July 1955.
The idealistic framework expanded on Brinkgreve's lecture
on living culture and cultural heritage; Van Saane devised
a business model based on NEMAVO's. Stadsherstel needed
to be a public limited company that met the same statutory
requirements of an 'authorised institution', so that the company
could enjoy the same fiscal benefits as a housing cooperative,
such as exemption from corporation tax and transfer costs.
Supplementary funding would come from restoration grants.
Things accelerated: the proposal was approved, a committee
further elaborated it, and Meischke, Van Saane and the real estate
agent C. Hoen set up an operating account as a pilot scheme
for two characteristic houses of the type that would be eligible
to Stadsherstel, Amstel 95 and 97 near the Magere Brug. They
concluded that development was feasible. K.W. van Houten
was appointed director and on 2 December the solemn decision
was made to found Stadsherstel. Six and his associates were on
the verge of proving that they could in fact do it all themselves.
The society now needed the municipality's blessing, in order to
receive 'an official statement of approval and support that would
to gain the confidence of future shareholders'. Brinkgreve's
role was once again a thorny issue in the Comité: should he
come along to the meeting with the municipal council? He had

26 J.H.W. Veenstra, 'Conserveringsplan voor de Amsterdamse binnenstad', undated typescript (Archives Stadsherstel)
27 Geurt Brinkgreve, 'Hoe Stadsherstel ter wereld kwam', undated typescript (Archives Stadsherstel)
28 Farewell speech Geurt Brinkgreve, 6 December 2002, in: *Binnenstad* 199, April 2003

only recently riled the municipal authorities by publishing
in full the municipality's memorandum on the city centre
in the conservationists's Heemschut magazine, accompanied
by extensive and stinging commentary. Brinkgreve, who
in addition to being the object of the debate took the minutes,
wrote in the draft minutes: 'The challenge resides in the
secretary. Although the plan for our society originated with
him, the committee cannot present itself to the city hall in his
company.' Chairman Six scrapped this line from the minutes
and the delegation went to the municipal council without
Brinkgreve. Brinkgreve withdrew, upon which Six wrote the
following on behalf of the others: 'My colleagues and I regret
that for practical reasons you, who initiated this matter after
all, have been unable to function (…) among the members
of this committee.' Six hoped that it 'will be possible one day
to repair this relationship, which has now been ended'.[27]
The 'practical reasons' that Six alluded to were in fact strategic
reasons. The matter at hand, not the person, was the priority,
namely the success of this infant initiative and the support
of the municipal authorities. Later, Brinkgreve admitted that
Six was right and consoled himself with the thought that
his work for Stadsherstel was finished anyway, but it would
always continue to rankle. Almost half a century later, he
summarised his feelings as follows: 'I am the only natural father
of Stadsherstel, whose fatherhood was officially kept silent.
He was banished before it was born.'[28]
The spiritual father may have left, but the child prospered under
its surrogate parents. The business case for the Amsterdamse
Maatschappij tot Stadsherstel N.V. was finalised in 1956. The
municipality agreed to cooperate, and Six courteously turned
the thumbscrews on his business partners so they would take
part financially; it is said he managed to round up 1.1 million
guilders with half an hour of phone calls. Stadsherstel was
formally established on 30 August 1956, and the last piece of
the puzzle, the ministerial 'authorisation', was put into place on

19 March 1957. The leap from a good idea to a serious operation was perhaps best expressed in the following newspaper headline: 'Institutional investors to protect old Amsterdam.'[29]

Name

How did the Amsterdamse Maatschappij tot Stadsherstel N.V. come about its name, especially the well-chosen word 'Stadsherstel'?

No explanation for the name is given in any documents from around the time of founding, nor in the 1955 memorandum. As far as we know, its founders never brainstormed about alternatives; they only played around with the preposition, changing 'of' to 'for'. 'Stadsherstel' seemed to have popped up from out of nowhere and has never been questioned since first being used. It is likely that the word 'stads-herstel' arose from talks held between Brinkgreve and Meischke, and was then organically transformed from a common noun to a proper noun. Several newspaper articles from the time still write about the 'Maatschappij tot stadsherstel', with a lower case 's'.

Why is it such a good name? The 'Stad' part is a reminder that the restoration and development of individual houses was not the company's ultimate aim, but a means to higher ends. Even more telling is the choice of 'herstel', an ambiguous concept that entails multiple meanings, associations and values. Related words, such as 'restoration', 'preservation', 'conservation' and 'heritage' are one-dimensional: they suggest that the past is the gauge for the present and they can therefore easily provoke the

---

29 *Leeuwarder Courant*, 31.08.1956
30 'Herstel en Vernieuwing'; Radio speeches of H.M. Koningin Wilhelmina and Z.Ex. Prof. Ir. W. Schermerhorn Minister-President on June 27 1945
31 Anton Groot and Max Cramer, *C.B. van der Tak*, Bussum/Amersfoort 2007, p. 314-345

accusation of conservatism. This is not the case with 'herstel'.
'Herstellen' can be used as a synonym for the verb 'to restore',
and therefore refer to a historical standard, but it can just
as easily mean 'heal' or 'correct an error', and therefore refer
to the future and leave behind it a past of wounds, wrong turns
and misguided paths. Moreover, 'herstel' also had a morally
authoritative ring to it during the years of post-war reconstruction. The first government address to the people after
liberation, in June 1945, was entitled 'Herstel en vernieuwing',
and the word 'herstel' appeared 25 times in the speech, in a
variety of guises, from democratic 'herstel', economic 'herstel',
'herstel' of the transport system, and 'a "hersteld" and
profound realisation of good and evil.' The term 'stadsherstel'
was still vacant among all these word combinations.[30]
The use of the word 'stadsherstel' in relation to preserving
cultural heritage made some insiders feel uneasy, because during
occupation the collaborator urban architect C.B. van der Tak
from Amersfoort used 'Stadsherstel' as the title for a photobook
about his restoration policy, which was released by the Nazi
publisher Hamer. It was a false start of a word that now deserved
to be used in a better way.[31]
It has remained an infallible name, and it got even better with
the introduction of the slogan that graced just about every
construction sign from 1966 onwards: '"Stadsherstel" "herstelt"
the city here too.' It is a constant confirmation of the close tie
between the city and the company, between the name and aim,
and between the individual house and the larger whole.

Doing business the slow way

The origins described in detail here reveal where Stadsherstel's
roots lay and still lie. The idea of combining an ideal with
business acumen has stood the test of time, as has the concept
of setting up the society as a company with a cautious and
prudent character, modest in size and profit, and with a dual
structure with a supervisory board full of heavyweights.

Stadsherstel: restoring order in the city

When Six van Hillegom went in search of board members in 1956, he did not accept anything but the absolute best. He hijacked chairpersons from the executive boards of major companies, especially banks and insurance companies, supplemented with the director of the Rijksmuseum, and the like. Stadsherstel thus had free access to the best financial advisors in the Netherlands. One of them, in later years, was the legendary ABN banker André Batenburg, who sat on the board from 1972 to 1994. 'When in doubt, I called Batenburg', says former director Wim Eggenkamp about that period. The bankers invariably advised the company to adopt a cautious policy and kept Stadsherstel from making costly blunders with speculative investments or 'accumulative loans', which many regular corporations took out. 'We also always had to do our best to underpin our plans well, because we knew that the board would not let us get away with shoddy work. A beneficial side effect for Stadsherstel is that people of their stature cannot afford to let the place go bankrupt. It's in their interest that we remain strong financially.'[32]

Stadsherstel had a hybrid structure from the very beginning: it was simultaneously a company, a housing corporation and a cultural heritage institute, and as a result the company could take a hit. It could take advantage of the benefits that all three had to offer and also mitigate losses. On the downside, this hybridity generated a lot of extra work. The standards used in post-war public housing, geared towards standardised, newly built mass housing, were often at odds with Stadsherstel, which specialised in the old, the deviating, in distributed ownership and complicated cases. For example, people's homes and workplaces in the old city are inevitably close to each other,

---

32 Interview Eggenkamp, 27.01.2016
33 Interview Meerstadt, 18.04.2016

often in the same building. But the public housing system is not fit to cope with such a combination of work and home; it is the product of a twentieth-century ideology that segregates purposes, that strictly separates living and work, and wants housing corporations to restrict themselves to residential dwellings. The maintenance of elaborate Stadsherstel houses is more costly on average as well. 'It's easy to imagine why that's the case,' says director Onno Meerstadt, 'and yet each time it's difficult to explain, because the Public Housing Authority is afraid that public housing funds will be used for a different purpose than for which they were intended, namely creating housing in the social sector.' It takes a lot of juggling to apply these kinds of general rules to a different and more specific reality. Moreover, public housing is subject to the vicissitudes of politics, whereas the style of Stadsherstel is one of constancy. When all this bureaucracy began to outweigh the benefits, Stadsherstel decided to largely say goodbye to the world of housing corporations. Winding that up took from 2009 to 2013; and since then only approximately twenty per cent of its total possessions are in the social sector.[33]

From the start, Stadsherstel allowed itself great freedom in its restoration philosophy. That is not a given, because there are strongly diverging views about what is correct restoration, which, moreover, change over time. The theoreticians of the State Monument Preservation Agency of the Netherlands (now called the Cultural Heritage Agency of the Netherlands) were usually much stricter than the more flexible municipal agency. Stadsherstel had already announced in the 1955 memorandum that it planned to follow a modest, pragmatic course. It did not intend to focus on individual top monuments, like the Hendrick de Keyser Association did, but on the *herstel* of houses as part of the city: 'Indeed, the restoration method needs to be based on completely different principles (...), namely use of the house for a modern purpose while maintaining the culturally valuable elements, on the one hand, and the opportunity for urban planning recovery, on the other hand.' To make a project feasible, it was not uncommon for an extra storey to be added in the 1960s. Decorative gables that were saved after demolition were used elsewhere later – a modus operandi that is no longer used because it is contrary to the prevalent standard of 'authenticity'. By not being strictly orthodox with each individual house, Stadsherstel was able to achieve more for the city, argues Eggenkamp: 'Take the Negen Straatjes. They would have disappeared if Stadsherstel had not intervened. No one is complaining about whether that is still authentic.'[34]

Finally, Stadsherstel keeps its distance from the daily business of politics. In 1954, Van der Does de Willebois expressed his desire for a 'non-political citizens' committee' and Six van Hillegom deliberately kept the company clear of the heat of the battle. 'We always did our work as far removed from politics as possible,' says former director Hengeveld, and the current director, Onno Meerstadt, elaborates on that: 'We stay away from anything that is polarising. We let others do the protesting, such as Heemschut, the Vrienden van de Binnenstad and the Cuypersgenootschap. It is important to know your role well. Our role is to implement. We would be vulnerable if we played the role of activist. We only take action once the die is cast. We work on the side-lines, away from the battle, so that we can be practical. This sense of practicality is strongly ingrained at Stadsherstel.'[35]

In all respects, Stadsherstel is a company for the long term that focuses on constancy. It is steadily growing at a rate of ten buildings per year, and it faithfully pays out a dividend of five per cent a year to its shareholders. It rarely sells its properties and thus has amassed an impressive portfolio, and the fact that

---

34   Interview Eggenkamp, 27.01.2016
35   Interview Hengeveld, 22.01.2016. Interview Meerstadt, 18.04.2016
36   *De Telegraaf*, 23.02.1968

it has long-term contact with tenants is a source of knowledge that can be used during subsequent restorations. The continuity among staff is striking as well. Many employees have been affiliated with the company for years, and thus Stadsherstel has managed to inconspicuously accumulate know-how that will not be lost anytime soon.

It is a special type of enterprise: idealistic and culturally informed, yet set up as a company; small scale yet carried by heavyweights; designed for continuity; set in its course yet not in a hurry; and a company that is constantly innovating but only gradually so. It shows that public affairs and the market can work together, but only if it happens with affection, intelligence and prudence. A healthy business operation goes hand in hand with community activity: many buildings are publically accessible, students are involved in every restoration, and the company has had an active Friends Association since 1980. It can be described as doing business the slow way.

In fact, there are examples of other companies in Amsterdam who approach business the same way, such as the bookshop Athenaeum, founded in 1966, and the weekly magazine *De Groene Amsterdammer*, founded in 1877.

A slow business plays a prominent role in the community, adapts to social change and actually changes society itself, but it does so like a long, undulating wave. Anyone looking back from this perspective at sixty years of interaction between a 'herstellende' city and Stadsherstel, can distinguish between three periods before, between and after 1975 and 1999.

1956 – 1975: working in a decrepit city

Around 1955, it was imperative that 'solutions would be presented in the short term of the city centre', but as it turned out this short term would take a long time. Thirteen years later, *De Telegraaf* stated again, or perhaps more accurately, was still stating: 'Amsterdam is working hard to transform itself from a city of bells and carillons to a city of alarm bells.'[36]

The city's appearance changed more slowly in the 1960s than anticipated. Cityfication struck in some places, mostly in the eastern part, but large areas remained untouched and derelict. In 1968 the city centre had 5,500 houses predating 1800, 'partly damaged and dilapidated, but *herstelbaar* (restorable)'. Since 1945 alone, 600 monumental buildings had been demolished, while 360 were kept standing with scaffolding and buttresses. Even though approximately a hundred houses were *hersteld* every year, according to the municipality, there was still a great deal to do.[37]

In contrast to this, the city underwent a radical cultural metamorphosis, not according to a top-down plan but from the bottom up as a result of the city's changing demographics and increasing prosperity. Billboards advertising domestic appliances and camping holidays appeared on the run-down city's fences, a hint of the prosperity elsewhere in the country. Baby boomers flooded the city to study, just as its former inhabitants were heading in the opposite direction. Amsterdam changed from a worker's city into a young people's city, with a new lifestyle, a new culture and new urban ideals. The counterculture Provo movement aimed to reclaim the streets from cars and protested against speculation, the lack of housing, slum clearances and cityfication. In 1967, an alternative city landscape was the subject of a 'teach-in', 'because we want to preserve small, old, cute little houses'. Sometimes this new movement cooperated with older conservationists, despite the massive cultural gap. Gradually the unrest in the city increased, culminating in a

---

37 *De Telegraaf*, 23.02.1968. Voorontwerp van de Tweede Nota over de Amsterdamse Binnenstad (Preliminary draft of the Second Memorandum on the Amsterdam Inner City), Gemeenteblad 1968, Bijlage C, p. 115
38 *Algemeen Handelsblad*, 06.10.1967. Poster *Amsterdaad '75*. Herman de Liagre Böhl, *Amsterdam op de helling*, Amsterdam 2010, p. 71

fierce battle concerning the construction of the underground through the Nieuwmarkt area in the early 1970s.[38]

This was the backdrop of Stadsherstel's work during its first twenty years. All that really mattered to Stadsherstel was the dilapidated city, and not the tumult and riots, because the company kept its distance from political and social commotion. While everyone was focusing on the Nieuwmarkt area, Stadsherstel was working elsewhere in the city.

When the city was at its worst, the Stadsherstel's working area was richer than ever. The reservoir of suitable ramshackle housing was inexhaustible, and in 1956 the company began to eagerly carry out its task. Stadsherstel planned to buy 25 houses in its first year, and 50 each in the second and third years, and the number of restorations in these years would increase from six to twelve to twenty. But before long, Stadsherstel's flying start turned into a tough learning process of trial and error. Ten years later, in 1966, the tally stood at eighty-four houses, twelve of which were completely restored and fourteen of which partially restored.

In retrospect, the teething troubles are easier to understand than the optimistic target figures. Stadsherstel was a pioneering company that needed to invent a new way of working; and anyone wanting to be a pioneer and act cautiously at the same time has to be willing to undergo a long apprenticeship. It was harder than the director, K.W. van Houten, probably imagined. He sought to achieve a balance between the number of purchased and restored houses, which he failed to find. He initially bought very little, then far too much. The supervisory board was not pleased with the imbalance between his many purchases and the scant restorations, and what is more, it turned out that the company paid far too much for some of its purchases. Van Houten suffered from long-term burnout and went into early retirement in 1965.

At that early stage, Stadsherstel also had to survive without its stern beacon, because chairman of the supervisory board Six van Hillegom had died in a car accident in 1961. His successor, former alderman Van 't Hull, was tasked in 1963 with turning the company into a mature enterprise, together with the new director J.M. Hengeveld, who was appointed in 1965. Soon the company began to flourish. The economist Hengeveld, who came from the paper manufacturer Van Gelder, introduced a strict business approach to the company. He raised extra money with a share issue to get the company going, the board members regained their confidence, and this all boosted momentum. Affairs were in order and the results on the streets were the best possible advertisement. Starting with the first restorations, such as Zandhoek 13, Langestraat 80 and Brouwersgracht 86, Stadsherstel's portfolio quickly filled up with spectacular 'before and after' photos. Along the Amstel River, in the dilapidated shopping streets that would later be renamed De Negen Straatjes, along the canals and in the alleyways, everywhere constructions signs appeared with the announcement: '"Stadsherstel" "herstelt" the city here too.' To generate maximum impact on the cityscape, the company preferred to buy corner buildings, such as the buildings at Vijzelgracht 1-3-5 on the corner with Prinsengracht. It was catching, according to Hengeveld: 'The contagious effect of our work was incredible. It showed the owners of buildings in the surroundings what could be done.' In the end, Van Houten's buying spree was even appreciated, because what was a bad buy in the early 1960s turned out to be an extremely wise investment years later.[39]

A mid-term review was carried out in 1976 on the occasion of the company's twentieth anniversary: in the first ten years,

---

39 Interview Hengeveld, 22.01.2016
40 J.M. Hengeveld, '40 jaar behoud en beheer van de Amsterdamse binnenstad; 1966 – 1976', in: Vereniging Vrienden van de Amsterdamse Maatschappij tot Stadsherstel, *Nieuwsbrief*, nr. 31, May 1996, p. 31

New plans circulating on the drawing board for
Vijzelgracht corner Prinsengracht, about 1963

26 houses were restored, and another 100 were restored in the following decade. 'That was an important contribution towards making the city centre habitable again,' wrote Hengeveld in his review, 'during a period in which not everyone thought there was much point to it.'[40]
But the period in which *Stadsherstel* had ruled the roost as a pioneer in the city centre inevitably came to an end.

1975 – 1999: a saturated city centre

In June 1973, a remarkable story appeared in the newspapers: British investors were pumping tens of millions of guilders into the city centre of Amsterdam. They were renovating warehouses and splitting up canal houses into a total of four hundred apartments. Amsterdammers watched in disbelief. Converting a warehouse into an apartment complex is 'a costly affair, which anyone involved in construction in Amsterdam is following with astonishment and suspicion,' the daily newspaper *De Tijd* reported. Even the director of the municipal Building Control Department was sceptical: 'I doubt whether our city's people will fall for this. The English will cure themselves of their extravagant desires once they've burnt their fingers.' The architect

Edo Spier, who designed the renovation of a warehouse for the English on Brouwersgracht, thought this was short sighted: 'I'm under the impression that Amsterdam will eventually regret its laxity in this respect. We easily could have done what the English are doing here. Those warehouses have been up for sale for ages. What's being done now will resonate for a long time. It will go much further than this.' Spier knew what he was talking about, because he had an office himself in an 'attractively renovated warehouse on Kromboomsloot, right on the underground frontier.'[41]

The English were quicker than the locals to realise that real estate in Amsterdam was cheap compared to international standards, wrote reporter Ben Kroon, and that the city centre would regain its residential purpose now that many offices had relocated to the city perimeter. 'The image of Amsterdam's city centre in the future, and especially the canal belt, will probably be determined by well-off singles or couples living in small but comfortable old houses or warehouses.' While the raging battle about the underground around the corner from Spier's place stole all the attention, 'capital and elan' quietly invaded Amsterdam 'to build an international dream city precisely in that city centre.'

The interest of British investors signalled a new era. Of course, Brinkgreve and Provo had already prophesied the revaluation of the old city centre in the 1950s and 1960s, but the business interest of investors was a different order of magnitude.

The year 1975 is a good symbolic choice for the start of the new era. The European Architectural Heritage Year increased interest in Amsterdam's unique heritage. This coincided with the celebration of the city's 700th anniversary and the violent

---

41 *De Tijd*, 02.06.1973

Nieuwmarkt riots in which a young generation proved that to them the old city was worth fighting for too. The municipality altered its policy to include a new kind of urban renewal in which expansions of the garden city variety were no longer the standard, but rather the existing urban and social structure, or 'Building for the neighbourhood'. The most spectacular break in the trend was that it actually materialised.
Stadsherstel's working area became increasingly saturated. That was welcome, because it made the city centre more habitable more quickly. Confidence in the future of the city centre was no longer a scarce good; rather, it had become the focus of policy. It quickened the pace of *herstel*, and Stadsherstel was doing better than ever. But it also gave rise to complications. When the municipality and the corporations started operating in the city centre, they automatically brought with them their wholesale methods from expansion areas. Though they did set to work on a smaller scale than in the west of Amsterdam or in the Bijlmer area, it was still pretty coarse compared to Stadsherstel's house-by-house approach. They had different considerations, more related to public housing and standardisation, and less related to restoration and uniqueness, and they were more prone to constructing new buildings. Their arrival also encroached on Stadsherstel's space, because each corporation was allotted part of the city centre; Stadsherstel were given two areas, Bethaniënbuurt and Kadijken.
The working areas did not need to be at each other's throats, but sometimes Stadsherstel deliberately sought confrontation, for example by purchasing a house in the Jordaan district in an area where a corporation wanted to demolish and construct new buildings. 'We liked to provoke them every now and then,' says Wim Eggenkamp. Conversely, the corporations were showing up on Stadsherstel's territory with increasing frequency. 'In those days, corporations had to carry out restorations too, but they approached it differently than we did. They put more emphasis on the housing, and less on the monument. You can

Stadsherstel: restoring order in the city

see the difference just by looking at the exterior, in the way the pointing is done, in the choice of brick, the window arrangements, how the window frames are recessed, the roof tiles. We look at these buildings very differently. We ask ourselves: what can we keep? For us, the more dilapidated the better. That makes it fun. Corporations, on the other hand, are quick to say: that can't be saved anymore, replace it. Of course, the difference is also that when we restore it is usually more costly.'[42]

Wim Eggenkamp became director in 1991, succeeding Jan Hengeveld. The entrepreneur was followed by a director with a more administrative background, because Eggenkamp had worked for the municipalities of Leiden and Haarlem for years on urban renewal and cultural heritage.

The period 1986–1996 was 'the most prosperous up until that point' for Stadsherstel. The number of properties it owned grew from 297 to 400, and the number of restored houses from 202 to 250. Yet the future was uncertain as a result of a fundamental shift in the market: 'In contrast to the first thirty years of Stadsherstel's existence, the purchasing opportunities in the last ten years have been severely limited. In 1987 we hit rock bottom. We didn't obtain a single house that year.' The comfortable situation in which decrepit city centre houses seemed to fall into Stadsherstel's lap was a thing

---

42 Interview Eggenkamp, 27.01.2016
43 W.M.N. Eggenkamp, '40 jaar behoud en beheer van de Amsterdamse binnenstad; 1986 – 1996', in: Vereniging Vrienden van de Amsterdamse Maatschappij tot Stadsherstel, *Nieuwsbrief*, nr. 33, December 1996, p. 3, 16
44 Interview Hengeveld, 22.01.2016
45 W.M.N. Eggenkamp, '40 jaar behoud en beheer van de Amsterdamse binnenstad; 1986 – 1996', in: Vereniging Vrienden van de Amsterdamse Maatschappij tot Stadsherstel, *Nieuwsbrief*, nr. 33, December 1996, p. 16, 46

of the past. 'After all, aside from the municipality and other corporations, there are private parties who are now willing to invest money in housing and do the restoration themselves. The demand for houses in the city centre is huge, and that is reflected in the spectacular increase of real-estate prices.'[43]

Eggenkamp's predecessor Hengeveld believes that Stadsherstel was in fact one of the causes of this market development: 'By buying houses, we essentially caused what has started to work against us. We experienced a time when there were still wrecks all over the place and no one was interested in the city centre yet. Our restoration work has made it increasingly difficult to find objects in the city centre, and that has made them more expensive. We are partly to blame for the price increases. We contributed to the changing climate. Stadsherstel no longer has the pioneering role that it once had.'[44]

Stadsherstel subtlety changed its course to regain its identity in the changing urban landscape. 'The working area is still primarily the city centre of Amsterdam', it wrote, looking back on the decade 1986–1996, but the focus now is 'mainly on less conspicuous streets and alleyways'. In addition: 'It made sense to start looking where we can do urgent restoration work outside the city centre, so that our expertise in the area of restoration will not be for naught.' And a third opportunity presented itself as well, which was first tried out on Stadsherstel's own premises in the Amstelkerk, restored in 1986–1990: an expansion to non-residential housing.[45]

1999– : great leaps forward

'The great battle for the city centre of Amsterdam' raged for more than the anticipated ten years, but can we even pinpoint a year when it ended? Symbolically, 1999 is a good candidate, because in that year the entire city centre of Amsterdam received status as protected cultural heritage. The value of the historical city had thus been officially recognised, and it was also a decisive step towards securing UNESCO World Heritage status, which the Canal Zone within the city centre obtained in 2010.

The city was in good shape around 1999. Public space had been spruced up, the canals and squares had gotten a makeover, and run-down areas such as Haarlemmerstraat were revitalised. Amsterdam benefited from the flourishing global economy and the removal of Europe's internal borders, the housing market wrested itself from the rest of the Netherlands and began to inch its way to the European urban level. In around 1999, low-cost airlines such as EasyJet and Ryanair appeared on the market, resulting in an explosive growth in the number of tourists visiting the city. Indeed, 'the saturated city' is a much talked about issue in 2016: will the city centre of Amsterdam succumb to its own popularity? It is tempting to quote the letter writer from 1955 again, who characterised Amsterdam as 'a jewel for any idealist, and for any materialist a goose that will lay more and more golden eggs.'

Today the city centre is not a major Central Business District nor a small-scale residential area. It is a 'modern historical city', as architecture historian Paul Meurs describes it: a contemporary city whose historical heritage is part of its contemporary function. In a certain sense, the entire city centre thus resembles a Stadsherstel house, where a historical form also coalesces with a contemporary and dynamic use.[46]

The need for Stadsherstel to restore houses in the city centre has diminished, though it still manages to snatch neglected historical houses from the jaws of demolition, as was recently the case on Foeliedwarsstraat. Stadsherstel's 450 buildings in the city centre form a 'critical mass' that is barely affected

---

46 Paul Meurs, *De moderne historische stad*, Rotterdam 2000
47 Interview Eggenkamp, 27.01.2016

by economic fluctuations caused by the market or politics. That is not only important for Stadsherstel but also for the city as a whole. 'What we have,' says Eggenkamp, 'and what we should cherish is what people in the corporation world call your "core assets". With our overall possessions, we own the core supply of cultural heritage monuments in Amsterdam. If we can manage to sustain that, then the city will never become as derelict again as when we started.'[47]

Stadsherstel has expanded its activities during this period in three ways. Increasingly, it owns a wider range of buildings with a purpose other than residential; these buildings are often outside of the Singelgracht perimeter, which encloses the city centre, and even outside Amsterdam; and frequently new uses have to be found for an old building. The first project that did not have a mainly residential purpose was the restoration of the wooden Amstelkerk in 1986–1990. The project became feasible by combining several purposes for which it would be used: an office space for Stadsherstel itself, a lettable hall, a restaurant and residences. A great leap forward occurred subsequently thanks to the merger with the Amsterdam Monuments Foundation (AMF) in 1999. This sister organisation added seven historical churches to the portfolio, including De Duif, the Vondelkerk, the Posthoornkerk and the Gerardus Majellakerk, as well as striking buildings such as the West-Indisch Huis, the Huis De Pinto, the 't Kromhout shipyard and two sewage pumping stations. Just as important as these new possessions was the pooling of expertise. This paved the way in the new millennium for new types of projects, such as Pakhuis de Zwijger, part of De Hallen, the former fire station 'Oud Nico' on De Ruijterkade, forts in the Defence Line of Amsterdam, and a growing number of churches, mills and pumping stations in an area that roughly comprises the metropolitan region of Amsterdam. Stadsherstel also operates abroad, providing advice on how to use the Stadsherstel concept in other cities, similar to the Stadsherstel organisations that were previously established elsewhere in the Netherlands following the example in Amsterdam.

Nevertheless, this expansion is not a break with the past, says Onno Meerstadt, who succeeded Wim Eggenkamp as director in 2007. '"Stadsherstel" is still the goal. We are here for the most endangered buildings. That used to mean residential buildings, but now it includes other types of buildings. The fact that they are having a hard time expresses itself in part in terms of business, because in the past we would have had to pay for some of these buildings, whereas now more often than not we are given money. Specific cultural heritage organisations for windmills, churches or the Defence Line of Amsterdam come to us for help because they cannot make ends meet on their own.'[48]

Today, both the business and social aspects are taken into account for each building. 'We are extremely prudent.' says Meerstadt. 'We do a feasibility study for each building, just as we did even before we were established.' Risks become manageable by combining purposes: debating centre and office space in Pakhuis De Zwijger, and offices, art studios and residential dwellings in the fire station 'Oud Nico'. A long-term lease was signed for the Majellakerk in the area called Indische Buurt with the Dutch Philharmonic Orchestra and the Netherlands Chamber Orchestra, who themselves invested in the acoustics and sound insulation.

Project leader Paul Morel emphasises Stadsherstel's social considerations. 'The aim is still to *herstel* the city. We refurbish buildings and give them a new life. This has a spill-over effect

---

48 Interview Meerstadt, 18.04.2016
49 Interview Morel, 22.04.2016. Interview Meerstadt, 18.04.2016
50 Confidential report in connection with the private issue of shares 'Amsterdamse Maatschappij tot Stadsherstel N.V. i.o. located in Amsterdam, undated, probably in early January 1956 (Archives Stadsherstel)

because the environment becomes more attractive as a result, there is less danger of high vacancy levels, and there are more investment opportunities. Tackling a single building can help to develop an entire area and reinforce social structures. A good example is Concertgemaal Noord. We renovated that and now it is an extremely popular meeting place. It is a catalyst for development in the area.'[49]

That points the way to the future. The city's *herstel* is still the aim, but the methods are changing. The working area is larger, but Stadsherstel remains primarily there for the atypical buildings. Those no longer only concern the odd ones out in public housing, but are relics from the industrial, religious, agricultural and perhaps educational heritage, which demand a wise approach in order to be successfully repurposed. More than ever before, users will be actively involved in the restoration, all the while also respecting sustainability requirements. The expansion of the working area was already anticipated sixty years ago, when Jan Six and his associates demarcated their working area in an almost ironic fashion: 'The society's activities could extend across the entire country. The group of Amsterdam citizens who took the initiative to establish this society were, however, especially focused on the city centre of Amsterdam, that part of the city bordered by Singelgracht and the IJ River. The intention for the present is to limit the working area to the part of town just described.'[50]

The words 'for the present' conceal a rich history and a promise of a long future.

Defence line of Amsterdam

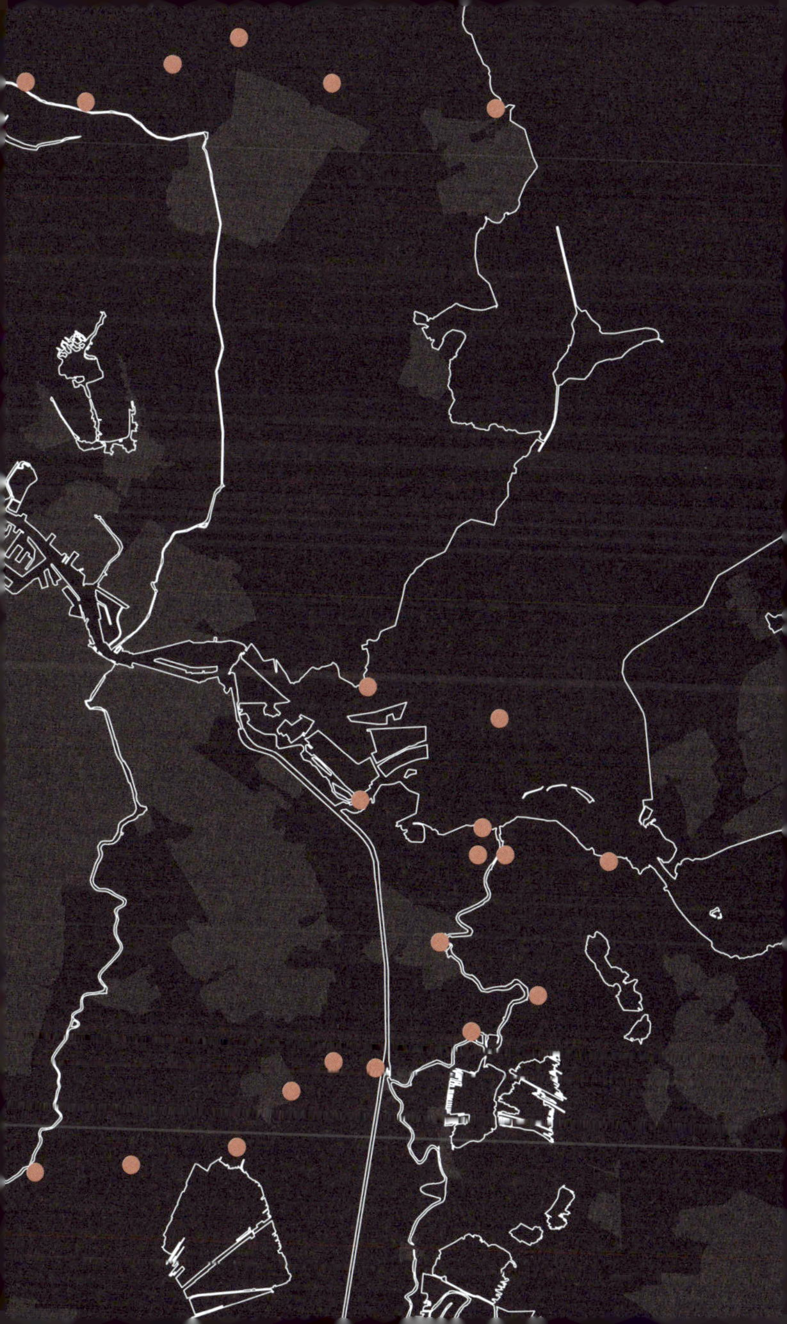

Landscape

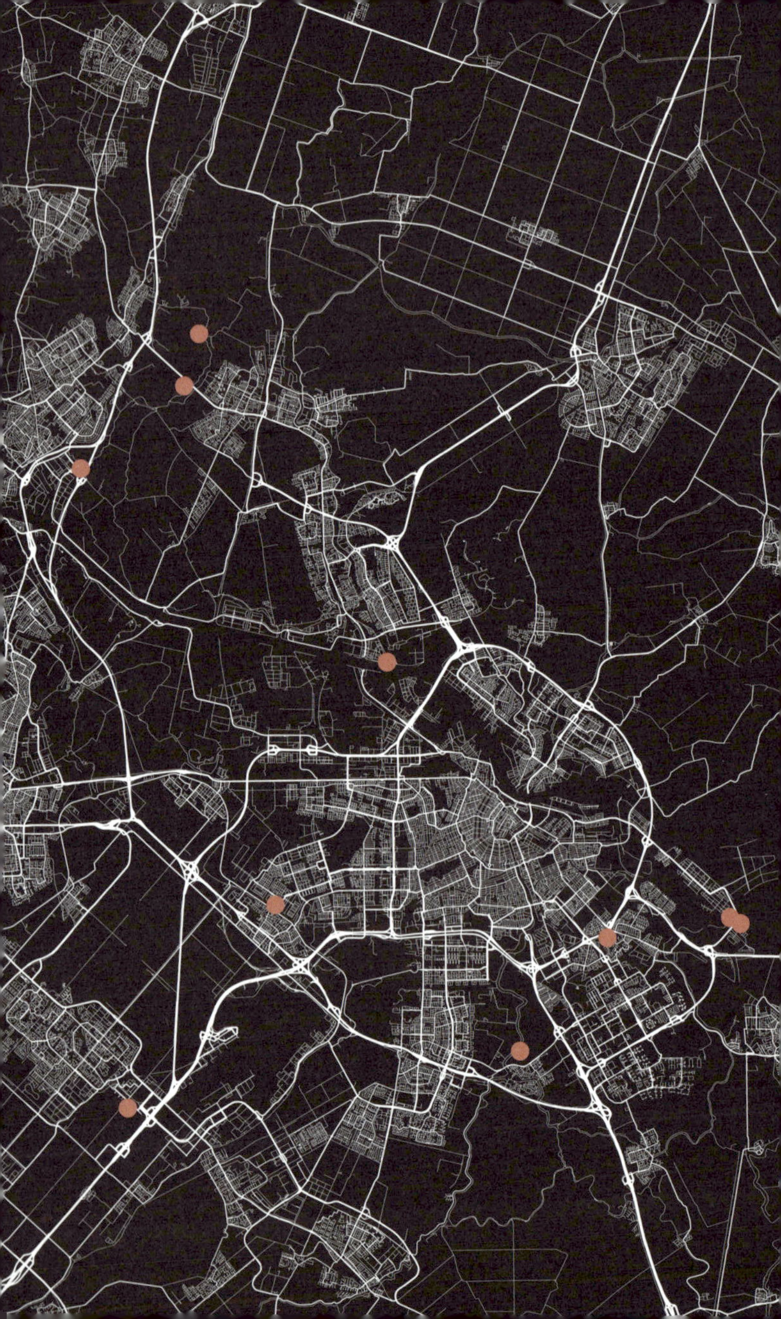

70	**Farmhouse den Burgh**, Hoofdorp
70	**Vensermolen**, Diemen
71	**Windmill de Zwaan**, Ouderkerk aan de Amstel
72	**Fort aan de St. Aagtendijk**, Beverwijk
82	**Fort aan den Ham**, Uitgeest
88	**Fort bij Krommeniedijk**, Uitgeest
96	**Akermolen Osdorp**, Amsterdam
104	**Fort Diemerdam**, Diemen
114	**Kringwetboerderij Zeehoeve**, Diemen
122	**Gebouw 197**, Zaandam

Stadsherstel has expanded its area of work to the Stelling van Amsterdam (Defence Line of Amsterdam). Within the 19th century line, Fort Diemerdam and the farm Kringenwetboerderij Zeehoeve in Diemen, the first provincial building of Stadsherstel, have been restored. The Akermolen in Osdorp, a mill that formed part of the hydraulic engineering works in the forerunner of the Stelling, was repaired. More recently, work began on the restoration of Fort aan den Ham, Fort aan de St. Aagtendijk and Gebouw 197, and this year will see the repurposing of Fort bij Krommeniedijk.

Windmill de Zwaan

Forts on the former line

The Stelling van Amsterdam, a 19th century defence line with a perimeter of 135 km, consists of 46 forts and batteries, dykes and locks in a circle of 15 to 20 kilometres around Amsterdam. It is an example of Dutch hydraulic engineering genius. With an ingenious system, the land surrounding the line could be placed approximately 50 centimetres under water. After flooding, the shallow lake created was not deep enough for enemy ships, but too deep for a man and horse with carriages. In the event of an attack on the Netherlands, the army and the government could withdraw within the ring. The forts are situated at locations where the water line is intersected by dykes, roads and railway lines.

Landscape

Fort aan den Ham

The water line was already out of date before completion with the arrival of the airplane. In 1996, the Stelling van Amsterdam was designated a world heritage site of Unesco. Today, the landscape is chiefly a green oasis in the Amsterdam metropolitan region with a number of opportunities for relaxation. Many suburbs of surrounding municipalities are located in the vicinity of the former line.

Landscape

Farmhouse den Burgh
Rijnlanderweg 878, Hoofdorp
2013

Vensermolen
Venserkade 112, Diemen
2014

Landscape

Windmill de Zwaan
Binnenweg 2, Ouderkerk aan de Amstel
2016

Fort aan de St. Aagtendijk

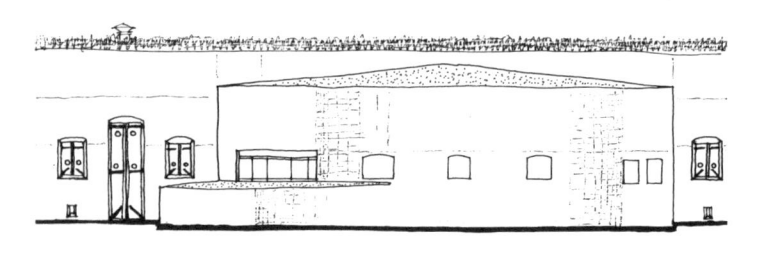

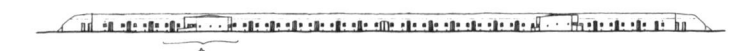

72

Address **Vuurlinie 1**	Built **1895/1899**	Restoration architect **Stadsherstel**
Town **Beverwijk**	Acquisition **2016**	Current use **Rehearsal room for musicians**
	Restoration **2016**	

Landscape

This fort served as defence of the St. Aagtendijk and the western quay of the Zuidwijkermeerpolder. The defensible earthwork was finished in 1895, the bomb-proof building in 1899. A 2.5 km-long defensive wall runs between the St. Aagtendijk and Zuidwijkermeer forts. A unique feature of this fort is the front caponier made of concrete: it's an extension to the centre of the fort's front wall, fitted on both side with embrasures that could be used to fire sideways. The caponier was protected against grenade fire by a heavy earth coverage. The original landscape around this fort has changed dramatically due to the construction of the A9 road. The motorway to the east of the fort runs directly alongside the engineer depot. The fort is now being used as a practice room for musicians and is regularly opened to the public.

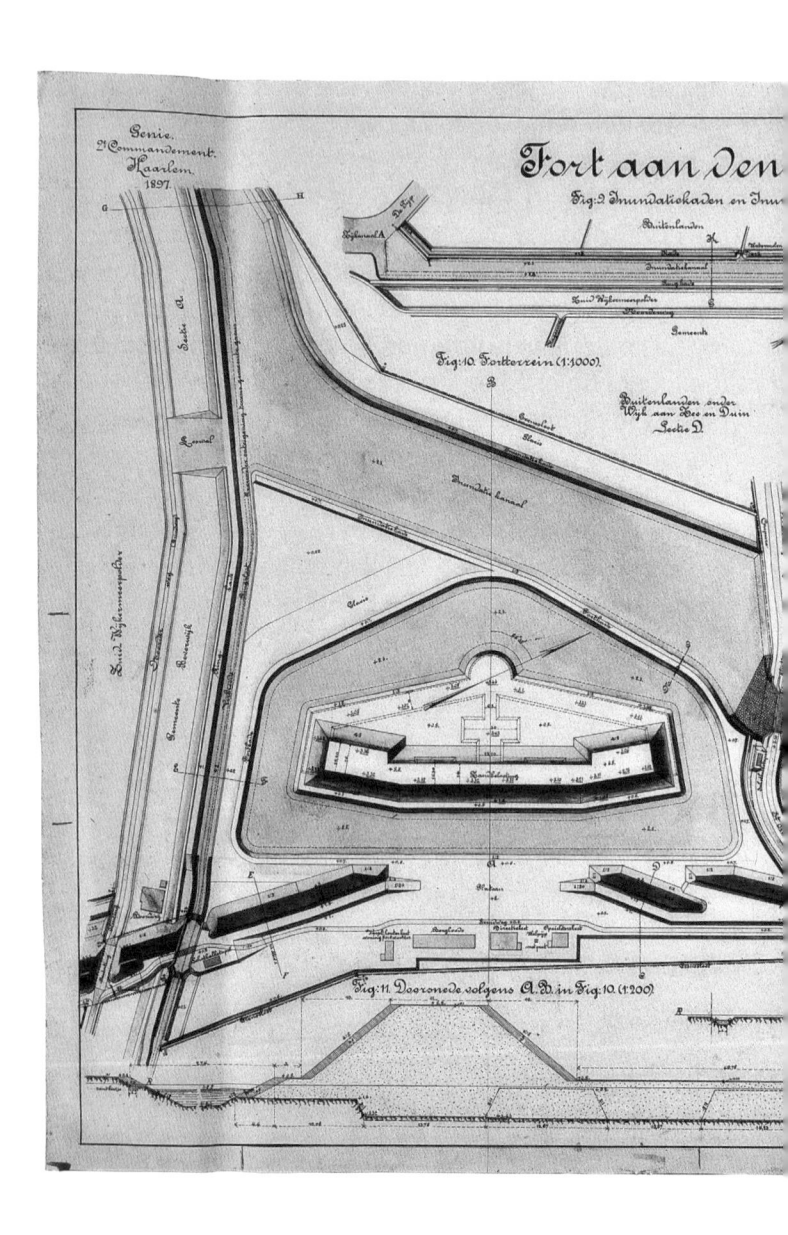

Fort aan de St. Aagtendijk

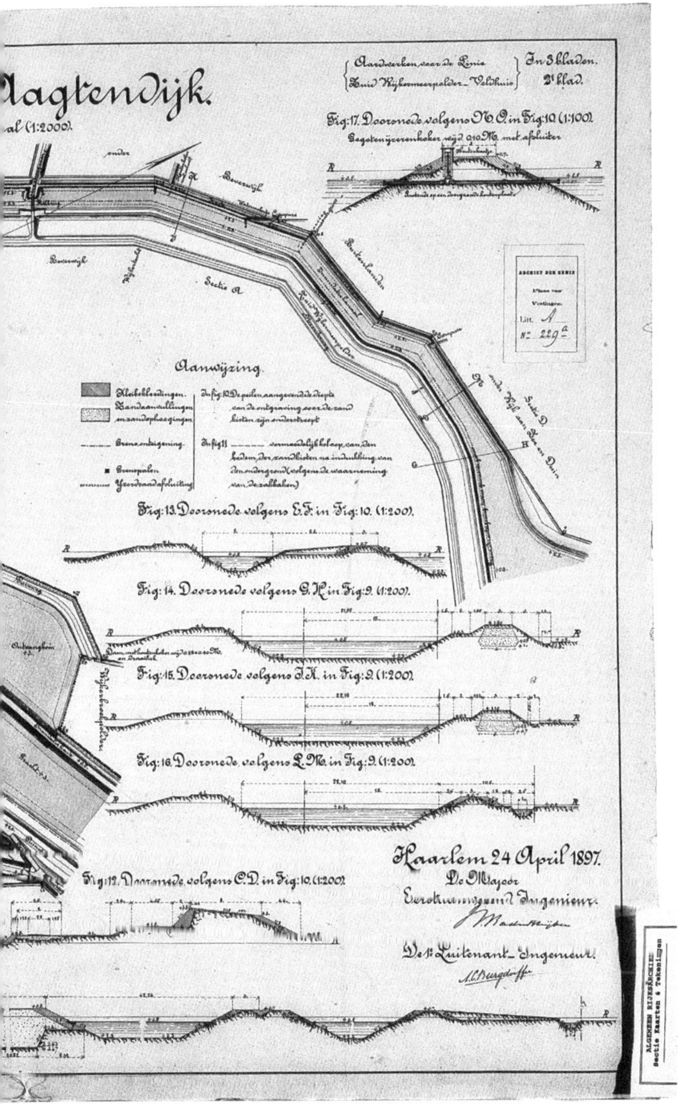
lagtendijk.
al (1:2000).
Aardwerken voor de Linie
Zuid Wijkermeerpolder – Veldhuis
In 3 bladen.
2e blad.
Fig:17. Doorsnede volgens N. O. in Fig:10. (1:100).
Aanwijzing.
Fig:13. Doorsnede volgens E.F. in Fig:10. (1:200).
Fig:14. Doorsnede volgens G.H. in Fig:9. (1:200).
Fig:15. Doorsnede volgens J.K. in Fig:9. (1:200).
Fig:16. Doorsnede volgens L.M. in Fig:9. (1:200).
Haarlem 24 April 1897.
De Majoor
De 1e Luitenant-Ingenieur.
Fig:12. Doorsnede volgens C.D. in Fig:10. (1:200).

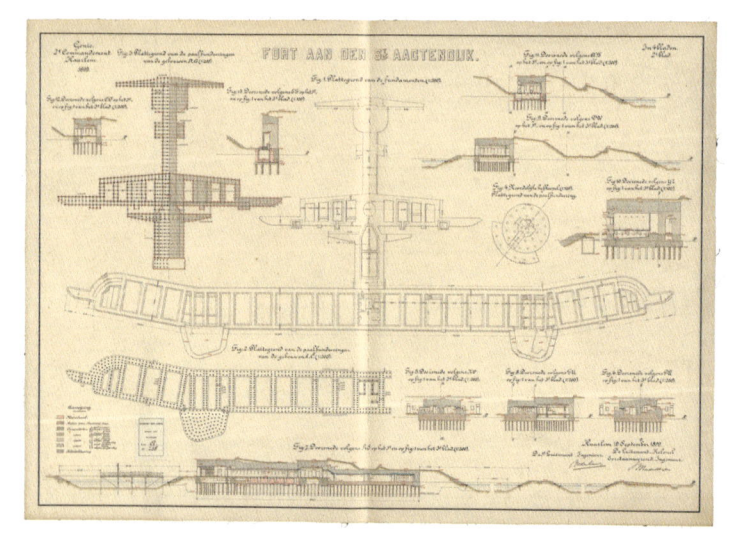

Fort aan de St. Aagtendijk

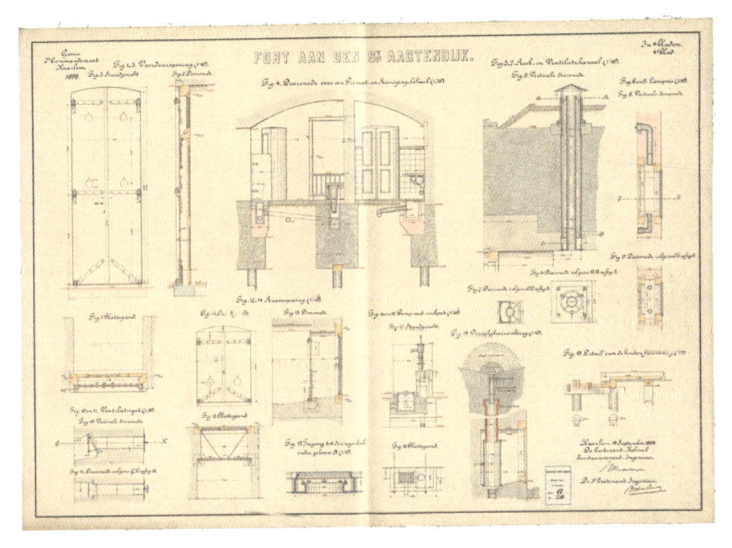

Landscape

Fort aan de St. Aagtendijk

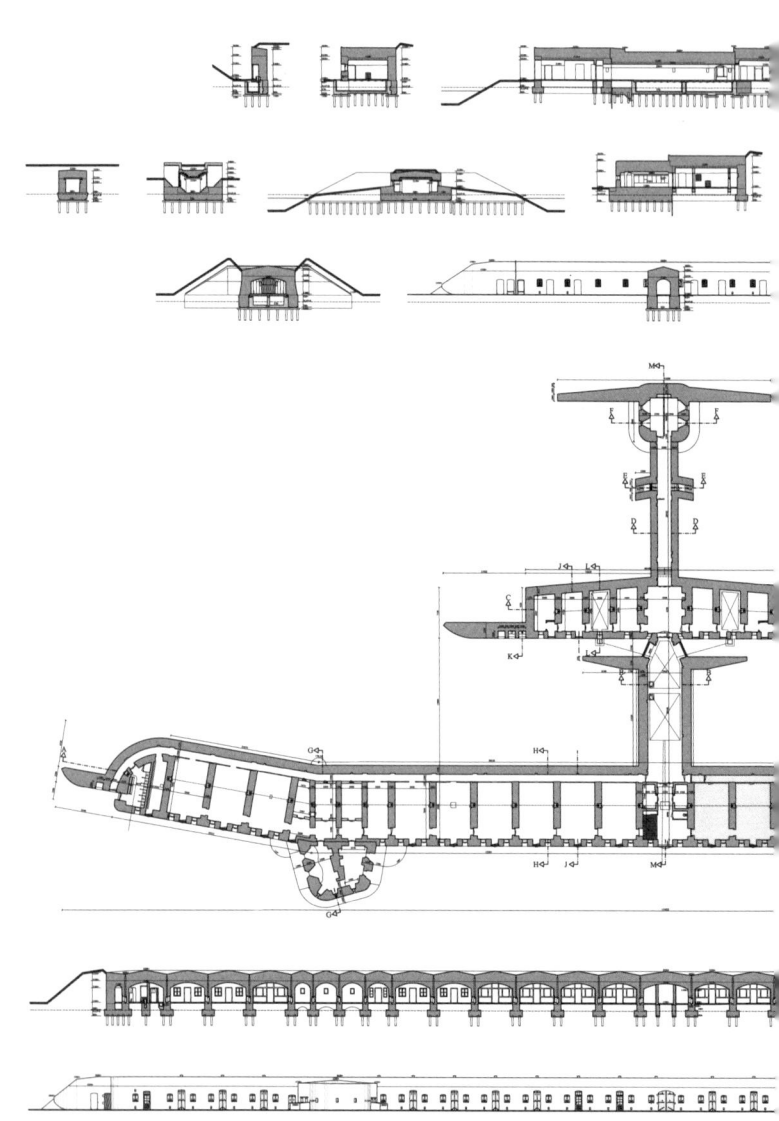

Floor plan, cross-sections and front view

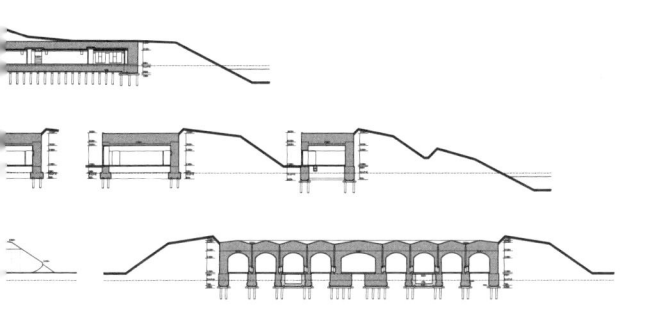

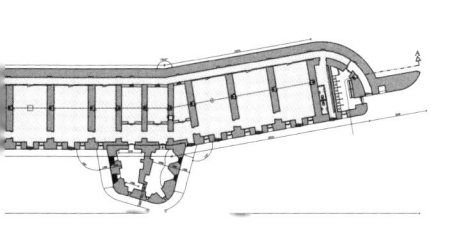

Landscape

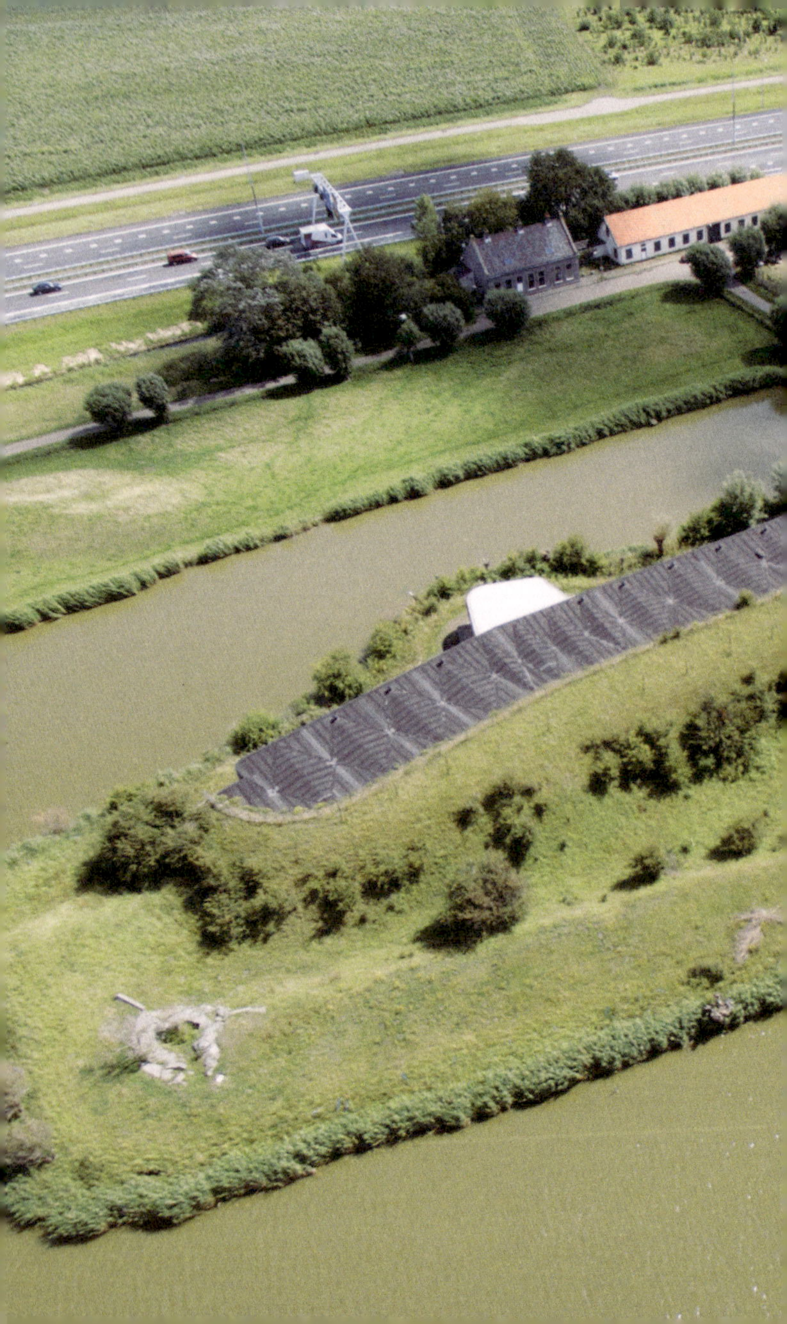

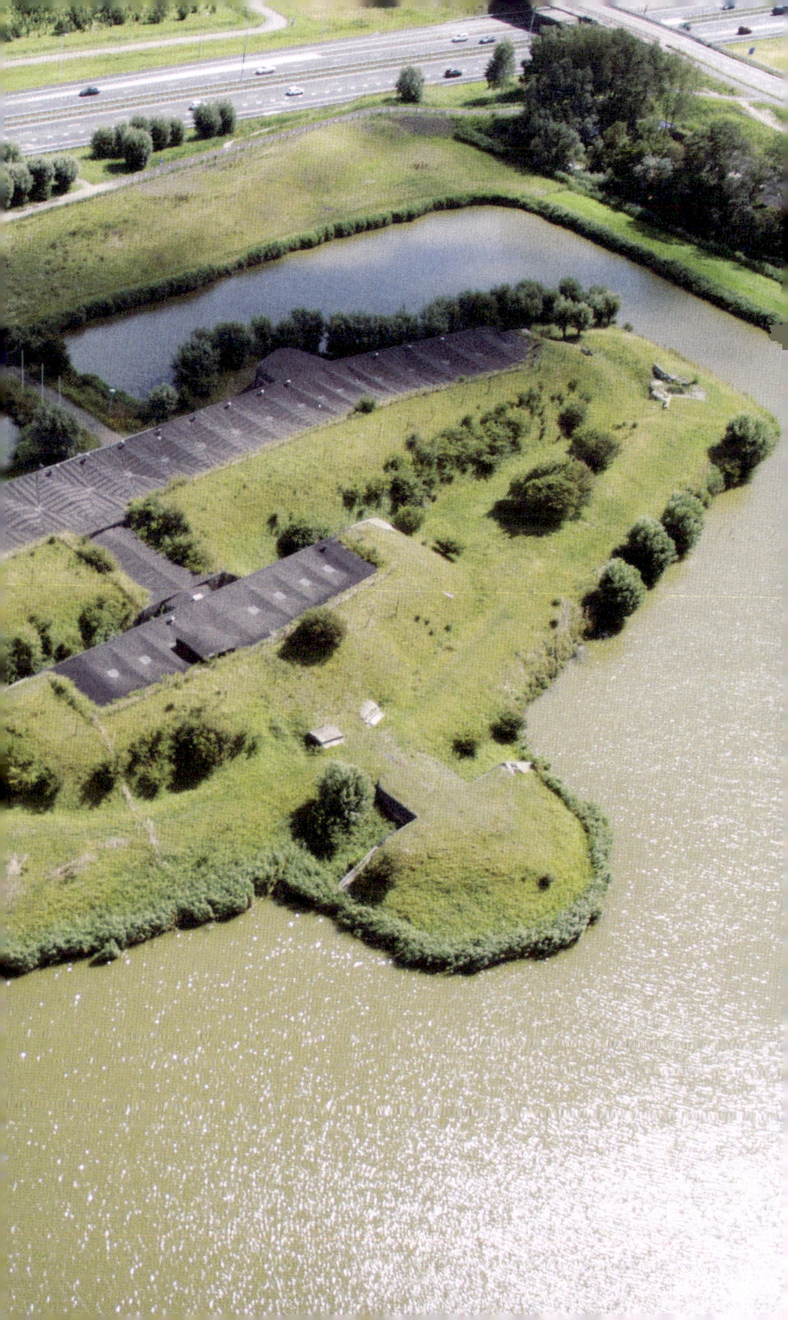

Fort aan den Ham

Address
Busch en Dam 13

Town
Uitgeest

Built
1896/1903

Acquisition
2012 (leasehold)

Restoration
2015

Restoration architect
Unknown

Current use
Military Museum

Landscape

The Fort aan den Ham was built between 1896 and 1903 and is located alongside the railway tracks and the N203 between Krommenie and Uitgeest. The necessity for this arose following the construction of the railway line from Amsterdam to Alkmaar on a slope, precisely between the larger forts Veldhuis and Krommeniedijk. In 1896, earth embankments were constructed on the fort grounds next to the railway line and several bombproof buildings followed in 1902 – 1903. In 1908, the concrete secondary battery was built on the southern side of the fort. The adjacent Rijksweg, the current N203, was completed in 1934 and runs parallel to the track. Fort aan den Ham had two lifting domes as main armament, each with a relatively small 6 cm canon in order to be able to fire on the flooded area and the railway embankment. The concrete main building, surrounded by a moat, is now a small military history museum. The engineer depot which belongs to the fort, a 19th century wooden depot just outside the moat on the rear side of the concrete main building, was used for the storage of the machinery and equipment in peacetime and was restored by Stadsherstel. Most of the 46 forts in the Stelling van Amsterdam has an engineer depot. Half of them still exist and several have been restored.

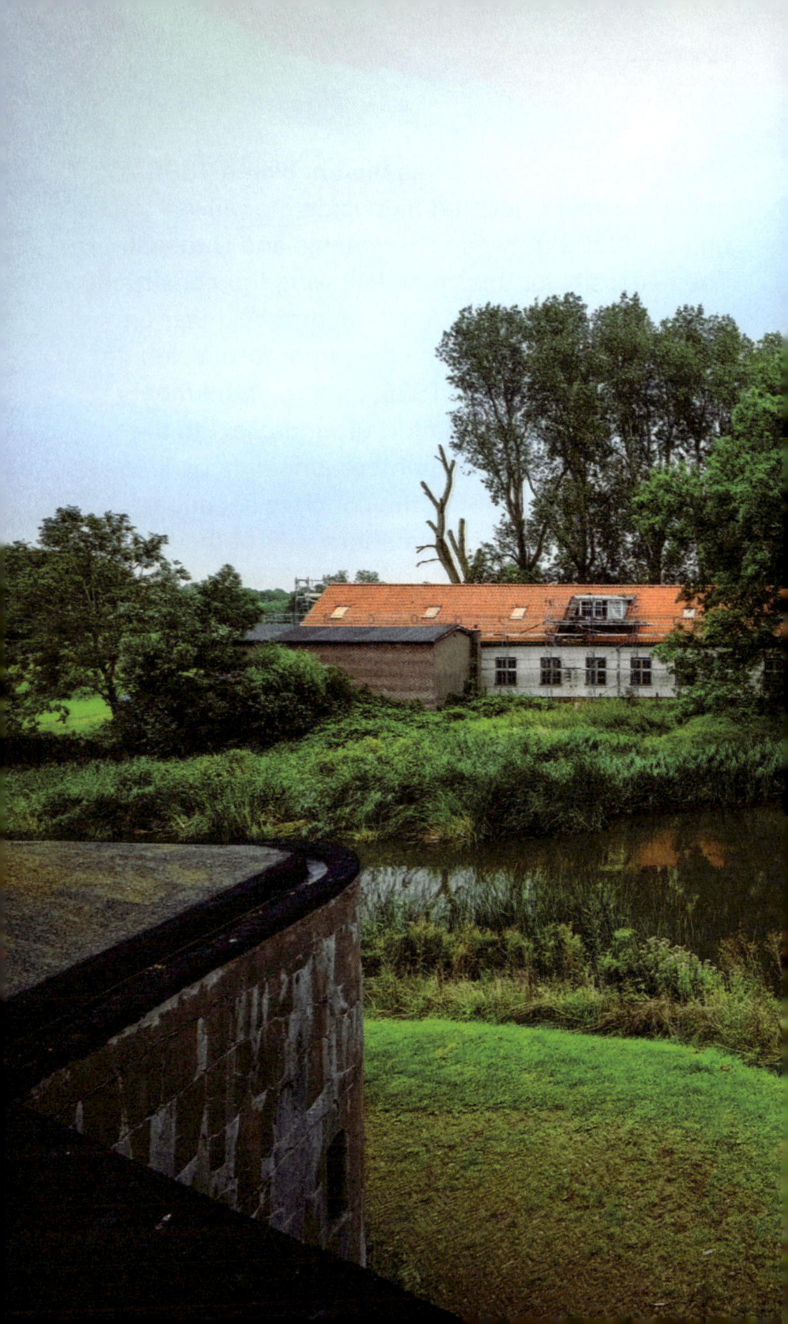

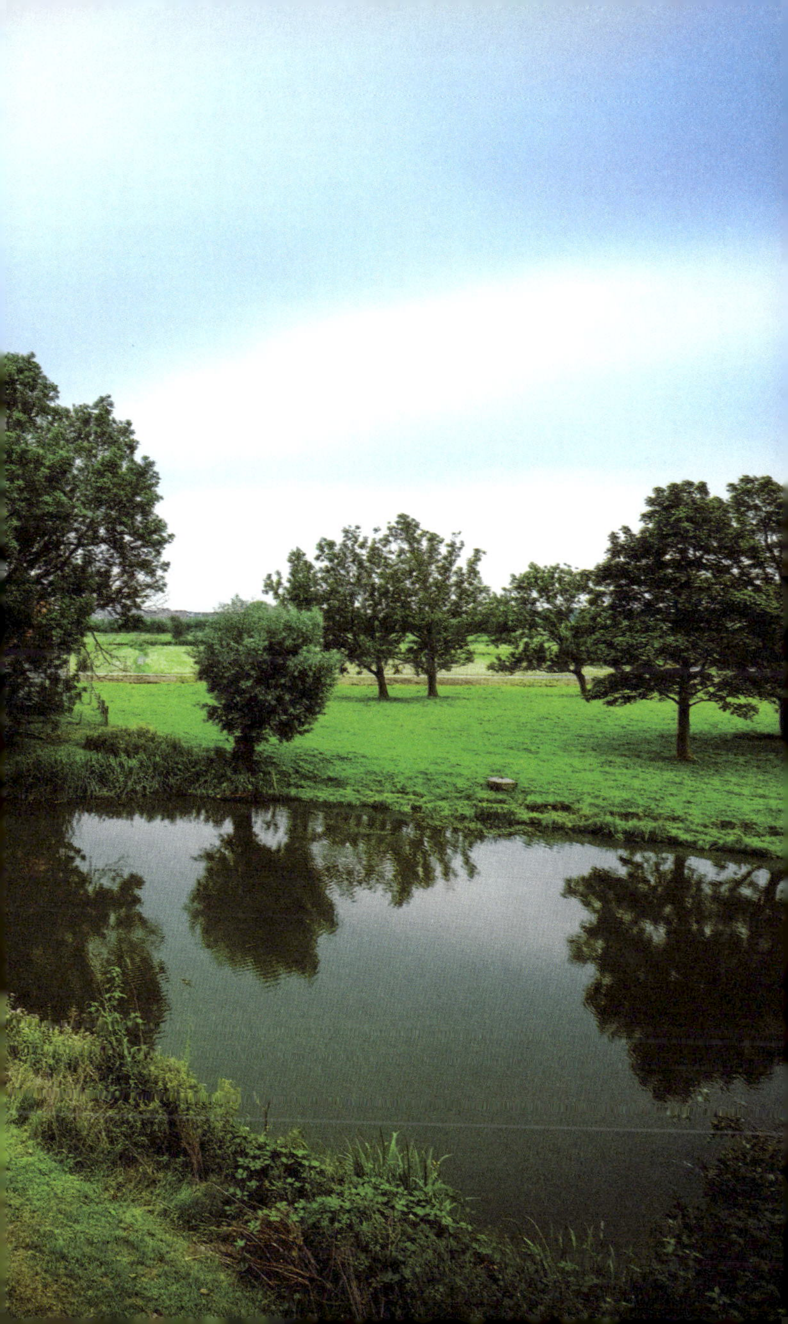

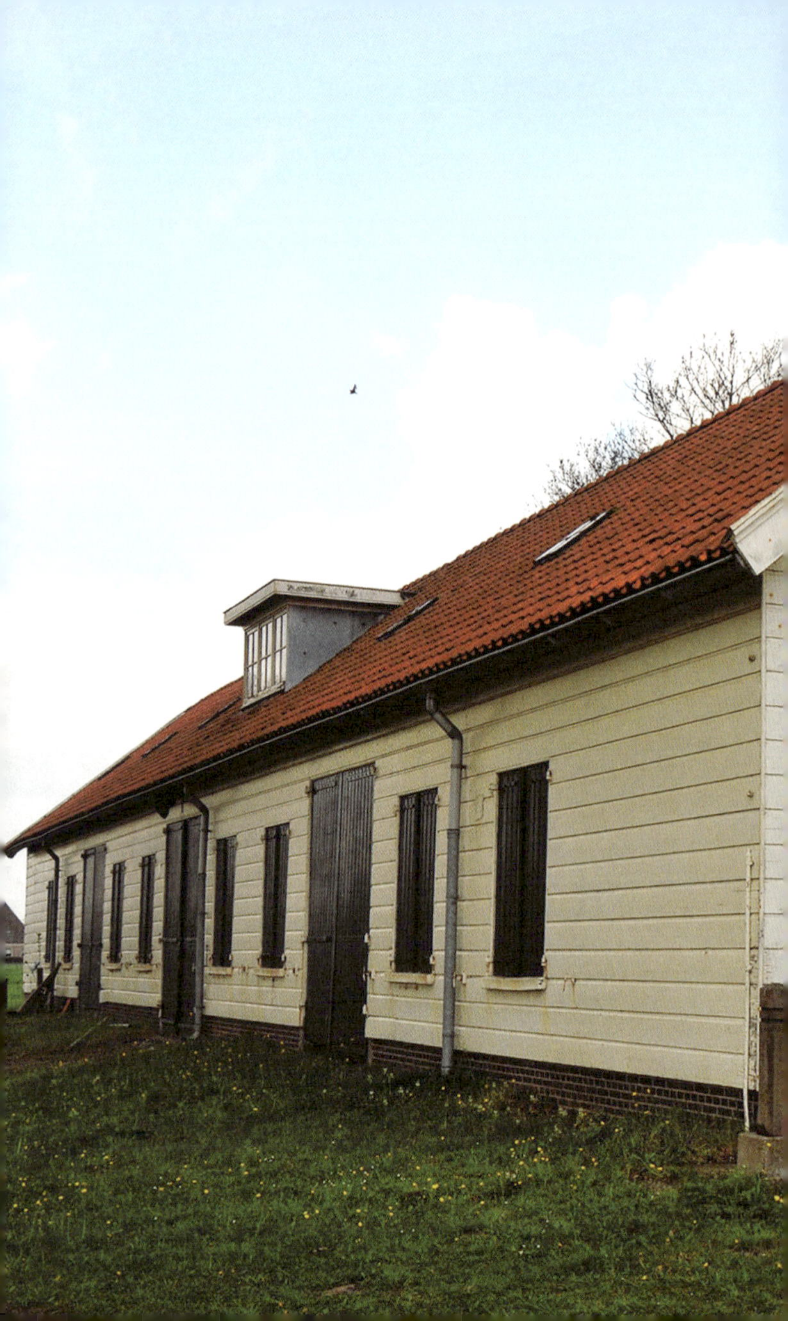

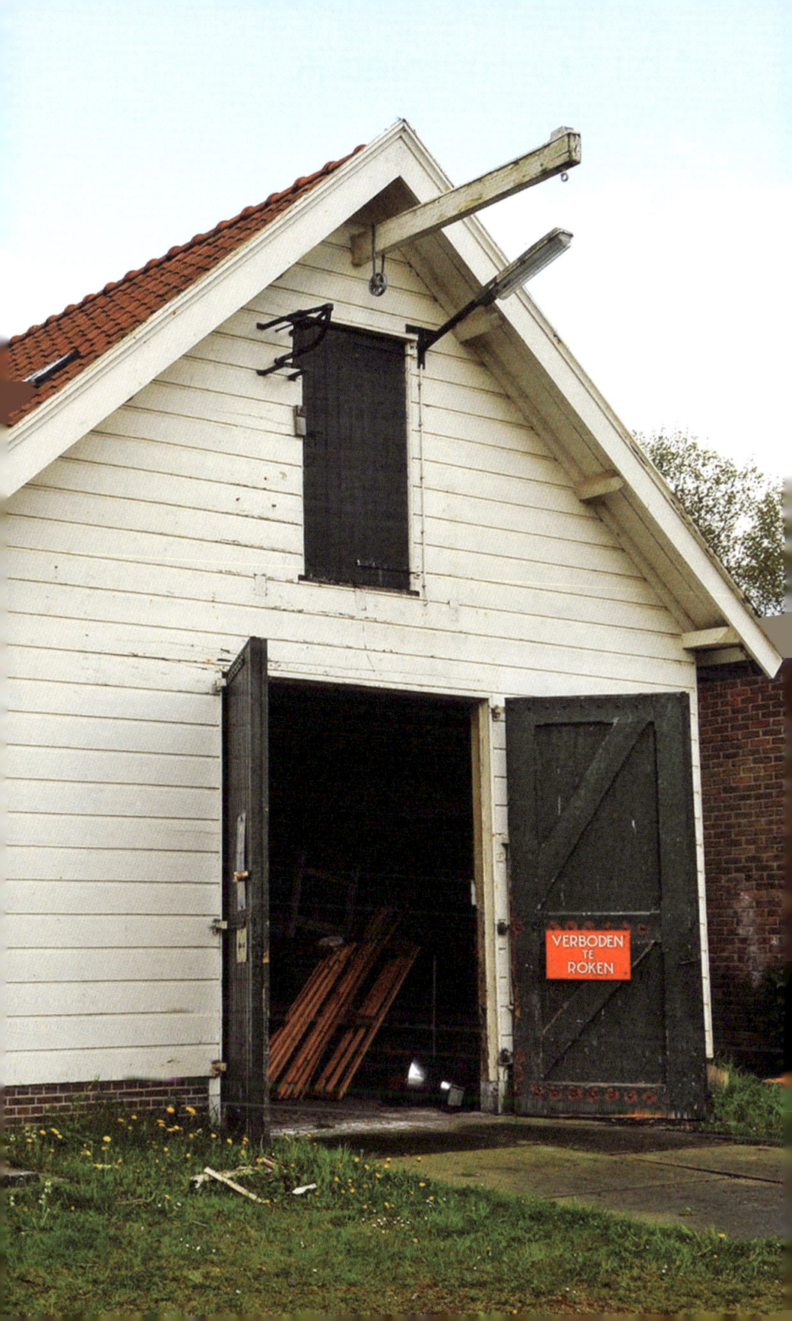
VERBODEN
TE
ROKEN

Fort bij Krommeniedijk

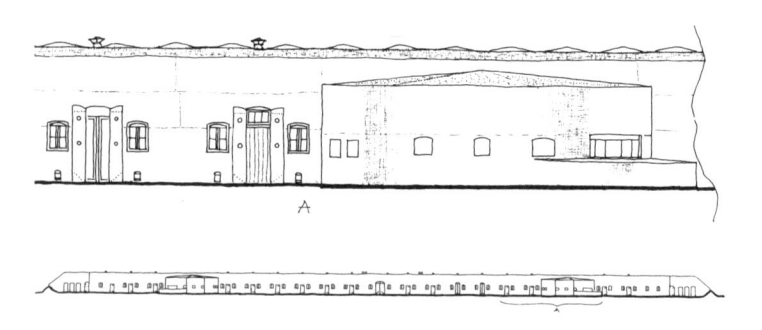

88

Address
Lagendijk 22

Town
Uitgeest

Built
1894

Acquisition
2016

Restoration
2017

Restoration architect
Hooyschuur Architecten

Current use
Future use as residential training centre for 26 autistic young adults and as a third visitor centre about the Stelling van Amsterdam focusing on natural values

Landscape

The Fort bij Krommeniedijk belonged to the most vulnerable part of the Stelling van Amsterdam. The width of the flooding area was small at the north-westerly-facing fort on the Lagendijk close to Uitgeest and also the high dune grounds in the vicinity ensured that construction of the first forts began here. The buildings of the fort were completed in 1903, the year in which the well-known landscape design firm and nursery Zocher received the assignment for, among other things, the planting of the outer moat with a single row of maples and Canadian poplars in the vicinity of the fort. The fortifications were officially closed in 1956, after which it was only in 1993 that it came into the possession of the foundation Landschap Noord-Holland. The original landscape around the fort has been preserved since then, with an open polder landscape, a meadow bird area, water around the defence line and the route of the Lagendijk road. The external layout of the fort grounds was designed anew after the acquisition, with terraces for visitors, parking places at both gorge branches of the fort and a bird observatory on the originally unpaved terrepleins. The new fort watchman's house was built based on a work by the Dutch designer Piet Hein Eek.

Fort bij Krommeniedijk

Landscape

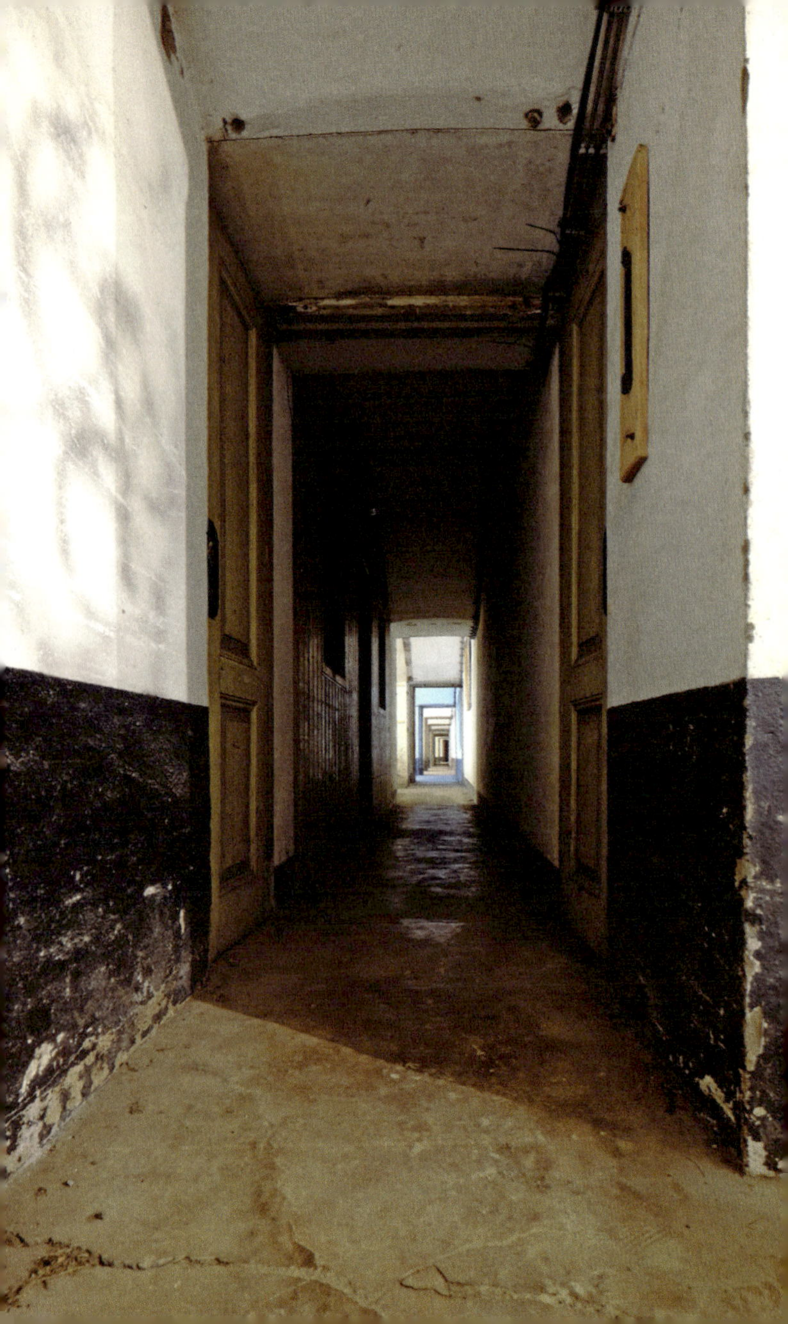

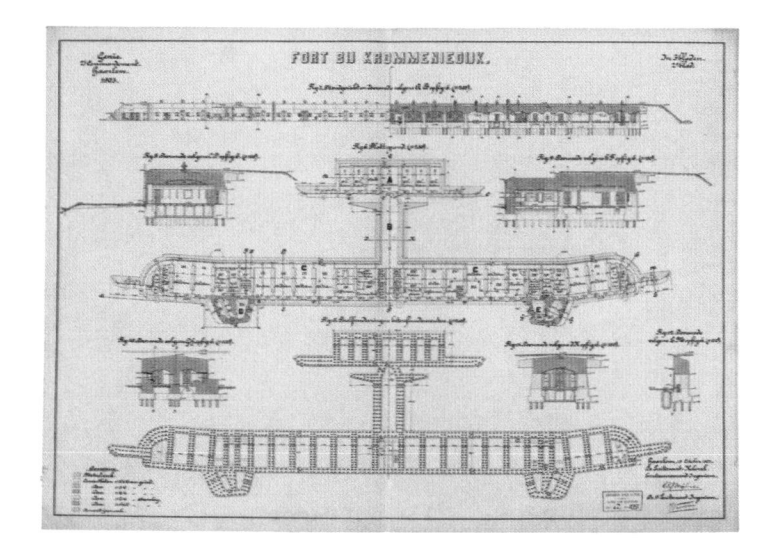

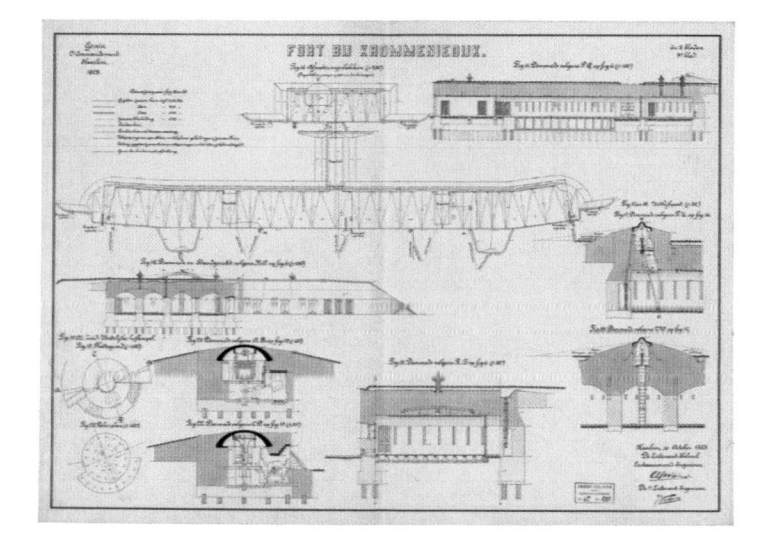

Landscape

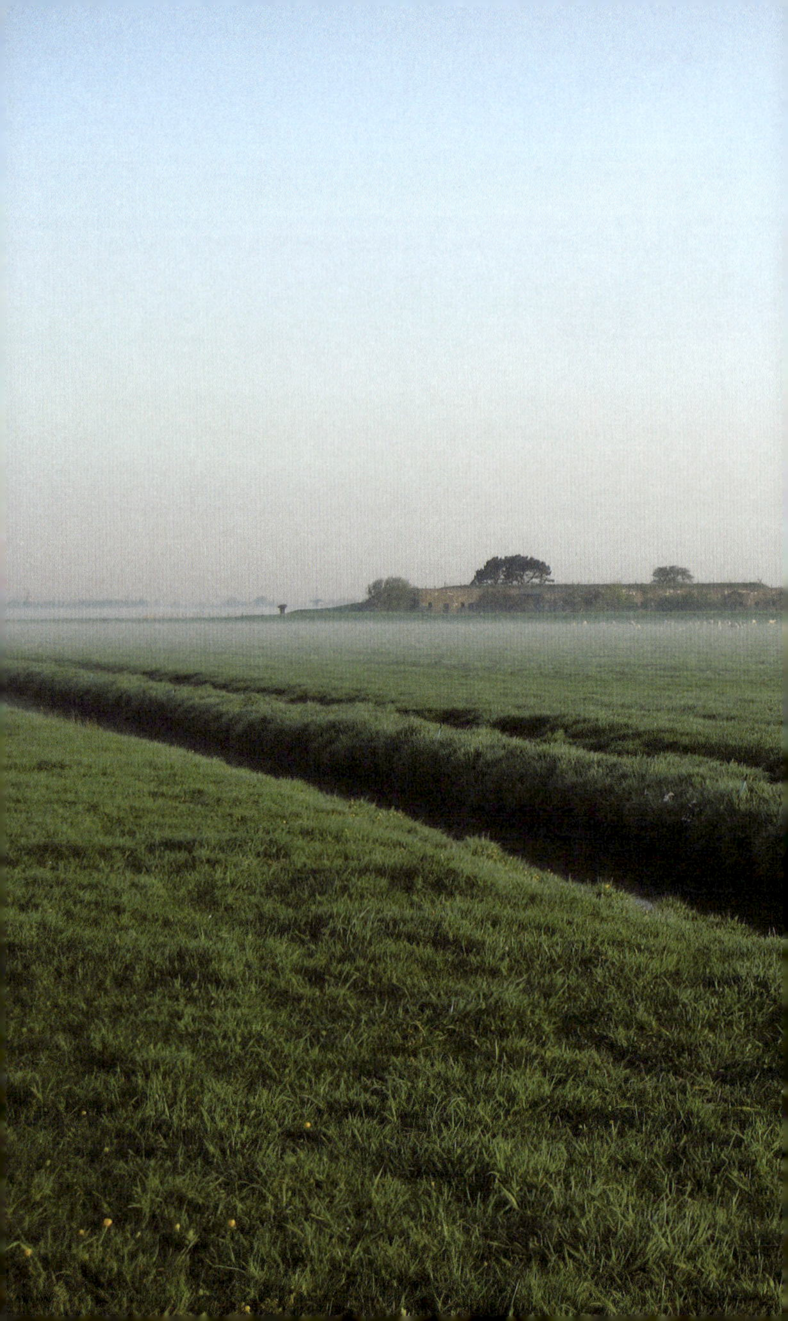

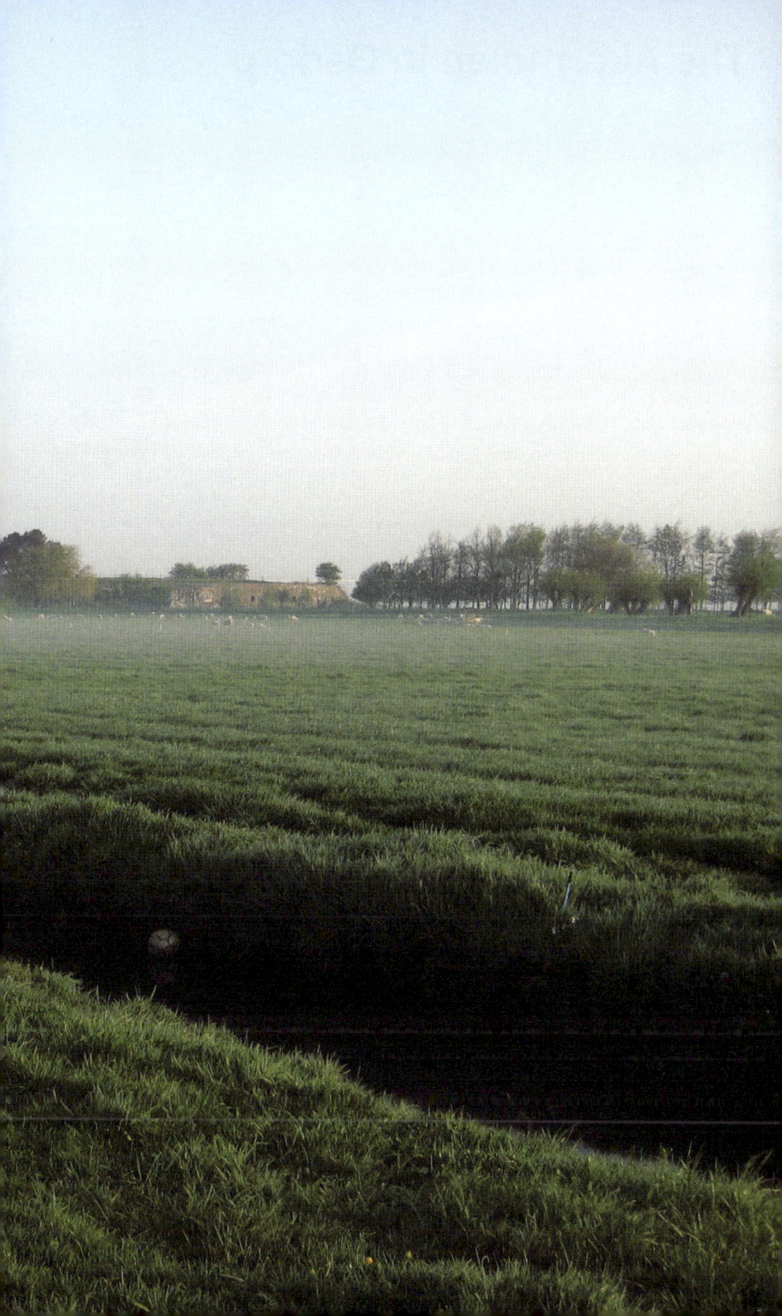

The Akermolen in Osdorp

Address
Zwarte Pad 30

Town
Amsterdam

Built
1874

Acquisition
2008

Restoration
2010

Restoration architect
R. van Dam

Current use
Information point, coffee- and tearoom

According to the minutes of de Dijkgraaf and Heemraden from the Haarlemmermeer Water Board, the Akermolen came from elsewhere before it was erected at its current location in 1874. The Oude Molen (Old Windmill), a modest little building at first glance, ensured that peat could be cut over the course of 20 years in the Middelveldsche Akerpolder in the 19th century. The water works that are still located underneath the mill stump, were not only used to keep the polder dry, but also formed part of the hydraulic engineering works in the Line during times of a threat of war. Of particular note are the old mill races which have been made visible through a glass floor that was fitted during the restoration around 2010. There is now a coffee and tea room at the mill.

The Akermolen in Osdorp

Landscape 99

'The old mill' (Akermolen), 2 July 1967

◁
Windmill De Akermolen pre 1921

The Akermolen in Osdorp

100

Akermolen before restoration

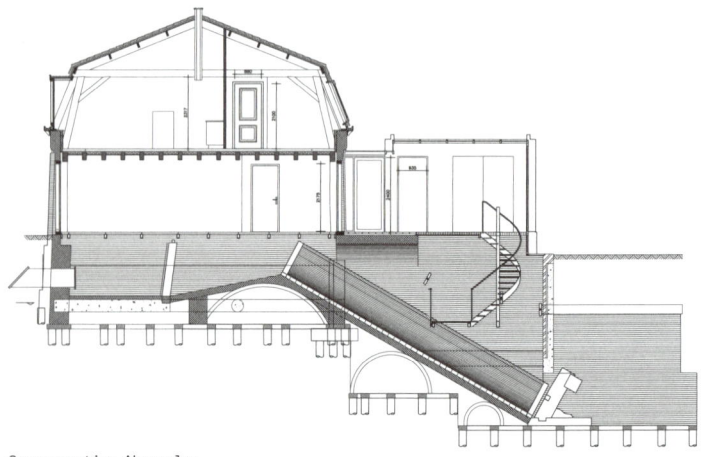

Cross-section Akermolen

Landscape

101

Interior restored Akermolen, first floor

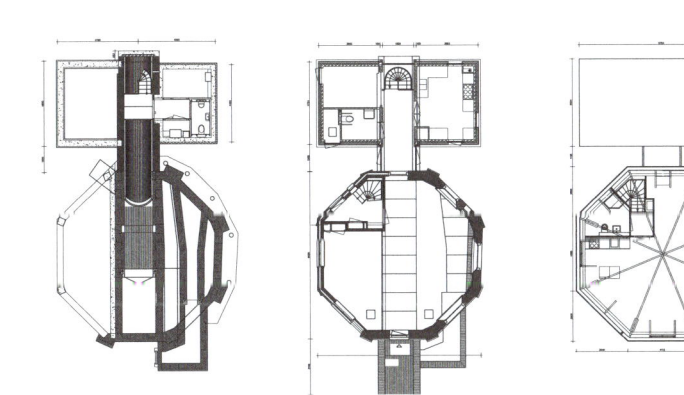

Floor plans: basement, ground floor, first floor

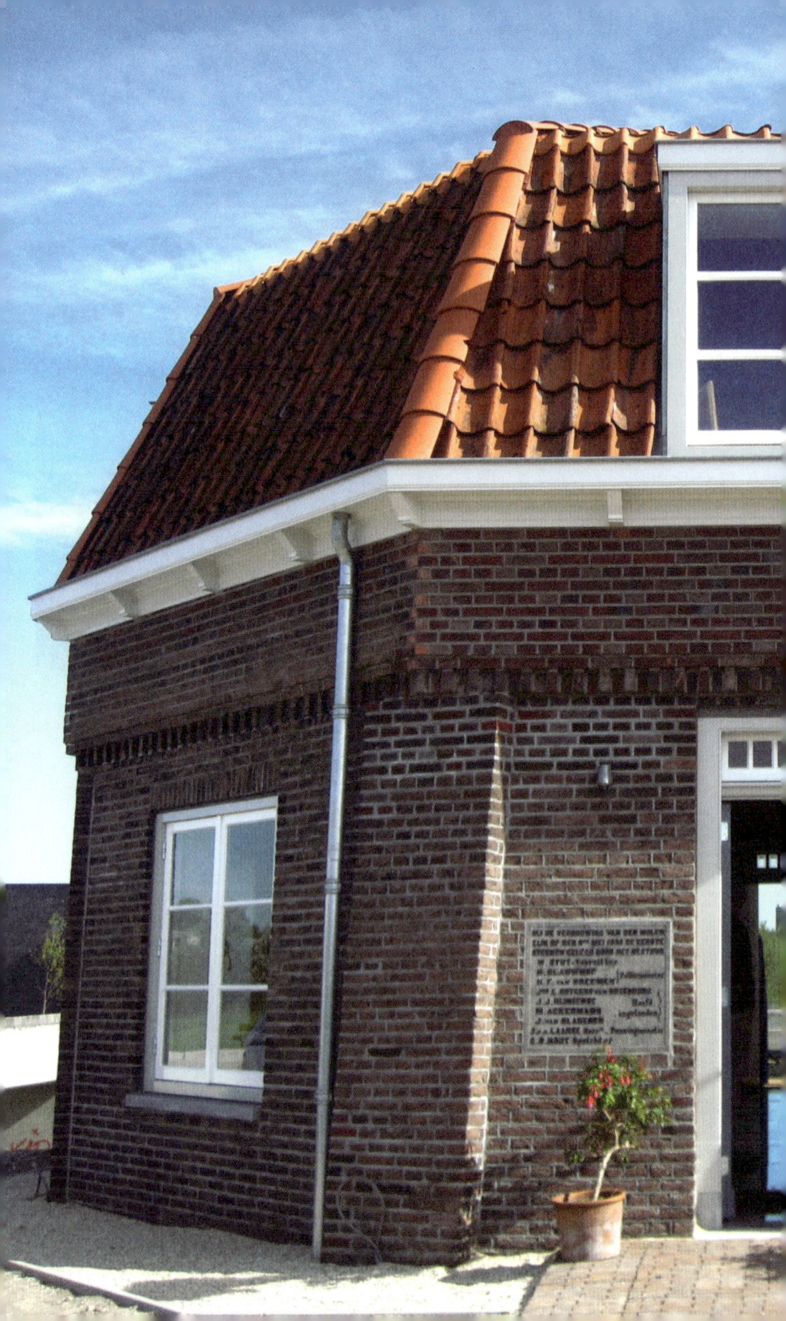

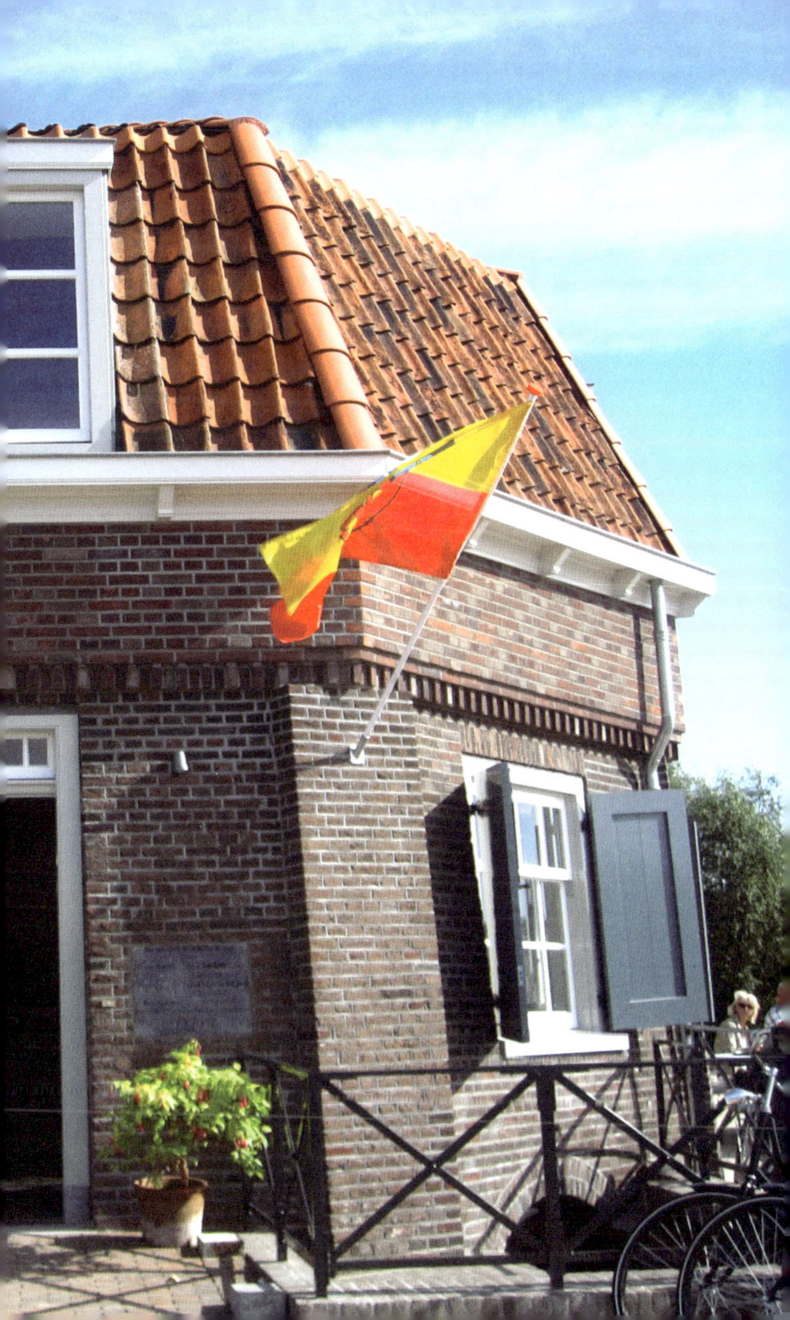

Fort Diemerdam

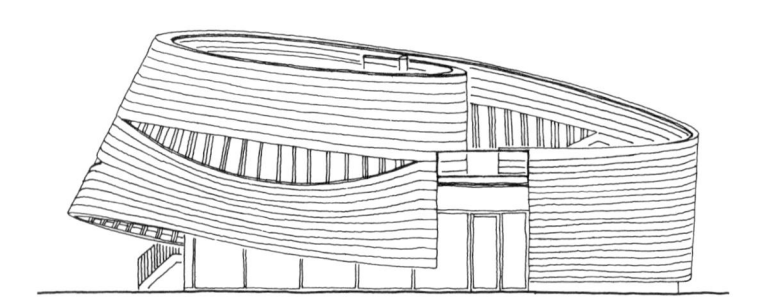

104

Address
Overdiemerweg 37

Town
Diemen

Built
2012

Acquisition
2006

Restoration
2012

Restoration architect
Rob Witsel

Current use
Hospitality pavilion

One of the few new building projects of Stadsherstel is a restaurant and café pavilion designed by Emma architects, which serves as main entrance at the green fortifications of Diemerdam coastal battery and the adjacent and previously refurbished Kringenwetboerderij Zeehoeve farm. The coastal battery was a site for a row of canons alongside the Zuiderzee (now IJsselmeer) for the protection of Amsterdam. There was already an earth rampart at this location, which later underwent all kinds of changes, new concrete buildings and gun emplacements were added, in order to become part of the Stelling in 1883. Paviljoen Puur was built on a historic floor plan according to regulations of the military fortification act, with a sunken plinth (60 cm) made from brick and a wooden superstructure. The wooden superstructure modelled on the various views of the surrounding landscape. The building is insulated with isovlas and clad with shingles made from untreated cedar.

Fort Diemerdam

Cannon in open coastal battery

Landscape

Fortwachter house

Hennipman family, Kringwelboerderij Zeehoeve (Fort Diemerdam)

Fort Diemerdam

108

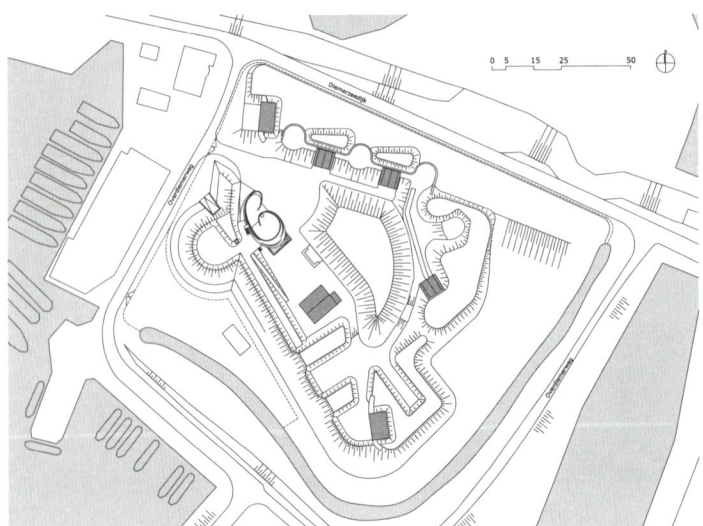

Site plan Fort Diemerdam after restoration

Landscape

Fort Diemerdam

110

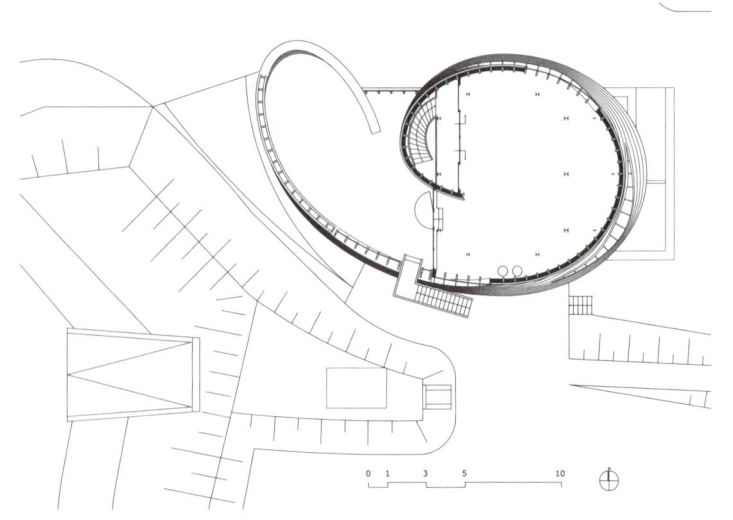

Site plan Pavilion Puur

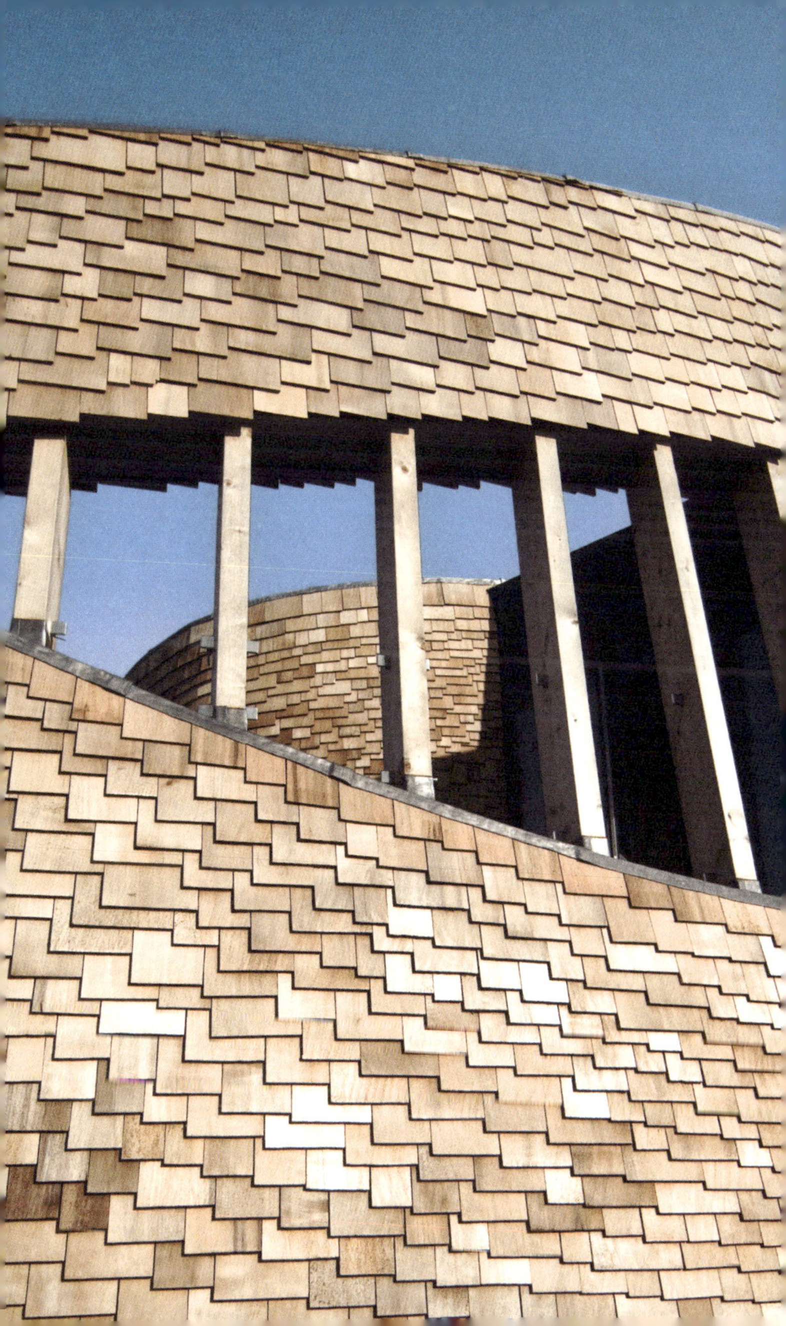

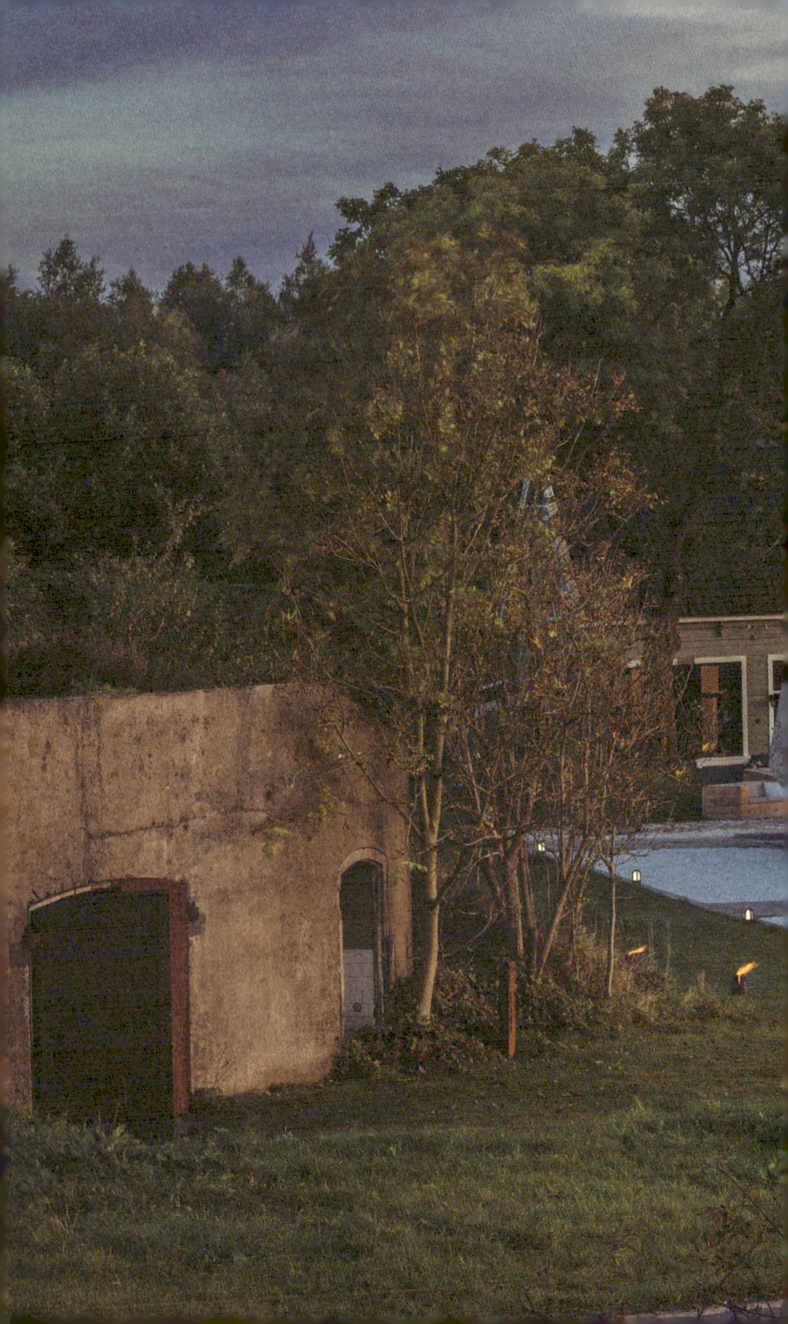

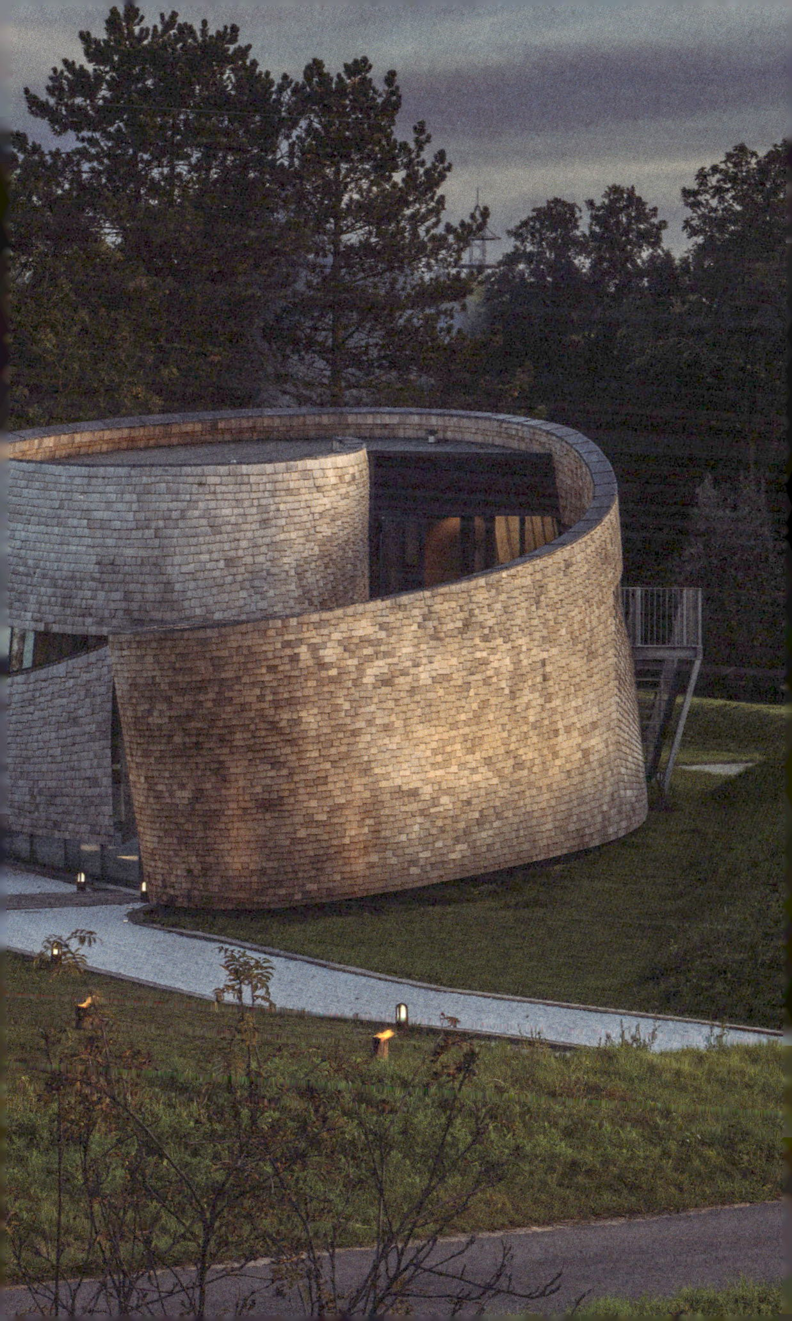

Kringwetboerderij Zeehoeve 114

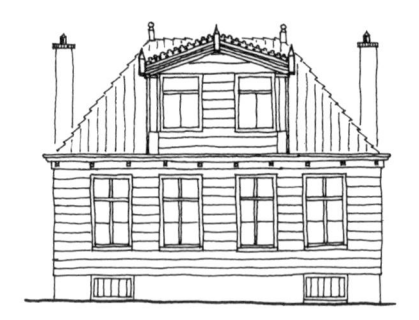

Address **Overdiemerweg 41**	Built **1847/1881/1923**	Restoration architect **R. Witsel**
Town **Diemen**	Acquisition **2003**	Current use **'Herstelling' Foundation**
	Restoration **2005**	

The provisions of the Military Fortifications (Building Restrictions) Act determined that no brick buildings were allowed to appear within the fort's field of fire. At the same time, the aim was to keep the meadowland low through grazing, so that the establishment of farms around forts could not be totally ruled out when building the defence line. The so-called 'kringenwetboerderijen' (military fortification act farms) met the requirement that they could be 'destroyed' quickly in times of war. It was only possible to build with wood on a brick foundation. The first dairy farm at the location of Zeehoeve – called 'Het Uijlenbosch' – was built in 1847 and was located within the circle surrounding the 'Batterij bij Diemerdam' (Battery near Diemerdam), a small fort originating from the 18th century that was erected close to the Stelling van Amsterdam in 1883.

Kringwetboerderij Zeehoeve

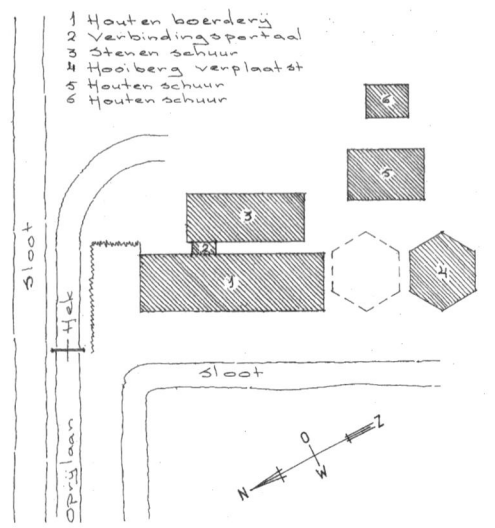

Location plan buildings Kringwetboerderij Zeehoeve

Landscape

The current wooden house – De Zeehoeve – dates from 1881 and has a rare floating cellar. It is a brickwork box, which can move up and down with the rise and fall of groundwater. The cellar is therefore actually separate from the construction of the house. The cowshed behind the living quarters of the farm was rebuilt on the wall footing of its precursor in 1923. Little remained of the shed following a storm in 2002. The grounds of De Zeehoeve was restored as much as possible to its state in around 1900. For example, the form cowshed was reconstructed with the original measurements and details, and reusing old materials as much as possible. The old fruit orchard and vegetable garden were restored on the basis of historical sources, as well as the greenery around the fort. A new addition to these grounds is the purification of the water through a halophyte field. The dirty water is guided through this field and purified. The farm is currently being used by the Stichting Herstelling (Repair Foundation) and offers a place where unemployed participants can gain work experience through tidying up and maintaining the farm and grounds. The young people work, among other places, in the vegetable garden, building and catering.

Kringwetboerderij Zeehoeve

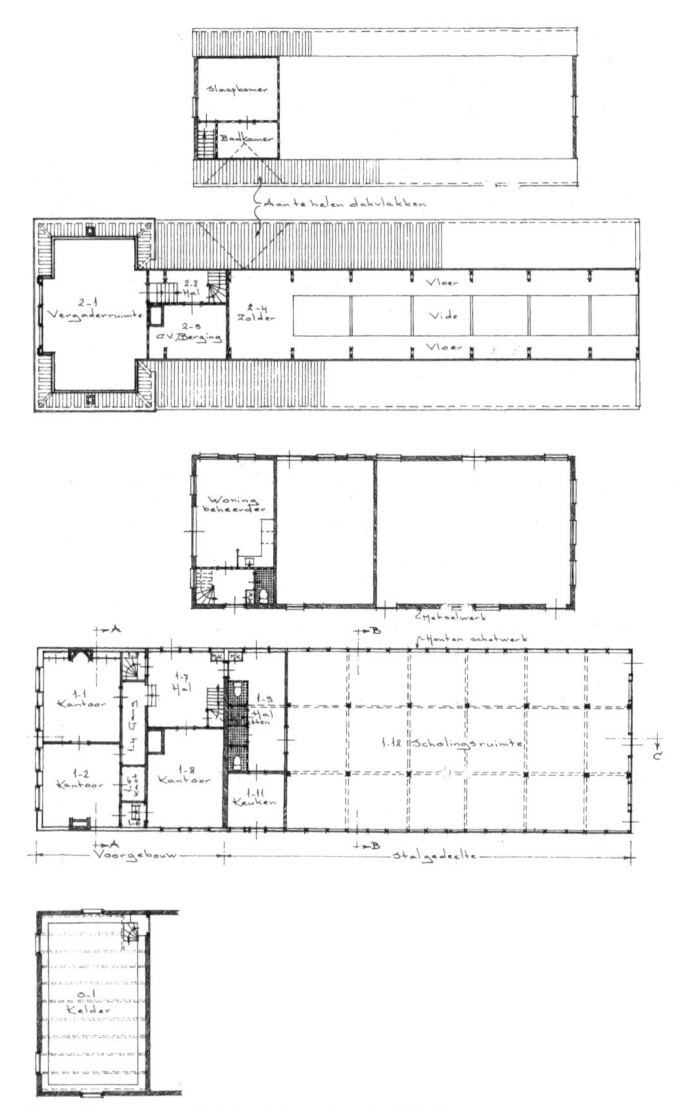

Floor plans current division Kringwetboerderij Zeehoeve

Landscape

Kringwetboerderij Zeehoeve

120

Front and back view, new situation

Landscape

Gebouw 197

122

Address	Built	Restoration architect
Havenstraat 157	**1918**	**Hooyschuur Architecten**
Town	Acquisition	Current use
Zaandam	**2015**	**Hospitality**
	Restoration	
	2016	

Landscape

Within the richly-wooded Hembrugterrein between the North Sea Canal and Zaandam, there are 60 industrial and empty buildings. The former chemical laboratory building, Gebouw 197 (Building 197), was very rundown and had partly collapsed when restoration started. The owner Central Government Real Estate Agency (Rijksvastgoedbedrijf) worked together with Stadsherstel in order to make the redevelopment of this piece of industrial heritage from 1918 possible. The site, in the middle of the Stelling, was put into used by the Department of War in 1895 for the production of weapons and ammunition. Ammunition was produced here until 2003. Since then, the buildings on the site, where thousands of people used to work, have fallen into further disrepair due to being left vacant. Gebouw 197 is part of a series of, at the time, heavily protected buildings, in various architectural styles, spread across the site. The raw, dilapidated architecture will probably become a provincial listed building. It was initially used as a chemical and metallurgy laboratory, and for inspection of ammunition. Work was carried out with combat gases in the laboratory. The laboratory waste was buried at various locations on the site and led to soil pollution. In 2012, a large-scale mustard gas inspection took place. In order to get rid of this image, more than 1 ha of soil was excavated.

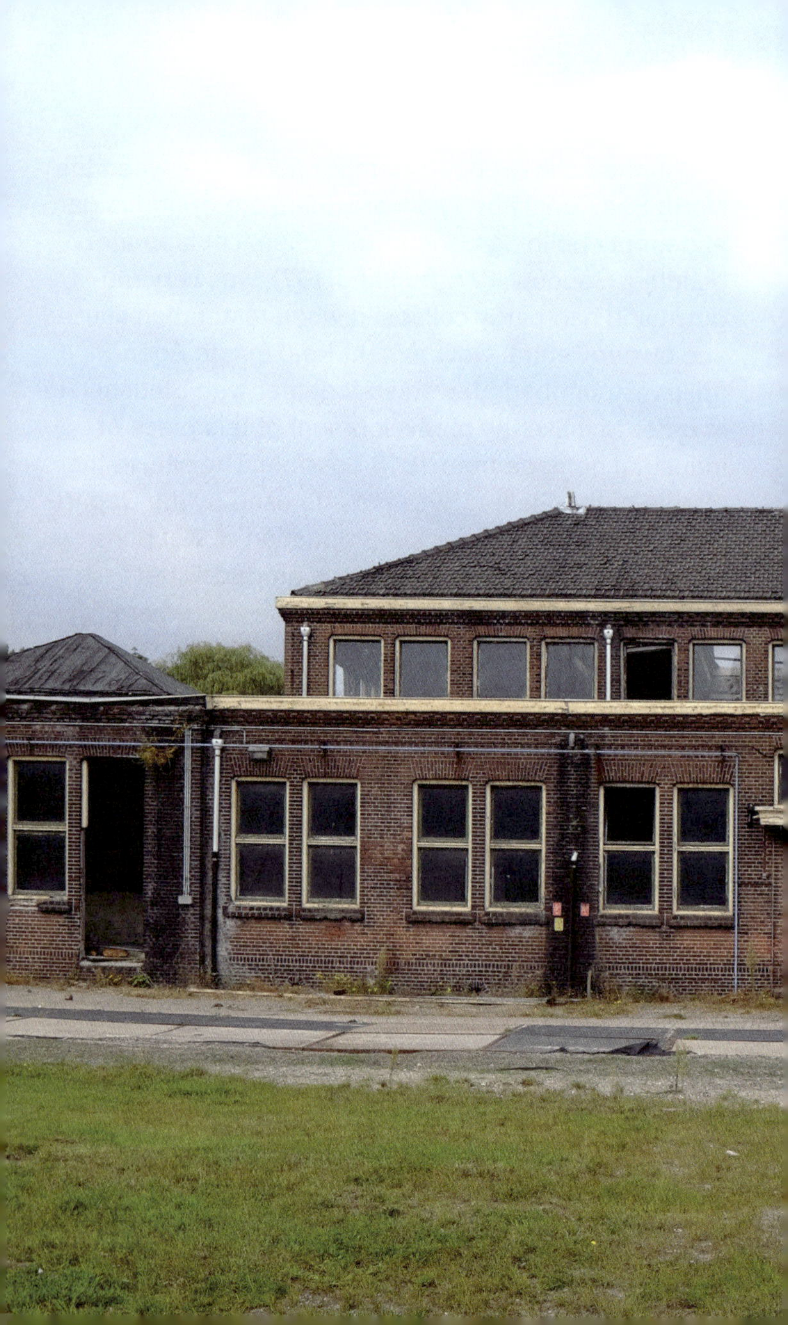

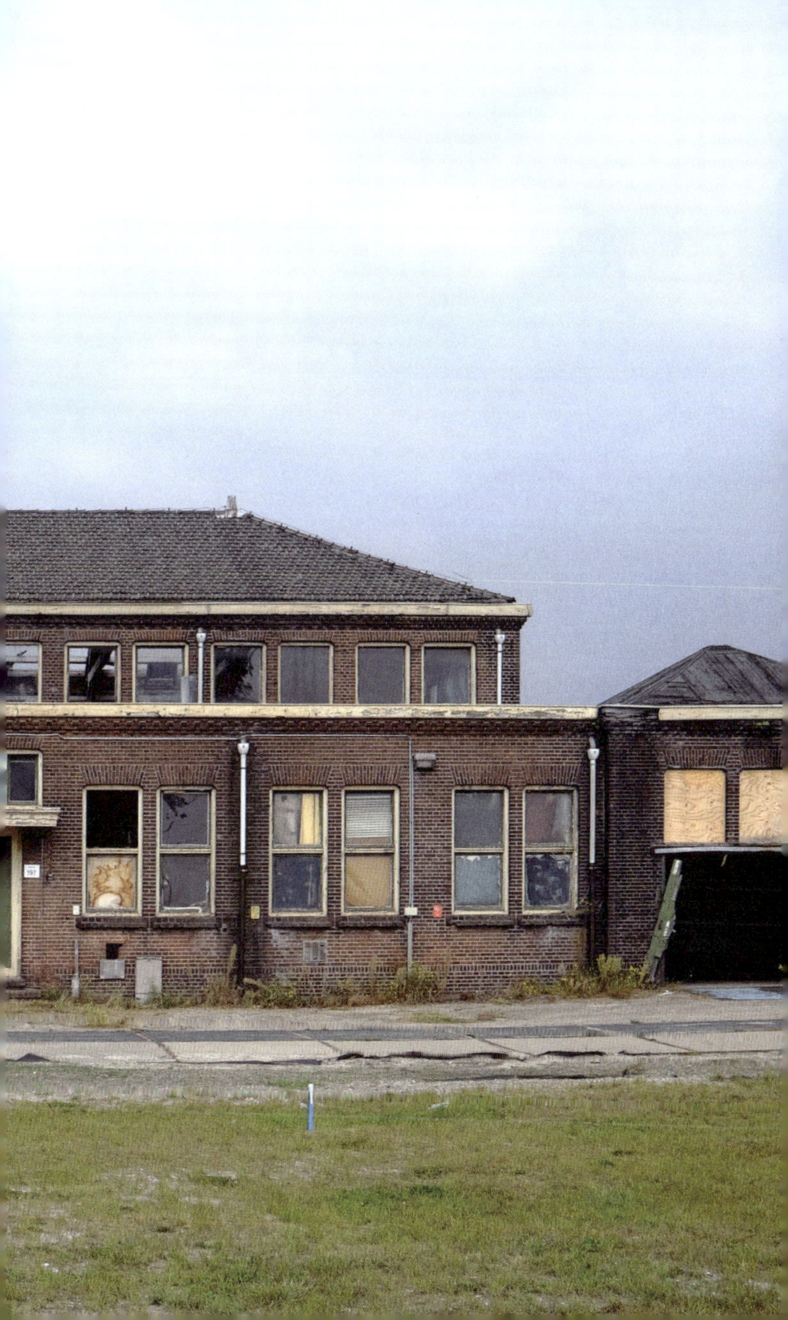
197

Gebouw 197

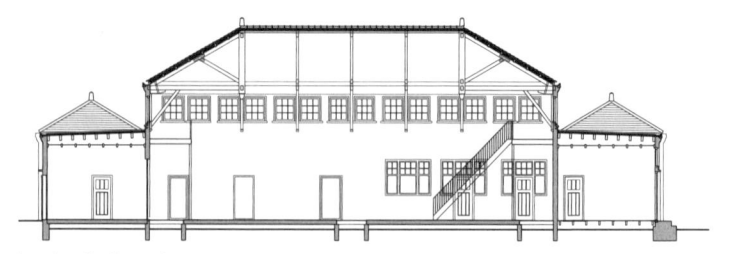

Longitudinal section

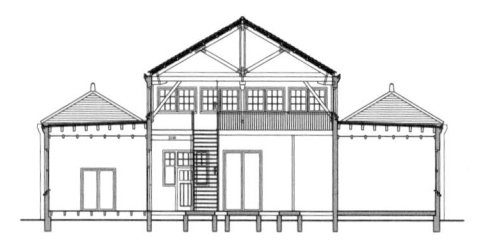

Cross-section

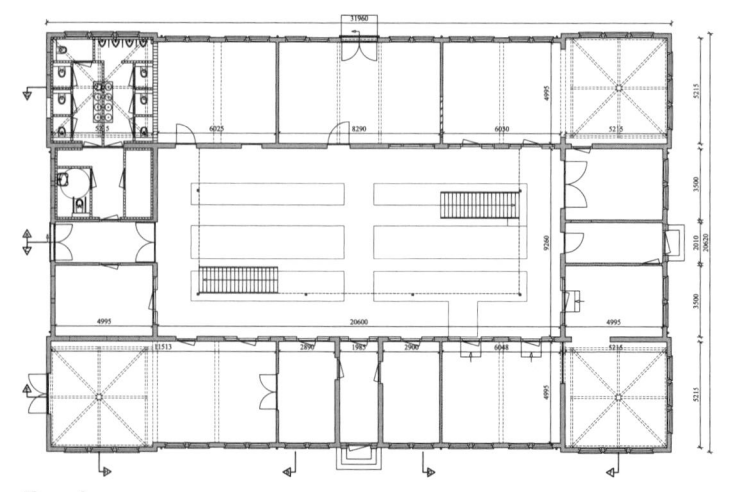

Floor plan

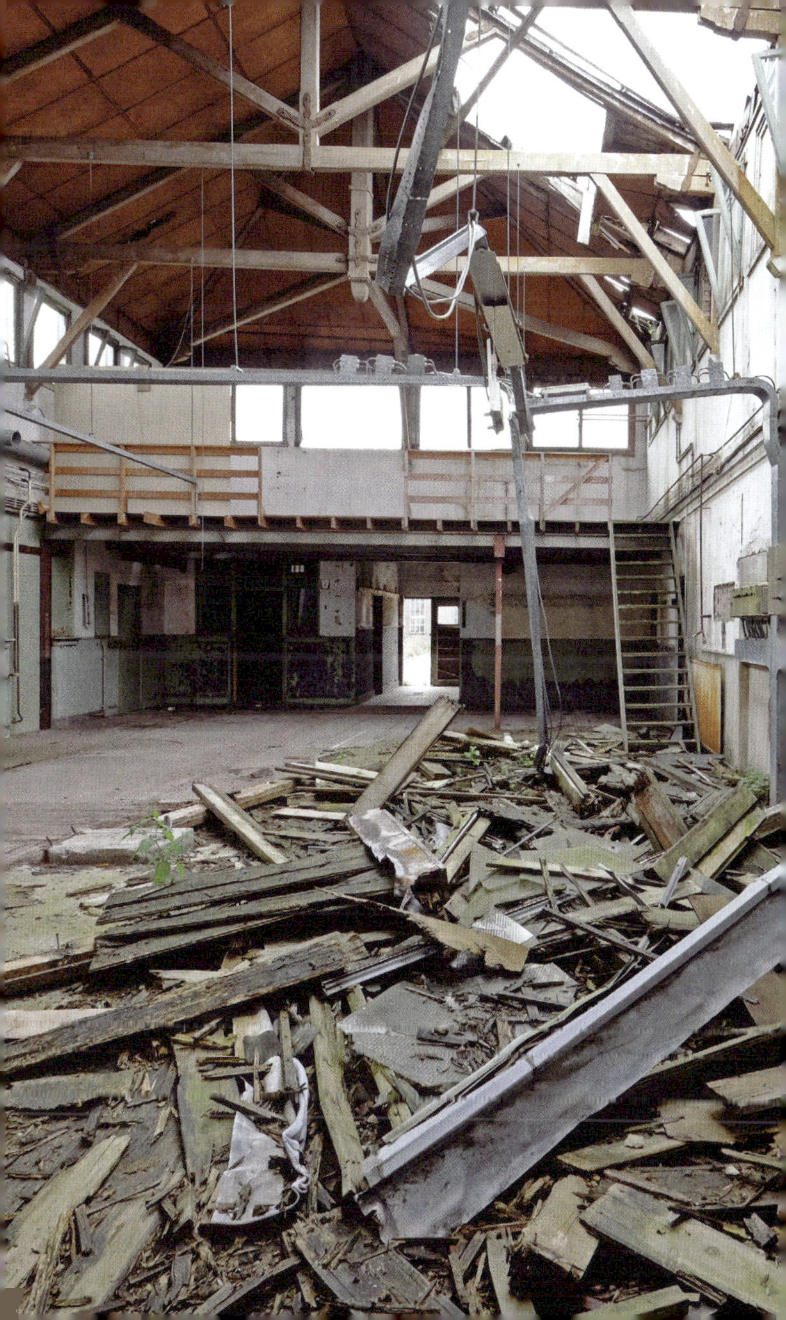

Gebouw 197

Roof construction

Romantic city portrait

In 'Geurt Brinkgreve 1917 – 2005', the commemorative edition of the magazine Binnenstad published by the Vereniging Vrienden van de Amsterdamse Binnenstad (Association of Friends of the Amsterdam Inner City), architectural historian Vincent van Rossem wrote an inspired article about the spiritual father of Stadsherstel Amsterdam N.V.. The visionary pioneer with an eye for the historical significance of the most important and most beautiful canal houses of Amsterdam was also aware of the gravity of the situation. Above all, according to Van Rossem, Brinkgreve waged a very practical campaign, which began in the 1950s when everything was on the verge of collapse. There was very little time for romantic thoughts back these days, because restoration was needed. The romantic ideas of Amsterdam had already been created around 1900 by artists such as Willem Witsen and L. W. R. Wenckebach, among others. These artists are currently attracting more and more interest with retrospectives in important museums. Earlier still, on 12 June 1971, the Amsterdams Historisch Museum (now the Amsterdam Museum) had opened a retrospective exhibition of cityscape painters entitled *Amsterdamse Stadsportretten / Views of Amsterdam 1700 – 1900*. Containing the pictures of a piece of the city, of squares, canals, streets and buildings as presented, perhaps with some artistic freedom, by the artist. The painted city portrait only emerged as an independent genre in the mid-17th century. The first well-known painters who made this their speciality were Gerrit Berkheyde (1638 – 1698) and Jan van der Heyden (1637 – 1712). The idealized images of the latter in particular have become well-known. At the end of the 19th century, painters like Breitner demonstrated, in an entirely unique artistic way, that new city portraits did not have to be less true to life.

▷ The paintings shown belong to the collection of the Amsterdam Museum.

Romantic city portrait

Hendrik Keun (1738-1787)
The Keizersgracht between the Molenpad and Runstraat, 1765

Romantic city portrait

Isaac Ouwater (1750-1793)
The Herengracht corner Leidsegracht, 1783

Romantic city portrait

Jan de Beijer (1703-ca.1785)
The Zuiderkerk seen from the Houtgracht (now Waterlooplein), 1785

Romantic city portrait

Romantic city portrait

Cornelis Springer (1817–1891)
Gasworks (demolished) along the Singelgracht, 1847

Romantic city portrait

Romantic city portrait

George Hendrik Breitner (1857-1923)
Breakthrough of the Raadhuisstraat near the Prinsengracht, 1898

Churches

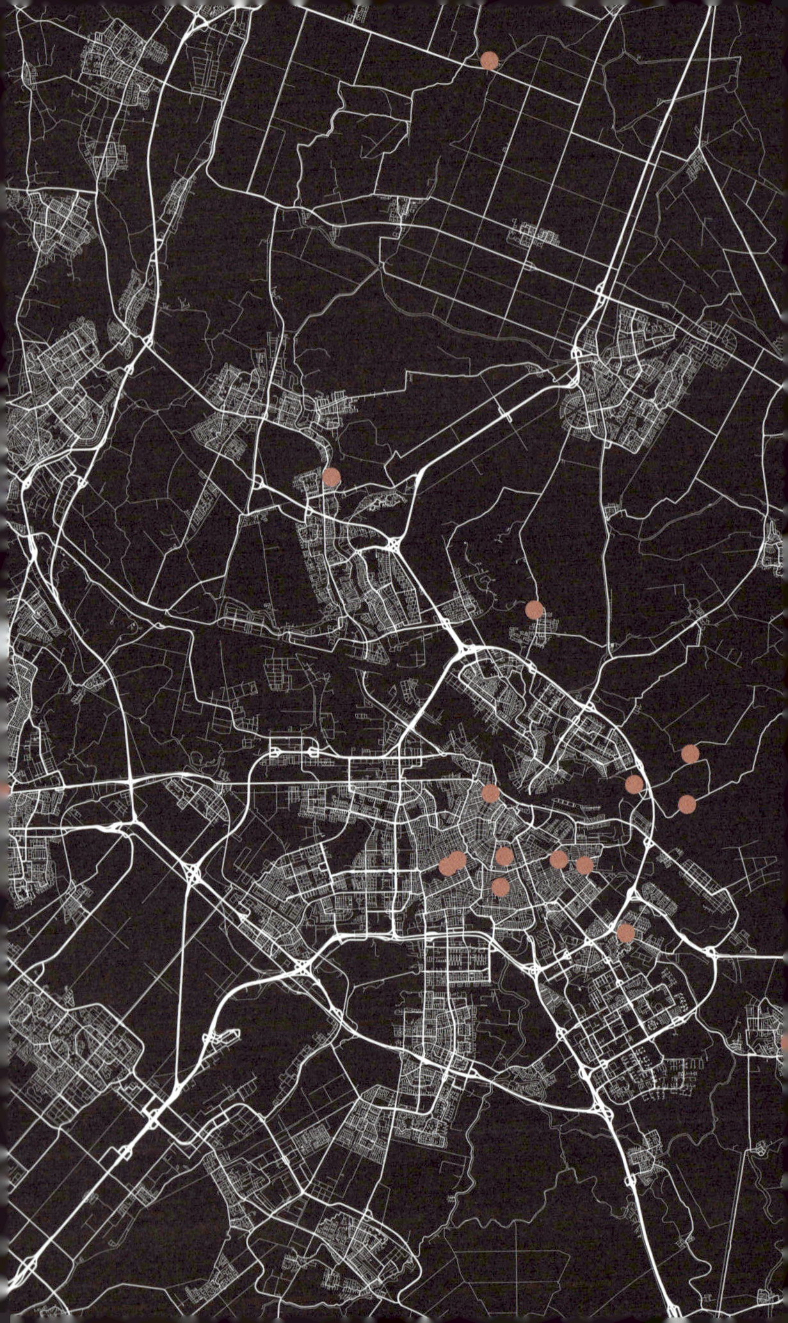

- 142 **Posthoornkerk**, Amsterdam
- 150 **Parkkerk**, Amsterdam
- **Pastorie Parkkerk**, Amsterdam
- 156 **Vondelkerk**, Amsterdam
- 164 **Amstelkerk**, Amsterdam
- 178 **De Duif**, Amsterdam
- **Pastorie de Duif**, Amsterdam
- 184 **Gerardus Majellakerk**, Amsterdam
- 196 **Zaandijkerkerk**, Zaandijk
- **Pastorie Zaandijkerkerk**, Zaandijk
- 198 **Kerkje van Evers**, Landsmeer
- 200 **Kerk van Ransdorp**, Ransdorp
- 202 **Kapel van Durgerdam**, Durgerdam
- 204 **Schellingwouderkerk**, Schellingwoude
- 206 **Muiderkerktoren**, Amsterdam
- 208 **Oranjekerk**, Amsterdam
- 210 **Grote Kerk**, Schermerhorn
- 216 **De Bakenesserkerk**, Haarlem
- 220 **De Hoop**, Diemen
- 228 **Van Houtenkerk**, Weesp

Stadsherstel focused on monumental houses up until the mid-1980s. Since the first purchases, the Amstelkerk and the Vondelkerk, 13 churches, a chapel, a church tower and a number of presbyteries have been restored, while two churches are currently being refurbished. This concerns religious cultural heritage, a term that makes it clear that not only the interests of the church community, the historic building community or local residents are being served. Stadsherstel is searching for solutions during the repurposing of these buildings, in which the visions of the interest groups reinforce each other and the public opening of the building is guaranteed. The preservation of the building also implies a new at the general public's disposal. The preservation of the building can become a focal point for identity and social cohesion or function as an attraction. The visual quality of, for example, a church tower as a distinguishing feature of a village or city is also a factor. For this reason alone, the preservation can often count on public support. The vacancy levels of religious heritage have increased enormously in recent decades. A lot of experience has been gained meanwhile through the purchase and repurposing of church buildings that have fallen into disuse, which were earmarked for demolition.

Amstelkerk

Zaandijkerkerk

Half of the projects are now in use as multi-functional spaces, where cultural events take place in the entire church or in the middle space. In addition, the buildings are often opened to the public with the help of a large number of volunteers. One of the newest acquisitions is the Grote Kerk van Schermerhorn. This church was built in the Dutch Golden Age with the financial help of well-to-do inhabitants, including several whalers. The stained glass windows are by Rubens. Stadsherstel conducted a feasibility study in advance in order to be able to restore this building immediately after acquiring it from the Foundation for Old Dutch Churches (Stichting Oude Hollandse Kerken, SOHK).

Grote Kerk Schermerhorn

Posthoornkerk

Address
**Haarlemmerstraat 124-126 ·
Haarlemmer Houttuinen 47**

Town
Amsterdam

Built
1861; towers 1887 – 1889

Acquisition
1996

Restoration
1998/2011

Restoration architect
André van Stigt

Current use
Offices and space for concerts and exhibitions

Churches

The Posthoornkerk was built on the Haarlemmerstraat in 1860 based on a design by the architect P.J.H. (Pierre) Cuypers. The church replaced the clandestine church De Posthoorn on the Prinsengracht and was constructed in two stages. Between 1860 and 1863, the chancel, transept, the crossing tower and the nave were built. The front consisting of two towers is from several decades later. The limited space on all sides forced an extra high design. The interior is fitted with galleries above the aisles. While the exterior has neo-Gothic characteristics, the Romanesque Munster Church (also by Cuypers) served as the model for the interior. The Posthoornkerk was withdrawn from service in 1963. And in spite of it obtaining the status of nationally listed building in 1972, there were demolition plans until the late-1980s. Thanks to the repurposing, the building still towers high above Haarlemmer neighbourhood.

Posthoornkerk 144

Birds-eye view Posthoornkerk, 1958

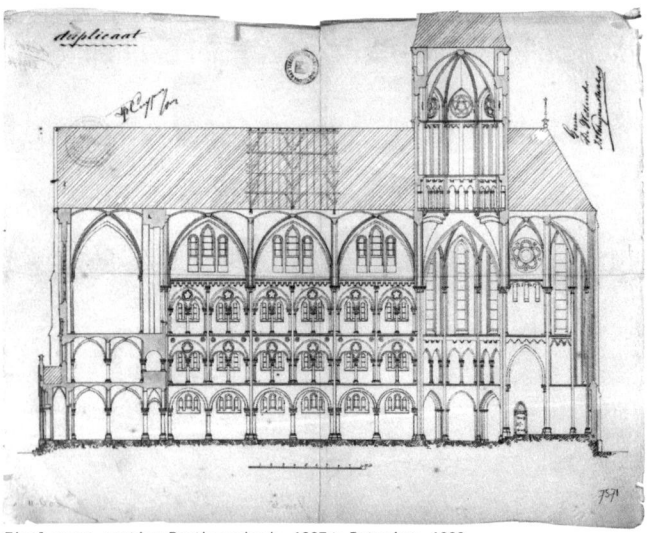

Final cross-section Posthoornkerk, 1887 ▷ Interior, 1988

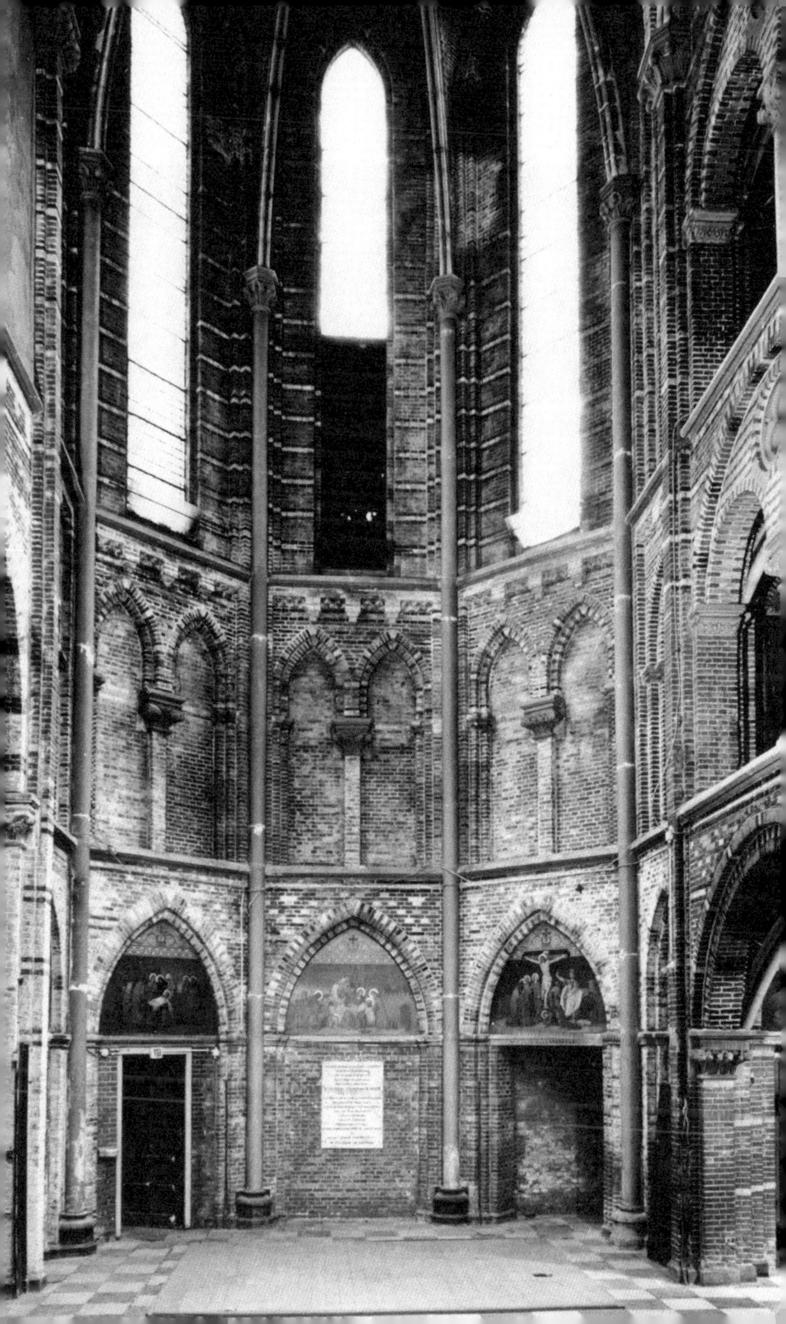

Posthoornkerk

Restoration wood construction

Repairs ironwork

Replaced windows

Churches

Restoration fresco above altar of Maria Kevelaer

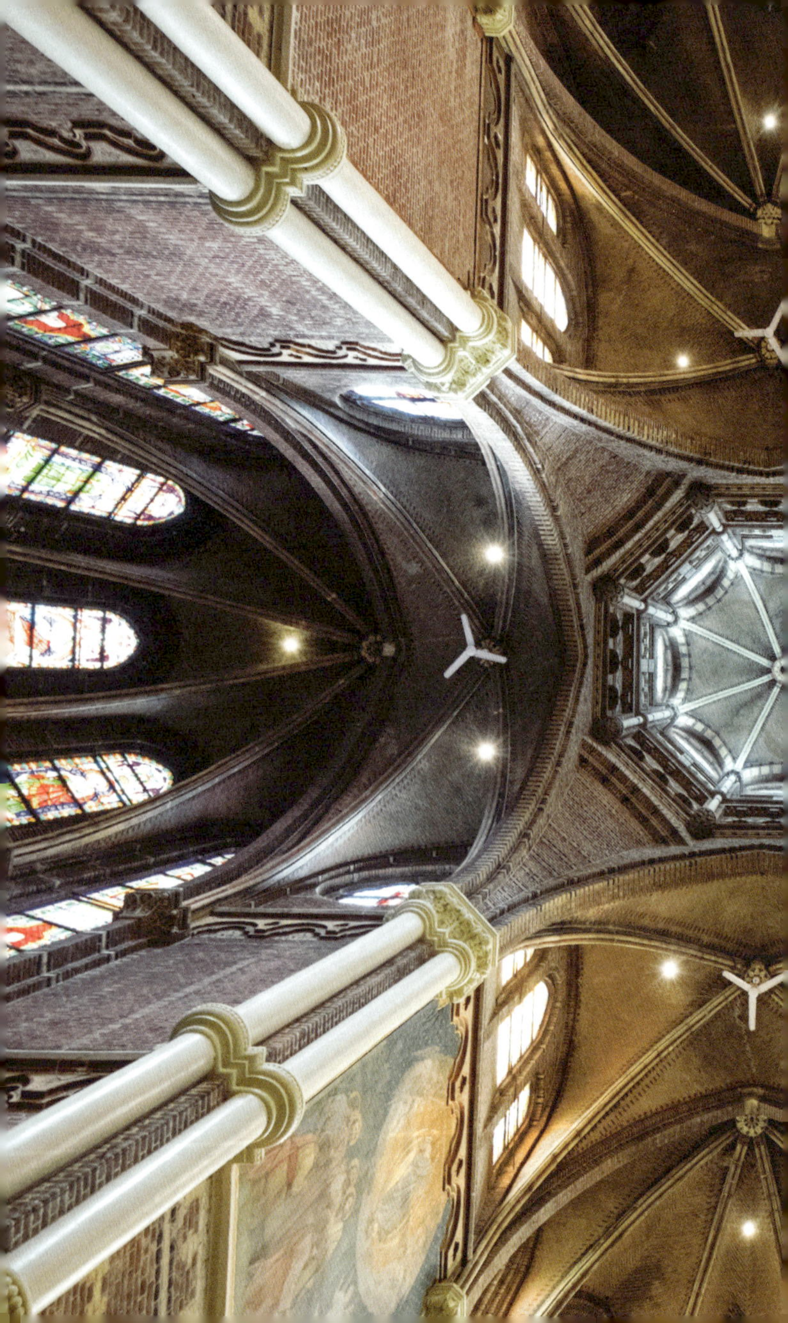

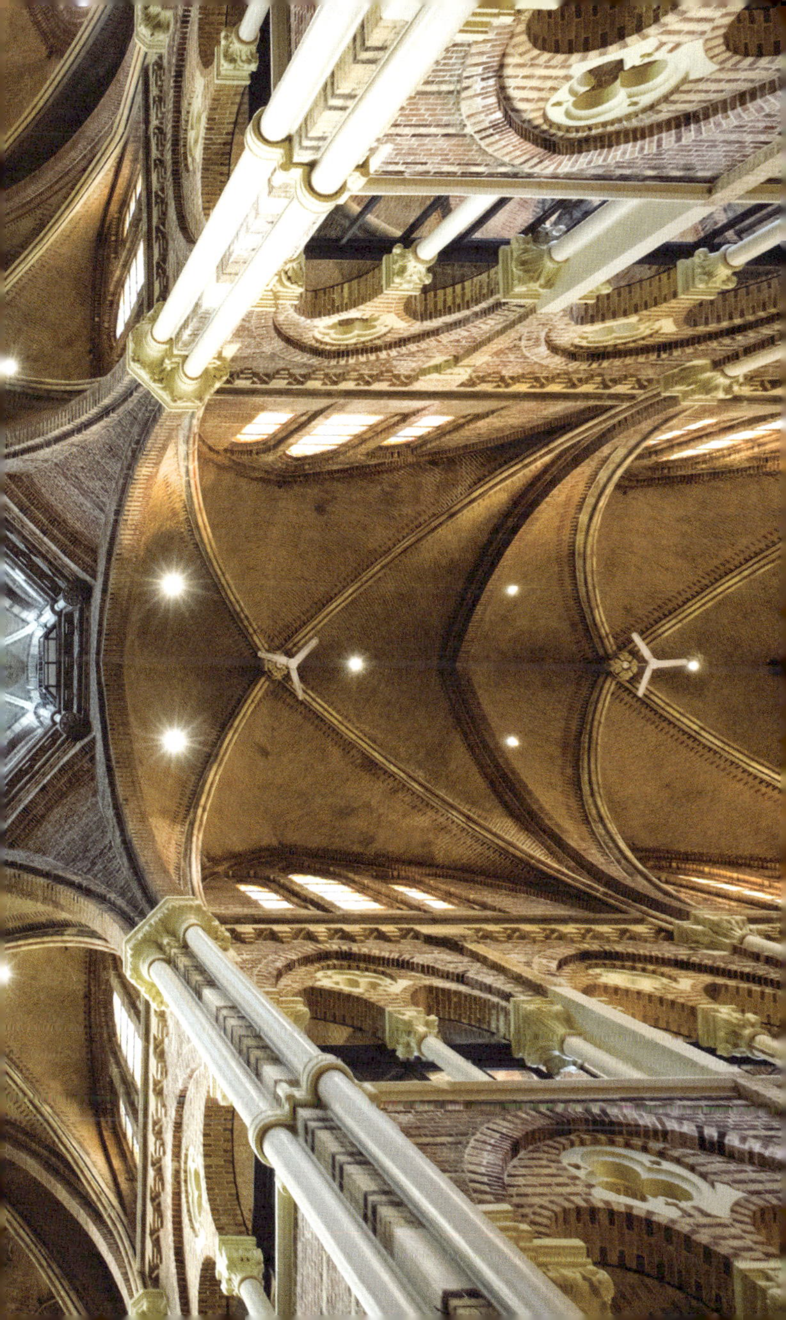

Parkkerk

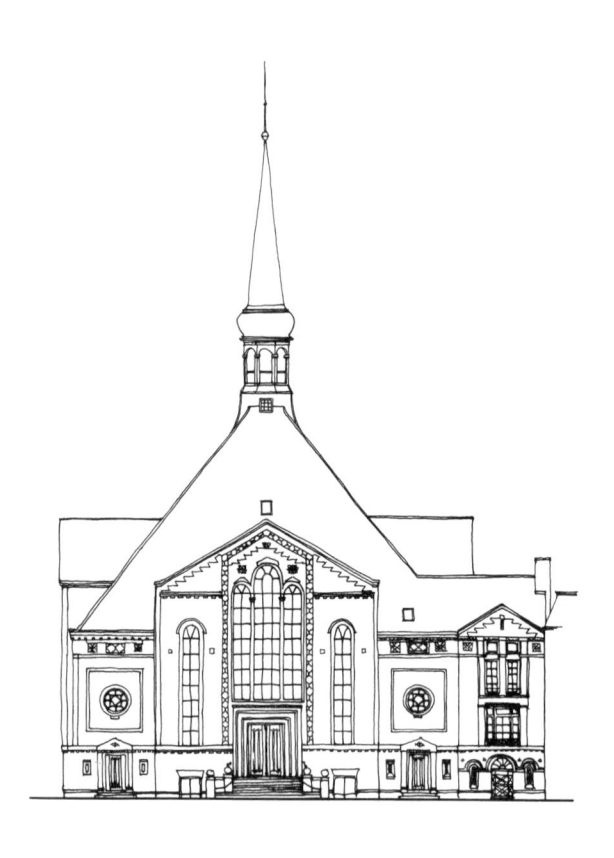

Address
Gerard Brandtstraat 26-28

Town
Amsterdam

Built
1916 – 1918

Acquisition
1995

Restoration
2006

Restoration architect
BD architectuur

Current use
Space for organ concerts

The church on the edge of the Vondelpark was designed by the architect E.A.C. Roest (1875 – 1952) and was put into use by the Reformed Church in 1918. At the end of the 1990s, the building was converted into an organ centre. It is extremely interesting architecturally as a late example of eclecticism. With an almost square floor plan, crowned by a slate-covered pavilion roof and a sizeable ridge turret, the brick construction is fitted with substantial gables and lunette vaults.
In addition to the architectural and urban design value, due to its location right by the park, the architectural spacial effect of the interior, the galleries, a stellar vault and a central clerestory, is of great importance. The wooden roof is finished off with stucco work and in addition the detailing and the woodwork, the stained glass in the dome, the pulpit, the baptismal font and the organ are important. The church was also lent significant from a church-historical perspective as a result of the creation of the Reformed Churched in Restored Community (Gereformeerde Kerken in Hersteld Verband).

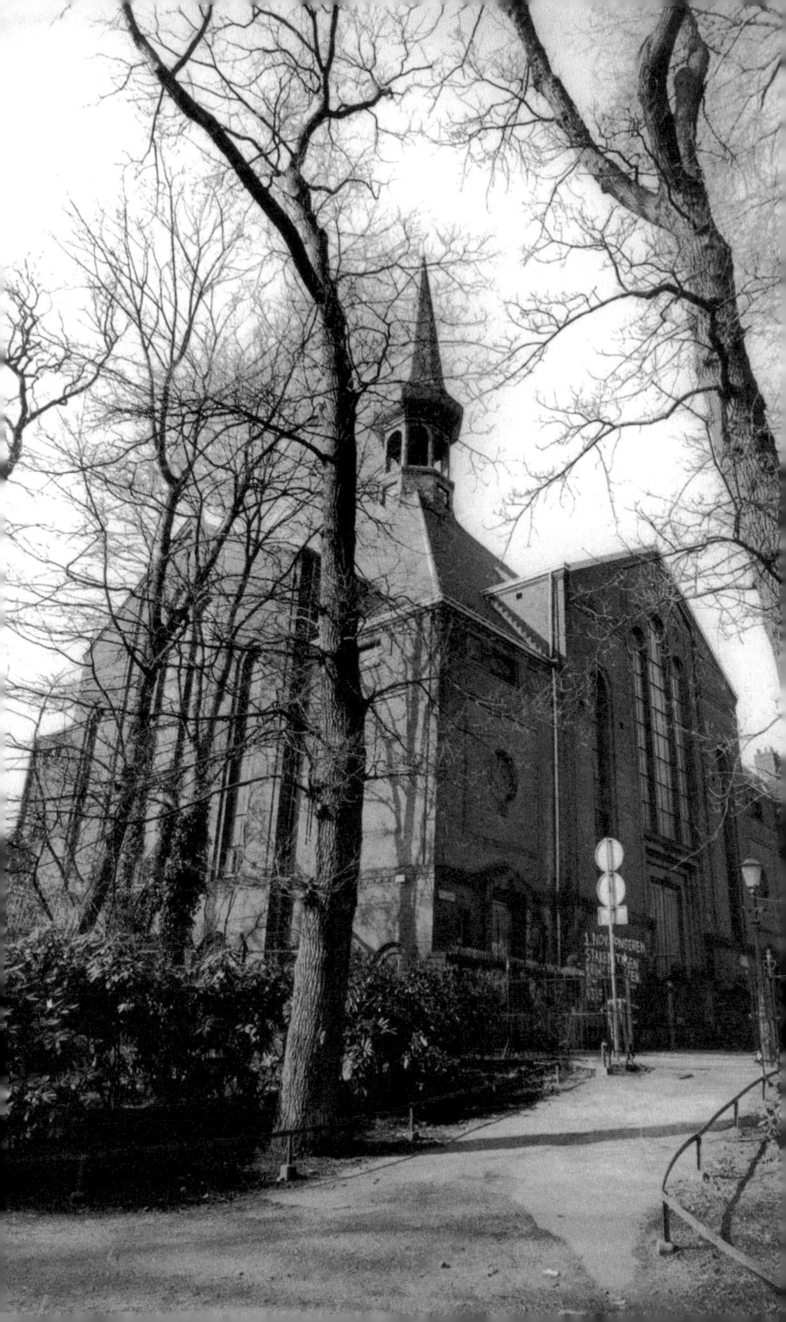

Churches

Stucco vault, 1991

Parkkerk

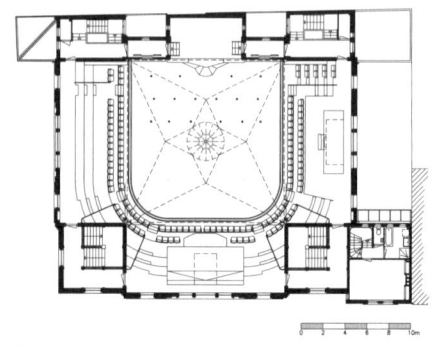

Balcony

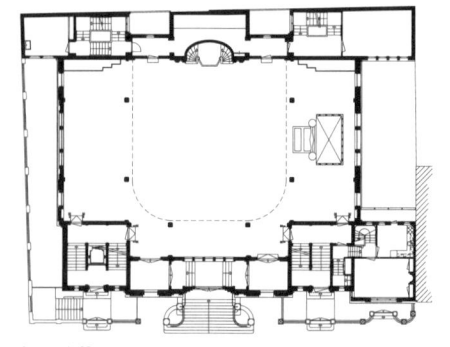

Ground floor

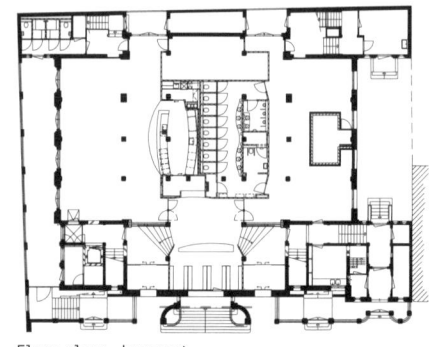

Floor plans, basement

Churches

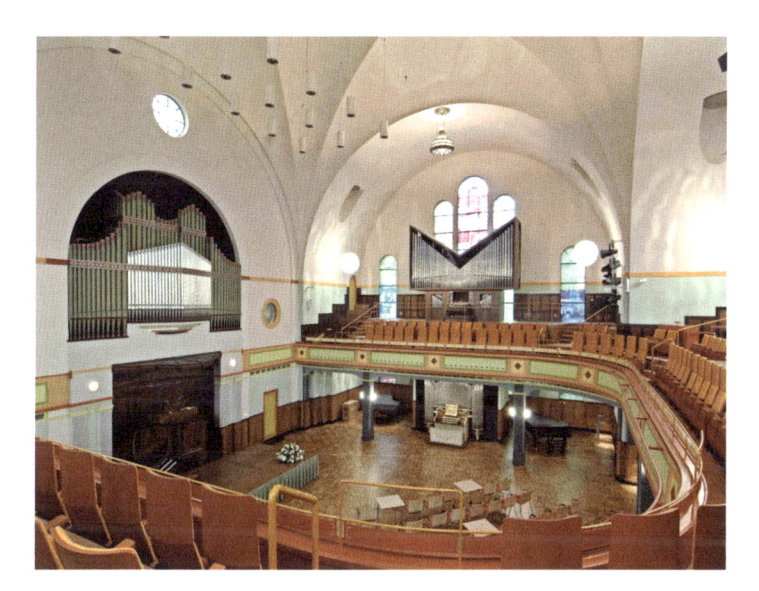

Vondelkerk

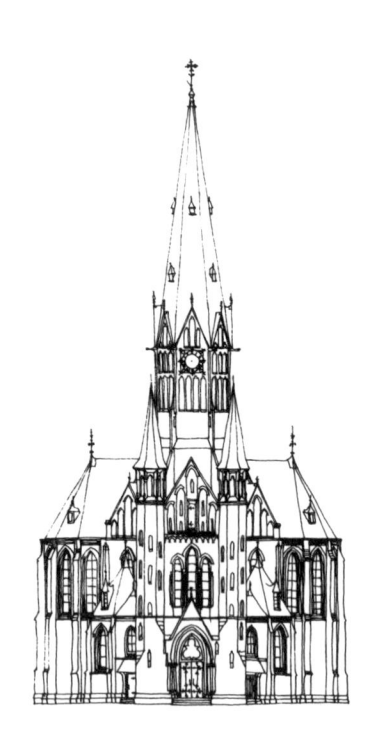

Address
Vondelstraat 120

Town
Amsterdam

Built
1872 – 1880

Acquisition
1996

Restoration
1986/2000/2004

Restoration architect
D. Bak

Current use
Nave on an occasional basis rented to cultural and social organizations, offices

Churches

Pierre Cuypers helped build the Vondelstraat as a property developer. According to his ideas about the ideal society, he designed the Vondelkerk in between the houses, the first brick of which was laid on 1 March 1872. When the severely neglected building was under threat of demolition about a century later, a repurposing plan was developed. A foundation established in 1980 managed to make a restoration and new use possible, as a result of which the historic cityscape, between classical and stately houses at the edge of the park, has been preserved. The central nave of the Vondelkerk can be reserved for a number of possibilities.

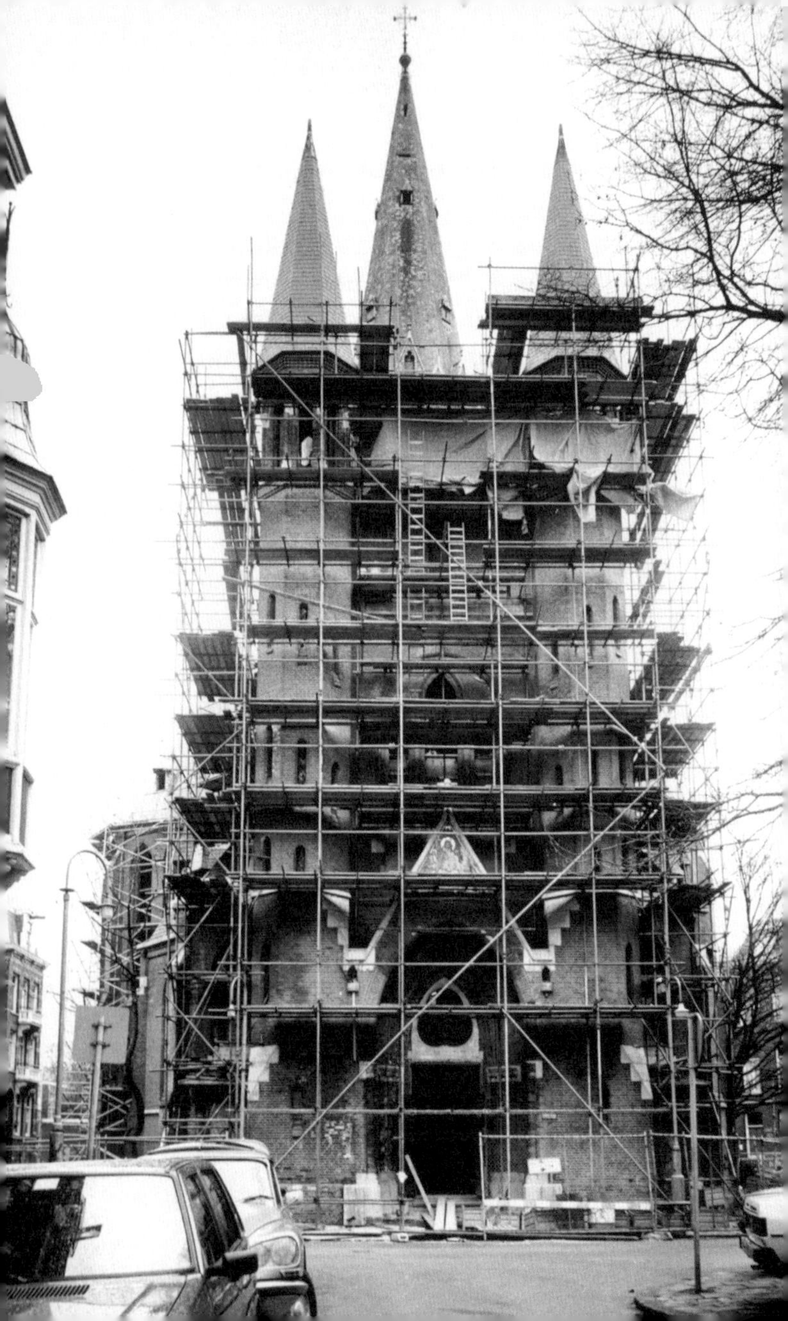

Churches

◁ Vondelkerk, April 1986

Vondelkerk

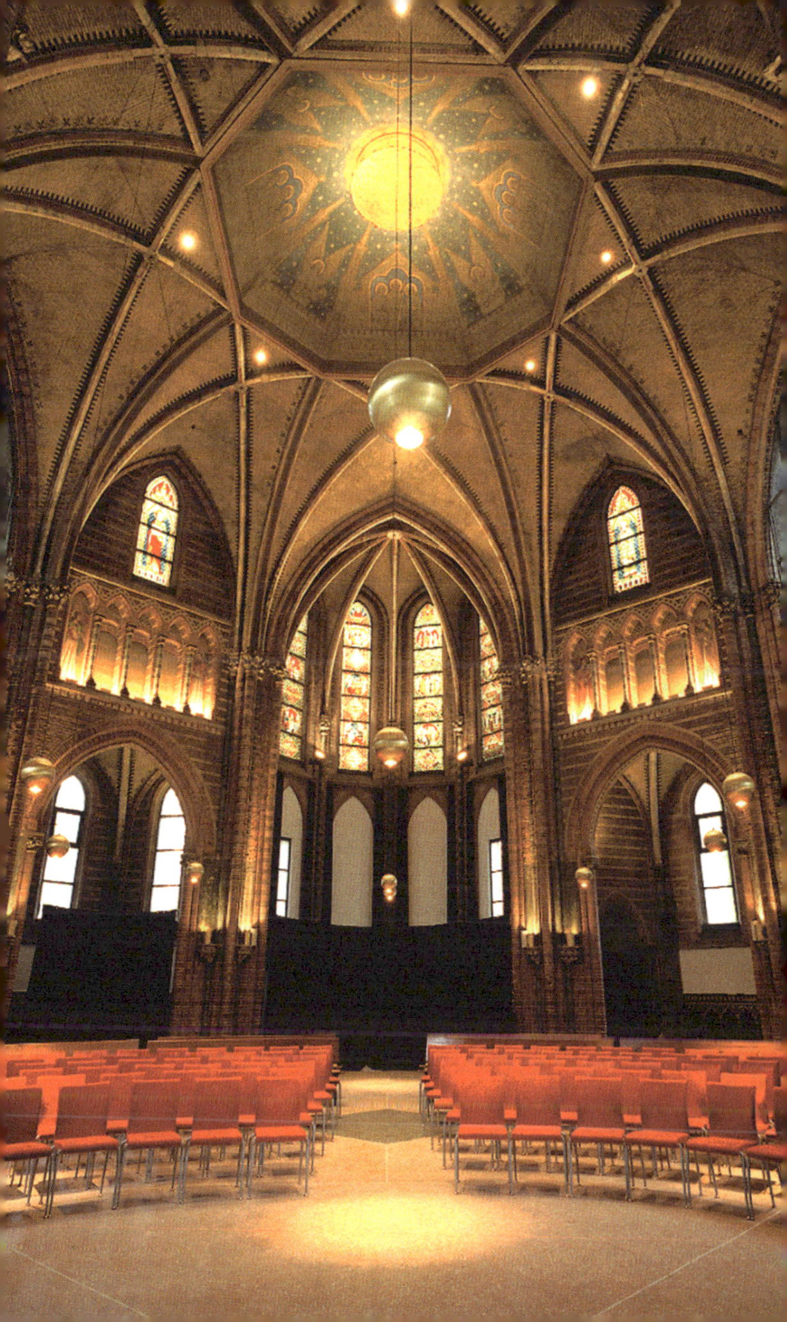

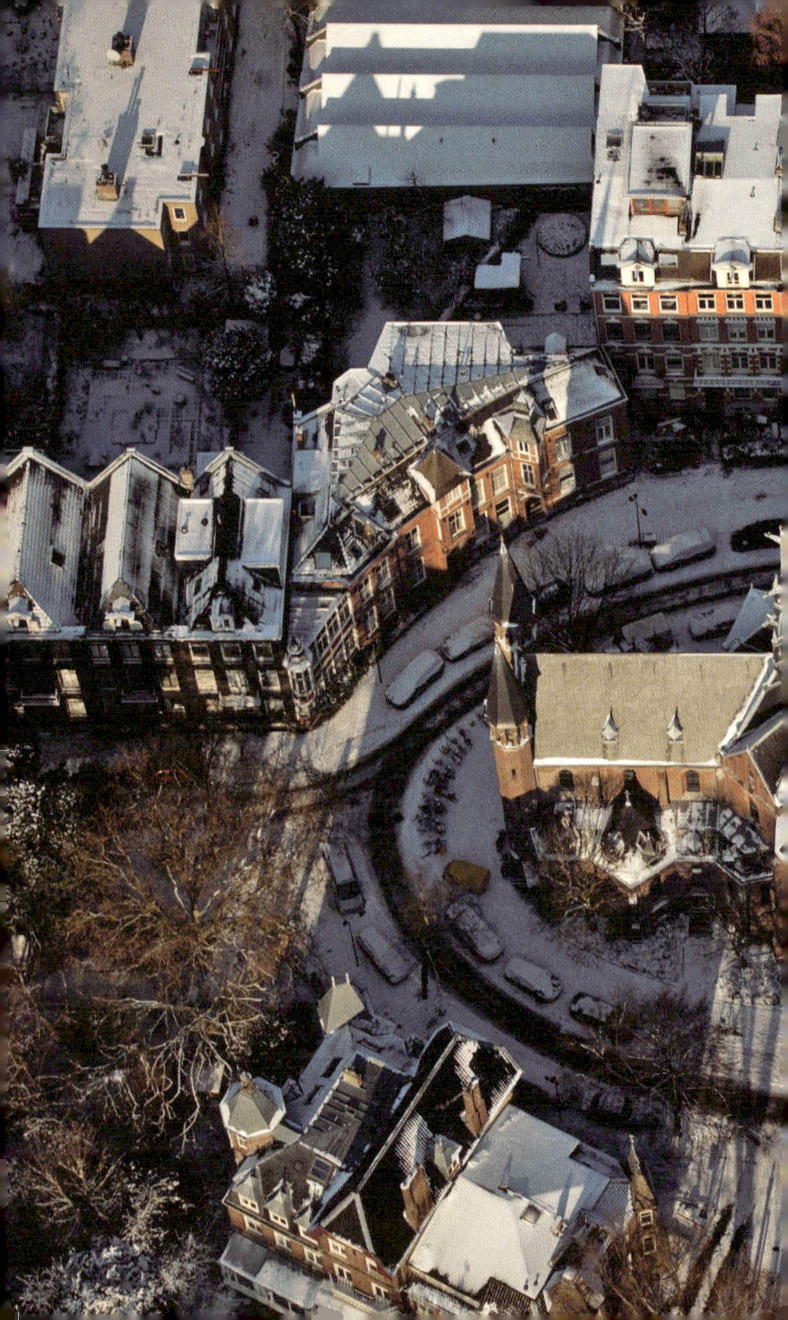

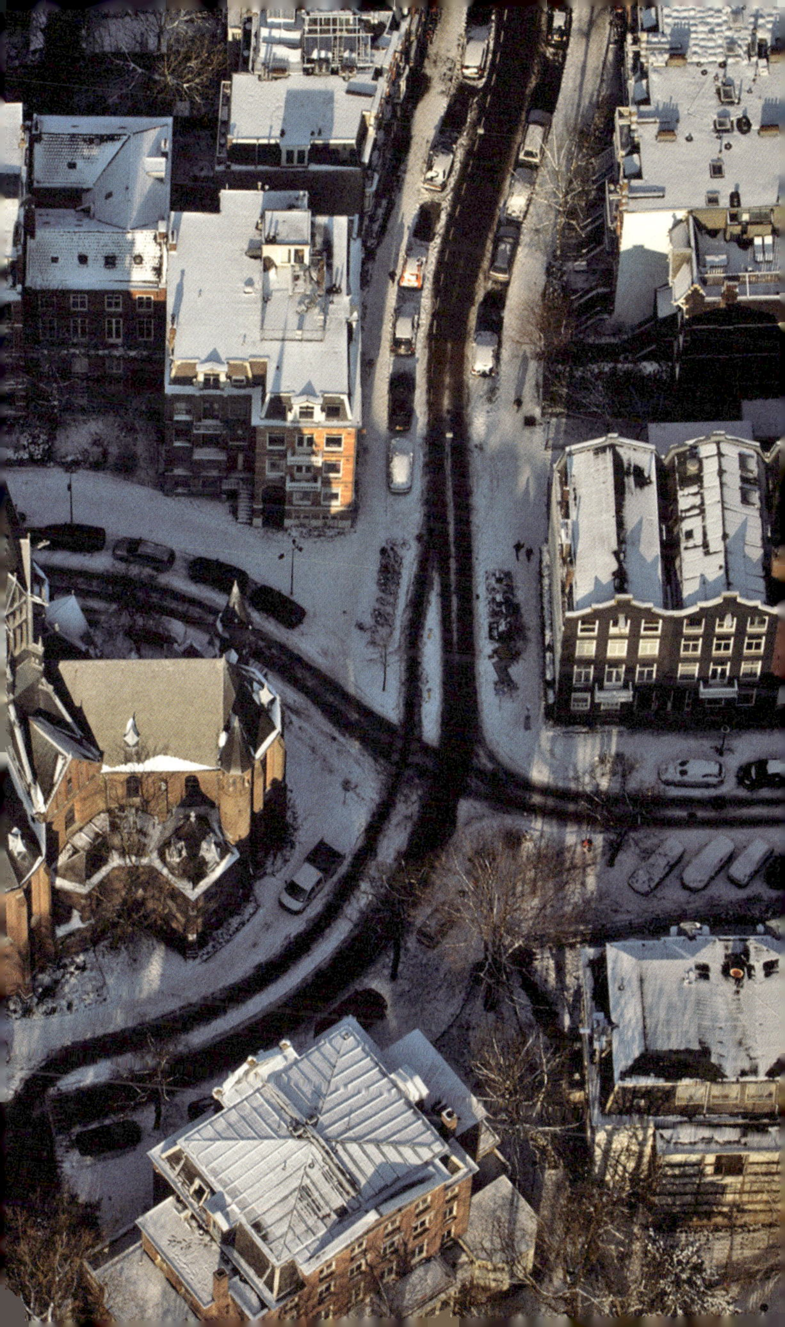

Amstelkerk

164

Address	Built	Restoration architect
Amstelveld 2-4-6-8-10-12	**1668 – 1670**	**Architectenburo Prins b.v.**
Town	Acquisition	Current use
Amsterdam	**1986**	**Office Stadsherstel, restaurant, housing**
	Restoration	
	1988/1990	

The original plan to erect a large church over the length of the entire square amounted to very little. In 1668, a temporary church was built on the corner at the side of the Reguliersgracht based on a design by city architect Daniël Stalpaert (1616 – 1676). The temporary church was made permanent. Apart from the wooden Amstel on the Amstelveld, a square in the centre of Amsterdam, Stadsherstel has restored 10 historic (shop) residences and the church building De Duif with accompanying presbytery, all in the vicinity of the Utrechtsestraat. Markets have been held on the square since 1876. The Monday morning market was one of the most famous ones in Amsterdam for a long time. Today, a weekly flower market is held under the distinctive planting of 46 Caucasian wingnut trees *(Pterocarya fraxinifolia)*. The square was created during the fourth urban extension of the canal ring in 1662.

Amstelkerk

Amstelkerk, Sermon barn, 1818

The church was constructed from unpainted pinewood, almost entirely free from any embellishment, with a paving brick floor. In 1673, a brick annex was added to the church on the Reguliersgracht and a brick sexton's house on the Amstelveld. The exterior was matched with the brick annexes through the use of a soft red colour. After receiving a legacy in about 1840, the interior of the old temporary church underwent a number of changes. The location of the pulpit was turned 90 degrees and woodwork made up of mainly gothic forms was installed over the original wooden construction. Vaults were added in the aisles and the semicircular fanlights made way for pointed arch windows. At the end of the 19th century, the stucco ceiling was revealed once again including large corbels with acanthus leaves, rosettes and volutes. The furniture was also revamped with, among other things, a beautiful organ.

Churches

Amstelkerk, new interior, 1840

This part of town was extremely run down in the 1970s and was affected by street prostitution when Stadsherstel started purchasing buildings there. Four of the 13 buildings purchased were shored up and only the bottom part of one building still remained. In 1971, Stadsherstel was offered the corner building Reguliersgracht 70 and did not hesitate to purchase this historic building. Indeed, special attention has been paid to corner buildings since the establishment of Stadsherstel. They often act as bookends for the buildings in poor condition in the row of facades and also encourage the neighbours to refurbish their buildings. The Amstelkerk also struggled with declining church attendance and poor maintenance. In 1990, Stadsherstel put the church into use as an office. The only remaining temporary church in Amsterdam was therefore rescued. The middle space of the building is rented out for cultural activities.

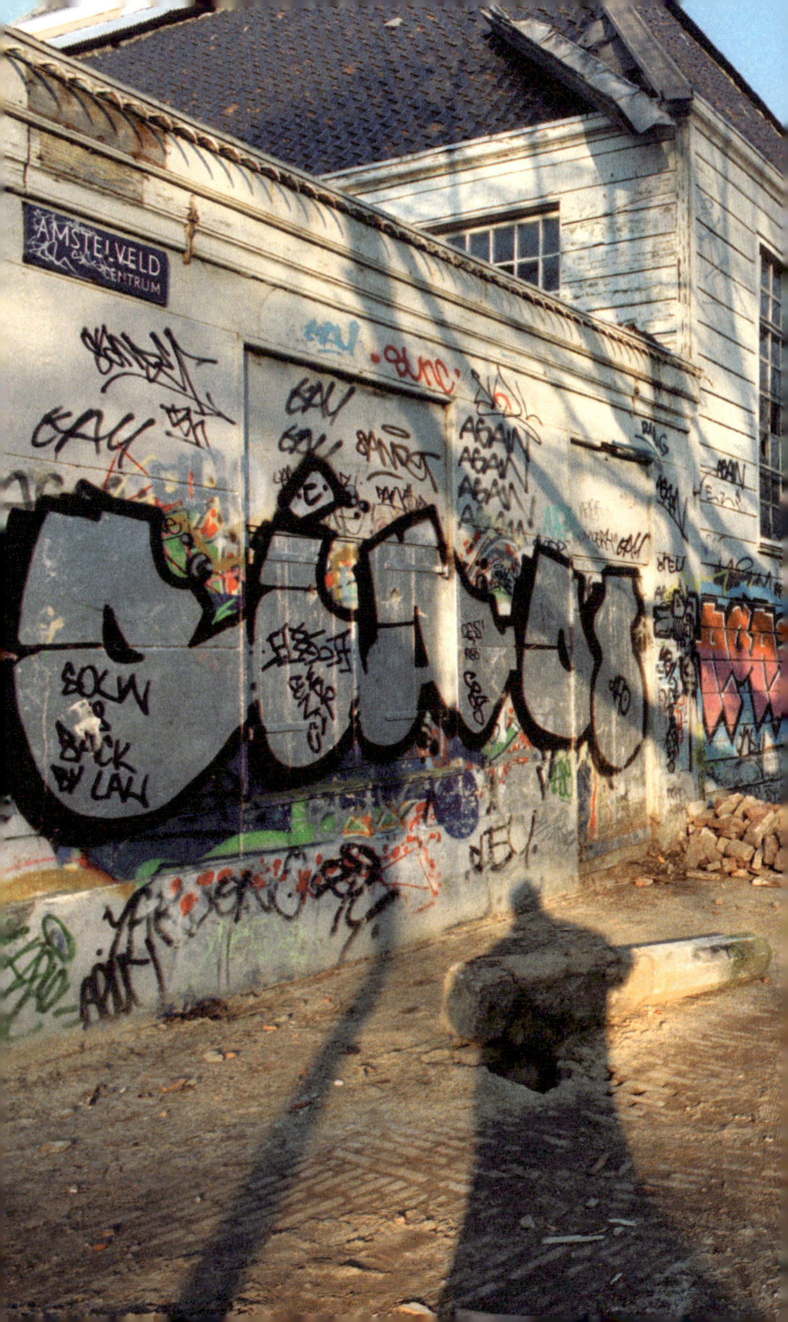
AMSTELVELD
CENTRUM

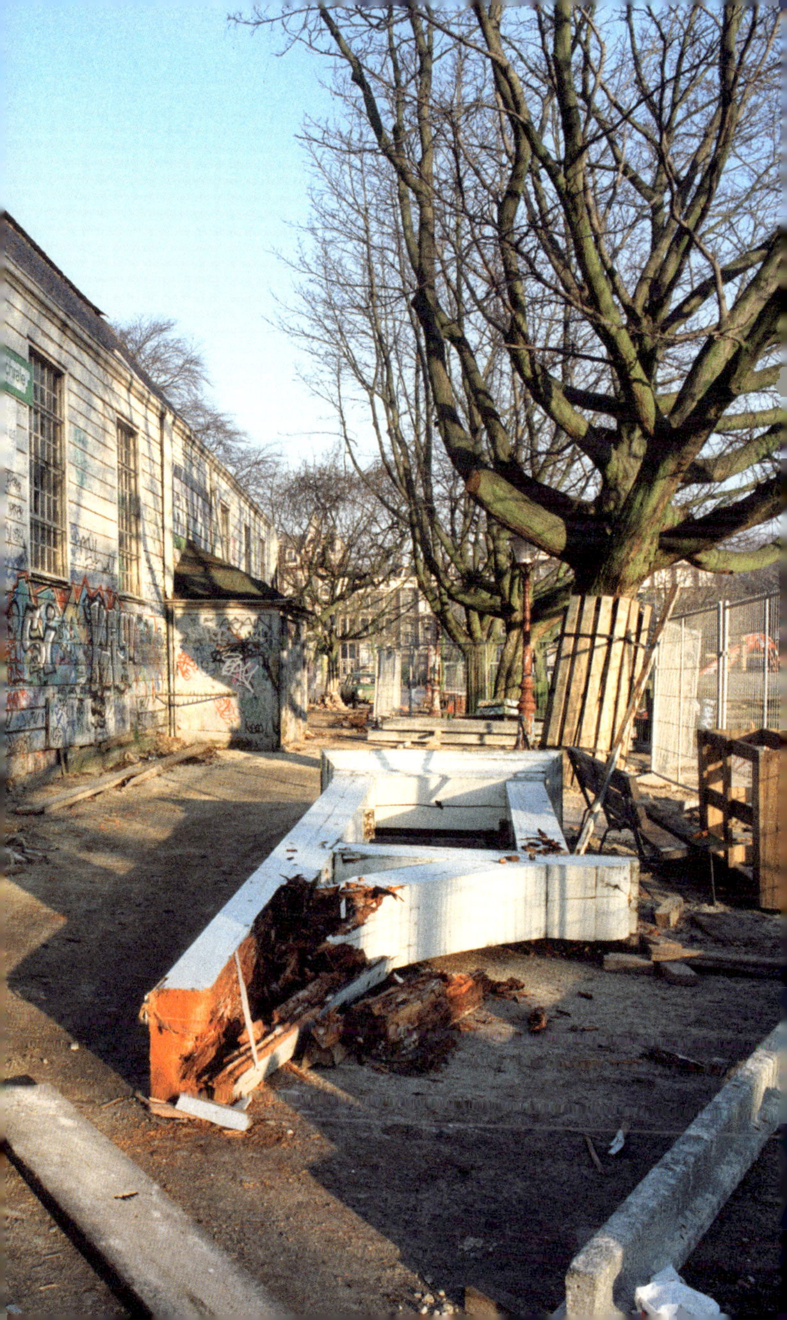

Amstelkerk

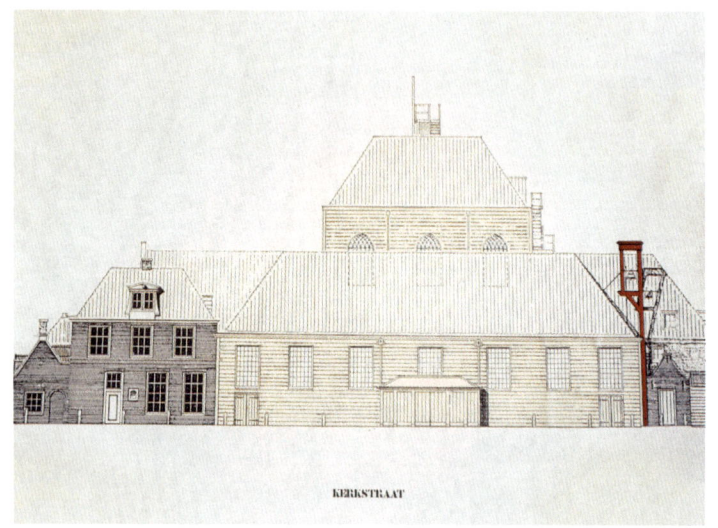

Front view

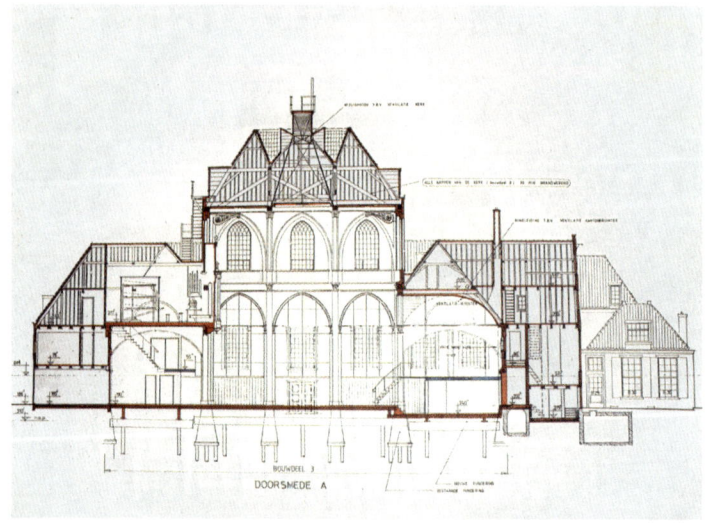

Cross-section

Churches

Lantern

Jan van der Heijden lantern

The finishing touch of the restoration of the Amstelkerk consisted of the fitting of wall-mounted lanterns by the Association of Friends of Stadsherstel. This outdoor wall lighting is a well-considered reconstruction of an earthenware model that was designed by Jan van der Heijden in 1669. In the course of a few years, the city was exceptionally beautifully lit. The lanterns were placed on a wooden pole and later also mounted on a wooden arm on the facade. Towards the end of the 17th and the beginning of the 18th century, such facade light fittings were made from iron, initially using the same form that the wooden arm had. Later, the wrought-iron arm developed into an ornamental arm with an inward and outward turning curl. The municipal electricity company recently followed up this initiative by placing the same lamps on wooden poles in the vicinity of the Prinsengracht. The lanterns fitted in well because the city lighting plan of Jan van der Heijden was approved in 1668, the year that the Amstelkerk was built. The corner building of the Kerkstraat Reguliersgracht 67 has been given the same lantern by the Friends.

Ritter lantern

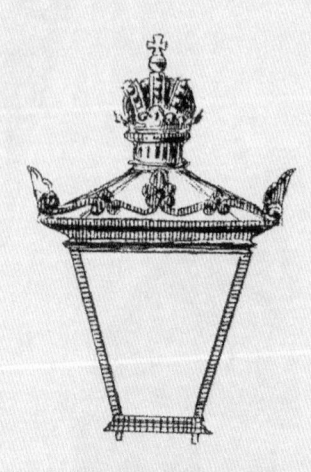

Crown lantern

Churches

Jan van der Heijden lantern

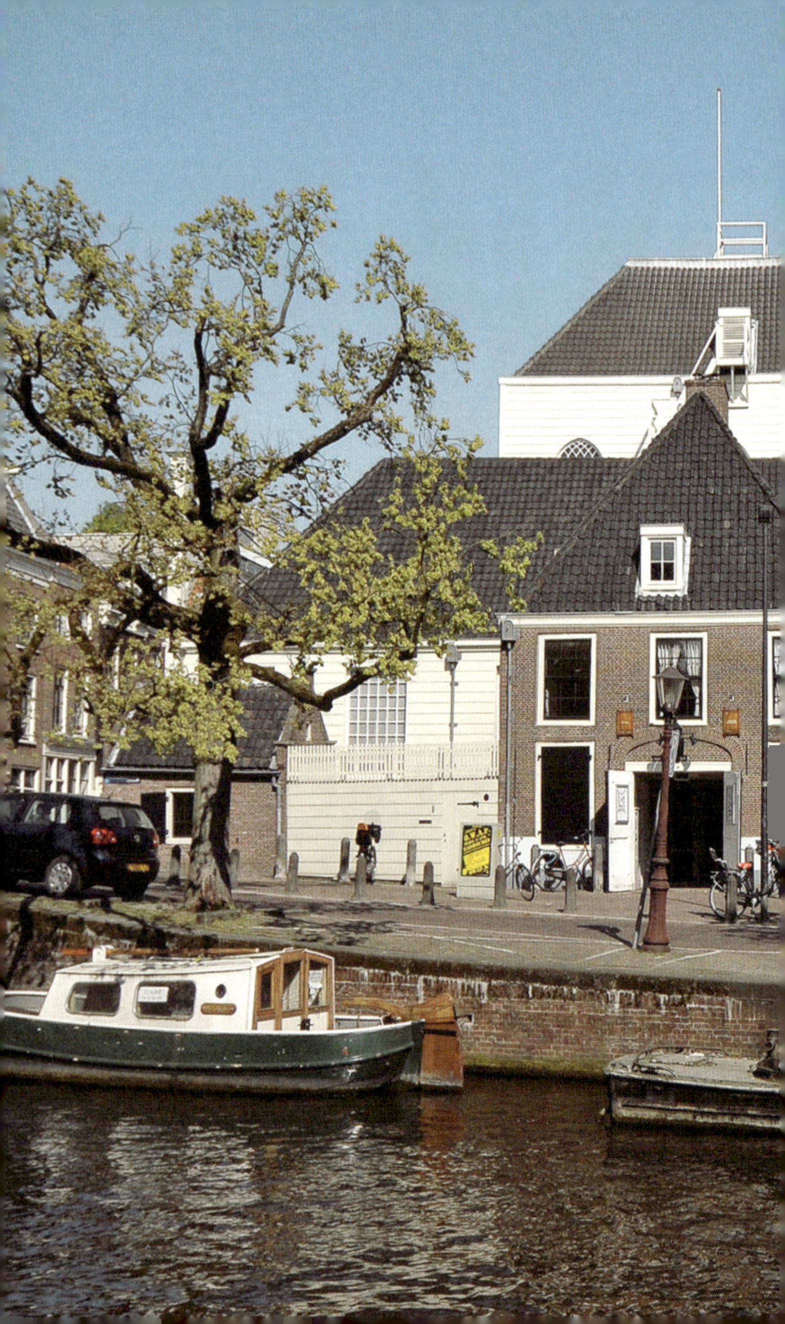

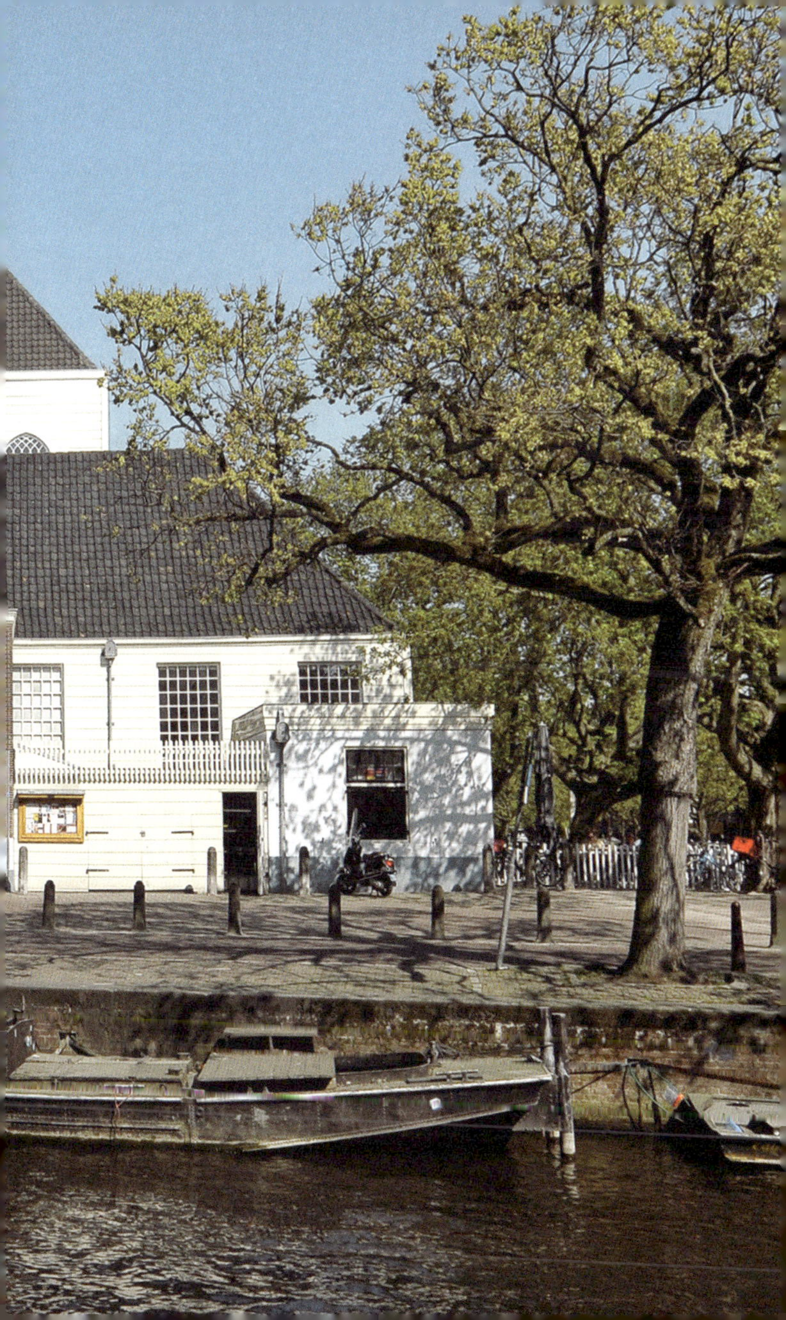

Amstelkerk

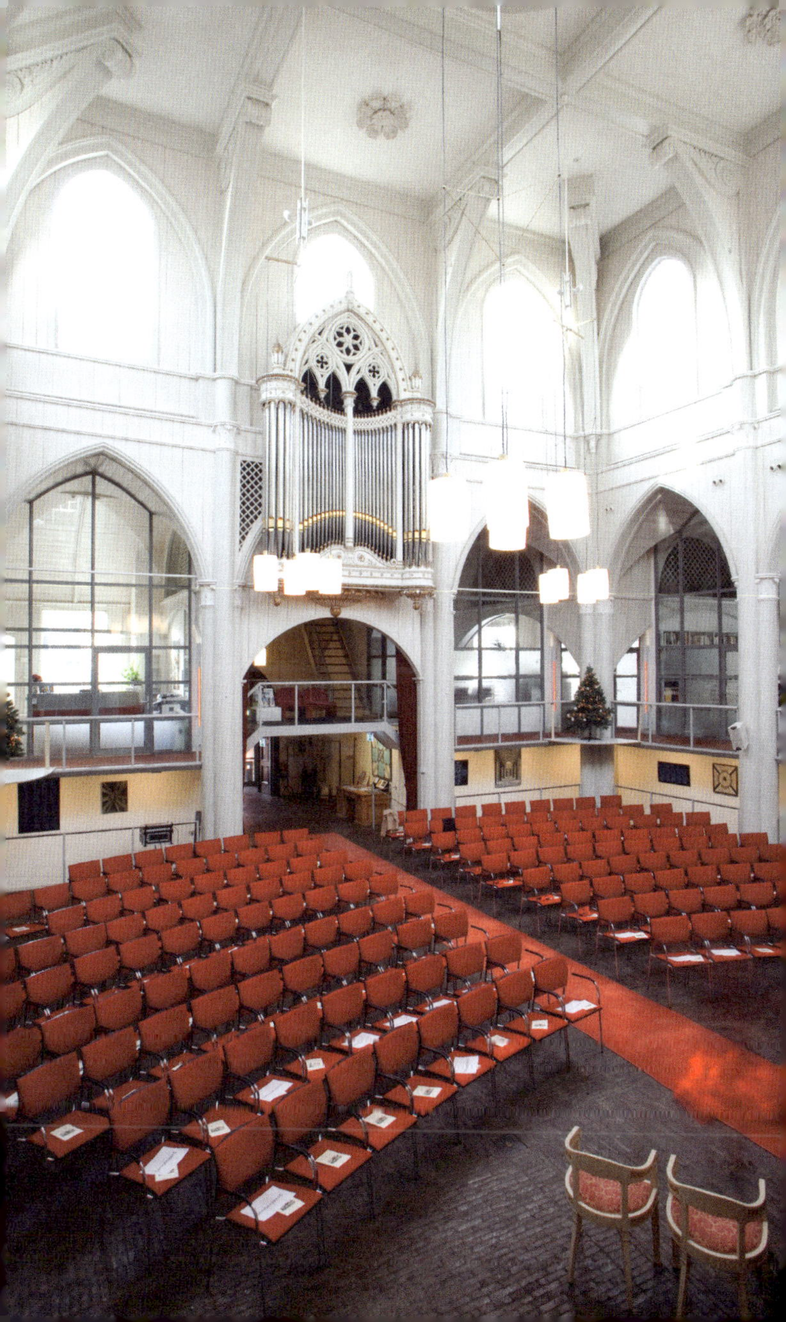

De Duif

Address
Prinsengracht 754-756

Town
Amsterdam

Built
1857

Acquisition
1995

Restoration
2002

Restoration architect
Architectenbureau Peters & Boogers

Current use
Occasional rental for events and as a wedding location

Church De Duif is located near the Utrechtsestraat between the stately buildings on the Prinsengracht. The church is built in a neoclassical style and the facade shows a variation on neo-Baroque style. With its modest facing facade, this nationally listed building from 1857 conceals a surprising spacious interior. The church replaced an older specimen and was built according to the design of the Leiden architect Theo Molkenboer (1796 – 1863). Molkenboer was the church architect of the Netherlands for a long time and De Duif is one of his later works. As knowledge of, and appreciation for, the Gothic style increased, appreciation for Molkenboer decreased and he lost his position as the most important church architect to Pierre Cuypers. Much of Molkenboer's work has now been demolished. This former Roman Catholic church was restored between 1999 – 2002, preserving all authentic details and is currently used as a location for events.

De Duif

Churches 181

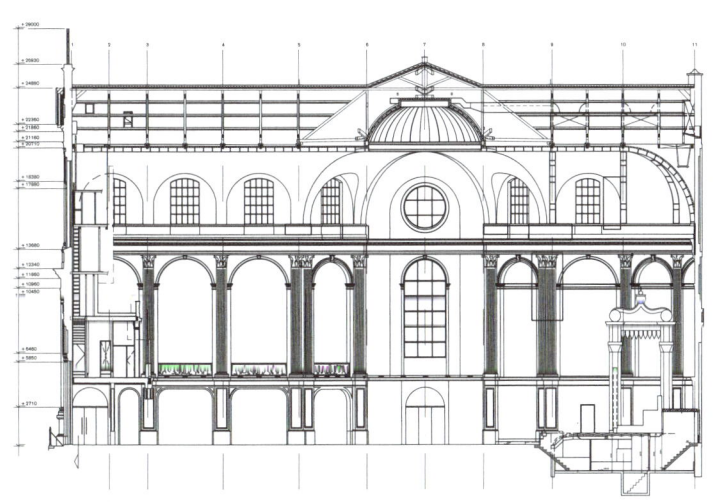

Longitudinal section

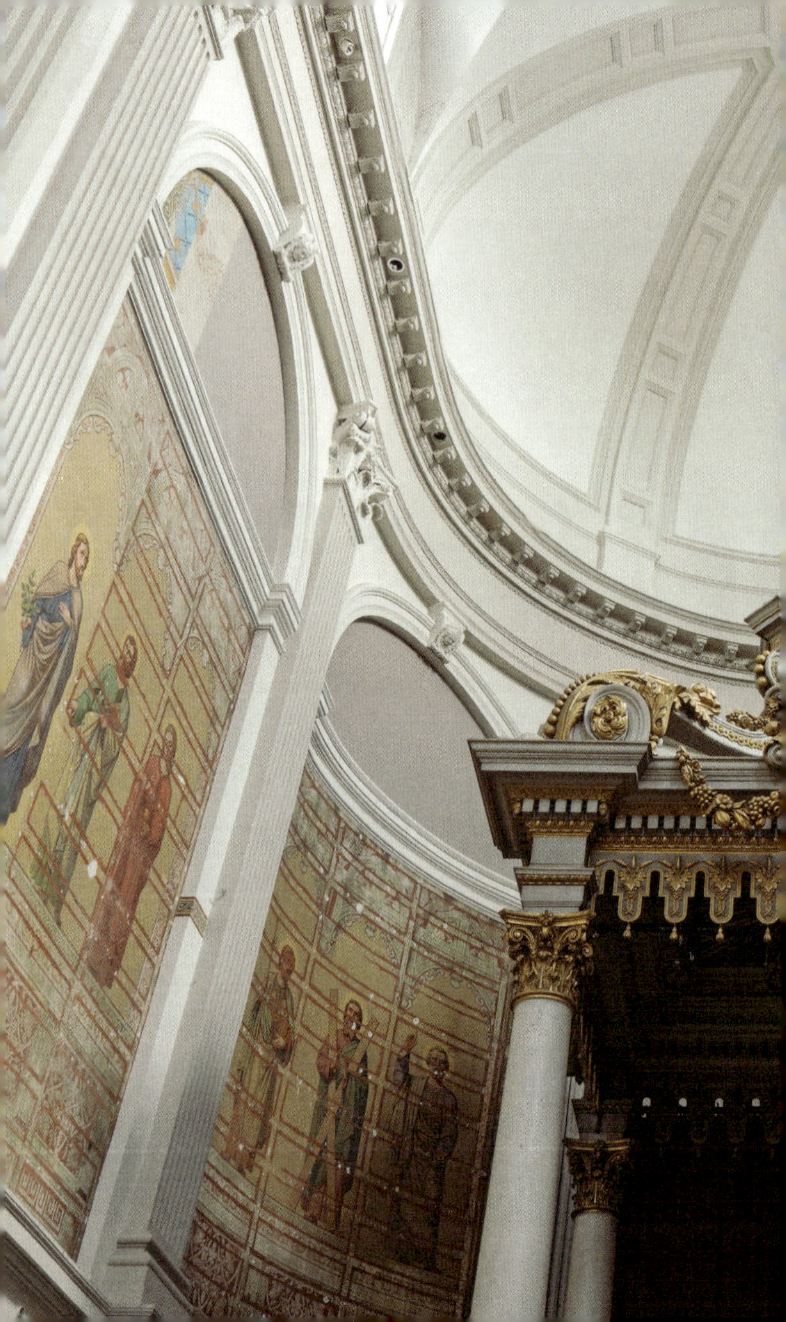

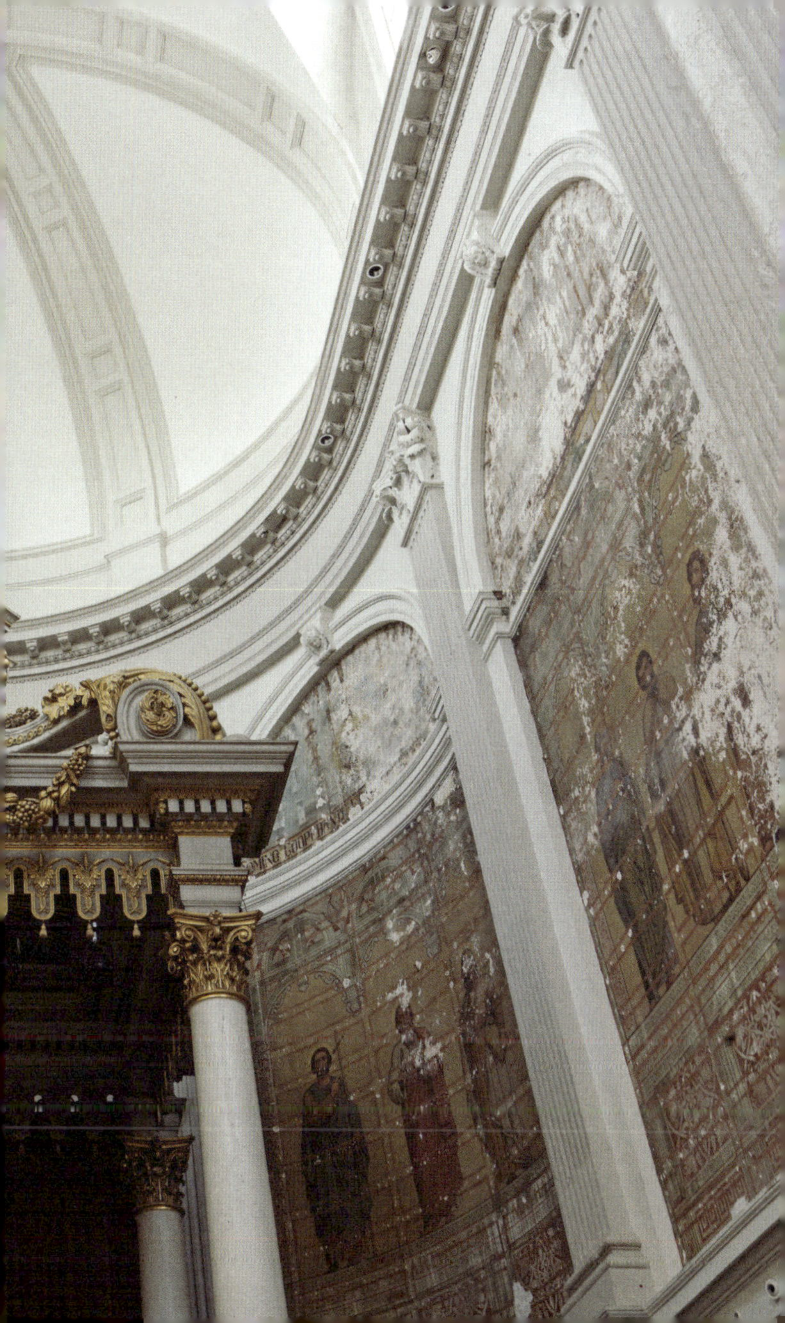

Gerardus Majellakerk

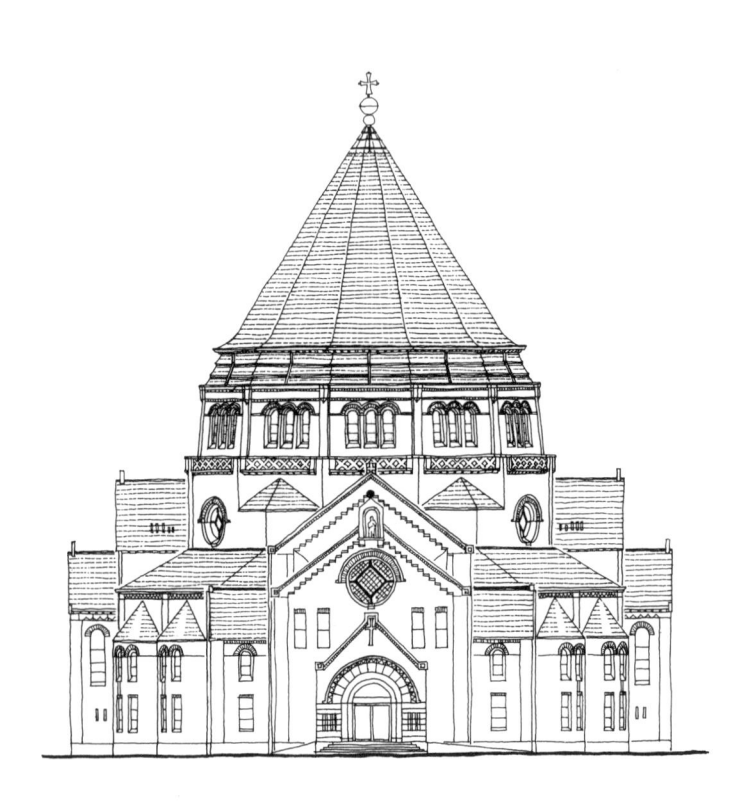

Address
Ambonplein 61-63-67-73-79

Town
Amsterdam

Built
About 1926

Acquisition
1992

Restoration
1993/2012

Restoration architect
André van Stigt

Current use
Offices and rehearsal space Netherlands Philharmonic Orchestra

Churches

The Indische Buurt (Indies Neighbourhood) in the eastern part of Amsterdam was built as an urban development district at the beginning of the 20th century. The Haarlem diocese established a new church community here for its Catholic followers and named the church after an Italian saint from the 18th century. Architect Jan Stuyt (1868 – 1934) already had a church design ready, which he made for the location on the Pijnackerstraat, where the Vredeskerk (Our Lady Queen of Peace church) by the architect Jos Bekkers now stands. In 1924, the parochial church council of the City of Amsterdam purchase a plot of approximately 6,500 m² bordered by the Ambonplein, the Obistraat, the Halmaheirastraat and the Batjanstraat. Apart from the Gerardus Majellakerk (1926), Stuyt also made the designs for a number of buildings surrounding the church. He was well know in the Catholic construction world and had previously designed, among other things, churches (especially in South Netherlands), schools, hospitals, town halls and villas, and worked many times with Jos Cuypers, son of the productive Pierre. In Amsterdam, he also built the Rozenkranskerk in the Jacob Obrechtstraat and the Boerhaavekliniek in the Johannes Vermeerstraat. Although the buildings surrounding the church appeared similar at first glance, they differed considerably from each other, in terms of both form and detail. This concerns schools for nursery, primary and advanced primary education, a presbytery and a nunnery.

Several surrounding buildings

Pastoor Hesseveld school, which was originally a girls' school for primary education, is situated on the north-eastern side of the complex. The corner building is located within the building line of the rectangular site of the Catholic enclave and is now being used as an office space for business startups. Kinderbewaarplaats, this former nursery school between the boys' and girls' schools has a rectangular plan with one floor, built with brick (cross bond) and a circumferential hip roof with braised tiles.

The oblong building of the former girls' school has two stories under a composite, roof fitted with braised *Tuiles du Nord*. The lower middle section and flattened saddle roof is situated between two hip roofs with lightly protruding corners placed transversely against the ridges. Ridges and hip rafters are furnished with ridge tiles. The box gutter

Churches

is incorporated in the roof overhang. The facades are built with brick (cross bond) and furnished with two circumferential ornamental bands made from red brick at the same height as the plinth. A colourful circumferential frieze with a tile picture finished off the facades. There are currently 13 music studios located there.

The Sint-Theresiaklooster, a freestanding building constructed as a convent is situated on the north side of the church. The building, with its broad facade that protrudes lightly to the right, is situated directly on the pavement. To the left, a high garden wall connects the facade with the adjacent classrooms. The Sint-Vincentiushuis, the former parish is now a studio building for artists.

Gerardus Majellakerk

Churches

Interior during restoration

The church is built in the form of a so-called central plan, a combination of a basilica and cruciform church. It is clearly visible, just like other churches designed by Jan Stuyt, that the architect was influenced as a designer by the Aya Sophia in Istanbul, which he had visited. The planned tower, inspired by the Saint Mark's Square in Venice, was never built due to a shortage of money, but the foundations are still in the ground. The details, both inside and outside, are borrowed from the Romanesque style. In 1992, the final mass was held and the parish moved to smaller premises. After a futile search by the owner and the diocese to give the empty building another use, demolition appeared to be the only outcome. Due to the peripheral location and the requirements of the diocese, the Majallakerk was an object that was very difficult to position in the market. On the other hand, it was of great value in urban design and architectural terms. The church, along with the surrounding buildings, obtained the status of nationally listed building due to its cultural-historical value, as illustration of social developments within Catholicism, whereby church and educational buildings were concentrated. It also has a group value due to the spacial, architectural and historical functional relationship with the other complex parts.

Gerardus Majellakerk

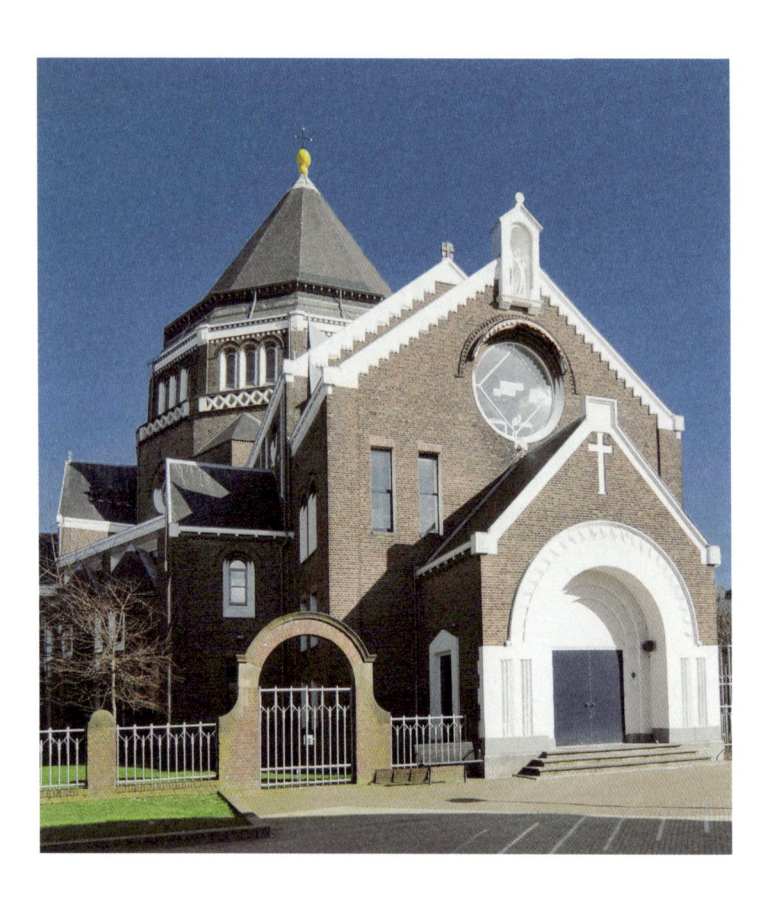

When Stadsherstel began restoration of the church (under restoration architect André van Stigt), the garden and the buildings around it did not look particularly healthy. A lot has improved since then. Most of the buildings have now been refurbished and the garden looks beautiful. As a result of the fences placed, it is perfectly possible to look at the garden and the buildings from different angles. Those people who work there can make use of the garden. A major refurbishment, including acoustic measures, has been carried out for the current tenants the Netherlands Philharmonic Orchestra. Offices have been built in the knave and the domed space has been made suitable for rehearsals and concerts (225 seats). The middle space can also be set up as one ground floor space and can be hired for special events.

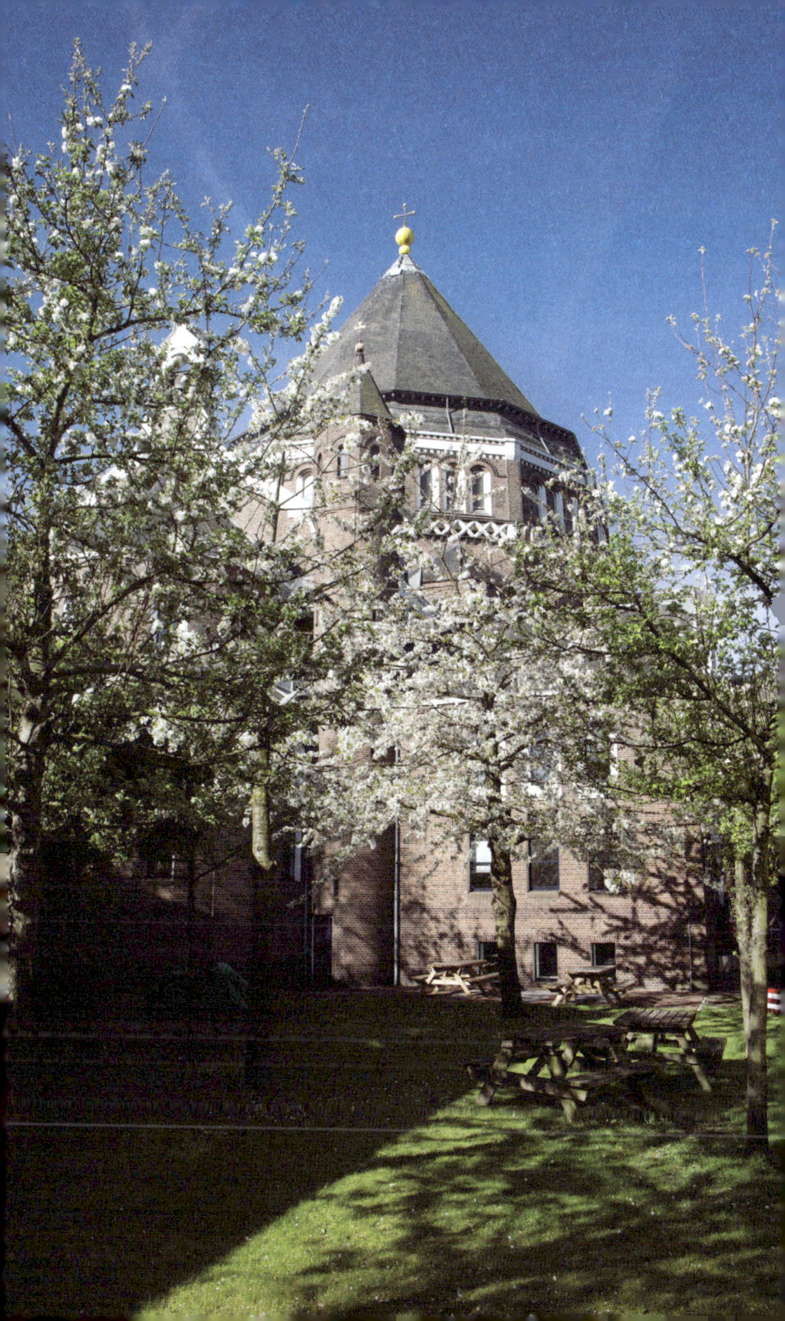

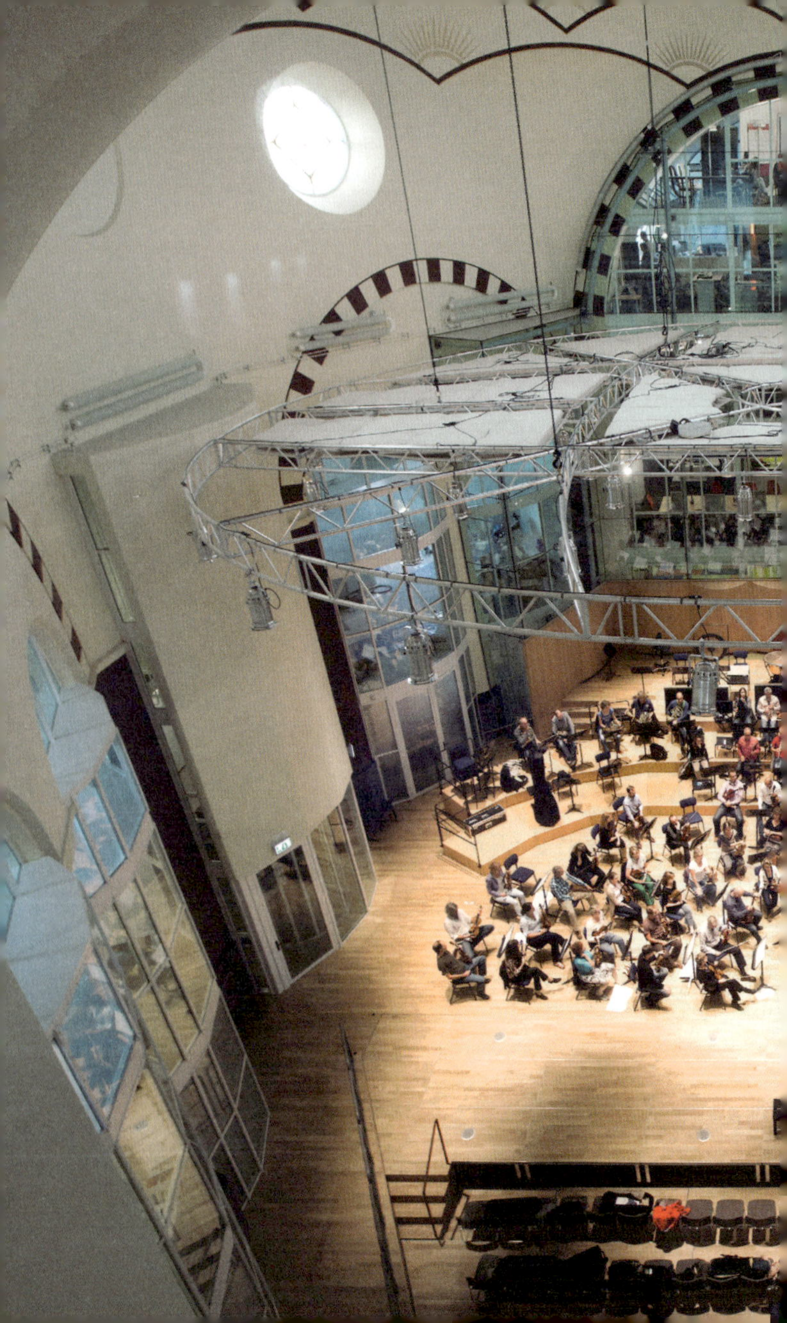

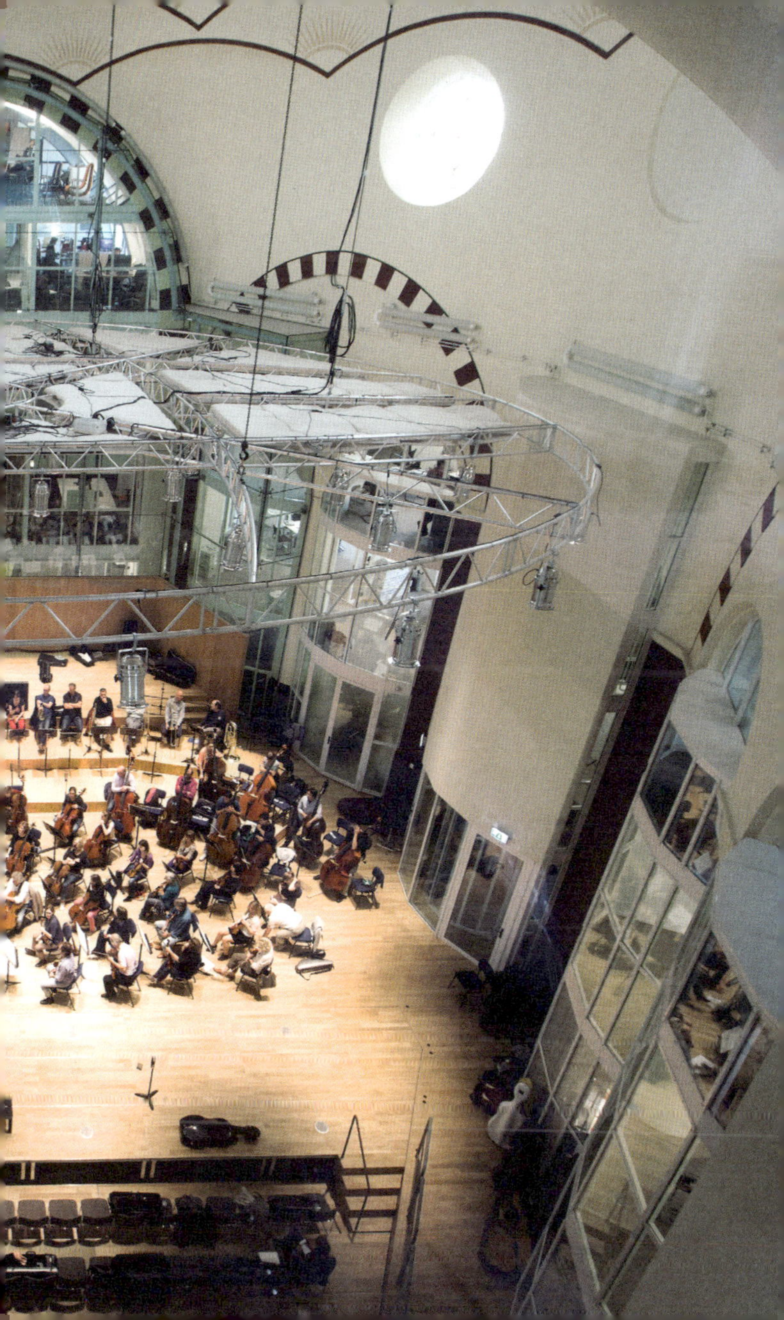

Churches

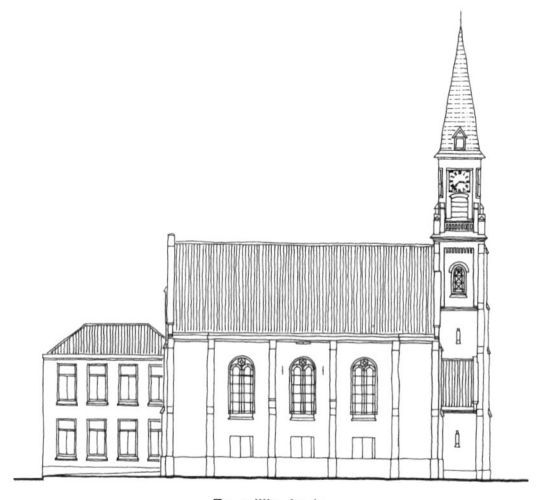

Zaandijkerkerk
Kerkstraat 9-10, Zaandijk
2016

Kerkje van Evers
Noordeinde 124, Landsmeer
2014

Kapel van Durgerdam
Durgerdammerdijk 101, Durgerdam
2013

Churches

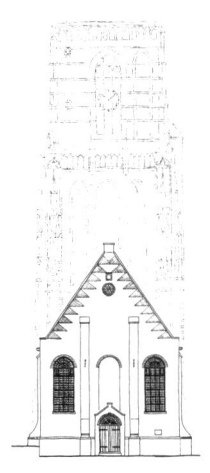

Kerk van Ransdorp
Dorpsweg 55, Ransdorp
2006

Schellingwouderkerk
Wijkergouw 6, Amsterdam
2000

Muiderkerktoren
Linnaeusstraat 37, Amsterdam
2012

Oranjekerk
Van Ostadestraat 149, Amsterdam
2000

Zaandijkerkerk

Zaandijkerkerk

Built **Rebuild after fire, 1880**
Acquisition **2013**
Restoration **2016**

The Zaandijkerkerk had been neglected for many years and was waiting for demolition. Thanks to the work of Stadsherstel, this could be prevented and restoration began in July 2015.

Churches

Isometric drawings of the Zaandijkerkerk with the incorporation of 11 apartments

Kerkje van Evers

Built **1861**
Acquisition **2014**
Restoration **2016**

This rare example of a religious timber-frame construction, which was built in 1861 for the Christian Reformed Church Landsmeer, has had various designated uses since 1927. The provincial listed building is popularly better known as 'het kerkje van Evers' (the church of Evers) and is an example of repurposing *avant la lettre*. The local monument committee drew Stadherstel's attention to this characteristic building, once a meeting centre, studio and 'paint shop'. The Evers family ran a well-known interior shop here and lived in the adjacent parsonage. The building is situated at a striking location on the Noordeinde road and with its spacious garden and the parsonage it has a distinctive

Churches

village-like character. Currently, only the pointed arch windows remain intact, but there also used to be a beautiful entrance in a Renaissance style and there were two characteristic air vents on the roof. As a result of joint efforts and a contribution from the province and municipality, as well as good contact with the Evers family, the complex has been given a new future and this piece of heritage will be preserved. Both buildings will house three apartments. During the Second World War, the painter Wim Schumacher (1894 – 1986) had his studio in the church. He went into hiding with the local doctor, together with well-known writers, the composer Karel Mengelberg and the architect Ben Merkelbach.

Kerk van Ransdorp

Kerk van Ransdorp

Built 1719/1936
Acquisition 2003
Restoration 2006

The oversized towers date from the early-16th century and were designed by Jan Poyt. These towers are reminiscent of the flourishing shipping industry, trade and economic activity that the village experienced especially in the 15th century. The medieval church was replaced in 1719 and significantly refurbished in 1833. In 1936, the church was rebuilt – on the old foundations - under the supervision of the architect J.C. Hoogendorp (1878 – 1952). Eighteenth century building materials were also reused then. The church is located on the village square and has a large garden.

Kapel van Durgerdam

Kapel van Durgerdam

Built **1687**
Acquisition **2009**
Restoration **2013**

The wooden building, actually a town hall from 1687, is the focal point of the former fisher's village on the Zuiderzee. It is now located between the dyke houses on the opposite side of the Amsterdam urban development district IJburg on the Buiten-IJ (Outer-IJ river) and is currently in use as a house. It is an important cultural historical listed building at a beautiful location. 'De Kapel' (The Chapel) probably got its nickname when mass was read here in the Middle Ages, because the nearest church was in Ransdorp. The restoration began at the end of 2012, following a thorough preliminary investigation. The architectural history was interesting, but the architectural condition was abominable. For example, the wooden construction still had many original details that were, however, severely damaged. Following the replacement of the foundations and rooftop unit, the enormous living room on the principal floor once again became the fantastic focal point of the restored chapel, with a view of all four points on the compass.

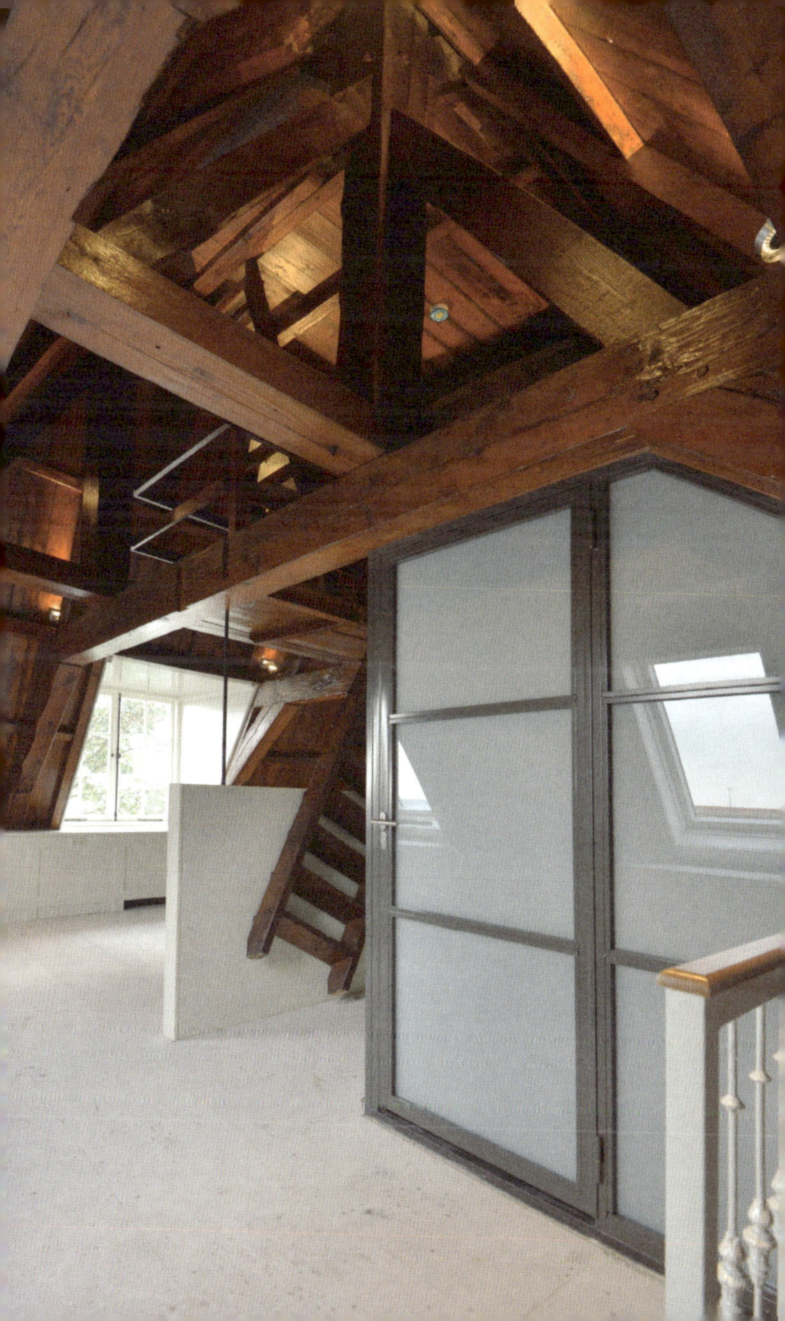

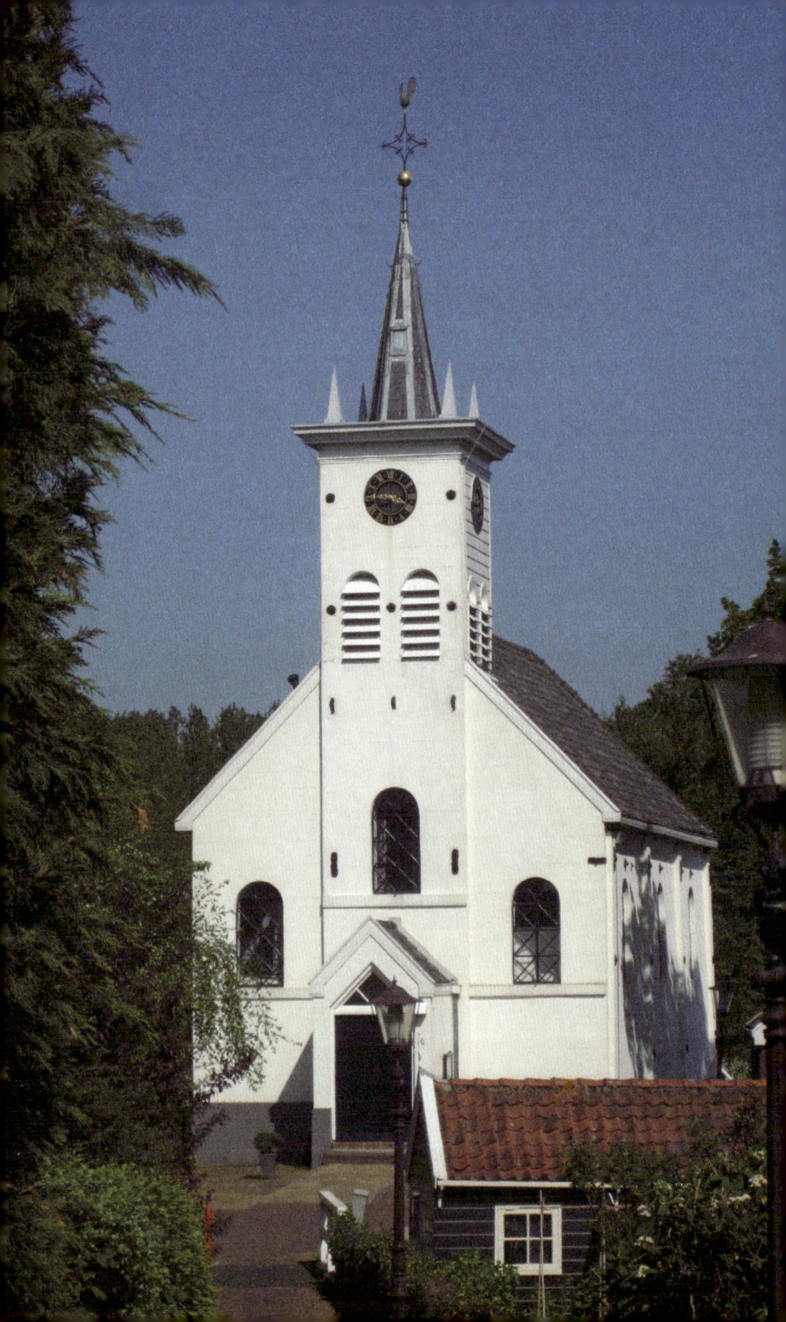

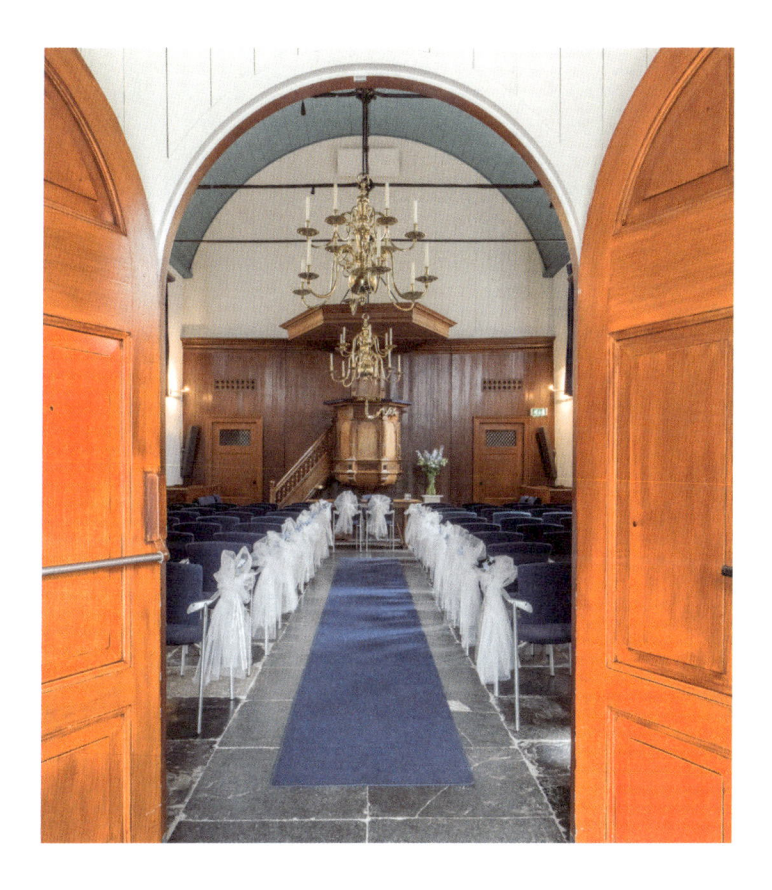

Schellingwouderkerk

Built **1866**
Acquisition **1998**
Restoration **2000**

The Waterstate style church of Schellingwoude is located close to the Oranjesluizen locks in Amsterdam-Noord (Amsterdam North) on a terp mound at the base of the dyke. An intimate white building with a rural location. Historical research before and during the restoration revealed that various churches have stood on the terp mound since the beginning of the 14th century. The current, originally Reformed, building dates from 1866. The restoration of the Schellingwouderkerk was completed in 2000. It is the smallest church of Stadsherstel. As a result of its rural and picturesque location, it is a romantic spot. The locks cooperate fully with outside visitors.

Muiderkerktoren

Built **1892**
Acquisition **2012**
Restoration **2012**

The Muiderkerk tower is the only remnant following the fire in the church on the Linnaeusstraat in 1989. New buildings are constructed behind the tower. The tower was acquired and restored in 2012.

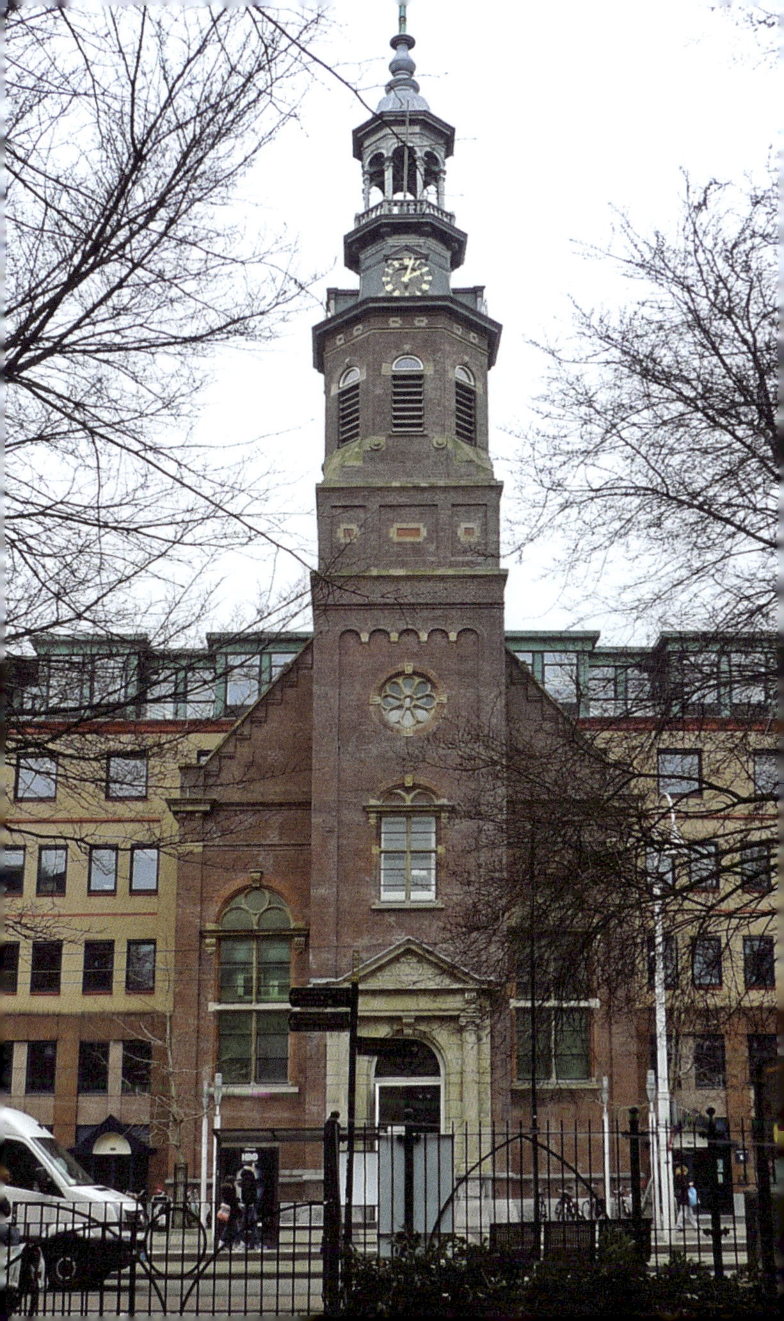

Oranjekerk

Built **1902**
Acquisition **1998**
Restoration **2000**

The Oranjekerk dates from a period in which the city was developing rapidly. There was no church building by the Sarpahtipark in the 19th century district De Pijp. Architect C. B. Posthumus Meyjes, who came from a family of pastors, is the designer and in 1903 the Amsterdam Reformed Congregation put the church – which is shaped like a Greek cross with octagonal transepts – into use. The main church space has not pillars, so that the pastor can be seen well from each spot. Whether or not the church would be given a steeple remained uncertain for a long time. In order to collect money, the Stuiversvereeniging Torenbouw Kerk YY (which was the name of De Pijp at the time) was established. This association managed to successfully collect the money required and the building of the steeple began in March 1902. At the beginning of the 1990s, restoration and a different use for the building followed fierce protests from the neighbourhood in reaction to demolition plans. The interior was completely changed based on a design by the architect Hans Wagner. The former main church space was replaced by smaller spaces, including a church space designed by the architect Leo Versteijlen and a foyer.

Grote kerk Schermerhorn

Address
Oosteinde 2

Town
Schermerhorn

Built
1634 – 1636

Acquisition
2016

Restoration
2016

Restoration architect
Fred Greven

Churches

The church built for the Dutch Reformed community in a Gothic style from 1634 – 1636 is shaped like a basilica. The windows with late-Gothic pointed arch shapes are among the best stained glass windows in the Netherlands (by P.P. Rubens). The wooden tunnel vault painted with flower motifs is also special. The interior is largely authentic. The original oak pews are still around the pillars. The church organ from the 18th century is in use again. As a result of the beautiful way the light falls on the interior and the pretty location in the Schermer (polder), this church is one of the highlights.

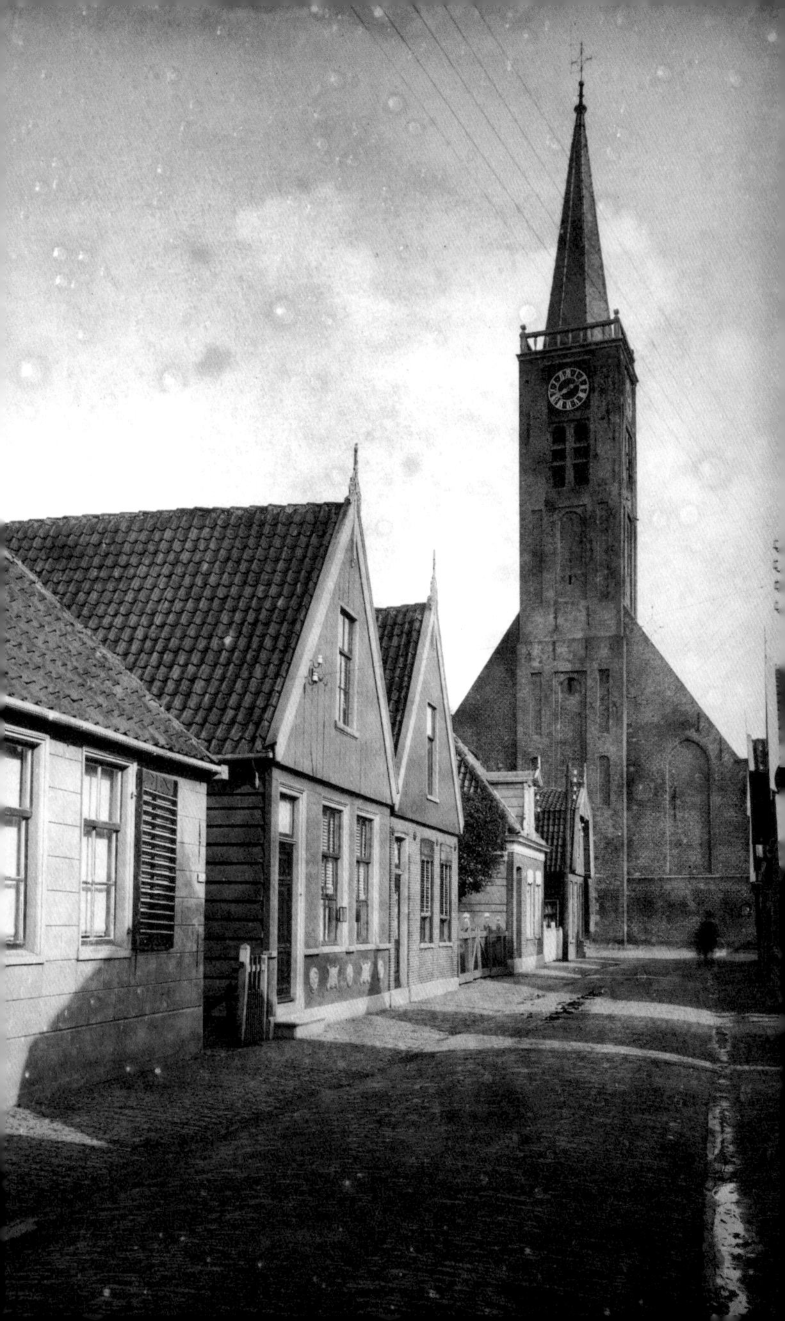

Churches 213

Grote kerk Schermerhorn

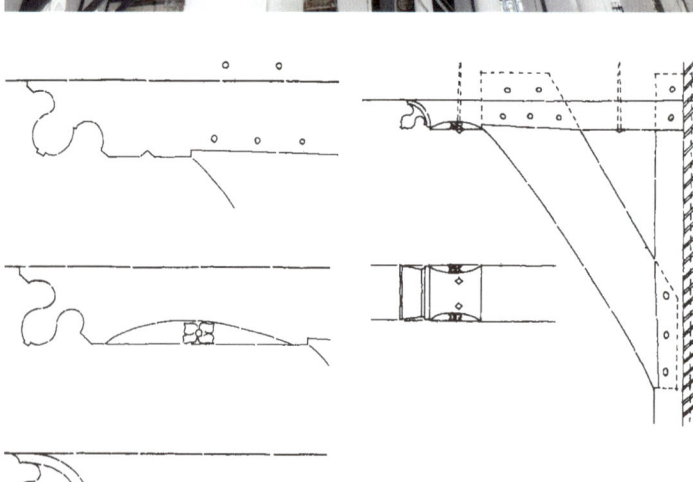

Corbel piece with nib

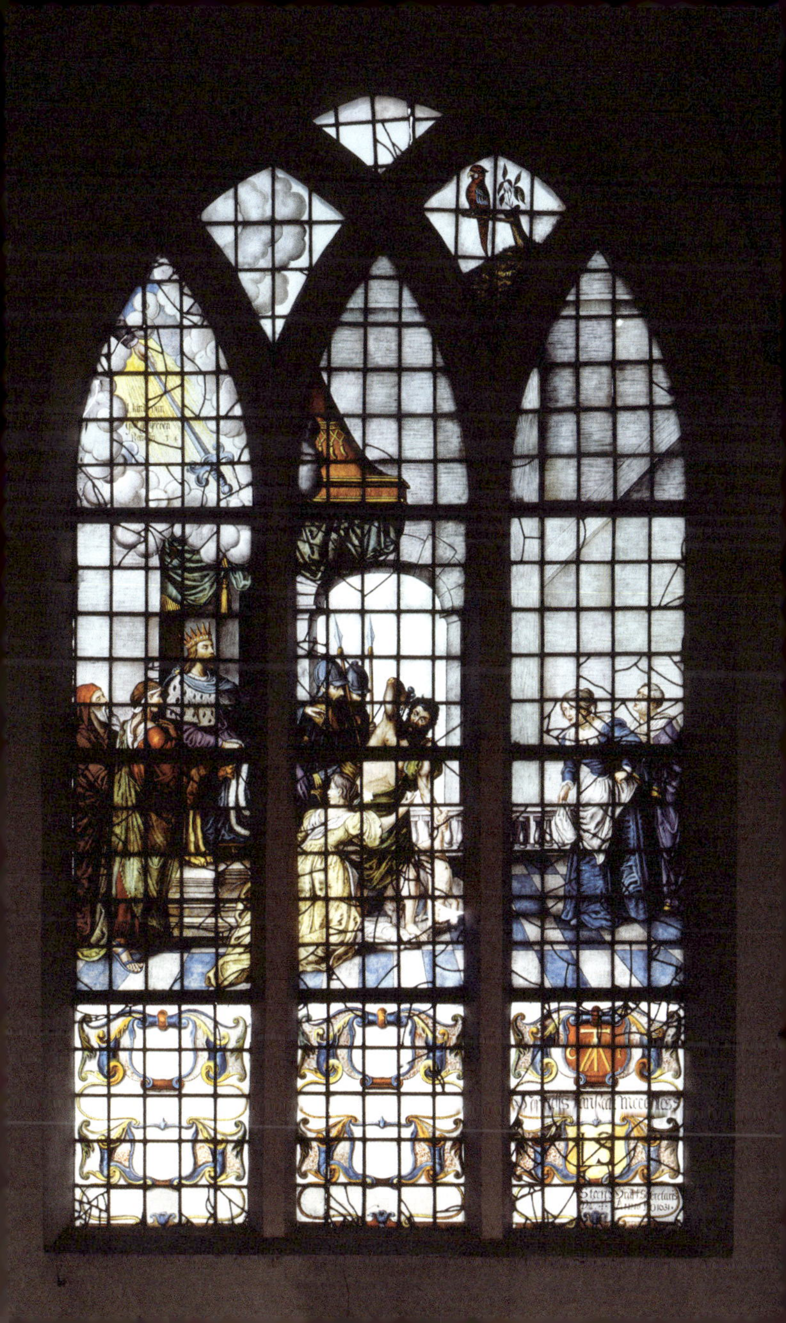

Bakenesserkerk

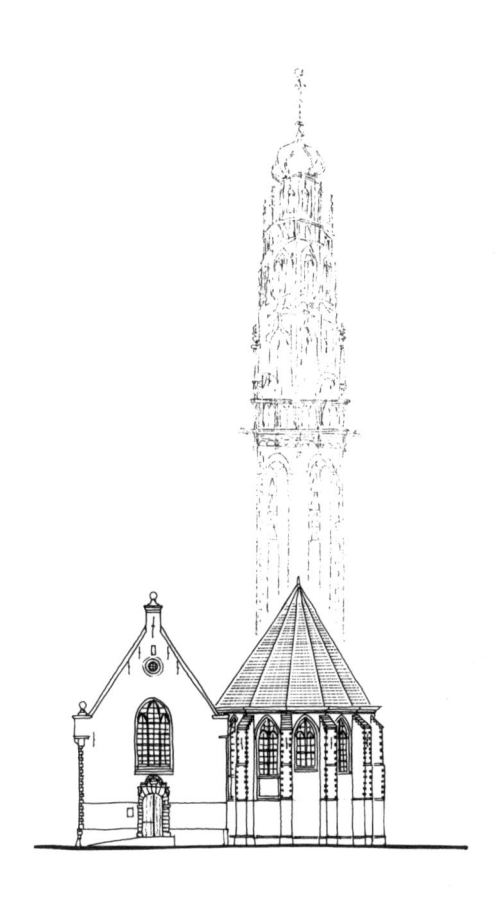

216

Address **Vrouwestraat 12**	Built **1415 – 1420**	Restoration architect **Martin Busker** **(Municipality of Haarlem)**
Town **Haarlem**	Acquisition **2009**	Current use **Multifunctional space, office, exhibitions**
	Restoration **2010**	

Together with the Sint Bavokerk, the Bakenesserkerk forms the striking silhouette, as a result of which Haarlem can be recognised from far away. The church started small around 1250, a simple wooden chapel on the Bakenes, a point of land on the bend of the river Spaarne and was replaced by a brick building soon afterwards. In 1530, the current tower was added and the church obtained its current form at the beginning of the 17th century. In January 2010, the restoration started and the building was assigned a new purpose as office and exhibition space.

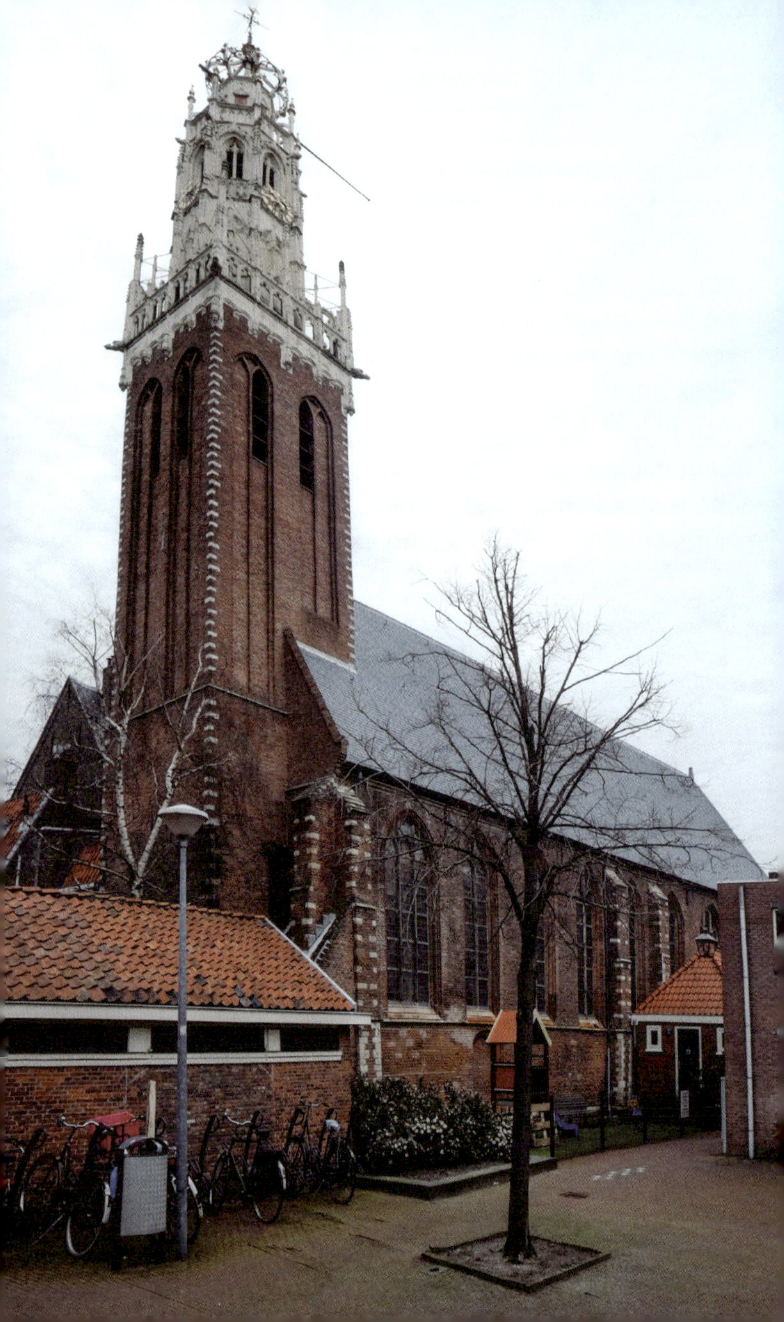

Churches 219

De Hoop

220

Address	Built	Restoration architect
Hartveldseweg 23	**1786 – 1787**	**Rappange & Partners B.V.**

Town	Acquisition	Current use
Diemen	**1996**	**Commercial space, events, dinners, receptions and concerts**

Restoration
1998

Behind the simple, characteristic facade, a rich and light interior is hidden. De Hoop in Diemen, built in 1786 – 1787, is the only remaining rural clandestine church in the vicinity of Amsterdam and was used as a church until 1910. The local population later used the building as a meeting centre, storage space and organ school. After a fatal fire in 1990, the listed building could be saved from demolition, followed by the restoration of the decorated interior.

De Hoop

Churches

DE HOOP

23

Clandestine churches

A clandestine church (or conventicle) is a church building that cannot be recognised as such from the outside. These places were used at the time of the Republic of the United Netherlands by Roman Catholics and other believers, because religious freedom was restricted to the Calvinist Reformed Church during the Golden Age. The clandestine churches appeared in many parts of the Netherlands and were mainly located in houses and warehouses in cities, while in the countryside a church usually had the appearance of a barn and were therefore also called barn churches. At the end of the 18th century, freedom of religion was introduced and the Catholics could build their own churches once again. Nevertheless, many clandestine churches still remained in use for a long time afterwards, especially in the west of the country. Most of them were ultimately demolished or unrecognisably altered and the Catholic Church started to built many neo-Gothic churches, including the replacement of the Posthoornkerk, at the end of the 19th century. Museum Ons' Lieve Heer op Solder (Museum Our Lord in the Attic), at the corner of the Oudezijds Voorburgwal and the Heintje Hoeksteeg, in the middle of the Red Light District, is probably the most well-known and frequently visited former clandestine church. A distinctive feature is that the building appears to be a normal canal house on the side of the Oudezijds Voorburgwal 40. Following refurbishment under the supervision of the architect Felix Claus (Claus and Van Wageningen), it was reopened to the public in 2015.

Museum Oudezijds Voorburgwal, 1935

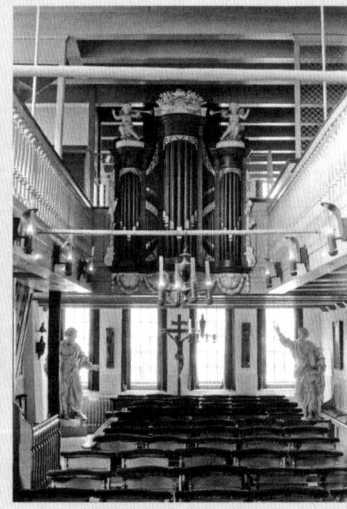

Interior Museum Ons Lieve Heer op Solder, 1975

Churches

Van Houtenkerk

Address
Oudegracht 69

Town
Weesp

Built
1906

Acquisition
2009

Restoration
2013

Restoration architect
Hooyschuur architecten

Current use
Office, church services and other uses

This church was constructed in 1906, commissioned by the Van Houten sisters, descendants of the famous chocolate-making family and is also, therefore, popularly called 'het Chocoladekerkje' (the Chocolate Church). The church is centrally located on the Oudegracht and has Romanesque references on the exterior. The interior is in the style of Art Nouveau with Jugendstil features and it was given the nickname 'auditorium' by the Protestant churchgoers. The chandeliers and wall-mounted light fittings, as well as the many stencils on the walls and ceilings, catch the eye. The innovations that occurred in the Dutch crafts and architecture around 1900 also had a so-called constructive or rational direction. The architect H.P. Berlage (1856 – 1934) was at the forefront of these innovations. In this school of thought, the appearance of the product was determined by its use and the nature of the processed material. The decoration was mostly sparing and secondary to the form. The constructive and rational direction was mainly imitated in Amsterdam and primarily stemmed from the need of socially engage artists to produce well-designed utensils for large groups of society. The Van Houtenkerk is an example of this art movement. Because the cost of the day-to-day management and maintenance had become too great after more than a century, the church was handed over to Stadsherstel in 2009.

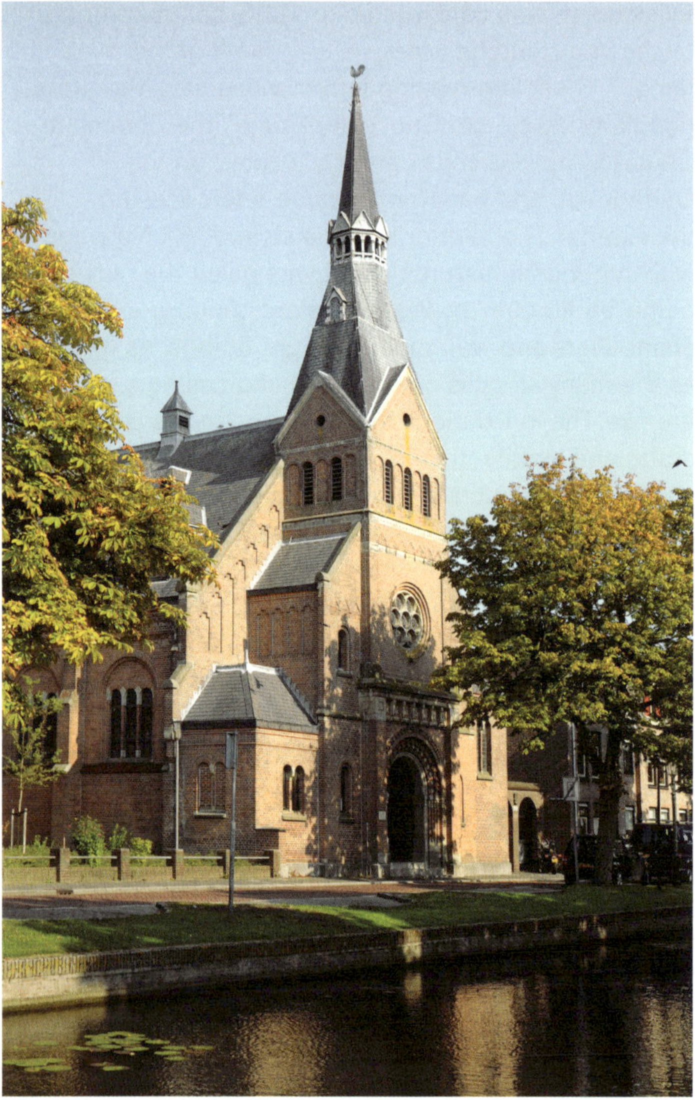

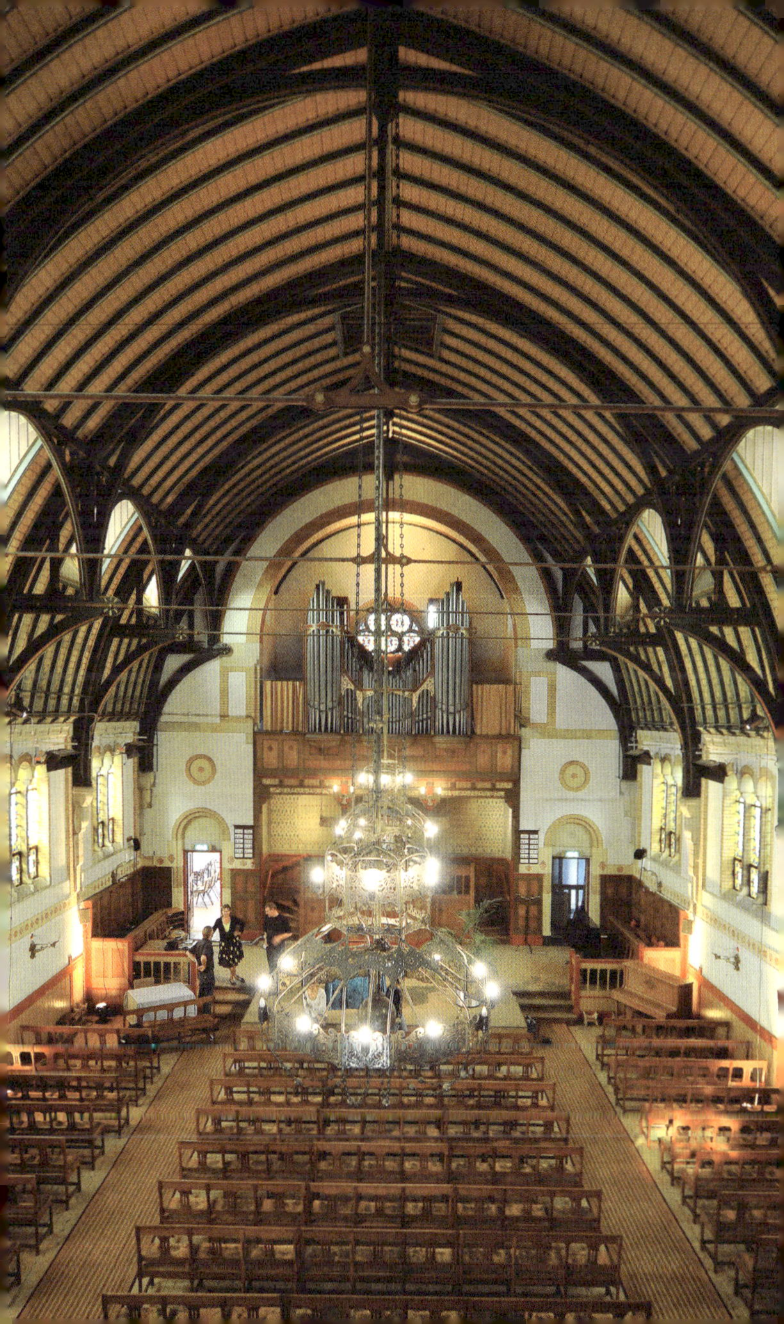

Van Houtenkerk

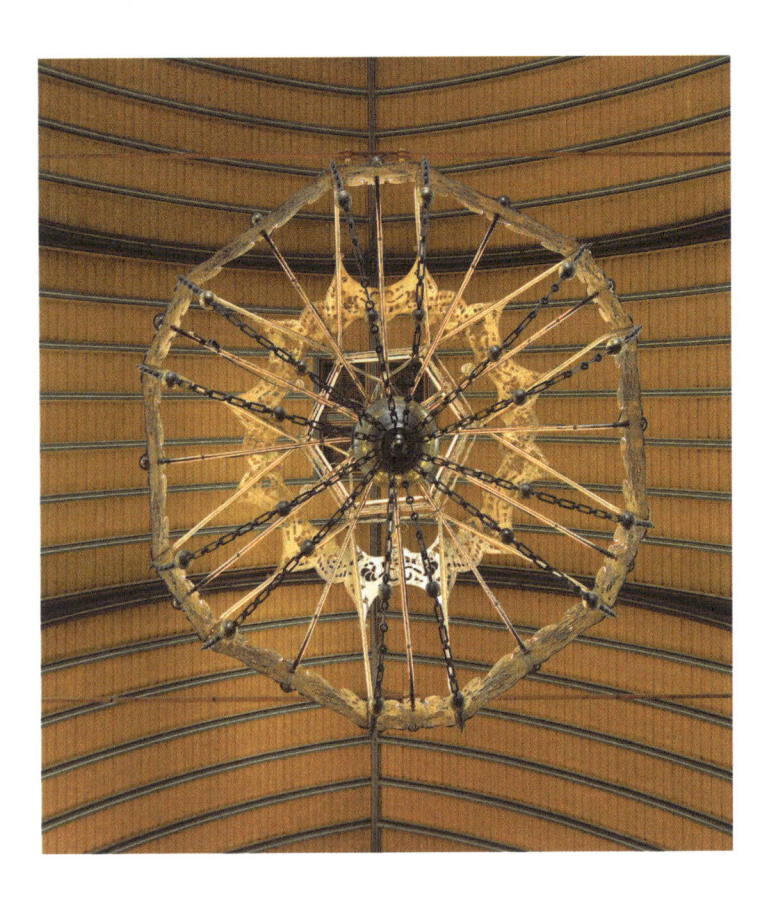

Windows and doors in the urban home

In the development of the house, windows and doors are the most rapidly changing elements. As a result of windows and doors, life in the house is also made visible and vice versa. In the 17th and 18th century, the window increasingly became part of the interior. The stained glass interior window, which we know from the paintings of Johannes Vermeer (1632 – 1675), served as protection against rain and cold with an open shutter. The separate secondary glazing was hung in a thin frame and hinged. The masterpiece for house carpenters involved making a cross window with four panes, as well as a double casement window frame and a Dutch leaded casement window. After 1700, there was a major shift in the development of windows and doors. Along with the changes to the interior, the rich decorative function that the ceiling assumed and the painting of beams, floorboards and wallpaper, there was also the introduction of the sash window with larger panes of almost clear glass, mounted in glazing bars. The sash window was based on the principal of a fixed fanlight with a lower window that could be slid upwards. The visual variety of external doors and panel doors in the Amsterdam urban home is unprecedented and traceable to each period in the construction history.

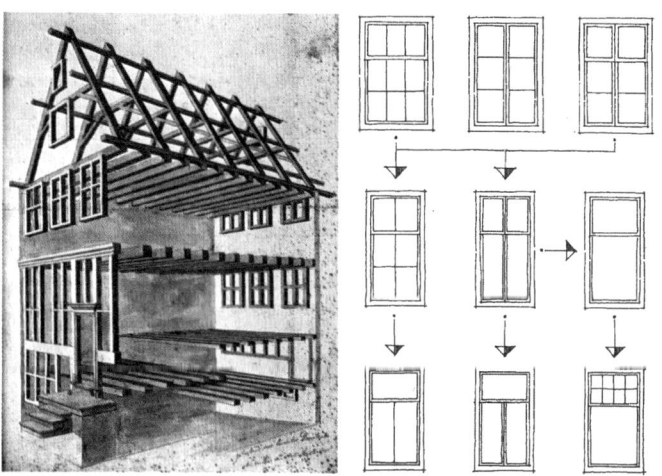

Windows related to the beams in a 17th century house

19th century development of a window

Windows and doors

Windows and doors 235

Windows and doors

Windows and doors

237

Windows and doors

Windows and doors

Windows and doors

Living

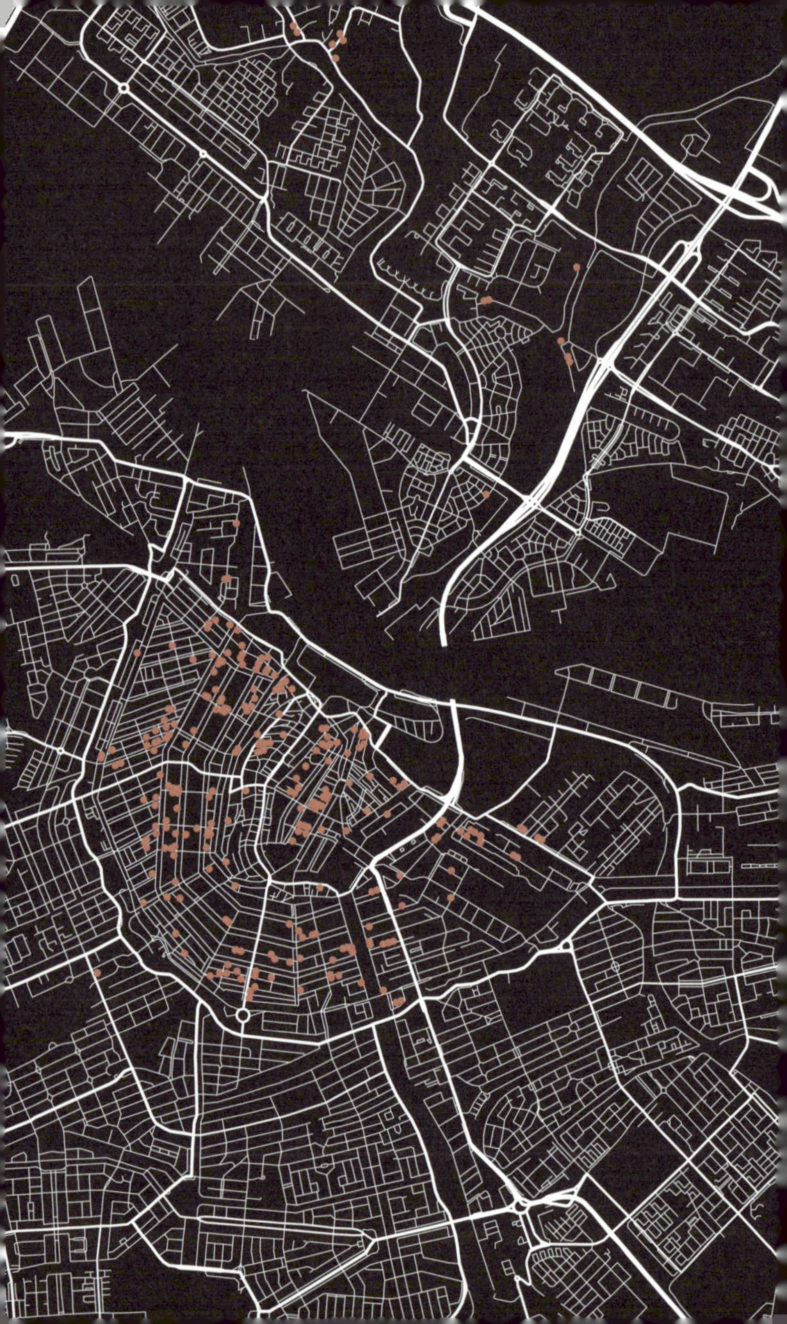

246 **Nieuwendijk**, Amsterdam
250 **Blaeu Erf**, Amsterdam
256 **De Wallen**, Amsterdam
260 **KLM Houses**, Amsterdam
272 **Grachtengordel**, Amsterdam
276 **Nine streets + two**, Amsterdam
290 **Raamsteeg 6**, Amsterdam
300 **Haarlemmerbuurt**, Amsterdam
304 **Jordaan**, Amsterdam
310 **Weteringbuurt and Amstel**, Amsterdam
316 **Plantagebuurt / Hortus / Artis**, Amsterdam
322 **Oostelijke eilanden and Kadijken**, Amsterdam
328 **Amsterdam-Noord**, Amsterdam
334 **Haarlem / Heemstede**

Henk Zantkuijl (1925 – 2012), was the pioneer of the building-historical research of urban houses. Following his architecture and construction engineering study, he started working on 1 August 1953 as a supervisor/draughtsman for the recently established Municipal Department for the Preservation and Restoration of Monuments and Sites (Bureau Monumentenzorg) in Amsterdam. In the years that followed, he made his name as a skilful restoration architect. He continued to be in charge of the municipal department until 1989, and supervised approximately 4,000 restoration case dossiers. His standard reference work *Bouwen in Amsterdam. Het woonhuis in de stad* (Building in Amsterdam. The House in the City, 4 editions) is still the basis for research into historical buildings. It appeared in 60 separate magazines between 1973 and 1992 and was published in one volume for the first time in 1993. The city of Amsterdam earned an international reputation in that period due to the systematic restoration of its architectural heritage. Zantkuijl's most important principle was that meticulous building-historical research should precede a thorough restoration. In retrospect, this would seem self-evident, but that was not always the case. The manner of consolidating, restoring or even reconstructing a historic building was the natural result of prior research. It also ensured reuse of sculpted gables that originated from demolished houses and that were stored in order to contribute to the overall silhouette of the city. The considerable knowledge that Zantkuijl managed to acquire about Amsterdam dwellings throughout the centuries has remained an important source for Stadsherstel, with all the information about roofs, wood, brick, natural stone, windows, doors, (pile) foundations, colour, style periods, interior, sources of heat, ceilings and staircases.

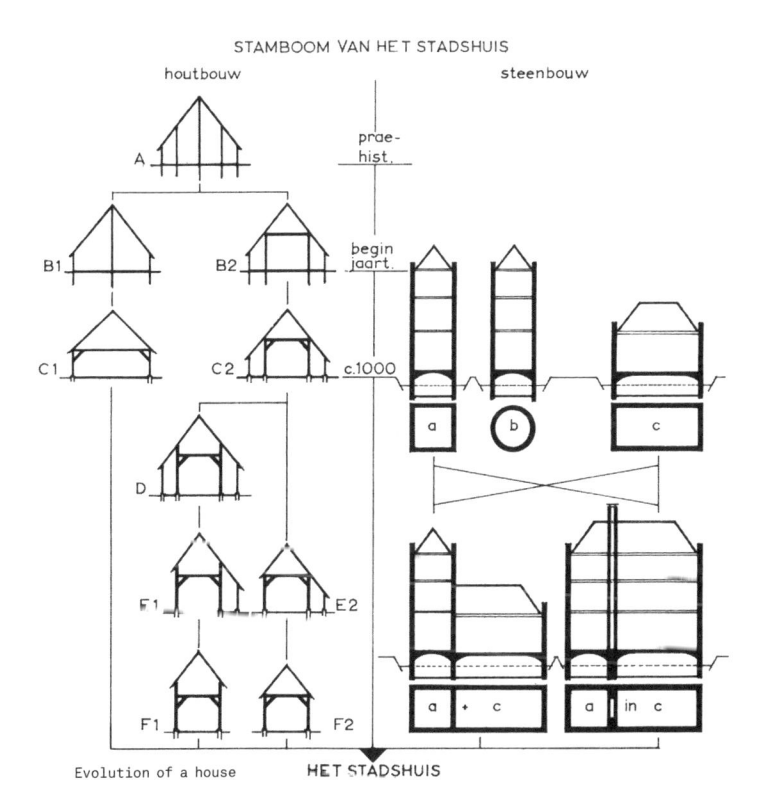

Evolution of a house

Nieuwendijk

1. Dirk van Hasseltsteeg 1-3
   2007
2. Dirk van Hasseltsteeg 2-4
   2007
3. Nieuwe Nieuwstraat 19
   1997
4. Nieuwe Nieuwstraat 27
   1997
5. Nieuwendijk 1 ·
   Prins Hendrikkade 1
   1978
6. Nieuwendijk 24
   1969
7. Nieuwezijds
   Voorburgwal 38
   1963
8. Nieuwezijds
   Voorburgwal 149 ·
   Paleisstraat 23-31
   1975
9. Nieuwezijds
   Voorburgwal 151
   1975/2011
10. Smaksteeg 24
11. Spuistraat 61
    2014
12. Spuistraat 255A-255B
    1990
13. Stromarkt 3
    2006
14. Stromarkt 4 · Singel 1
    2005
15. Stromarkt 5-15
16. Stromarkt 17-23

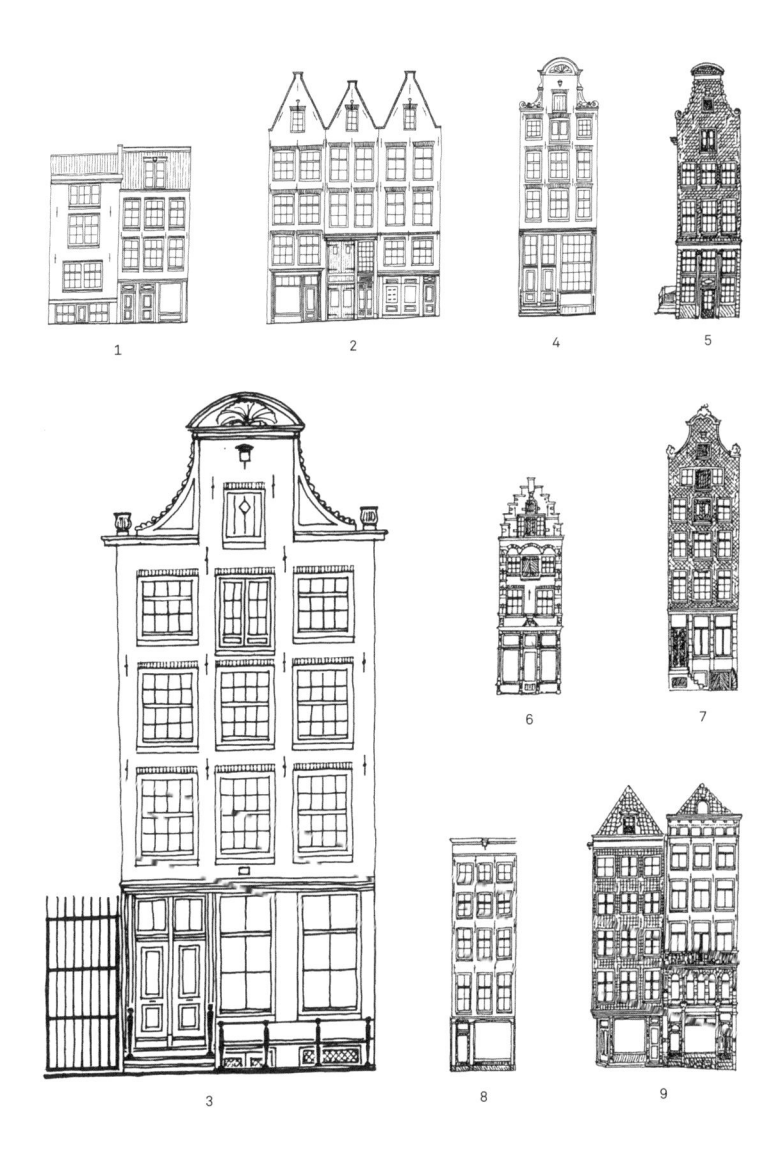

Living

247

Nieuwendijk

248

10

11

12

13

14

15

16

Medieval Amsterdam

The parcelling between the Nieuwendijk and the Nieuwezijds Voorburgwal is one of the oldest in the city. The slanting course of the streets and alleyways can be directly related to the reclamation of the Amstel banks in the late-12th century. By digging drainage ditches, the water flowed from the peat to the river. The ditches die not lie perpendicular, but slanting inland, in order to prevent intake of the river water. The ribbon development on the drained ditches grew into the current urban proportions with, among others, the Gravenstraat, the Sint Nicolaasstraat and the Dirk van Hasseltssteeg. We also find the crooked street pattern in the Jordaan neighbourhood. The Sint Nicolaasstraat and the Rozenstraat in the Jordaan are actually in line with each other. It was thus originally one ditch prior to construction of the canal ring. Today, the Nieuwendijk and surroundings is a shopping district aimed at tourists. Up until the 1970s, the current pedestrian area was still, albeit to a limited extent, accessible to cars.

Blaeu Erf

250

Nieuwezijds Voorburgwal 87-95

Nieuwezijds Voorburgwal 97-99

Sint Nicolaasstraat 46-58

Sint Nicolaasstraat 49-51

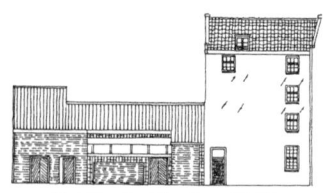

Sint Geertruidensteeg 15-18

Address
Nieuwezijds Voorburgwal 87-99 / Sint Nicolaasstraat 49-50, 51-57, 52-64, 59, 63-75, 66-78, 67, 71, 75, 80-84, 88, 90 / Sint Geertruidensteeg 15-18

Town
Amsterdam

Built
1600 – 1700

Acquisition
1978

Restoration
1982 (SN 49, 51-57, 59, 63-75), 1985 (NV 87-99 / SN 67, 71, 75, 80, 82, 88, 90 / SG 15-18)

Restoration architect
G. de Klerk / Stadsherstel

Current use
Shops, offices, housing, HAT-units

The well-over 20 buildings of Stadsherstel around
the Blaeu Erf are in the vicinity of the Nieuwezijds
Voorburgwal between the Sint Geertruidensteeg and
the Romeinsarmsteeg. This area behind the Nieuwe
Kerk is named after Joan Blaeu who printed the world-
renowned Blaeu atlases past 'de Son' archway between
1666 and 1672. In the night of 16 February 1672,
the map printing works and publisher went up into
flames resulting in more than 380,000 guilders damage.
After this disastrous incident, the widow of the printer
submitted a plan asking to be allowed to erect 28 small
houses on the devastated spot, which she gained permission for in January 1675. Since the 19th century,
the purpose of the buildings in the narrow alleyways
has been changing. From 1953, the buildings were purchased by the textile wholesaler G. van Wees en Weiss.
It later came into the hands of house trader Tabak, who
had to stop his plans for a car park by the municipality.
The empty buildings were squatted around 1970 and
after a lethal fire (1974) with fatal results in the building
on Sint Nicolaasstraat 58, every kind of weather was given
free reign in the boarded up houses until Stadsherstel
took over responsibility for the complex. On the basis
of architectural research, a decision was taken to restore
the seriously run-down neighbourhood in two phases
while preserving the small-scale parcelling amidst larger
buildings that had sprung up in the surrounding area from
the end of the 19th century. Fourteen of the houses are
on the monuments register. Nieuwezijds Voorburgwal 87
was refurbished following complete dismantling.

Nieuwezijds Voorburgwal during restoration

Nieuwezijds Voorburgwal after restoration

Blaeu Erf

Sint Nicolaasstraat 38 after restoration

Sint Nicolaasstraat 56

This building was completely reconstructed in 18th century form with a 19th century cornice. As in the case of a number or neighbouring buildings, a HAT-unit was erected here.

Sint Nicolaasstraat 54

Before Stadsherstel carried out the restoration, this building had a cornice, similar to number 56. The cornices were placed at the same height during refurbishment in 1930. Both buildings were given a flat roof. In order to accentuate the original point of departure, a decision was taken to place a bell gable to increase the variety of facades.

Sint Nicolaasstraat 52

The crow-stepped gable was rebuilt at the same time as the neck gable of number 50 in the 1930s. In addition, the historic components such as the natural stone tables, the *oeil(s)-de-boeuf* and the relieving arches above the windows were reused. The buildings of number 50 and 52 are now inhabited by female students. Number 50 still contains parts from the original skeleton construction. By applying tuck pointing, the modern appearance of the facades has been somewhat concealed.

Sint Nicolaasstraat 48

A drawing of the original building before the demolition of 1944 can be found in the municipal archives. This shows that a bakery used to be located here. There was a stone plaque in the neck gable with the inscription 'De Blauwe Haan A° 1731'. This stone is now displayed in the facade of a villa elsewhere in the city.

Sint Nicolaasstraat 46

Only the base of the building remained, so it was decided that there should be a modern new building. It was the first time that Stadsherstel carried out a new building.

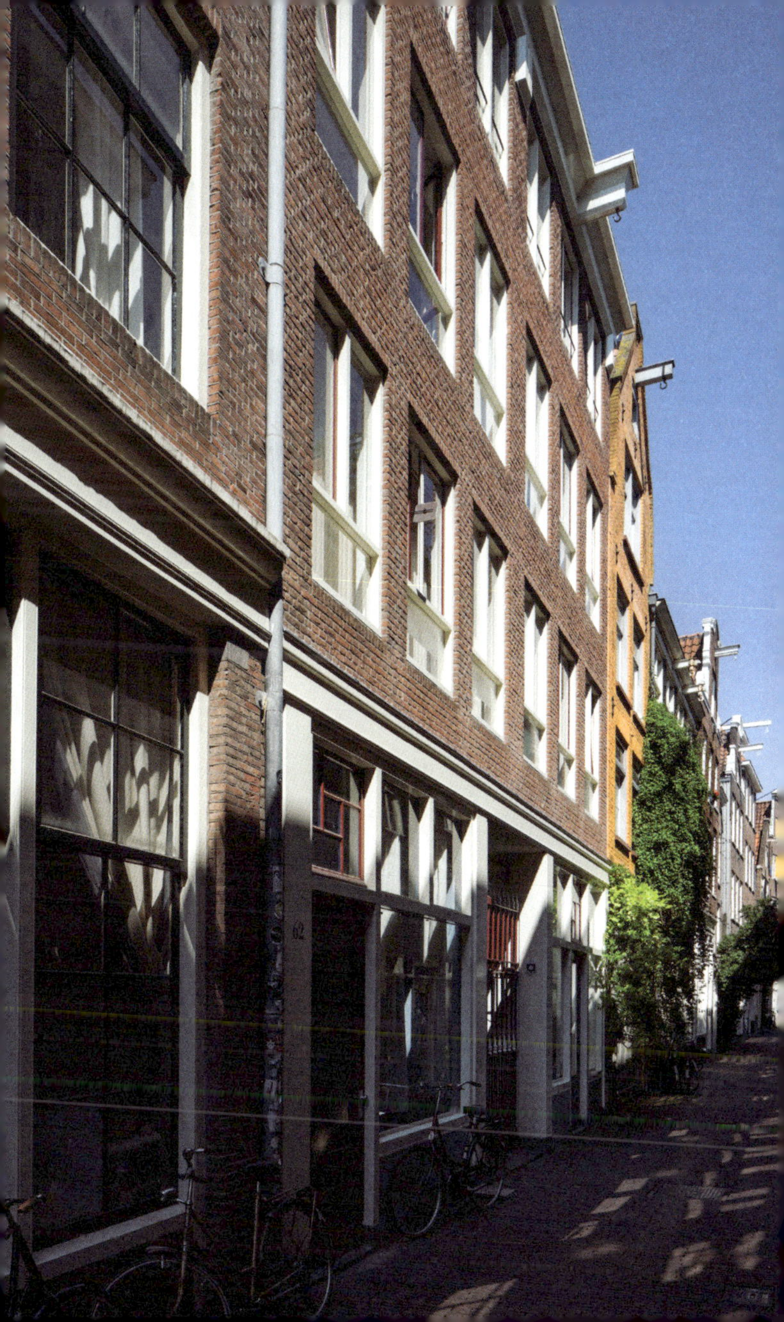
62

De Wallen

1. Barndesteeg 8-16
   1992
2. Bethaniëndwarsstraat 1-7
   1992
3. Bethaniënstraat 3-7
   2000
4. Bethaniënstraat 10
   1992
5. Bethaniënstraat 14
   1992
6. Bethaniënstraat 37-39
   1990
7. Binnenkant 36-37
   1973
8. Binnenkant 50
   1971
9. Binnenkant 51 ·
   Kalkmarkt 12-13
   1971
10. Enge Kerksteeg 3 ·
    Oudekerksplein 32
    1994
11. Geldersekade 3
    1959/2012
12. Geldersekade 10 ·
    Oudezijds Kolk 1
    1992
13. Geldersekade 12
    1984
14. Geldersekade 14 ·
    Oudezijds Kolk 3
    2002
15. Geldersekade 15
    1992
16. Geldersekade 53
    1963/1996
17. Geldersekade 78
    2004
18. Geldersekade 121
    1982
19. Guldehandsteeg 1
20. Guldehandsteeg 11-17
    1990
21. Kalkmarkt 7
    1999
22. Kalkmarkt 10
    2004
23. Kalkmarkt 11
    1971
24. Kalkmarkt 12-13 ·
    Binnenkant 51
    1971
25. Kloveniersburgwal 6-8
    1980
26. Kloveniersburgwal 14
    1990
27. Kloveniersburgwal 22-24
    2007
28. Kloveniersburgwal 38
    1969
29. Kloveniersburgwal 40
    1971
30. Kloveniersburgwal 44
    2014
31. Kloveniersburgwal 57
32. Koestraat 13
    1993
33. Koestraat 16B
    1996
34. Koestraat 20-22
    1994
35. Koestraat 24-30
    1990
36. Korte Keizersstraat 11
    1980
37. Kromme Waal 13
    1963
38. Lange Niezel 10
    2013
39. Lange Niezel 22
    1992
40. Oude Hoogstraat 17
    1990
41. Oude Schans 52
    1977
42. Oude Waal 6
    1984
43. Oudemanhuispoort 1A
    2012
44. Oudez. Achterburgwal 143
    1990
45. Oudez. Achterburgwal 156
    2013
46. Oudez. Achterburgwal 164
    2007
47. Oudez. Achterburgwal
    189-195
    2006
48. O.z. Achterburgwal 199 ·
    Rusland 3-5
    2002
49. Oudezijds Voorburgwal 1
    1993
50. Oudezijds Voorburgwal 2
    1994
51. Oudezijds Voorburgwal 4
    1975
52. Oudezijds Voorburgwal 7
    1999
53. Oudezijds Voorburgwal 61
    1958
54. Oudezijds Voorburgwal 67
    2012
55. O.z. Voorburgwal 224-226
    · Servetsteeg 11
    1997
56. O.z. Voorburgwal 228-230
    1994
57. O.z. Voorburgwal 232
    1995
58. Pijlsteeg 33-41
    1996
59. Pijlsteeg 57-63
    1995
60. Rusland 10-12
    2003
61. Rusland 27
    2002
62. Sint Annenstraat 10-16
    1995
63. Huis de Pinto
    Sint Anthoniebreestraat 69
    · Sint Anthoniesluis 25
    1975
64. Sint Jansstraat 24-46
    1992
65. Spinhuissteeg 1A ·
    Dwars Spinhuisteeg 9-13
    1993
66. Spinhuissteeg 3 ·
    Dwars Spinhuissteeg 7
    1993
67. Spinhuissteeg 5 ·
    Dwars Spinhuissteeg 5
    1993
68. Spinhuissteeg 12
    2014
69. Warmoesstraat 15
    2012

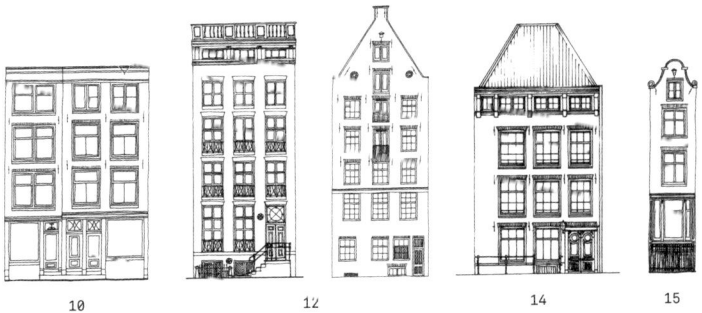

Living

257

De Wallen

20

22

27

30

33

34

35

38

39

40

56/57

Living

58

58

60

61

62

62

63

KLM Houses

Address
Oudezijds Armsteeg 6-28, Oudezijds Voorburgwal 28 (Veilinghuisje), Oudezijds Voorburgwal 30, Oudezijds Voorburgwal 32-34

Town
Amsterdam

Built
2010 (OA), 16th century (OV28, OV30, OV33-34)

Acquisition
2008 (OA), 2001 (OV28), 1995/1996 (OV30, OV33-34)

Restoration
2010 (OA), 2007 (OV28), 2006 (OV30, OV33-34)

Restoration architect
Architectenbureau Rappange en Partners

Current use
Housing and hospitality

Living

The block of buildings of project ARM is in the northern part of the Red Light District between the Oudezijds Voorburgwal, Oudezijds Armsteeg, Warmoesstraat and the Heintje Hoekssteeg. Stadsherstel has been active here for a considerable amount of time and is working together with the municipality on the creation of a new development. It starts with the purchase of a few bad buildings and an inner courtyard where six building once stood. More precisely, the project consists of the restoration and repurposing of Oudezijds Voorburgwal 30 (of houses and a beer shop (completed 2006 – 2008), the restoration and repurposing of Oudezijds Voorburgwal 32 of houses (completed in 2007), the demolition of a base and reconstruction of the canal building Oudezijds Voorburgwal 34 (completed in 2007), the restoration and extension of the municipal listed building the 'Veilinghuisje', number 26 in the inner courtyard, which has been converted into a small-scale artisan beer brewery (completed in 2008). With the building of the KLM Houses, the run-down Oudezijds Armsteeg 6 – 28 was given a new stimulus. Stadsherstel took the land on a long lease at a time when the bases had already been demolished. The architecture of the six buildings was inspired by the Delft blue houses that the airline company hands out on some flights. At the end of 2010, the handing over of the rental homes, business spaces and the tasting room of the artisanal and social beer brewery 'De Prael' took place. The site was designed as construction training project for the promotion of continuity of the restoration profession.

YOUTH
LAST WATERHOLE
LIVE MUSIC
BAR DISCOTHEEK
HOTEL
Heineken

Living

263

Plot layout before renovation

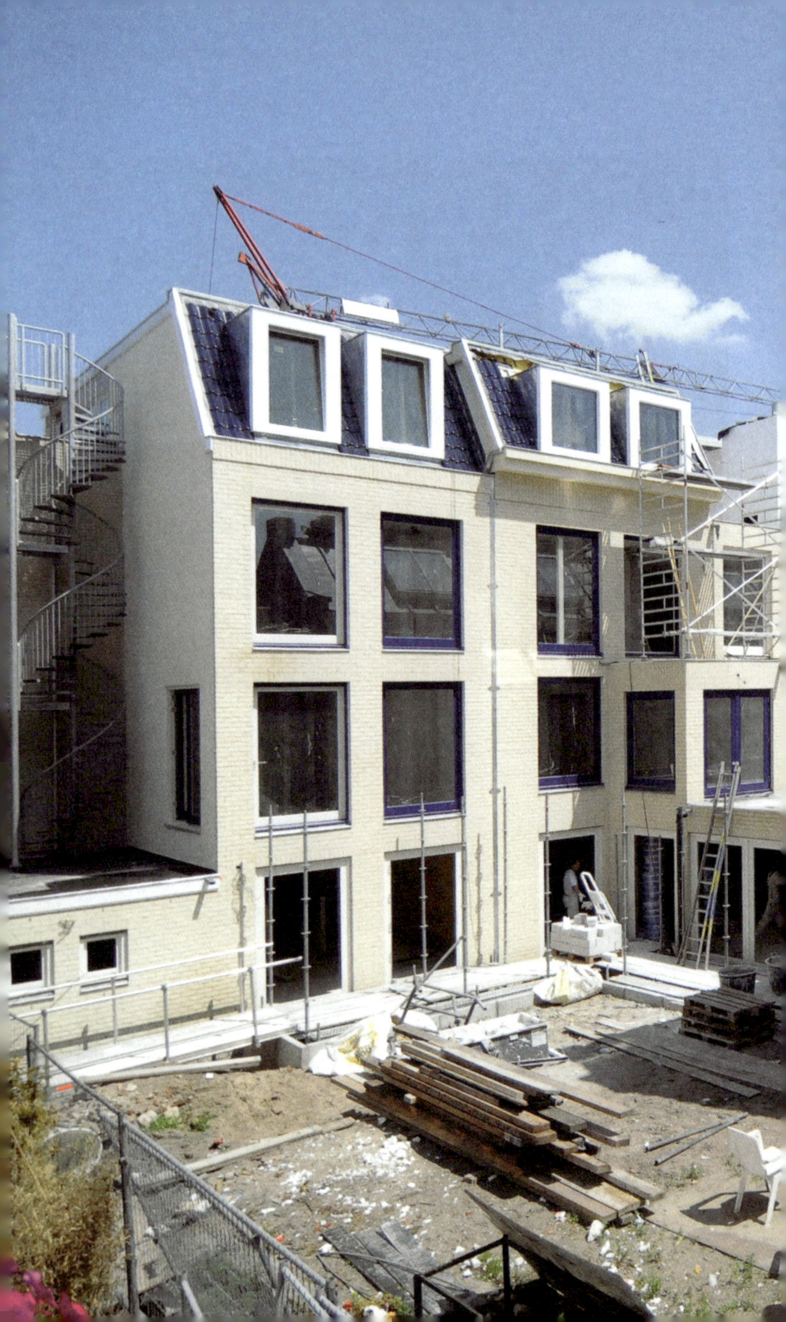

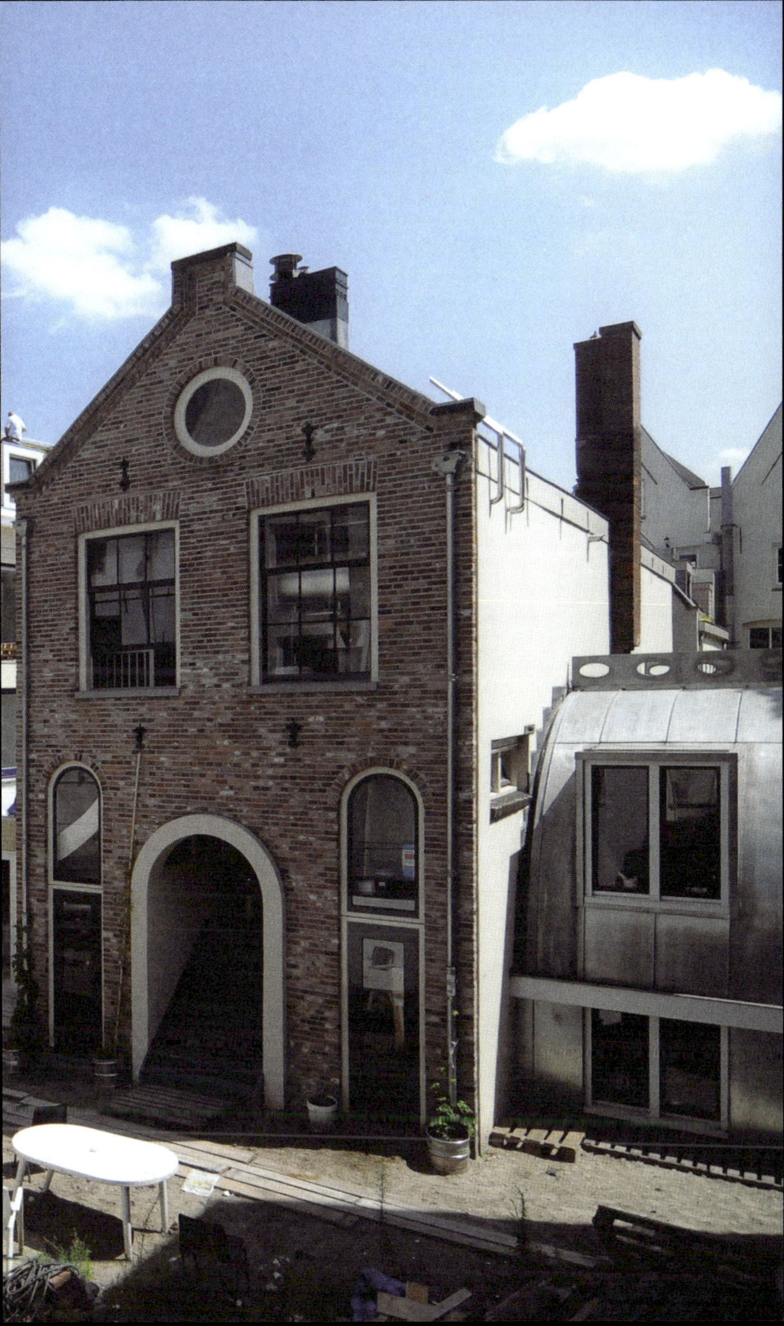

KLM Houses

266

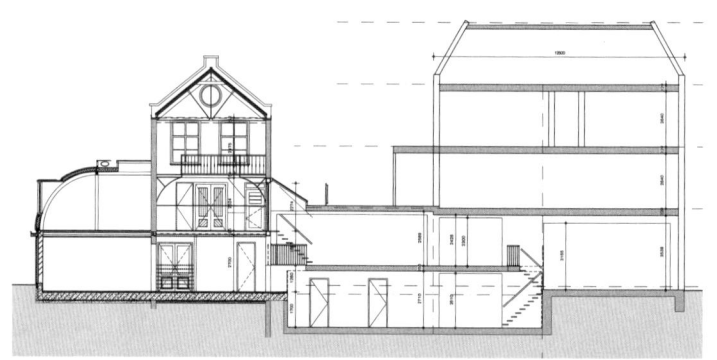

Cross-section, left Veilinghuisje and right the KLM Houses

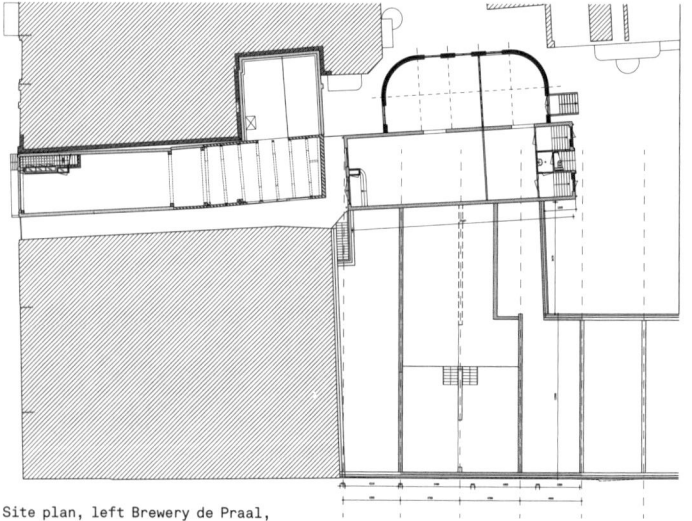

Site plan, left Brewery de Praal,
right above Veilinghuisje, and below the KLM Houses

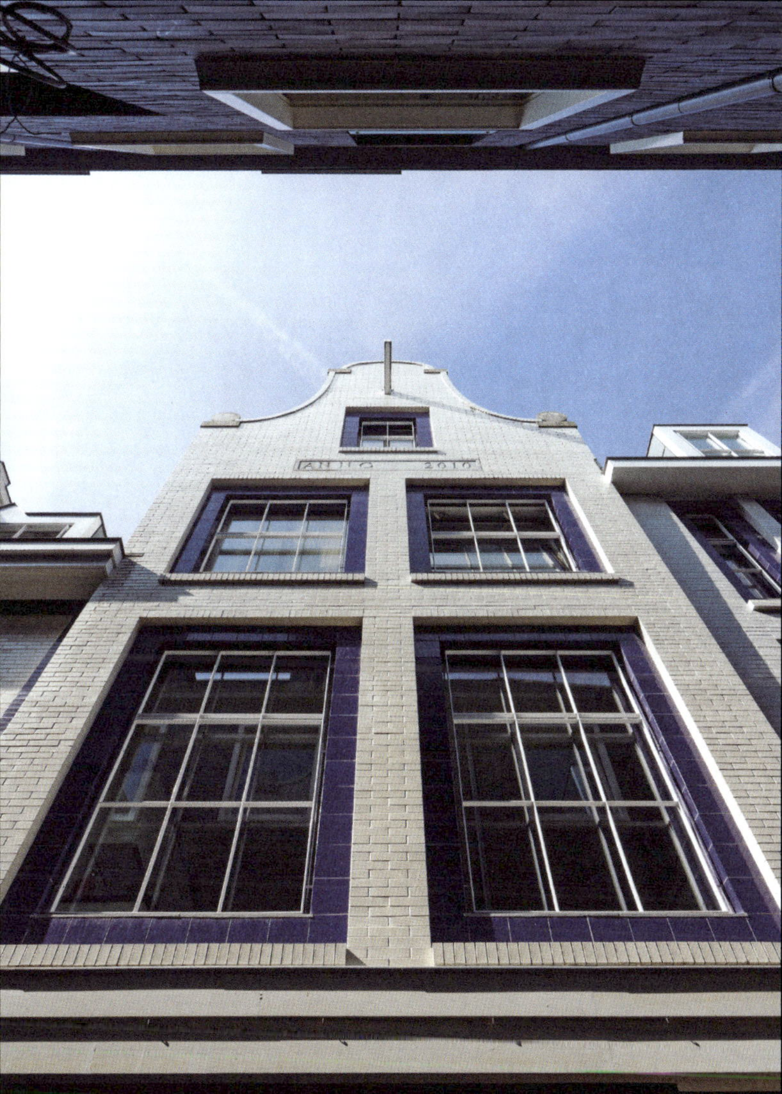
ANNO 2010

KLM Houses

Original facade wall Oudezijds Voorburgwal

Bought houses

Living 269

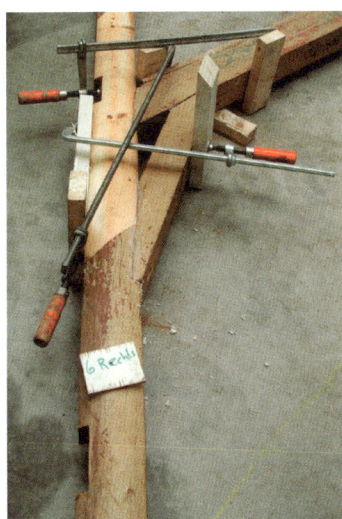

Exposing and reconstruction structure of beams

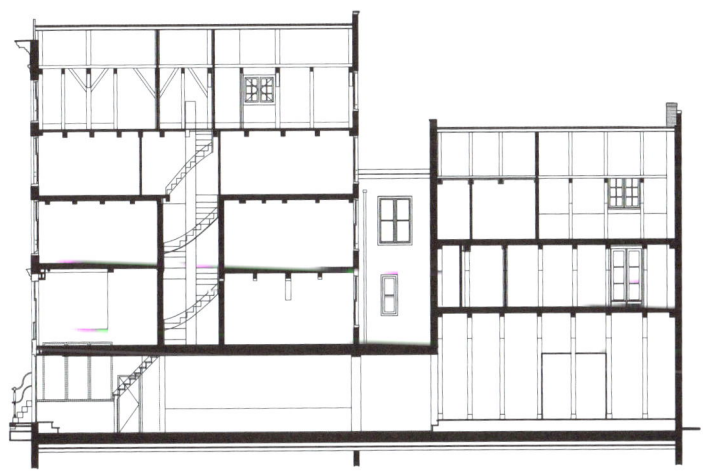

Cross-section restoration

KLM Houses

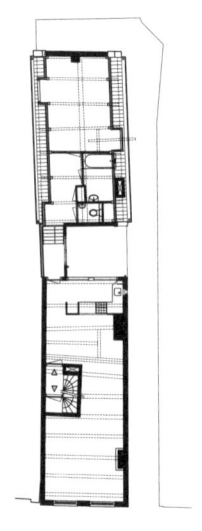

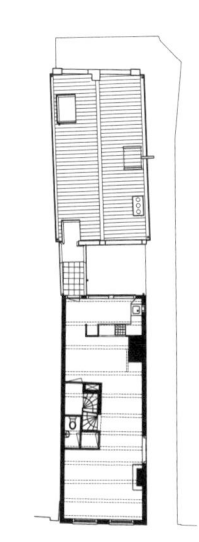

Second floor

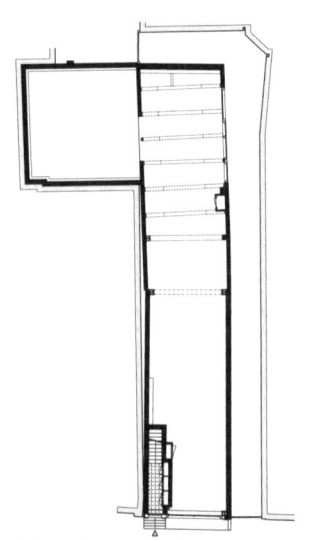

Third floor

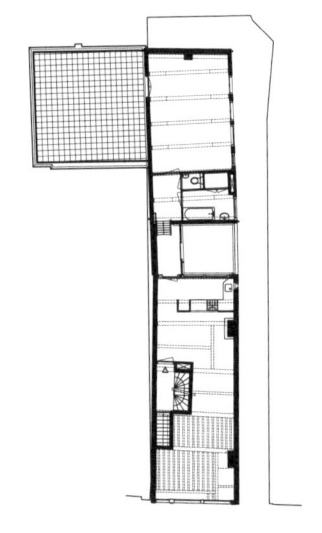

Oudezijds Voorburgwal 30, ground floor

First floor

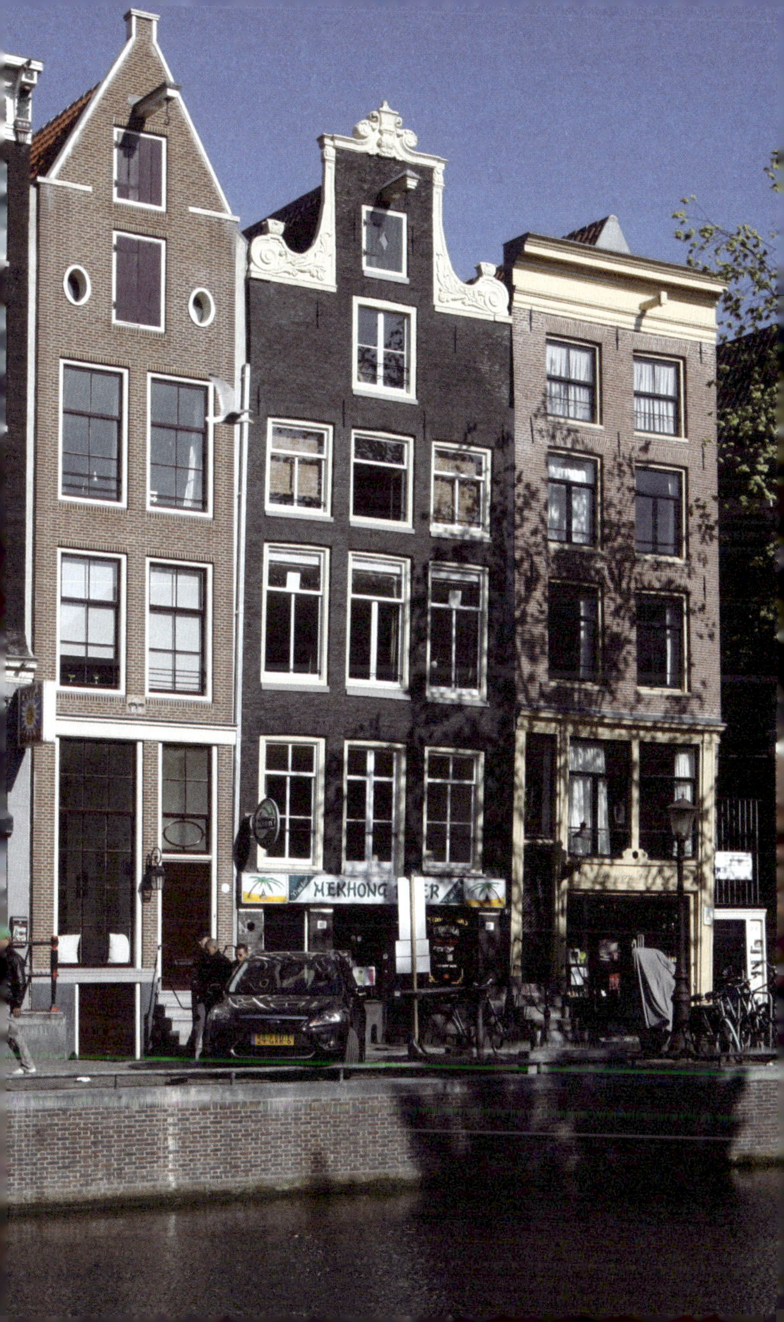
MEKHONG

Grachtengordel

1. Bergstraat 2-4
   2013
2. Herengracht 35
   1964
3. Herengracht 249
   2010
4. Herengracht 325
   1989
5. Herengracht 361
   (leasehold)
   1962
6. Herengracht 532 ·
   Reguliersgracht 2
   2012
7. Keizersgracht 62
   1973
8. Keizersgracht 95B ·
   Herenstraat 41
   1967
9. Keizersgracht 97
   1970
10. Keizersgracht 99
    1971
11. Keizersgracht 172A ·
    Leliegracht 36
    1964
12. Keizersgracht 184-188
13. Keizersgracht 278-280
14. Keizersgracht 323
    1972
15. Keizersgracht 326-328
16. Keizersgracht 396-402
17. Keizersgracht 414-418
18. Keizersgracht 527
    1978
19. Keizersgracht 539 ·
    Nieuwe Spiegelstraat
    22A-22D
    1984
20. Keizersgracht 541
    1984
21. Keizersgracht 543
    1984
22. Keizersgracht 677
    (leasehold)
    1963
23. Keizersgracht 695
    1988
24. Keizersgracht 697
    1988
25. Keizersgracht 703
    1970
26. Korsjespoortsteeg 5
    1983/2005
27. Korsjespoortsteeg 8
    2015
28. Korsjespoortsteeg 17
    2009
29. Langestraat 35-37
    1986
30. Langestraat 76A-76B
    1975
31. Langestraat 80
    1959/2001
32. Leidsegracht 61
    1973
33. Leidsegracht 106 ·
    Raamdwarsstraat 9-11
    1999
34. Nieuwe Spiegelstraat
    22B-22C-22E
    1984
35. Paardenstraat 1
    (leasehold)
    1970
36. Prinsengracht 1A
    1986
37. Prinsengracht 3
    1986
38. Prinsengracht 5
    1986
39. Prinsengracht 8
    1967
40. Prinsengracht 25
    1969
41. Prinsengracht 142-144
    1966
42. Prinsengracht 146
    1966
43. Prinsengracht 148
    1966
44. Prinsengracht 206
    1987/2003
45. Prinsengracht 300
    1962
46. Prinsengracht 333
    1967
47. Prinsengracht 335
    (leasehold)
    1967
48. Prinsengracht 337
    1967
49. Prinsengracht 339
    1967
50. Prinsengracht 451
    1974
51. Prinsengracht 457
    1986
52. Prinsengracht 459
    1986
53. Prinsengracht 600 ·
    Weteringstraat 1
    1977
54. Prinsengracht 602
    1978
55. Prinsengracht 646
    1971
56. Prinsengracht 648
    1971
57. Prinsengracht 1075
    1982/2015
58. Roomolenstraat 11
    1968
59. Singel 1 · Stromarkt 4
    2005
60. Singel 135
    2009
61. Singel 157
    1983
62. Singel 159
    1983
63. Singel 346
    2001
64. Singel 368
    1986
65. Singel 413
    1969
66. Singel 415
    1971
67. Singel 417
    1971
68. Singel 419
    1968
69. Singel 496
    1965

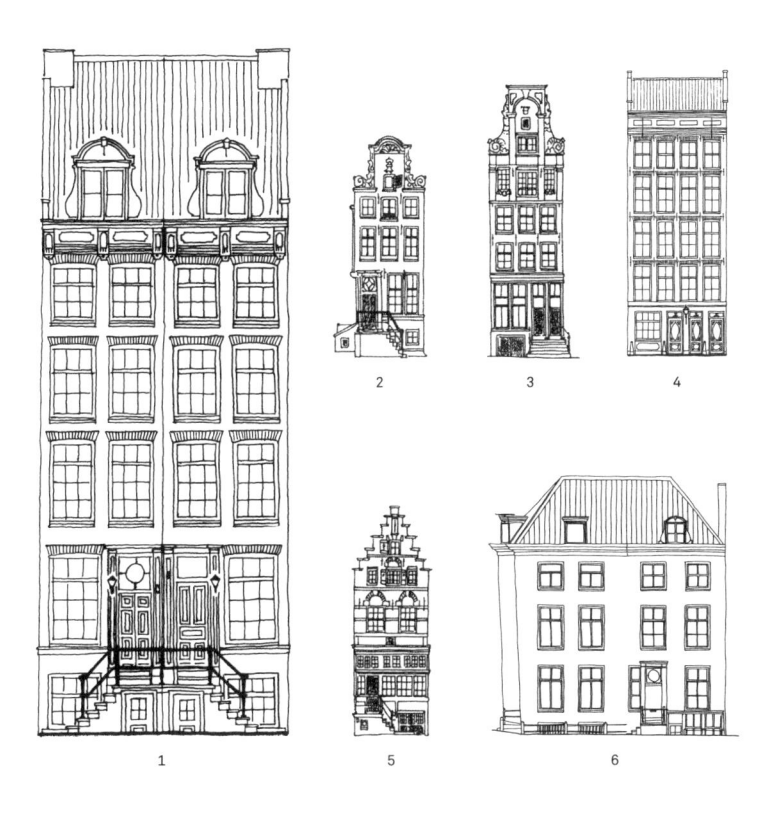

Living 273

1

2

3

4

5

6

9/10

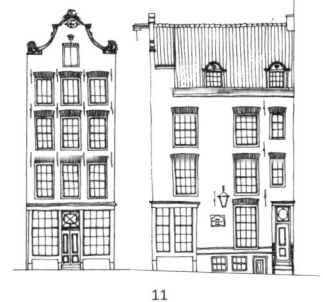

11

18

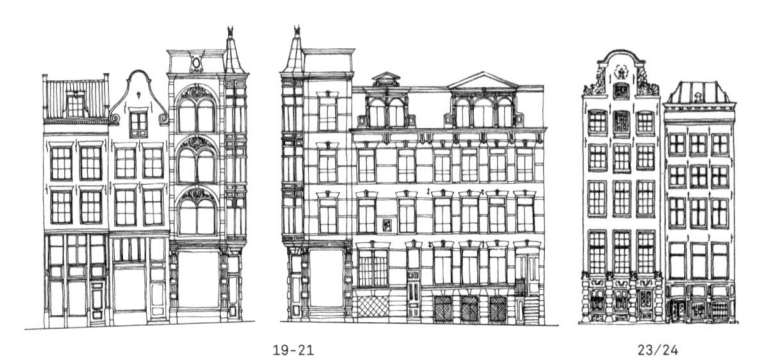

Grachtengordel 274

19-21   23/24

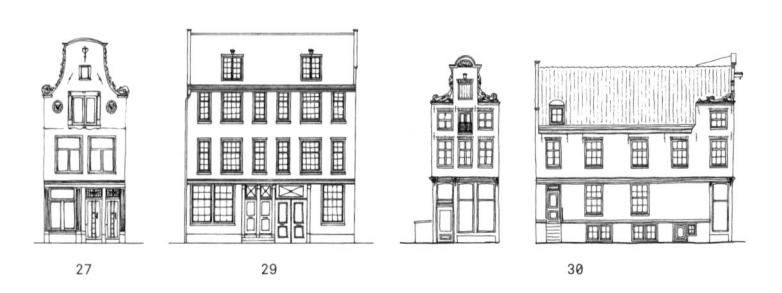

27   29   30

32   33   35

Living 275

Nine streets + two

1. Beulingstraat 15
   1982/2011
2. Beulingstraat 17
   1982/2011
3. Gasthuismolensteeg 8
   1988
4. Herenstraat 29
   1969
5. Herenstraat 31
   1968
6. Herenstraat 33
   1968
7. Herenstraat 34
   1991
8. Herenstraat 35
   1967
9. Herenstraat 36
   1997
10. Herenstraat 37
    1967
11. Herenstraat 38
    1980
12. Herenstraat 39
    1967
13. Herenstraat 41 ·
    Keizersgracht 95B
    1967
14. Oude Spiegelstraat 1A ·
    Singel 350
    1983
15. Prinsenstraat 18
    1973
16. Prinsenstraat 20
    1972
17. Prinsenstraat 22
    1972
18. Raamsteeg 6
    2012
19. Reestraat 2-6
    (leasehold)
    1970
20. Reestraat 5
    1982
21. Reestraat 7
    1982
22. Reestraat 8
    (leasehold)
    1981
23. Reestraat 15
    1977
24. Reestraat 17
    1977
25. Reestraat 19
    1971
26. Reestraat 30-32
    1973
27. Runstraat 4
    2009
28. Runstraat 29
    1997
29. Wolvenstraat 1A ·
    Herengracht 300
    1987

Living 277

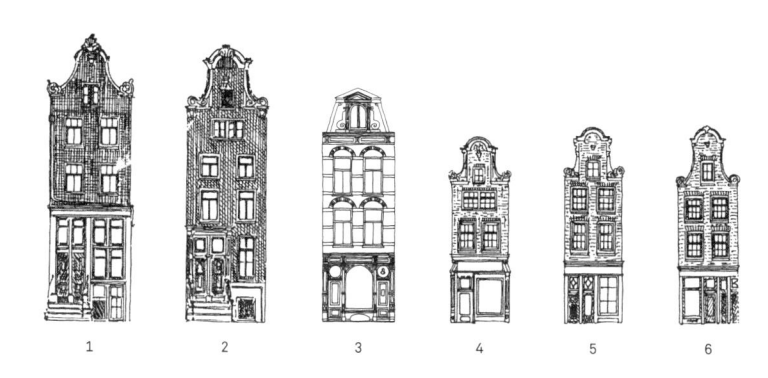

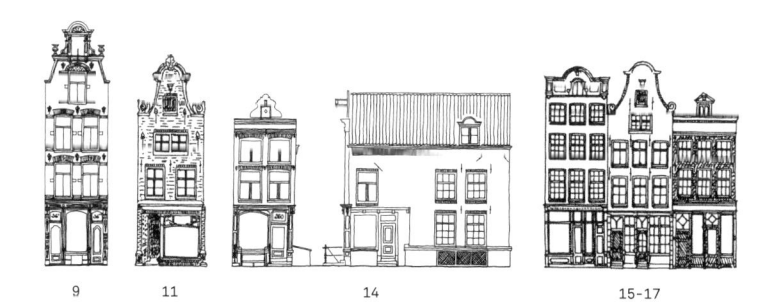

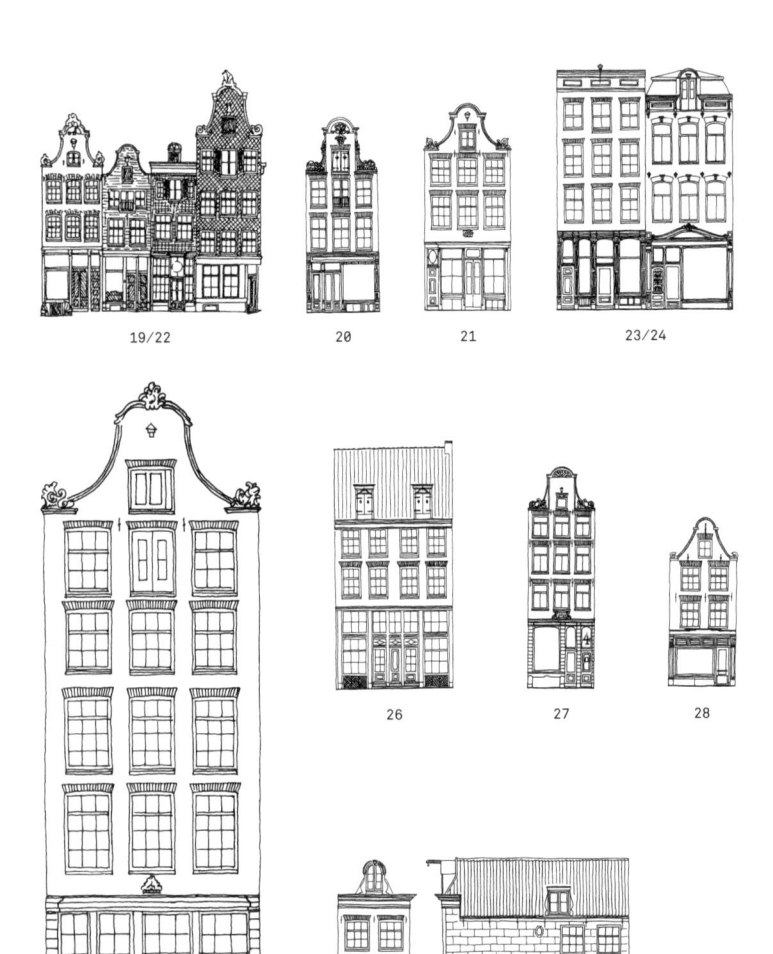

Nine streets + two

278

19/22

20

21

23/24

25

26

27

28

29

A number of side streets in the canal ring between the Raadhuisstraat and the Leidsegracht are currently known as 'De 9 Straatjes' (The Nine Streets) for marketing reasons. The canals are intersected at three locations by three shopping streets that are constantly in line with each other. Together they make up a neighbourhood with unique shops, coffee houses and restaurants. From the Prinsengracht in the direction of the Singel, there is, in succession, the Reestraat, Hartenstraat and Gasthuismolensteeg; the Berenstraat, Wolvenstraat and Oude Spiegelstraat; and the Runstraat, Huidenstraat and Wijde Heisteeg. The names of the outermost six streets, built around 1614 during the third extension of the city, are reminiscent of a neighbourhood where traders and craftsmen once worked and lived in the tanning sector. The plots in the side streets were much smaller than the parcels on the canals and could be completely developed.

Together with the bordering Prinsenstraat, the Herenstraat, where Stadsherstel manages nine buildings, forms a tenth and eleventh street, located between the Leliegracht and the Brouwersgracht, in view of the similar range of shops.

Hartenstraat 10 and 12, about 1903

Based on an 18th century snapshot of the occupancy, the Hartenstraat appears to be the richest side street. Here lived bakers, a butcher, three grocers, four fabric salesman, a tailor, two cabinetmakers, two watchmakers, a silversmith, two barber surgeons, as well a schoolteacher, cook, publican, reserve office candidate, ironmonger, tobacconist, cheese retailer, glove salesman, stocking retailer, candle maker and a 'salesman'. At the end of the 1970s, the neighbourhood slowly began to change. Some of the offices on the canals began to make way for apartments and attracted increasingly rich residents. As a result of that, one traditional shop in the Hartenstraat after the other changed ownership. At the moment, there are many boutiques in the more expensive segment and branches of exclusive fashion chains have found their way to the neighbourhood.

Fa. BENNINK
CENTRALE VERWARMING
OLIESTOOK-EN
AARDGASINSTALLATIES
FORD
XA-43-57

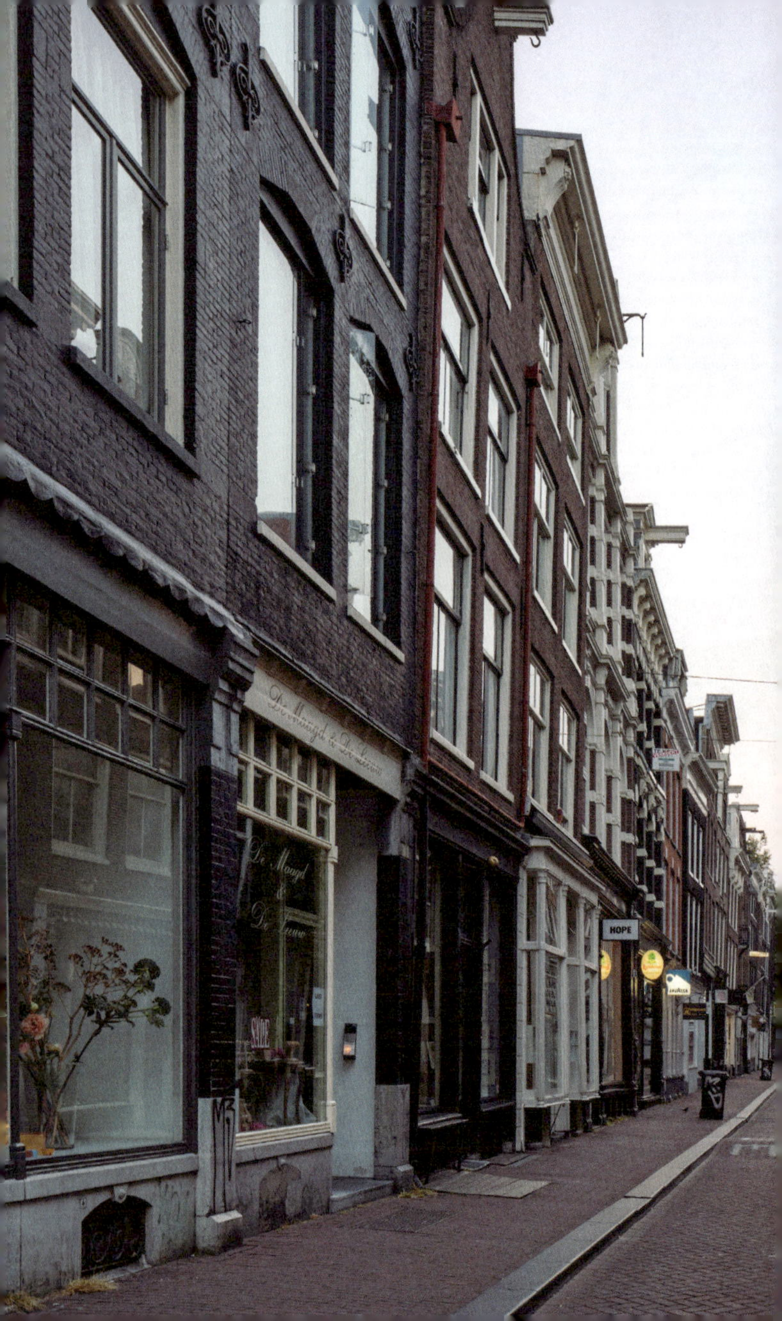
De Maagd & De Leeuw
HOPE

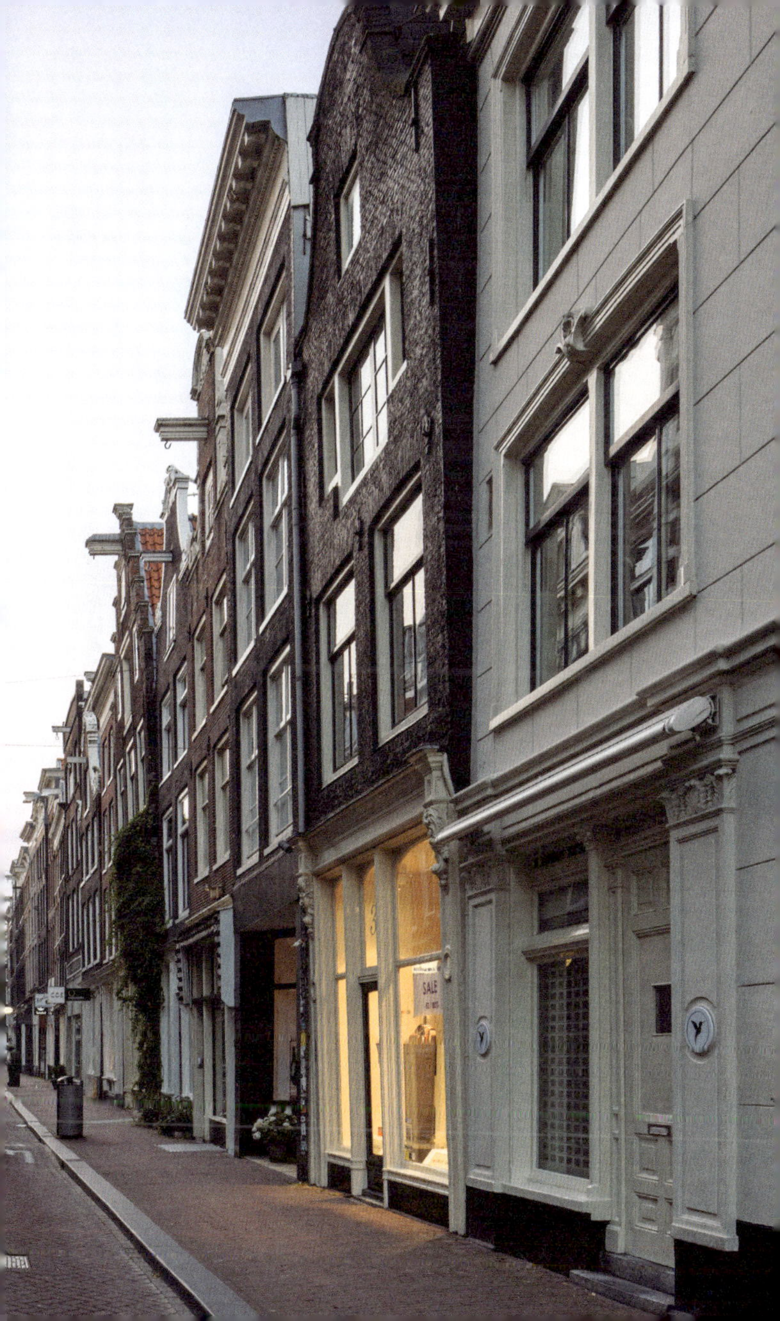
SALE

Reestraat 5-7

Built 1725 – 1750 (on the pediment of no. 5: 1714)
Acquisition 1980 (5), 1975 (7)
Restoration 1982

After the replacement of the foundations at number 7, it turned out the load-bearing walls, the rear facade and the roof also needed replacing, so that only the front facade of the building was actually preserved.

Reestraat 8 (Reerust)

Built 1600 – 1625
Acquisition 1978
Restoration 1981

A roe deer is depicted in the gable crowning and this building has been known as the house 'with the roe deer in the facade' since the 18th century.

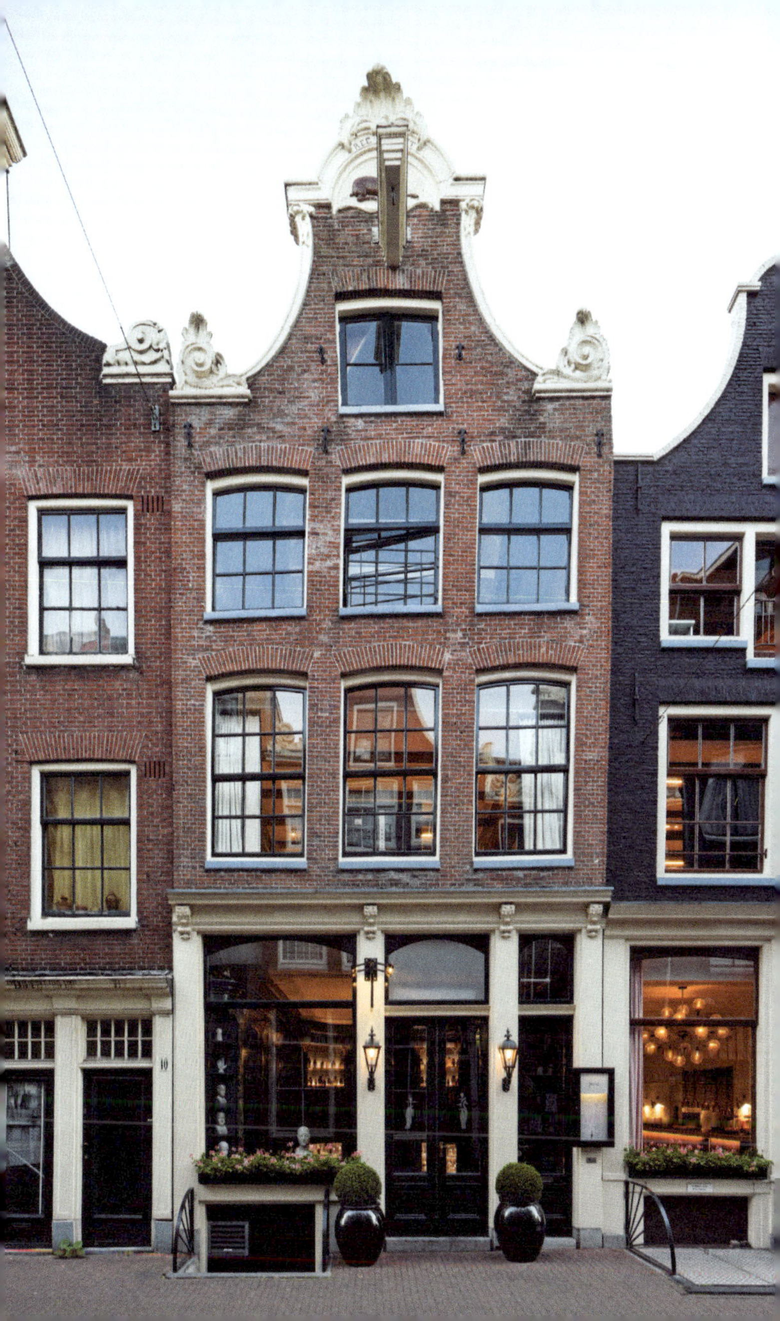
10

RED WING SHOES
15
RED WING SHOES
AMSTERDAM
LINEMA
PHOTOGRAPHY

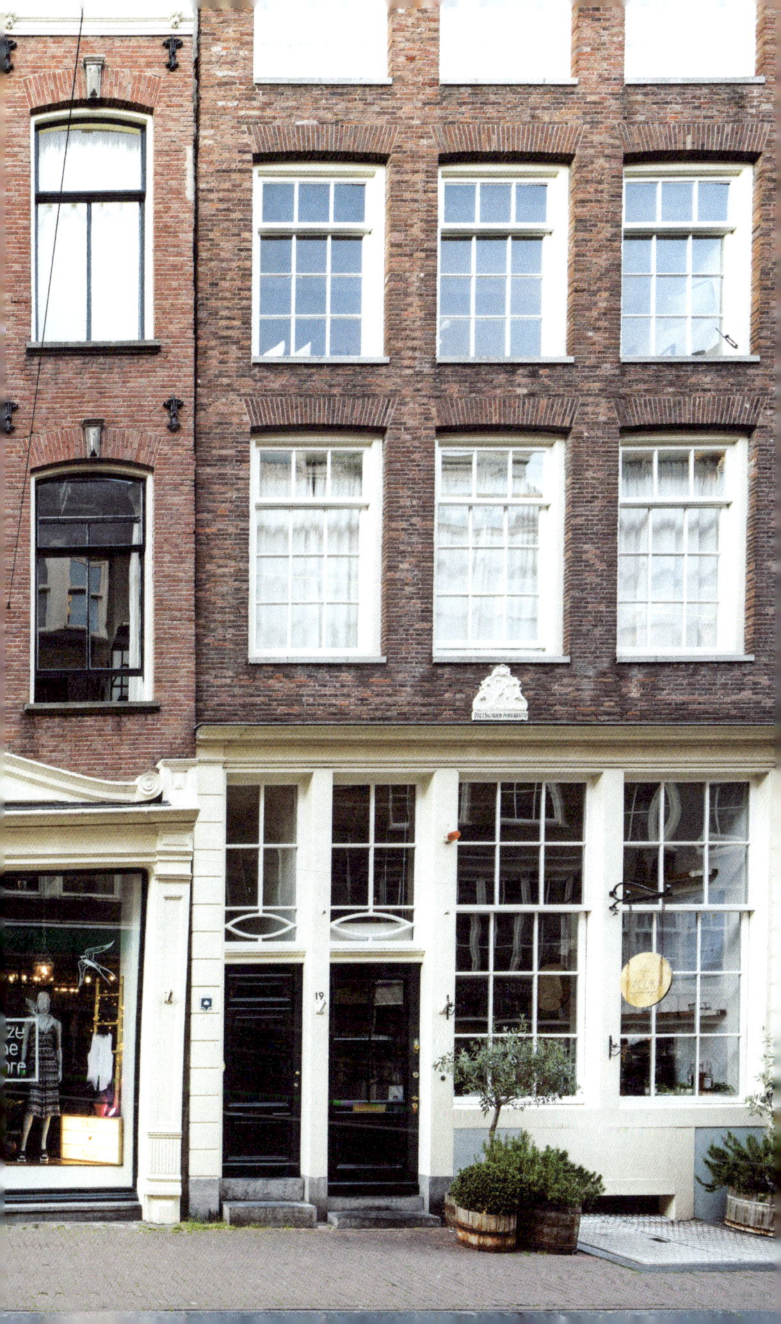
19

Runstraat 29

Acquisition **1966**
Restoration **1997**

The specific period features of the front from 1923 was restored with great attention to detail. The work was carried out as construction training project in which all aspects were dealt with on a small scale.

beauregard

Raamsteeg 6

290

Address
Raamsteeg 6

Town
Amsterdam

Built
17th century

Acquisition
2010

Restoration
2012

Restoration architect
Architectenbureau Vroom

Current use
Shop house

Stadsherstel has been busy with this problem case since 2007, but did not initially buy the house, because the owner was asking too high a price for only 30 m^2 surface area. A project developer who quickly discovered that restoration was too difficult and financially unfeasible applied for a demolition permit in order to be able to switch to new development and the official heritage authorities gave permission due to far-reaching deterioration of valuable interior parts. In reaction to this, the Association of Friends of the Amsterdam Inner City strived to preserve the facade so that the building still served, for a while, as the centre of discussion with regard to the topic of the neglected buildings in the historic centre. However, the building could still be thoroughly rescued ultimately. An architectural firm drew up a restoration plan preserving the original wooden frame and the proper glass panes in the windows. Surprising discoveries emerged from the architectural and building-historical research.

Raamsteeg 6

Profile of the corbels

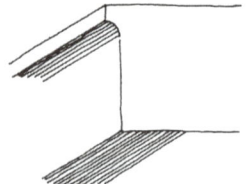

Prior to the restoration, further wood research was conducted, so-called dendrochronological research, whereby a date us determined on the basis of the annual rings of the sapwood. The wood samples, which were taken from the beams with a hollow drill, revealed that the rear part of the house was built around 1635, while the front part of the house was built in or soon after 1655. It should be noted that the date based on this wood research does not or hardly differs from the stylistic dating, on the basis of 'timber corbels' found under the beam ends. According to the classification of Zantkuijl's monumental study and bookwork *Bouwen in Amsterdam* (Building in Amsterdam), the profile of the corbels in the front and rear part of the house point to a date from the second quarter of the 17th century. The research also provided traces of building work from the beginning of the 17th century, with a particular type of bricks from that time. The long building history makes Raamsteeg 6 a very interesting shop house. It tells us a lot about the origin of the building and the street to which the restoration was added in the 21st century.

Living

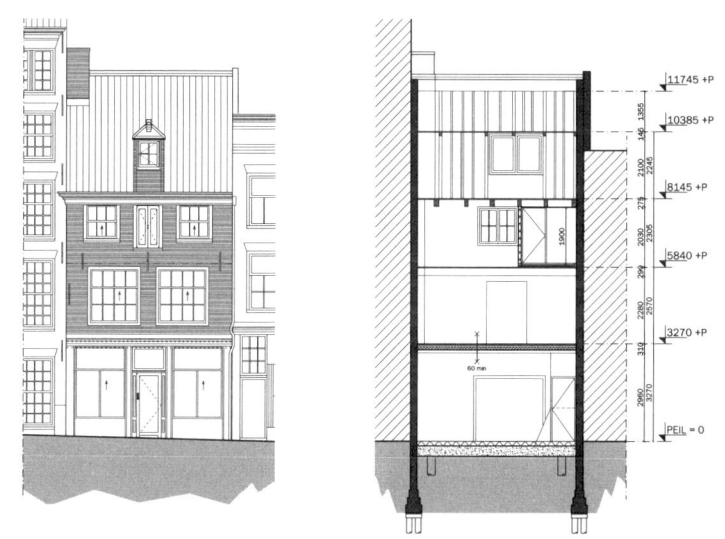

293

Restoration drawings, front and back facades

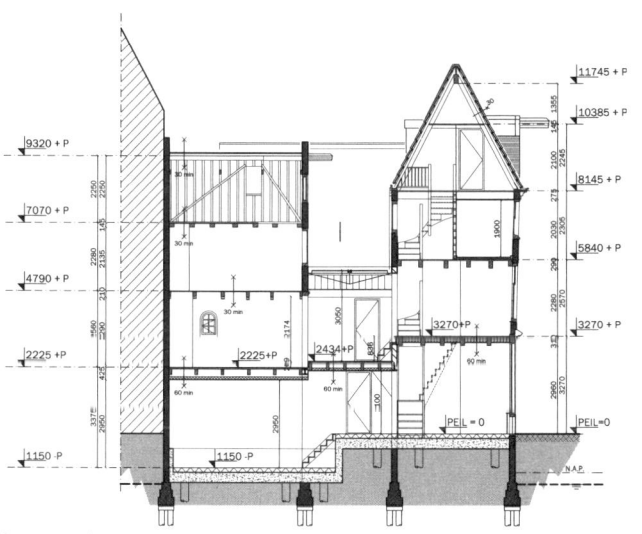

Cross-section

The Raamsteeg is a small street, within the inner city canal of 1425, in the Medieval part of Amsterdam. In the 17th century, it became part of the traffic route Berenstraat – Wolvenstraat – Oude Spiegelstraat – Raamsteeg – Rosmarijnsteeg where, as a rule, shop houses were being built. The street has managed to preserve that function up until today. On the right-hand side of the street, there are a row of houses at right angles to the road with two stories and identical roofs, in which Raamsteeg 6, or at least the front part of the house, is recognisable. The houses were probably built in

Living

295

about 1500. A house at right angles to the road is a type of building with a roof, the ridge of which runs parallel to the street. The placement perpendicular to the street is more common in Amsterdam. The shop house, a type of building that can be recognised by a wooden lower front with large windows and an entrance on street level, appears to be early 19th century at first glance due to the wooden cornice, but if you look closely you see that these largely consist of 17th century brickwork with the 'quarter bats' and quarter bricks at the corners.

Raamsteeg 6

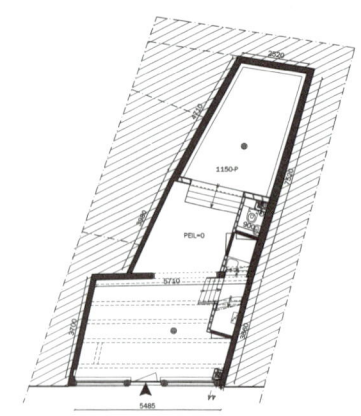

Floor plans ground level

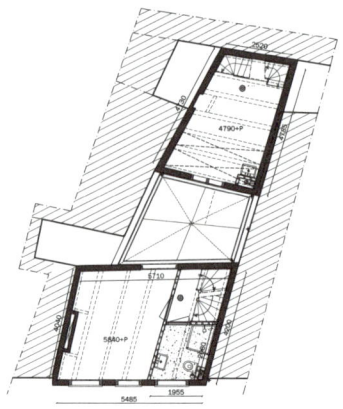

First floor

Living

Raamsteeg 6

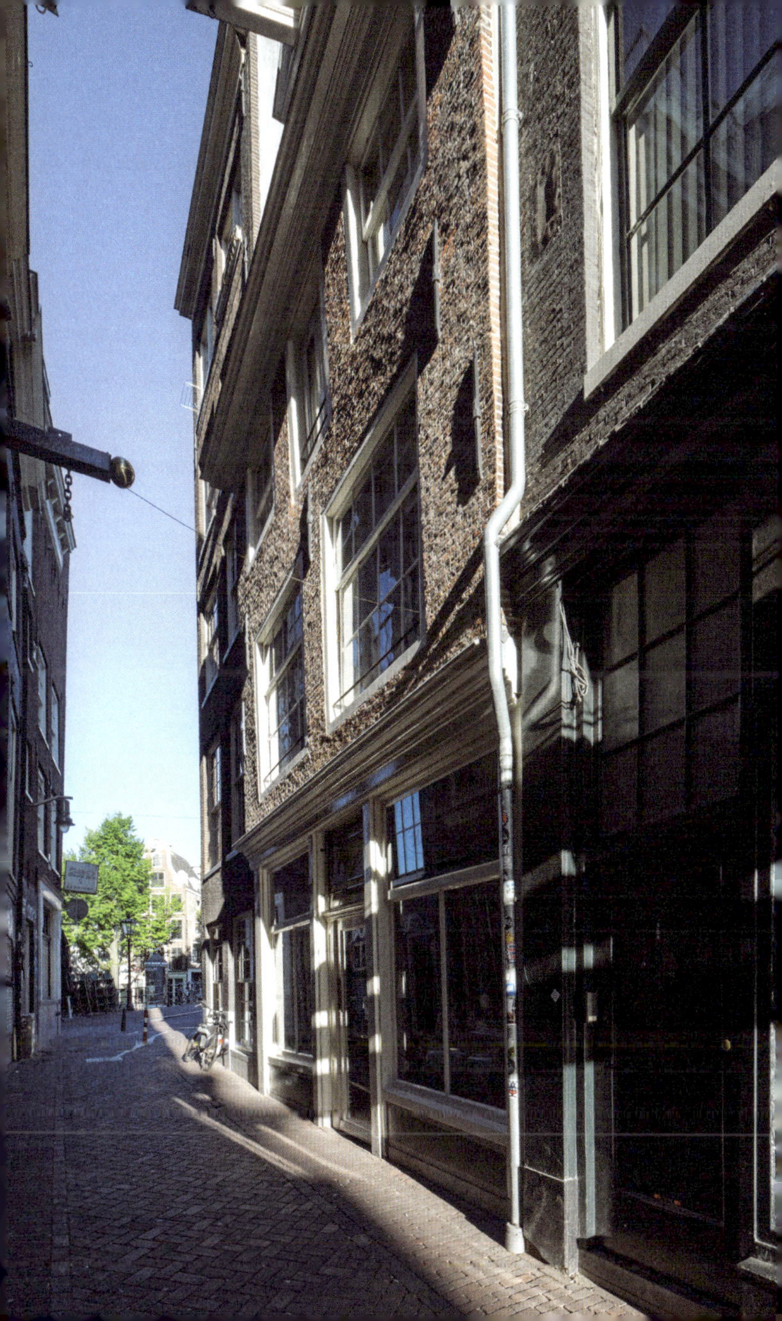

Haarlemmerbuurt

1. Binnen Brouwersstraat 2
   1993
2. Binnen Brouwersstraat 16
   2001
3. Binnen Brouwersstraat 20
   2001
4. Binnen Brouwersstraat 22
   1994
5. Binnen Vissersstraat 9-11
   1997
6. Binnen Vissersstraat 13-15A
   1997
7. Binnen Vissersstraat 15B-17
   1997
8. Binnen Vissersstraat 19-21
   (leasehold)
   1997
9. Binnen Vissersstraat 23
   1997
10. Brouwersgracht 62 ·
    Herenmarkt 23-27
    1976
11. Brouwersgracht 86 ·
    Binnen Brouwersstraat 37
    1960/2003
12. Brouwersgracht 95
    1972
13. Brouwersgracht 97
    1972
14. Brouwersgracht 99
    1972
15. Brouwersgracht 101 ·
    Prinsengracht 1
    1972
16. Brouwersgracht 135
    1989
17. Droogbak 17 · Buiten Wieringerstraat 1
    1976
18. Gouwenaarsteeg 13
19. Haarlemmer Houttuinen 65A · Korte Prinsengracht 5
    1964
20. Haarlemmerdijk 55
    1986
21. Haarlemmerstraat 1
    1996
22. Haarlemmerstraat 3
    1996
23. Haarlemmerstraat 46
    2012
24. Haarlemmerstraat 48
    1984
25. Haarlemmerstraat 115
    1973
26. Herenmarkt 9
    1984
27. Herenmarkt 19
    1984
28. Herenmarkt 21
    1972
29. Korte Prinsengracht 6
    1998
30. Korte Prinsengracht 7
    1964
31. Korte Prinsengracht 9
    1964
32. Vinkenstraat 55
    1986
33. Vinkenstraat 68
    1986
34. Vinkenstraat 74
    1991
35. Bickersgracht 30
    1978
36. Grote Bickerstraat 35
    (unbuilt)
    1974
37. Zandhoek 13
    1959/1996
38. Zandhoek 14-15
    1978

Living

301

Haarlemmerbuurt

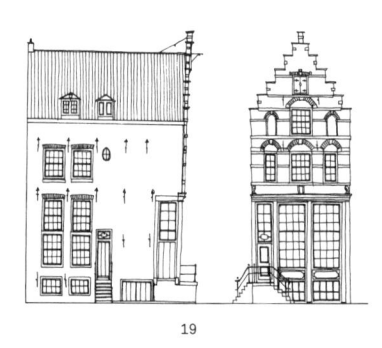

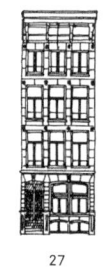

17   18   19

20   21/22   23/24   25

26   27   28

Living   303

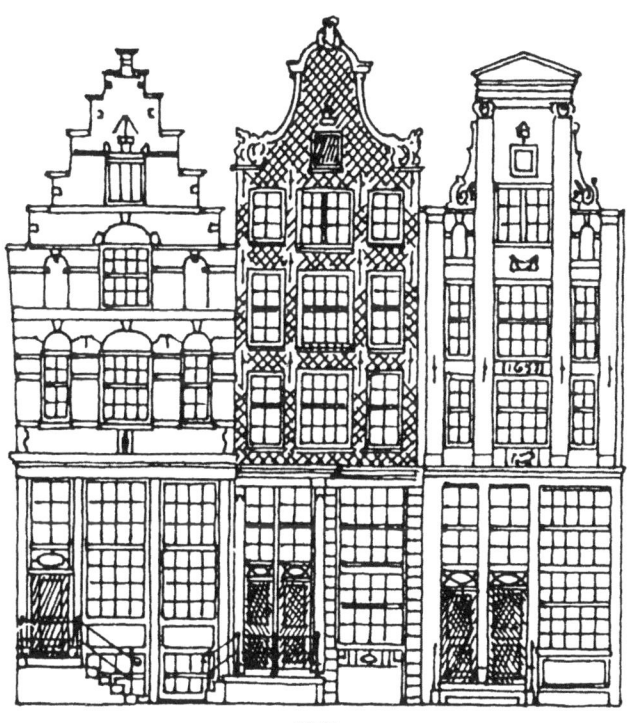

30/31

29   32   33   34

Jordaan

1. Bloemgracht 4
   1968
2. Bloemgracht 32
   1970
3. Bloemgracht 34
   1963
4. Bloemgracht 35
   1971
5. Bloemgracht 36
   1963
6. Bloemgracht 37
   1977
7. Bloemgracht 39
   1992
8. Bloemgracht 42
   1999
9. Bloemgracht 76 · Tweede Leliedwarsstraat 25-31
   1978
10. Bloemgracht 125
    1972/1999
11. Bloemgracht 127
    1972
12. Bloemgracht 145-147
    1993
13. Bloemgracht 166
    1992/2008/2011
14. Eerste Egelantiersdwarsstraat 2-4C · Tuinstraat 51
    1987
15. Eerste Lauriedwarsstraat 50
    2001
16. Eerste Looiersdwarsstraat 11 · Oude Looiersstraat 55
    1995
17. Egelantiersgracht 5
    1978
18. Egelantiersgracht 13
    1978
19. Egelantiersgracht 35
    1979
20. Egelantiersgracht 37
    1979
21. Egelantiersgracht 39
    1979
22. Egelantiersgracht 46
    1987
23. Egelantiersgracht 48
    1987
24. Egelantiersgracht 51
    1974
25. Egelantiersgracht 53
    1974
26. Elandsgracht 43
    1984
27. Lauriergracht 12
    2006
28. Lauriergracht 19-21
    1989
29. Looiersgracht 2-4
    1979
30. Marnixstraat 58
    1998
31. Marnixstraat 291-295
    2012
32. Nieuwe Leliestraat 75
    1992
33. Nieuwe Leliestraat 183
    2009
34. Nieuwe Looiersstraat 25-27
    1997
35. Noorderkerkstraat 2
    2008
36. Oude Looiersstraat 55
37. Oude Looiersstraat 61
    1995
38. Passeerdersgracht 6
    1985
39. Tuinstraat 53-55
    1987
40. Tuinstraat 57
    1987
41. Tuinstraat 59-61
    1987
42. Tweede Goudsbloemdwarsstraat 6
    1990
43. Tweede Goudsbloemdwarsstraat 10
    1990
44. Westerkade 24-25
    2013

Living 305

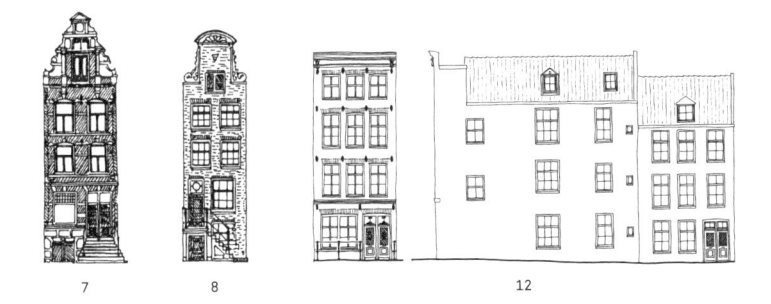

1 2 3 4 5 6

7 8 12

13 15 16 17 18 26

Jordaan 306

25 27 30 31

33 34 35 36 39

14 40/41 42 43 44

The Jordaan district became overpopulated and run-down in the 19th century. In some case numerous large families inhabited a floor in separately rented rooms next to each other. Cellars and attics were divided. Slums gave access to fully built-up inner courtyards where daylight barely penetrated. In the 1950s, large sections of the Jordaan were in a dilapidated state and plans were made for large-scale demolition and new buildings. The plans, however, could not count on any support. The urban renewal was continued within the existing urban structure. A turbulent period of protest preceded that. Amsterdam citizens worried about the loss of the historic city centre. Since the 1960s, much has been restored.

▷ Bloemgracht, 2016

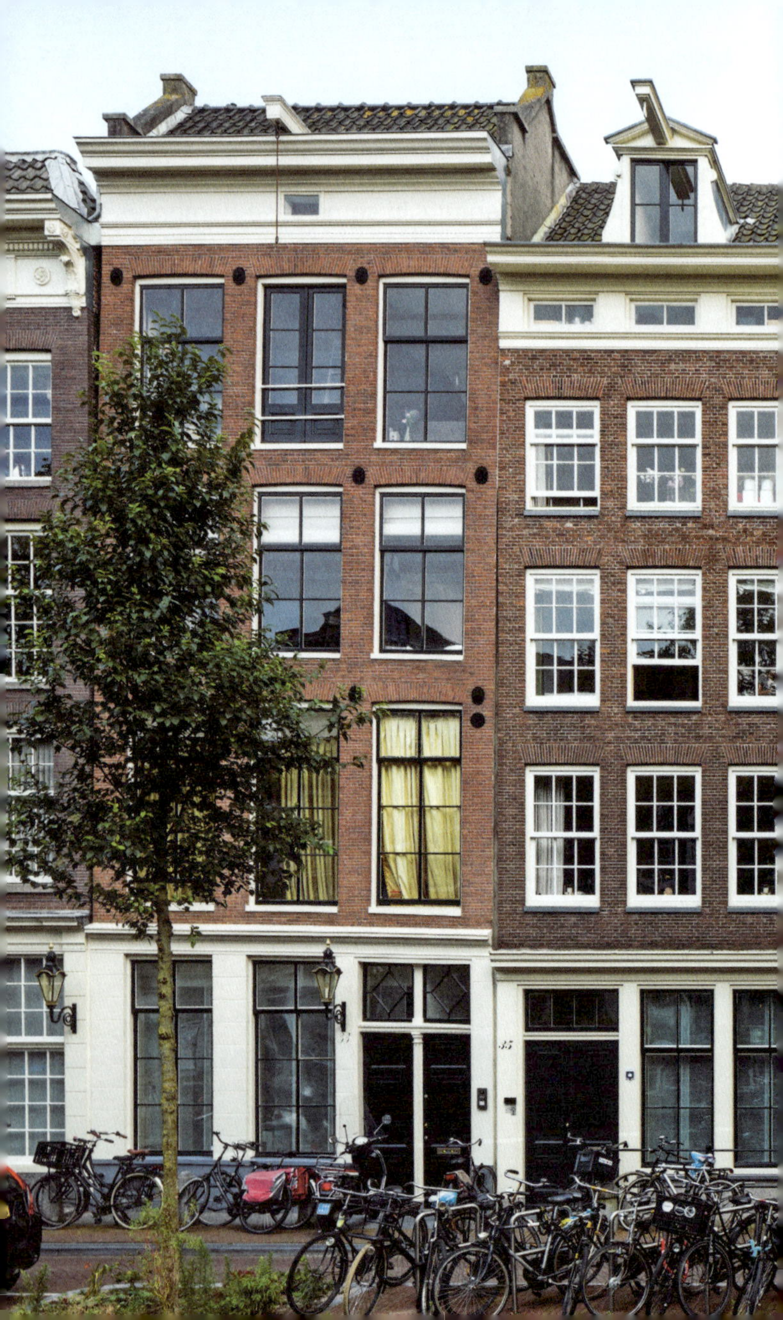

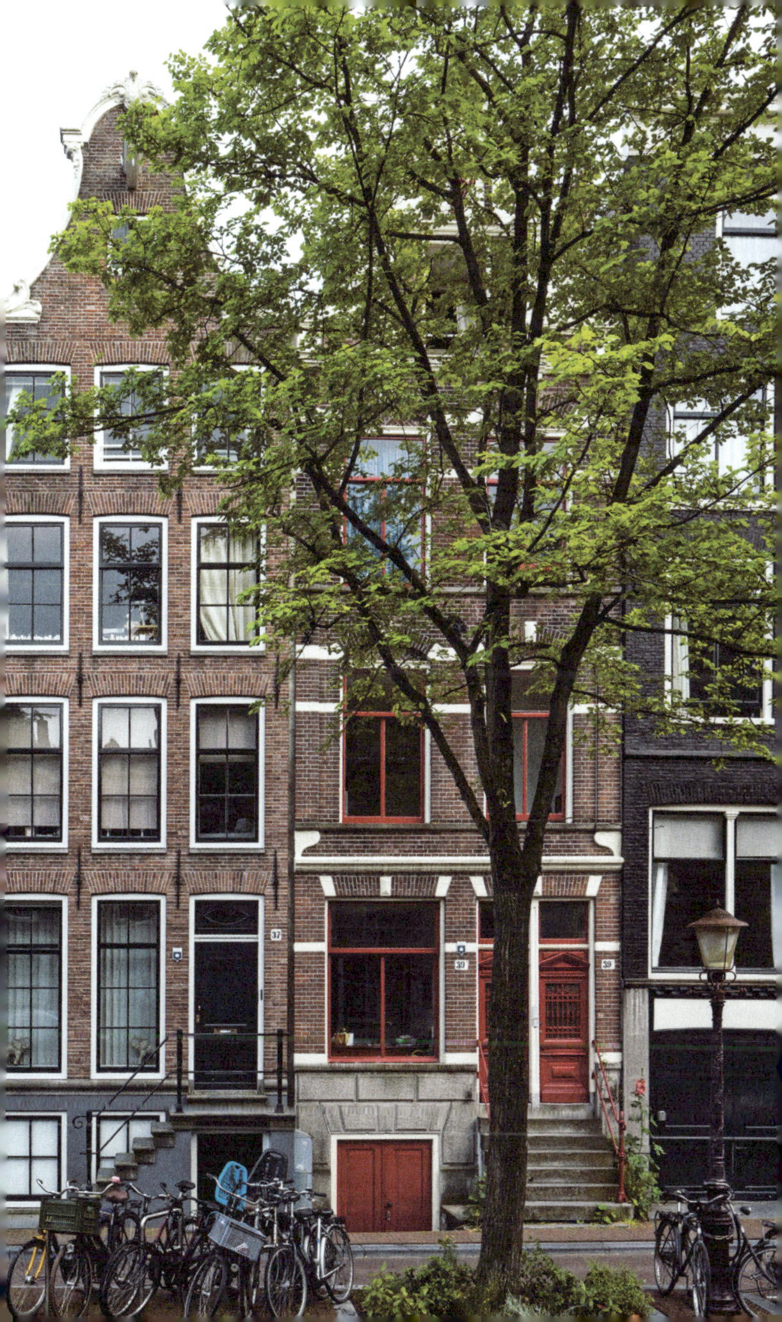

Weteringbuurt and Amstel

1. Achtergracht 34
1973
2. Amstel 81 ·
Nieuwe Kerkstraat 2
1973
3. Amstel 87
1962
4. Amstel 95
1972
5. Amstel 97
1971
6. Amstel 99
2009
7. Amstel 176
1989
8. Amstel 262
1964/1998
9. Amstel 264
1969
10. Amstel 266
1969
11. Amstel 268
1967
12. Amstel 282
2013
13. Amstel 316-318 ·
Achtergracht 36-38
1973
14. Eerste Weteringdwars-
straat 30
2006
15. Eerste Weteringdwars-
straat 70 · Vijzelgracht 4-8
2011
16. Hodshon Dedelhofje
Eerste Weteringdwars-
straat 83-105
1985
17. Kerkstraat 15
2013
18. Kerkstraat 17
2013
19. Kerkstraat 184
1989
20. Kerkstraat 186
1989
21. Kerkstraat 188
1989
22. Kerkstraat 192
1998
23. Kerkstraat 194
1998
24. Kerkstraat 196
1998
25. Kerkstraat 198
1998
26. Kerkstraat 273
1985
27. Kerkstraat 278
2002
28. Kerkstraat 280
2002
29. Kerkstraat 321
1990
30. Kerkstraat 323
1993
31. Kerkstraat 326
1967
32. Kerkstraat 328
2000
33. Kerkstraat 328 ·
Reguliersgracht 70
2000
34. Kerkstraat 329
1995
35. Kerkstraat 396-398
1978
36. Kerkstraat 400
1978
37. Kerkstraat 402
1978
38. Kerkstraat 414
1963
39. Kerkstraat 416
1963
40. Kerkstraat 418
1963
41. Korte
Leidsedwarsstraat 70
2014
42. Lange
Leidsedwarsstraat 31
2008
43. Noorderdwarsstraat 7
2010
44. Noorderstraat 39A-C-E-G
1991
45. Noorderstraat 39B-D-F-H
1991
46. Overtoom 371-373
2004
47. Reguliersgracht 11-13
1982
48. Reguliersgracht 19
1961
49. Reguliersgracht 65-67
1990
50. Reguliersgracht 70
2000
51. Reguliersgracht 95
2007
52. Tweede
Weteringdwarsstraat 5-7
1975
53. Tweede Weteringdwars-
straat 71-73
2005
54. Utrechtsedwarsstraat 106
2003
55. Utrechtsedwarsstraat 71 ·
Utrechtsestraat 135
1991
56. Utrechtsestraat 141
1975
57. Vijzelgracht 1
1971
58. Vijzelgracht 3
1971
59. Vijzelgracht 5
1971
60. Vijzelgracht 39
2001
61. Vijzelgracht 47
2009
62. Vijzelgracht 63
2003
63. Vondelstraat 41
2013
64. Weteringstraat 19
1974

Living

311

3 4 5 6 7

8 9 10 11 12

13/1  19-21

Weteringbuurt and Amstel 312

22-25

26

27/28

30

31

34

35-37

41

42

43

44/45

46

Living 313

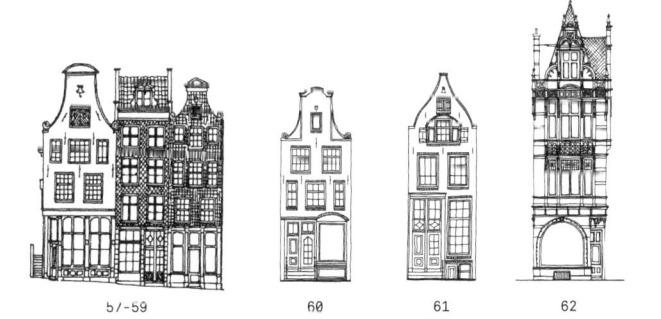

47

50

51

52

53

54

55

56

57-59

60

61

62

Mantelpieces and fireplaces

Mantelpieces and fireplaces

An important reason for the petrification of the wooden house was fire prevention, in which the manner of heating and the discharge of smoke played a large role. At the end of the 17th century, the traditional high smoke flue in the wealthier interiors was often replaced by the low mantelpiece, which was mostly made of marble. The mirror was placed over that, framed with rich ornamentation. The search for a heating method to create a lot of heat with little fuel continued. Much heat was lost through the chimney with the attractive open wood fire. This loss could be partly solved with high heathers with better distribution.

Ca. 1750-60

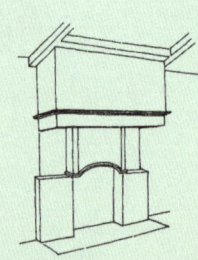

Mantelpiece ca. 1730

Coal stove, about 1820

Mantelpiece Reguliersgracht 63

Mantelpiece Weaver's House, Zaanse Schans

Living 315

Mantelpiece Merchants house Beverwijk

Plantagebuurt / Hortus / Artis

1 Henri Polaklaan 20
2001
2 Jonas Daniel Meijerplein 52
· Nieuwe Herengracht 55
1993
3 Muiderstraat 24-30
1995
4 **Nieuwe Herengracht 45**
1993
5 **Nieuwe Herengracht 47**
1993
6 **Nieuwe Herengracht 49**
1993
7 **Nieuwe Herengracht 51**
1993
8 **Nieuwe Herengracht 53**
1993
9 **Nieuwe Herengracht 71** ·
Muiderstraat 28-32
1995
10 **Nieuwe Herengracht 189**
11 **Nieuwe**
Herengracht 219-221
1979
12 **Nieuwe Keizersgracht 37**
1964/1996
13 **Nieuwe Keizersgracht 39**
1964/1997
14 **Nieuwe Kerkstraat 2A**
1973
15 **Nieuwe Prinsengracht 29**
1968/2011
16 **Nieuwe Prinsengracht 43**
2014
17 **Nieuwe Prinsengracht 45**
2014
18 **Nieuwe Prinsengracht 47**
2014
19 **Nieuwe Prinsengracht 49**
2014
20 **Nieuwe Prinsengracht 51**
2014
21 **Nieuwe Prinsengracht 53**
2014
22 **Plantage Kerklaan 21**
2000
23 **Professor Tulpstraat 14**
2005
24 **Professor Tulpstraat 16-20**
2005
25 **Professor Tulpstraat 22-28**
2005

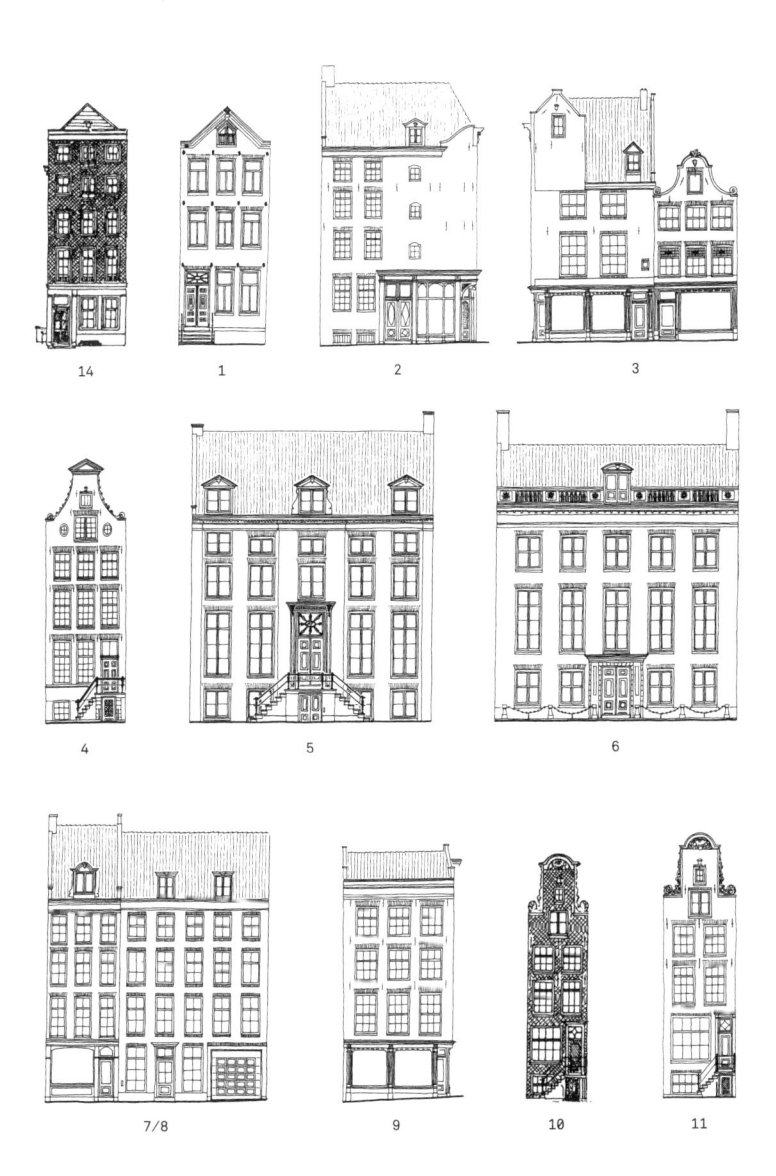

Living

14 1 2 3

4 5 6

7/8 9 10 11

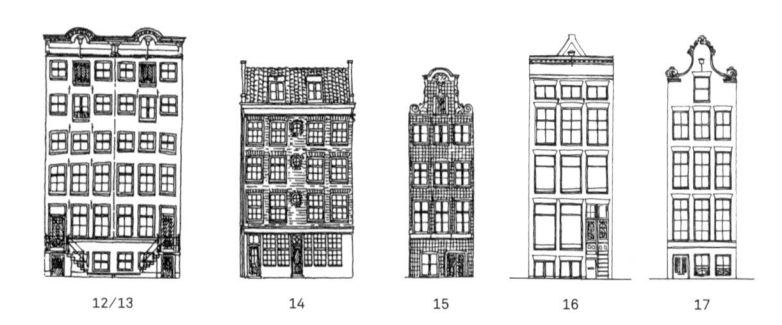

Plantagebuurt / Hortus / Artis 318

12/13

14

15

16

17

18

19

20/21

22

23-25

In the 17th century, there were many pleasure gardens situated in the Plantage neighbourhood where Amsterdam citizens could walk among greenery. The rich collections of plants and trees of the Hortus Botanicus has already been here since 1682 and originated from a Hortus Medicus (a garden with medicinal plants). The zoo Artis has been located in this neighbourhood since 1838, and now has 27 monumental buildings including a beautiful library and an aquarium building. At the end of the 19th century, more houses were built and the Plantage became an entertainment district with theatres. The green character has, however, remained intact up until today.

TANDARTSPRAKTIJK

JONAS DANIEL MEIJER
PLEIN

TANDARTSPRAKTIJK DE HORTUS

Oostelijke eilanden and Kadijken

1. Foeliedwarsstraat 40-42, 50-52
   2014
2. Hoogte Kadijk 12
   2005
3. Hoogte Kadijk 16
   1992
4. Hoogte Kadijk 18A-18C
   1992
5. Hoogte Kadijk 50
   1992
6. Hoogte Kadijk 52
   1992
7. Hoogte Kadijk 62
   1992
8. Hoogte Kadijk 74 · Tussen Kadijken 17-19-21
   1992
9. Hoogte Kadijk 97-101-105
   1988
10. Hoogte Kadijk 99-103
    1988
11. Hoogte Kadijk 107-111-115
    1988
12. Hoogte Kadijk 113-117 · Overhaalsgang 1
    1988
13. Kadijksplein 5-12 · Laagte Kadijk 1-2
    1997
14. Laagte Kadijk 10-12
    1997
15. Prins Hendrikkade 87
    1992
16. Prins Hendrikkade 101
    1975
17. Rapenburg 93
    2014
18. Tussen Kadijken 3-5-9
    1992
19. Tussen Kadijken 7-11
    1992
20. Tussen Kadijken 13-15
    1992
21. Wittenburgergracht 33-35
22. Wittenburgergracht 59
23. Wittenburgergracht 197-201
    1987
24. Wittenburgergracht 205-209
    1987
25. Wittenburgergracht 297-301
    1989

Living 323

Oostelijke eilanden and Kadijken

13

13

Living 325

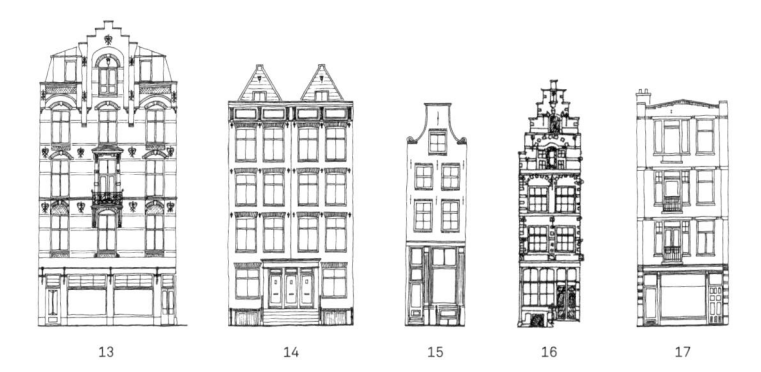

13 14 15 16 17

25

The brick

The brick industry got going in the second half of the 12th century. People learnt how to make a fully-fledged construction material from inferior types of clay. The clay was an erosion product of natural stone supplied by the sea or the rivers. The result was a compact thick brick. Up until the 17th century, a combination of brick types continued to define architecture. The small brick was already found at an early stage in Amsterdam. From the 17th century, the Vecht size (21x10x3,8cm) dominated. Colour has always been important in brick architecture. In order to obtain the ideal of a single-coloured material, people painted the brickwork red. It was only in the 19th century that a change in the appreciation of the 'pure' material followed.

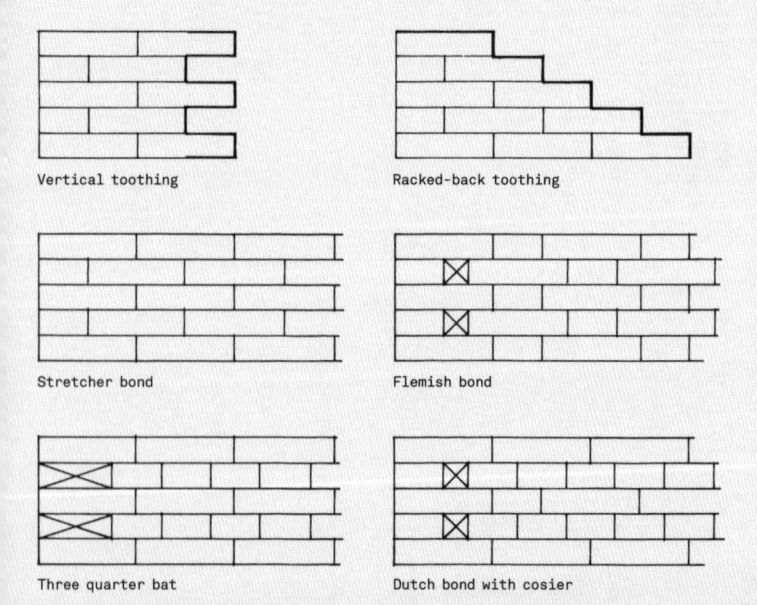

Vertical toothing

Racked-back toothing

Stretcher bond

Flemish bond

Three quarter bat

Dutch bond with cosier

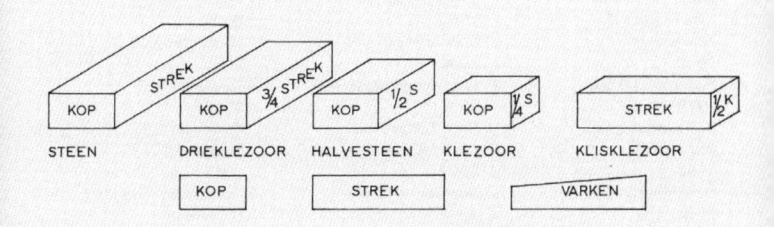

Living

327

STEEN — KOP / STREK
DRIEKLEZOOR — KOP / 3/4 STREK
HALVESTEEN — KOP / 1/2 S
KLEZOOR — KOP / 1/4 S
KLISKLEZOOR — STREK / 1/2 K

KOP STREK VARKEN

- Course of stretchers
- Course of headers
- Bed
- Vertical joint

Vertical bond with bat

Dutch bond with three quarter bat

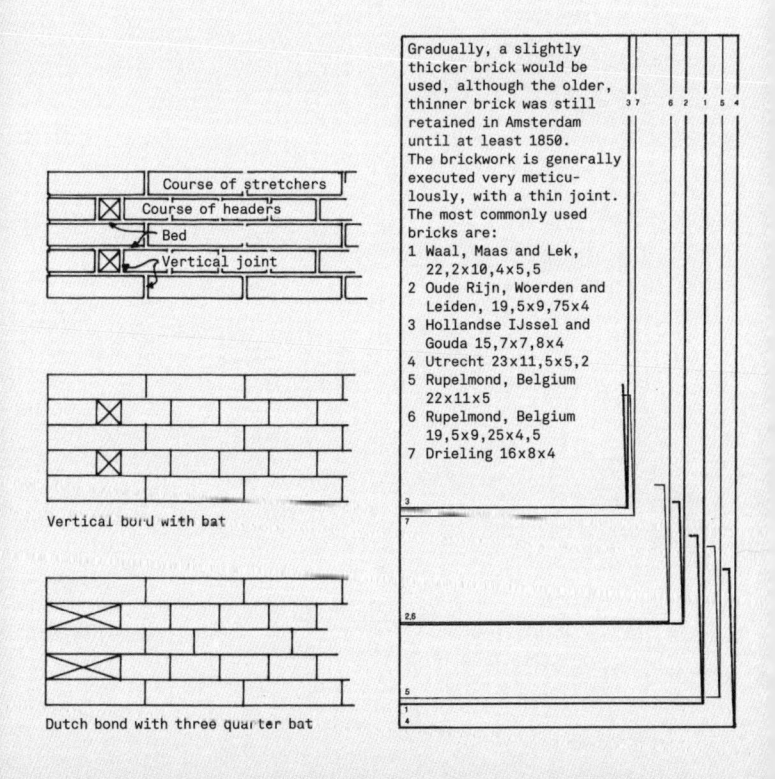

Gradually, a slightly thicker brick would be used, although the older, thinner brick was still retained in Amsterdam until at least 1850. The brickwork is generally executed very meticulously, with a thin joint. The most commonly used bricks are:
1 Waal, Maas and Lek, 22,2x10,4x5,5
2 Oude Rijn, Woerden and Leiden, 19,5x9,75x4
3 Hollandse IJssel and Gouda 15,7x7,8x4
4 Utrecht 23x11,5x5,2
5 Rupelmond, Belgium 22x11x5
6 Rupelmond, Belgium 19,5x9,25x4,5
7 Drieling 16x8x4

Amsterdam-Noord

1. Broekergouw 10
   Zunderdorp
   2002
2. Broekergouw 12
   Zunderdorp
   2002
3. Buiksloterdijk 224
   1974
4. Buiksloterdijk 228
   (leasehold)
   1983
5. Buiksloterdijk 230
   (leasehold)
   1986
6. Buiksloterdijk 254
   2002
7. Buiksloterdijk 434
   2002
8. Buiksloterdijk 444
   2002
9. Landsmeerderdijk 45
   2004
10. Noordhollandsch-
    kanaaldijk 24
    2002
11. Noorder IJdijk 109
    2002
12. Stoombootweg 1
    2002
13. Stoombootweg 4
    2002
14. Stoombootweg 17
    2002
15. Wingerdweg 28-34
    2005
16. Zuideinde 422
    2002
17. Zuideinde 428-430
    (leasehold)
    2013
18. Durgerdammerdijk 97
    Durgerdam
    2005/2011

Living 329

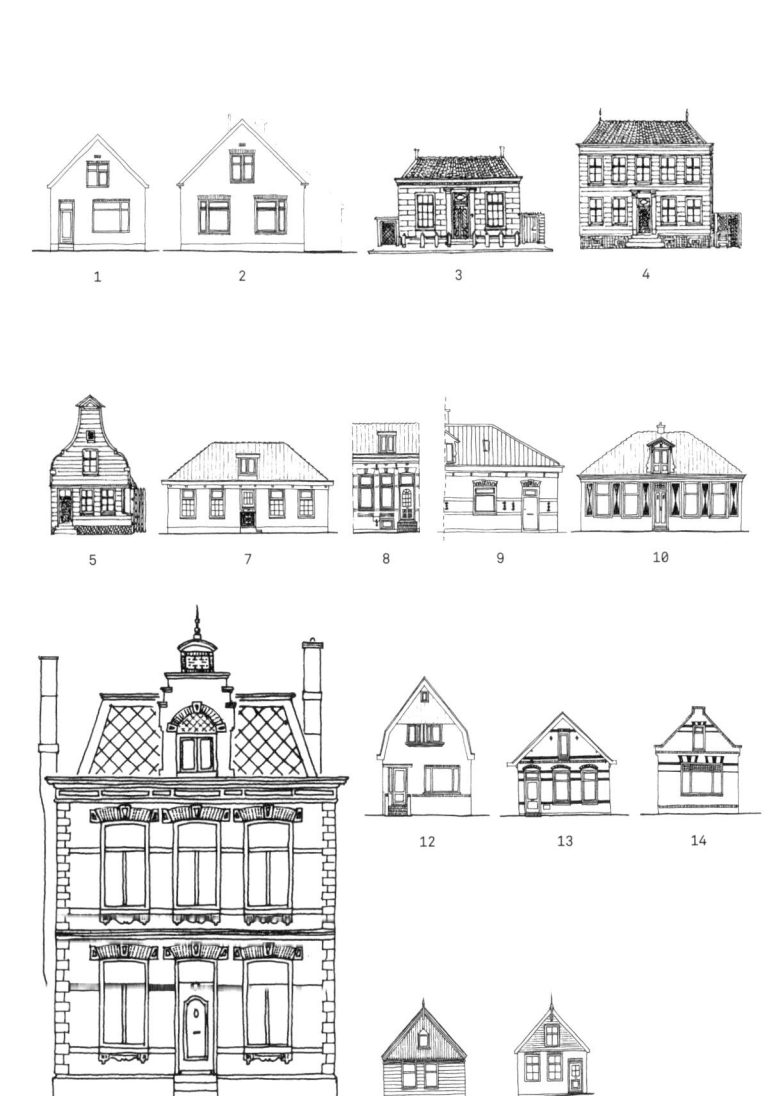

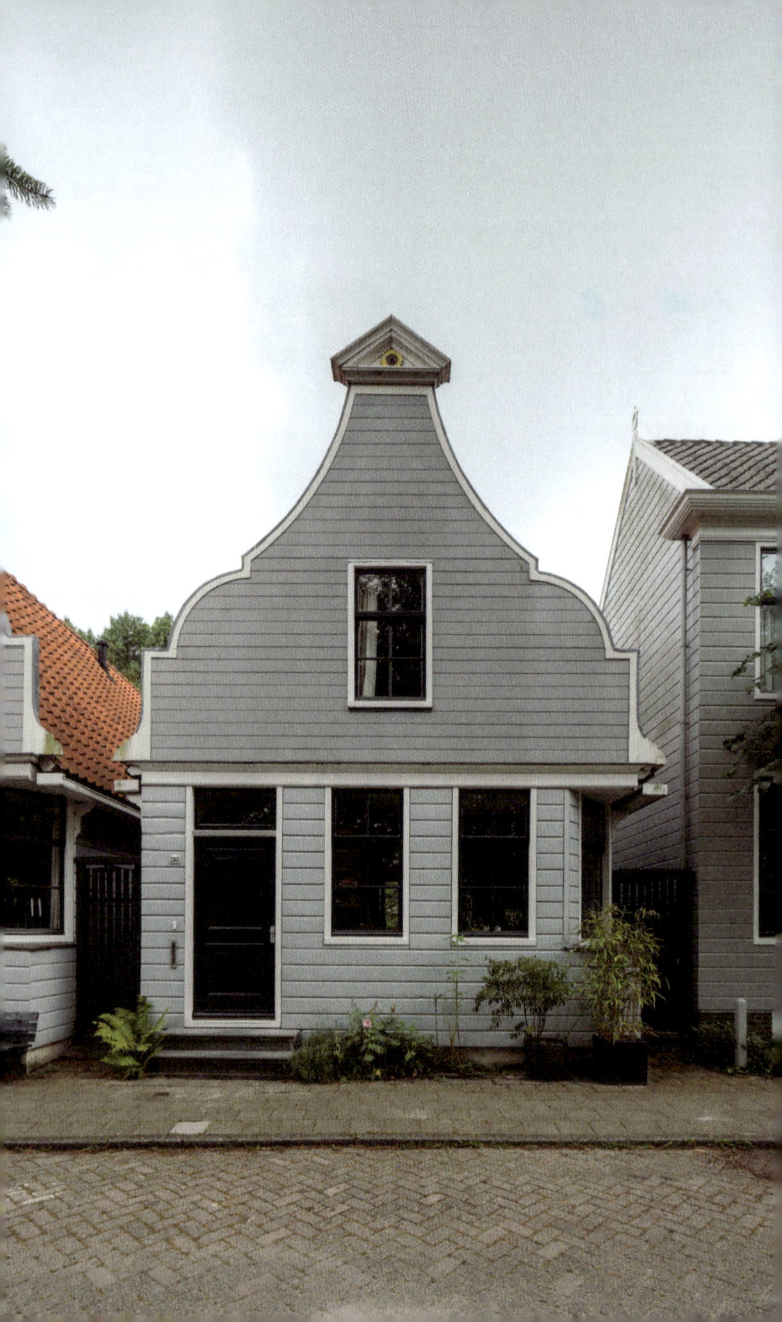

Living

Amsterdam-Noord (Amsterdam North) is situated on the opposite side of the IJ River and solely reachable by ferry until 1957. In 1957, the first cross-river connection was created, the Schellingwouderbrug (Schellingwouder Bridge), followed by the Coentunnel in 1966, the IJtunnel in 1968 and the Zeeburgertunnel in 1990. With the construction of the North-South metro line, the attraction of the district as a place to live increased enormously, which led to new development on the banks of the IJ. The small villages of the pastoral North have now been restored to their former glory.

▷ Buiksloterdijk at the level of house number 228, 2016

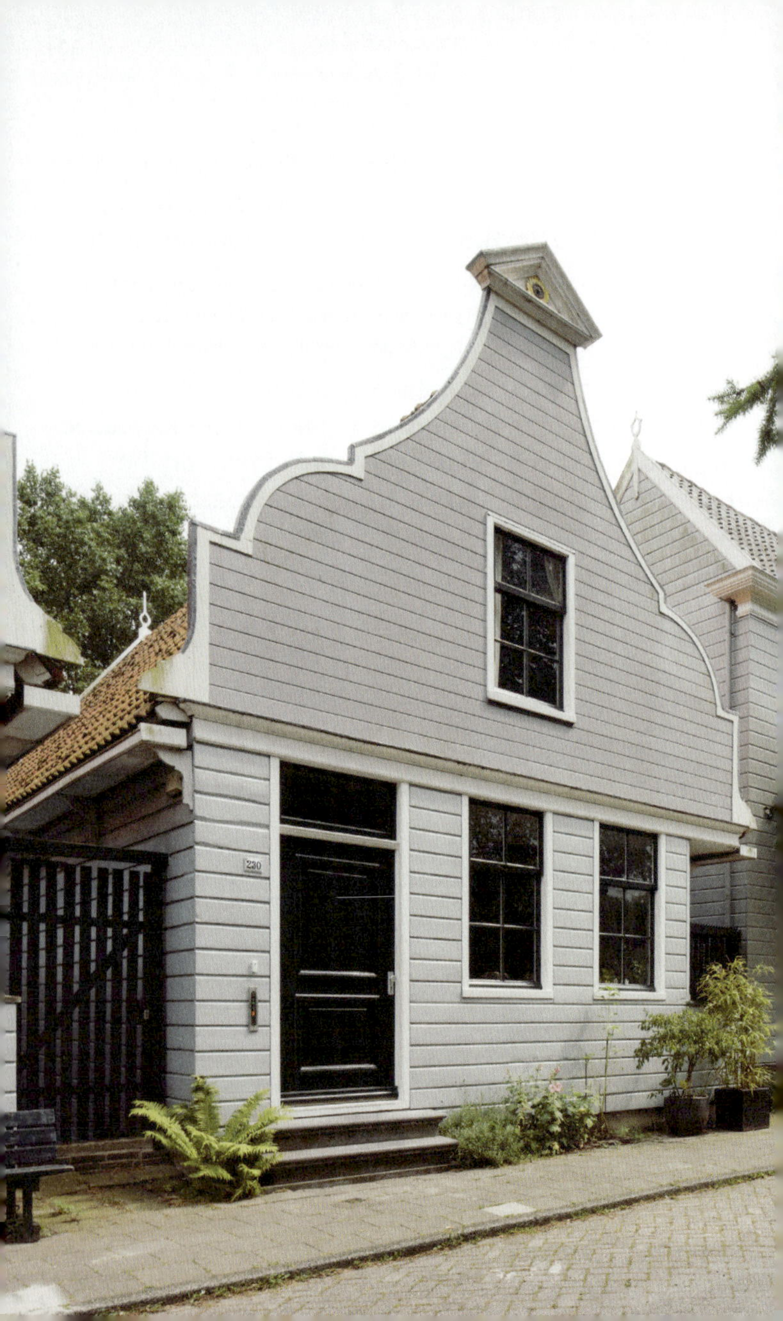
230

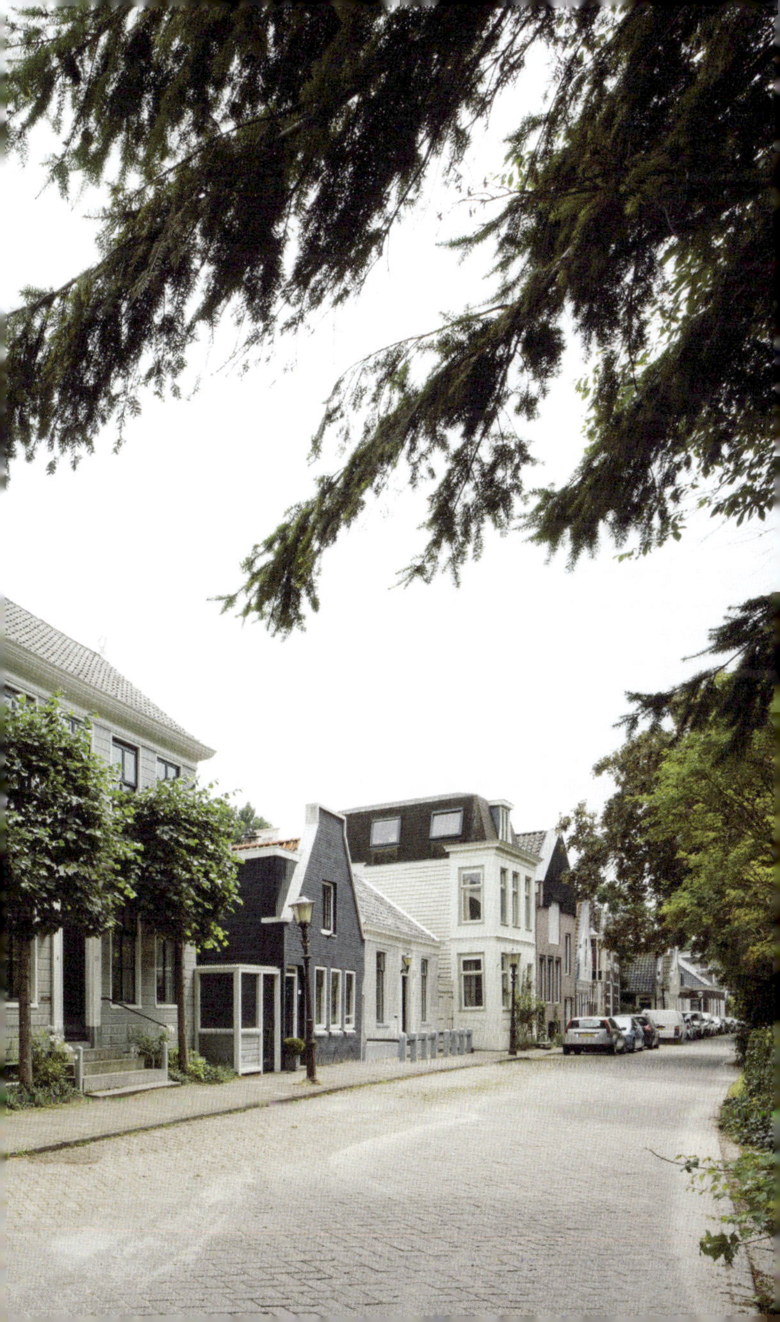

Haarlem / Heemstede

1. Rosenstock
   Huessy Huis
   Antoniestraat 5-7-11 ·
   Hagestraat 2-12
   Haarlem
   2015
2. Begijnhof 20
   Haarlem
   1972
3. Groot Heiligland 26
   Haarlem
   2011
4. Kleverlaan 9
   Haarlem
   2015
5. Spaarne 11
   Haarlem
   2009
6. Spaarnwouderstraat
   68-68A
   Haarlem
   2011
7. Spaarnwouderstraat
   72-72A-72B
   Haarlem
   2011
8. Spaarnwouderstraat 74 ·
   Spiegelstraat 2B
   Haarlem
   2011
9. Spaarnwouderstraat 76 ·
   Spiegelstraat 2A
   Haarlem
   2011
10. Spiegelstraat 4
    Haarlem
    2013
11. Spiegelstraat 6-8
    Haarlem
    2013
12. Spiegelstraat 8A
    Haarlem
    2013
13. Wilhelminaplein 4-6
    Heemstede
    2013
14. Wilhelminaplein 12
    Heemstede
    2015

Living

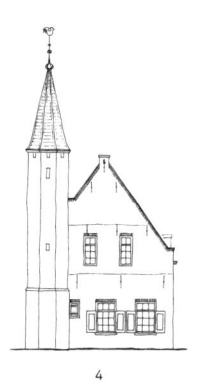

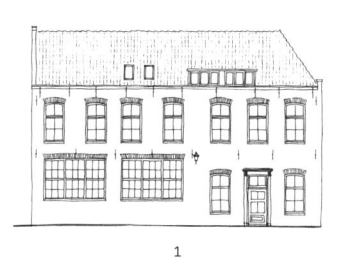

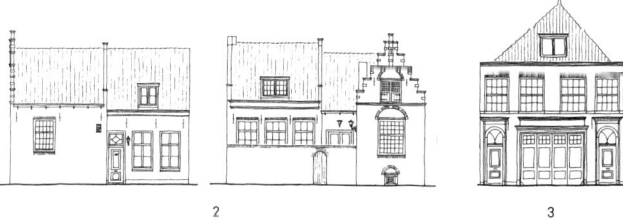

335

4

1

1

2

3

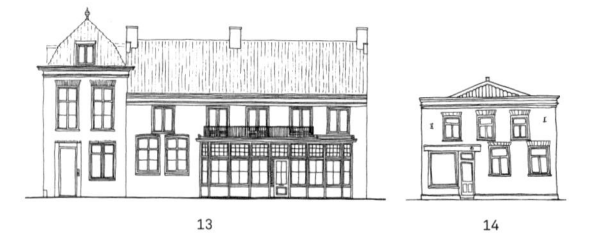

Haarlem / Heemstede

5

6-9

10-12

13

14

Staircases and balustrades

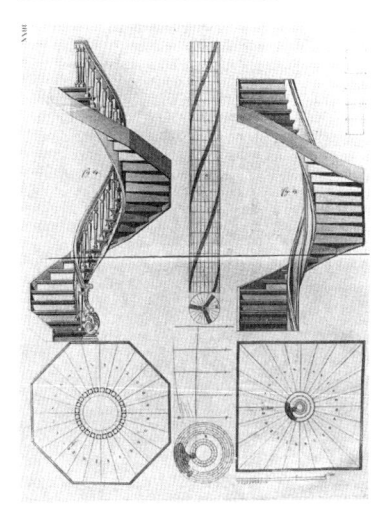

Bored newel and winding staircase (18th century), the reinforcement of the sense of space through continually rotating around the axis. The staircase was given a decorative function.

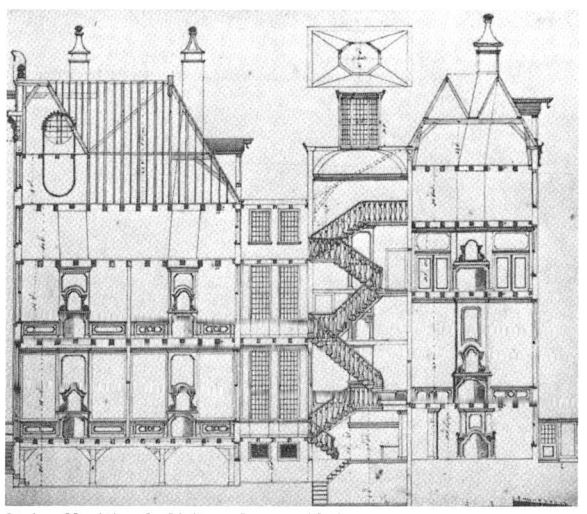

Stairwell with a fanlight or lantern if the staircase did not border the inner courtyard.

Staircases and balustrades

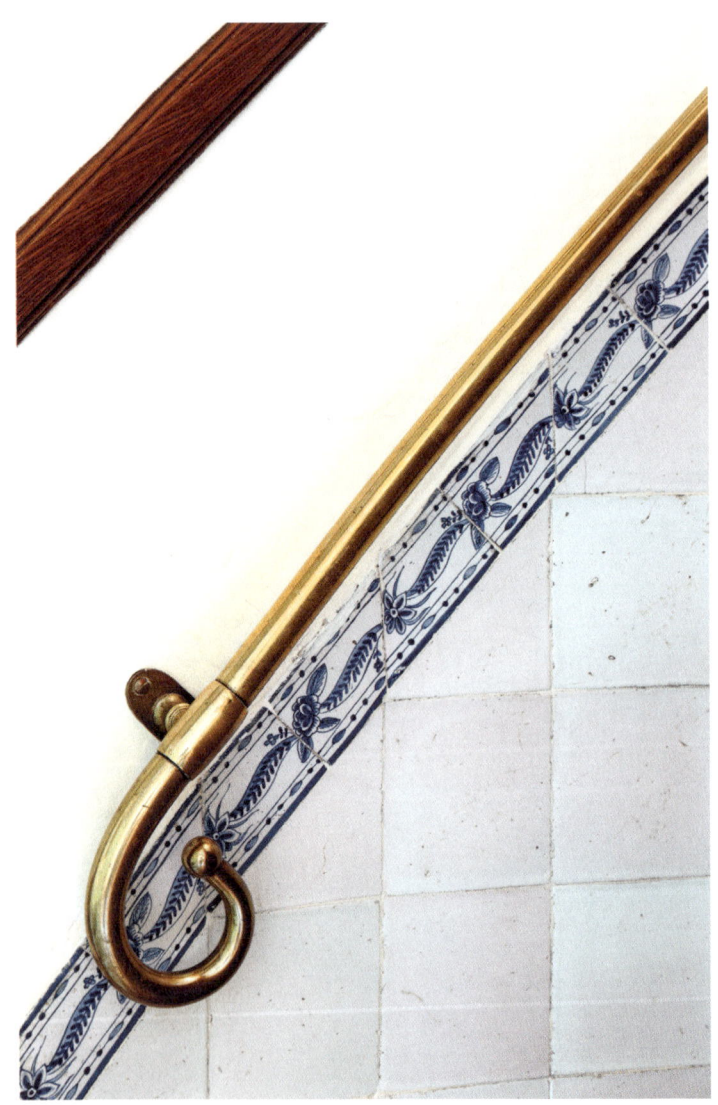

338

19th century staircase Reguliersgracht 63

Staircases and balustrades

Staircases and balustrades

18th century staircase former Merchant's house Beverwijk

Staircases and balustrades

Staircases and balustrades

Merchant's house Breestraat Beverwijk

Staircases and balustrades

Staircases and balustrades

Keizersgracht 62

Interior

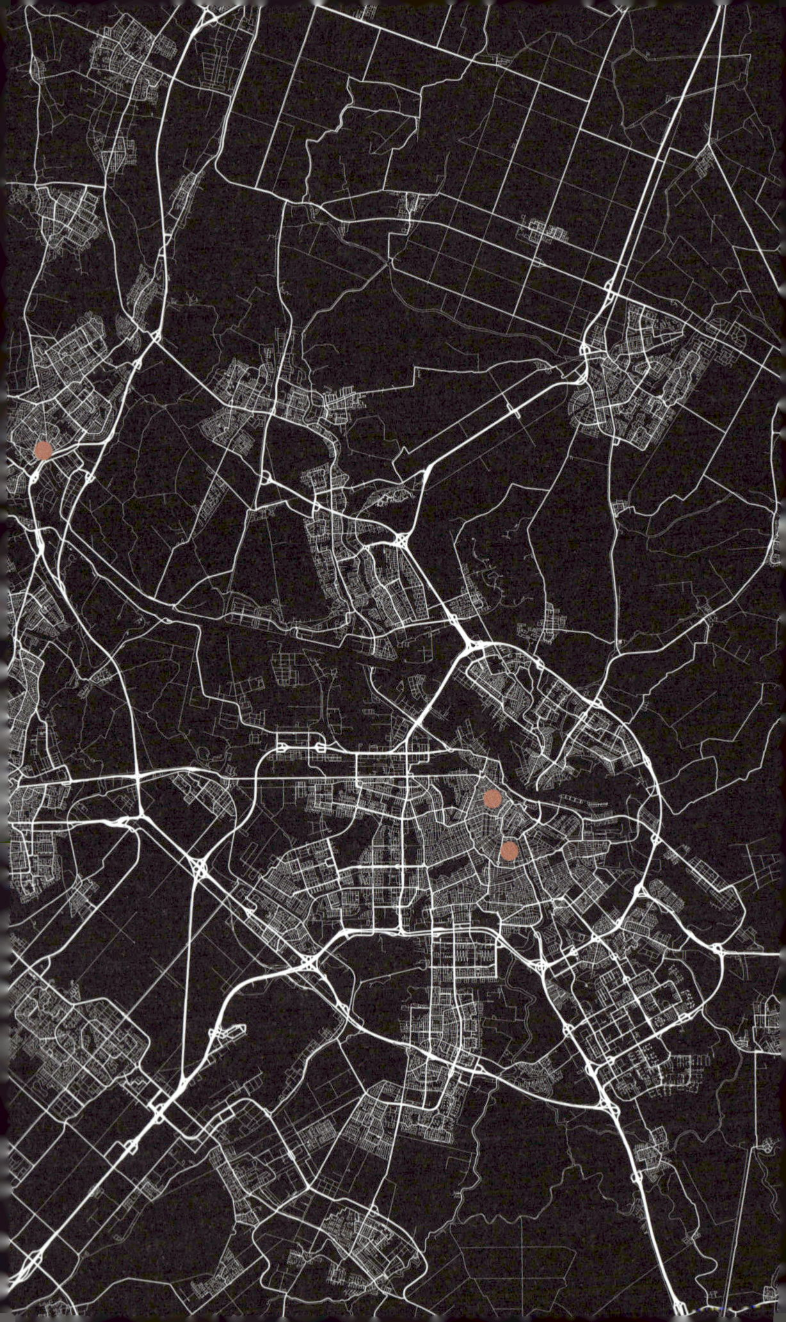

350 **Keizersgracht 64**, Amsterdam
372 **Reguliersgracht 63**, Amsterdam
396 **Beverwijk presbytery**, Beverwijk

Many interiors of Stadsherstel have been opened to the public, ranging from churches, industrial and military heritage to houses, a number of which have a unique historical layout. For example, the period room in the former merchant's house in Beverwijk has been completed to its former glory with the return of a unique hand-knotted carpet following a restoration that took one year. The historic wallpapers with scenic images had already been tackled earlier. Revenue from hiring it out or visitors is generally the main objective of the property. Many locations are ideal for holding lectures, symposia, dinner parties and receptions. The prestigious locations are well suited to business use or the presentation of a company, or as a wedding location or sometimes even for a religious service. A number of buildings have a good acoustic for recitals and concerts, or are suitable for dance performances. The owners of a historic building often faced with issues and problems related to maintenance and repair, or with questions with respect to determining the cultural historical value of the interior. One of the most important matters when tackling these issues is whether to restore or replace the interior of a building. Stadsherstel collaborates with specialists in the field of historical interior research. The qualities of a well-designed interior are often barely noticed at first glance. In many cases, this concerns a well

Period room former merchant's house Beverwijk

thought out design and a lot of craftsmanship. The real quality only comes to light after further research. This also applies to high-quality restoration projects, including those which show respect for the original design and construction. A short while ago the district Amsterdam Centrum started a project drawing up an inventory of historic interiors. In this way, better protection can be offered against interiors being sold or thrown away in containers.

Sliding door with a portrait of architect Jacob van Campen

Keizersgracht 64

Address
Keizersgracht 62-64

Town
Amsterdam

Built
1738

Acquisition
1962

Restoration
1973

Restoration architect
H. F. Rappange

Current use
Commercial spaces

Interior

The restoration of the nationally listed building on the Keizersgracht 64 in 1973 was the largest and costliest project of Stadsherstel up until that point. The ceiling paintings were repaired in the laboratory of the Rijksmuseum and the garden house was replaced. The original house dates back from 1616. The seafarer Jan Mol, to whom the stone plaque 'De Mol' above the door refers, owned the property. The building, a 5.5 metre-wide merchant's house, was thoroughly refurbished by the new owner in 1738, which consisted of raising the front part of the house by two stories and building a large rear annexe. The principal floor, in particular, is very richly detailed. The hallway has a stucco ceiling and alcoves in the walls, while the inner room has an original ceiling. Ceres, the goddess of grain crops, is depicted sitting on a cloudscape in the large middle section. She is holding a bundle of wheat in her right hand, while grasping a melon in her left hand. A floating young man with four dragonfly wings offers her a basket of fruit. The two original privies have been preserved in the inner courtyard with a wooden ornamental wall between them, which is bordered by pilasters. The privy by the front part of the house was accessible from the inner room. The interconnecting section also has a beautiful stucco ceiling. A small stair case leads to a landing, from which the large hall and the small room in the rear annexe are accessible. A richly decorated staircase leads up from the landing. The rear hall also has its original woodwork and ceiling. The large ceiling painting depicts Father Time as an

Keizersgracht 64

old naked man with a long beard large wings and an hourglass on his head. Geometry sits next to him with wings in her hair. She points with a compass to a plate on which, among other things, a triangle, a circle and square are depicted. She has an astrolabe (a ball constructed from bands) under her left arm. Nobody knows who made the painted ceiling canvases.

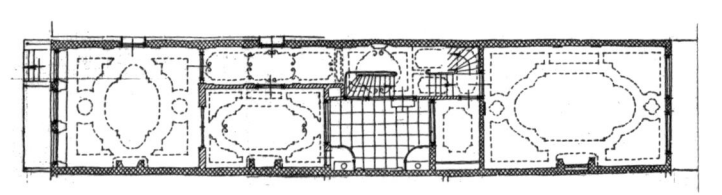

Ceilings first floor

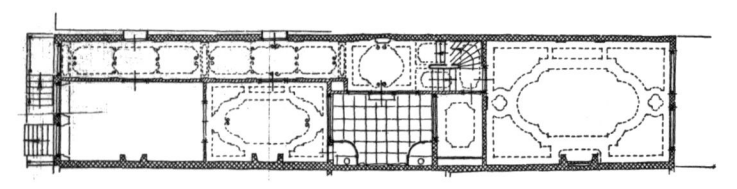

Ceilings entrance level,
(centre) toilets on the inner courtyard (see page 367)

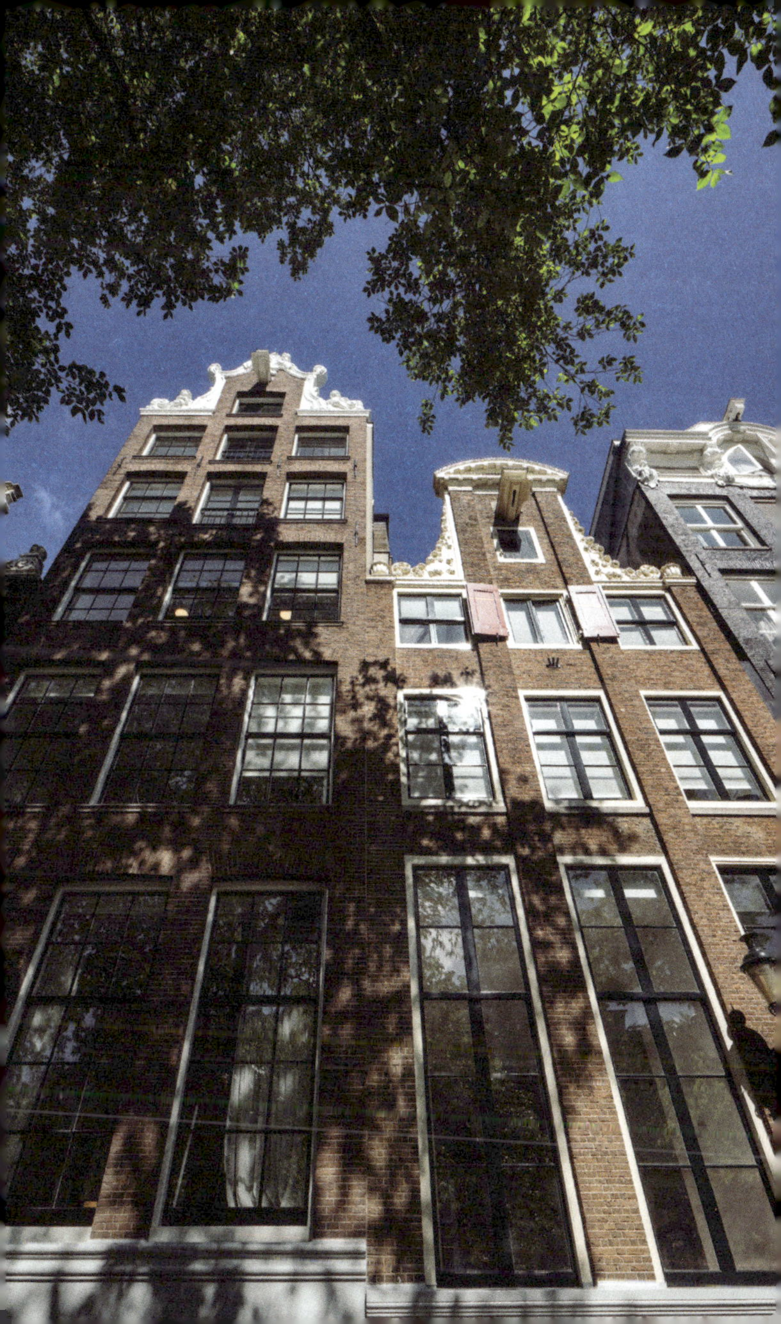

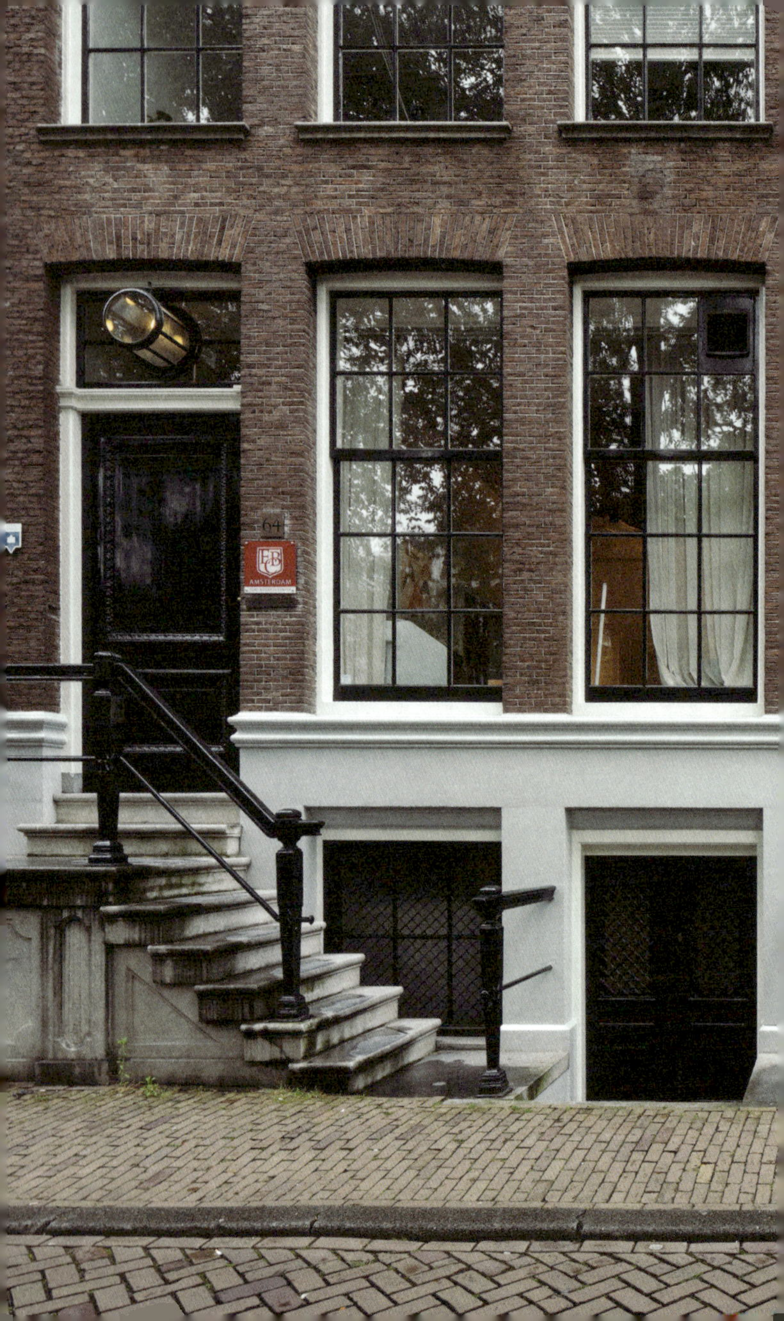
64
EBC
AMSTERDAM

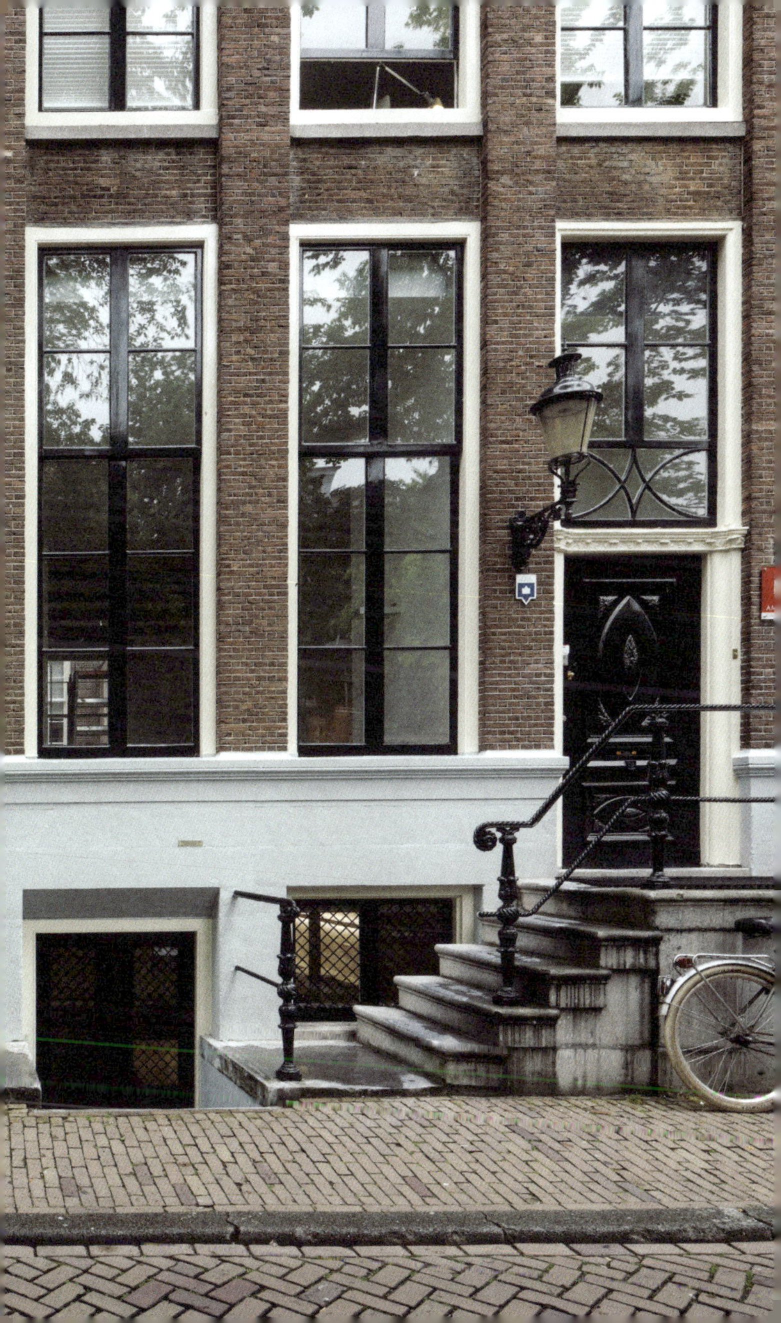

Keizersgracht 64

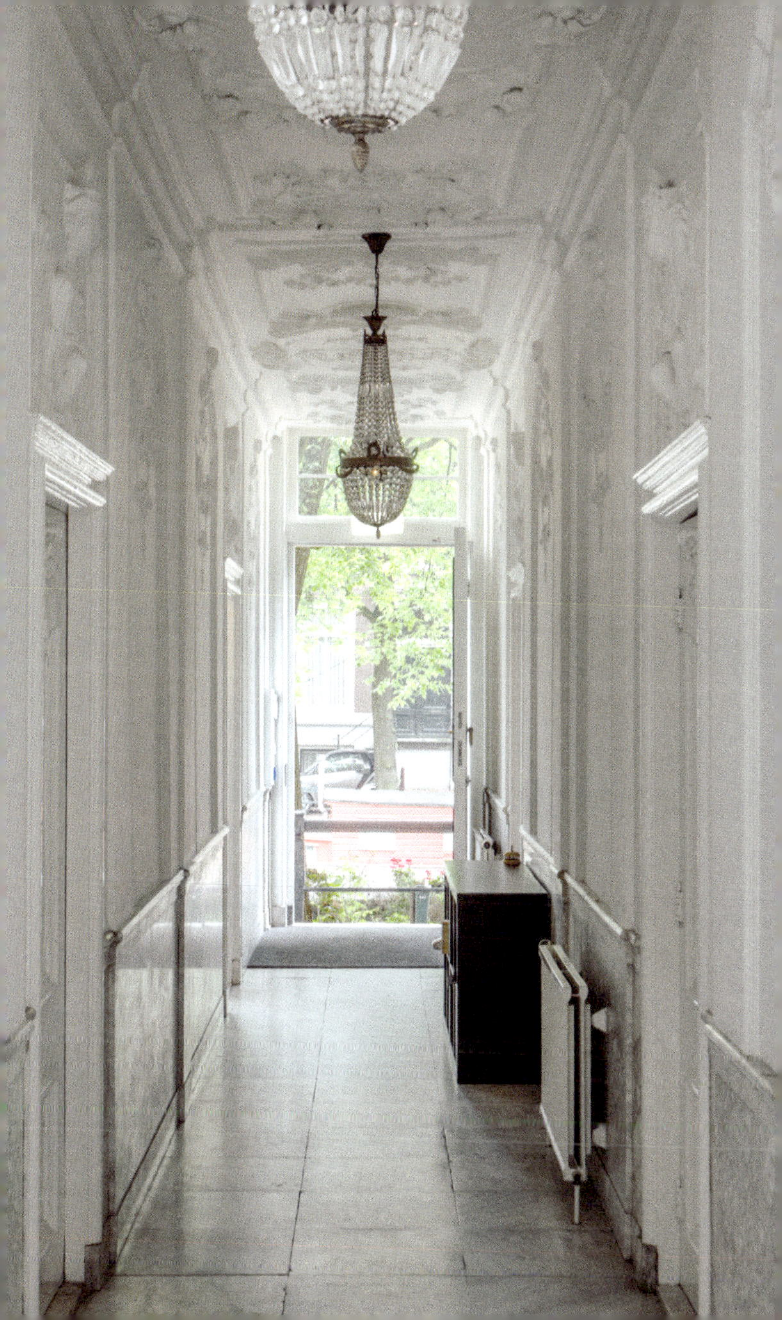

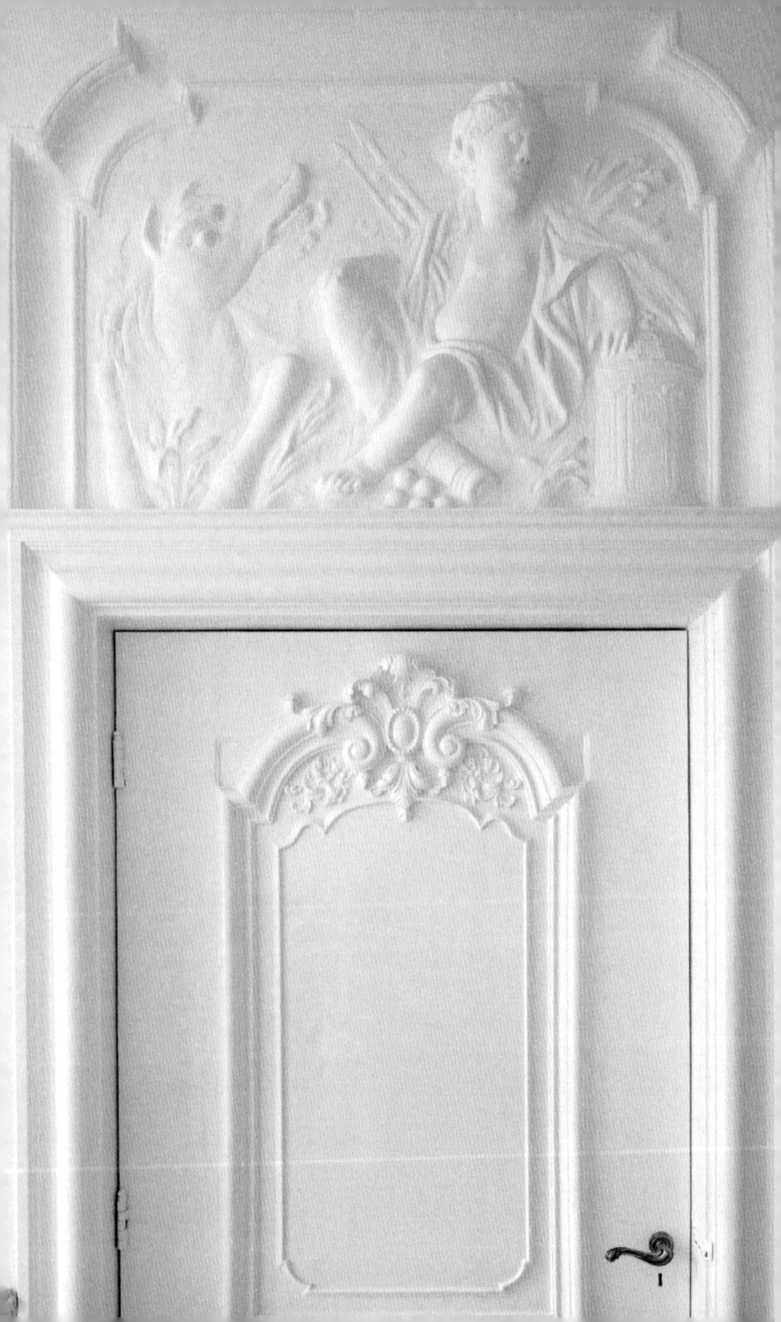

Interior

Keizersgracht 64

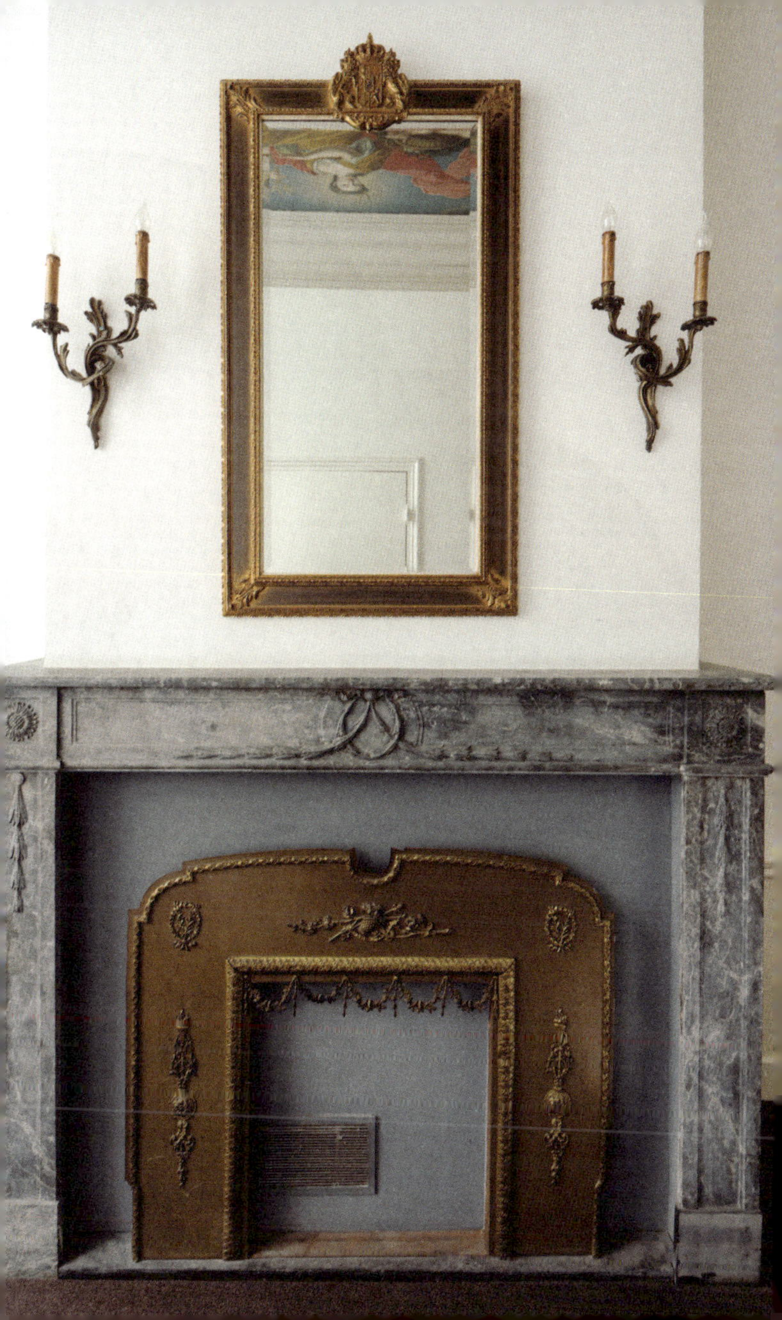

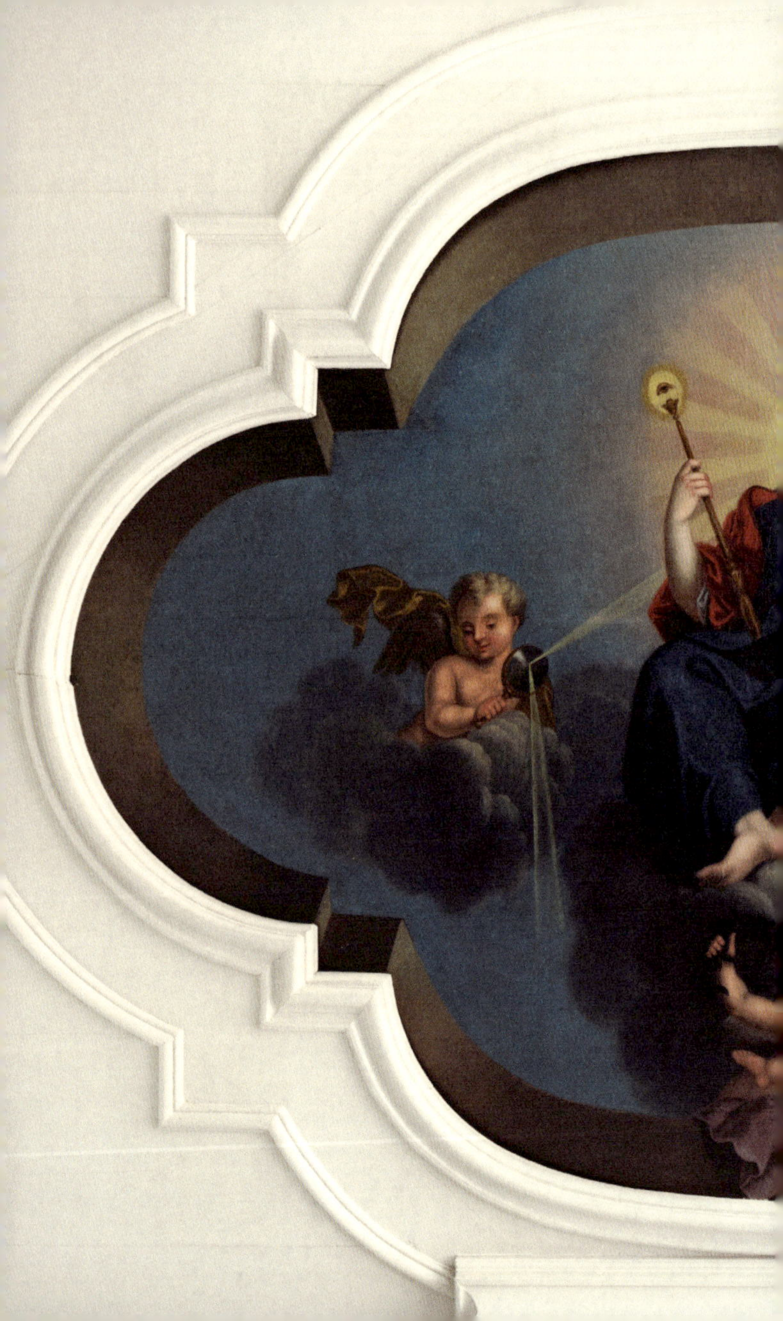

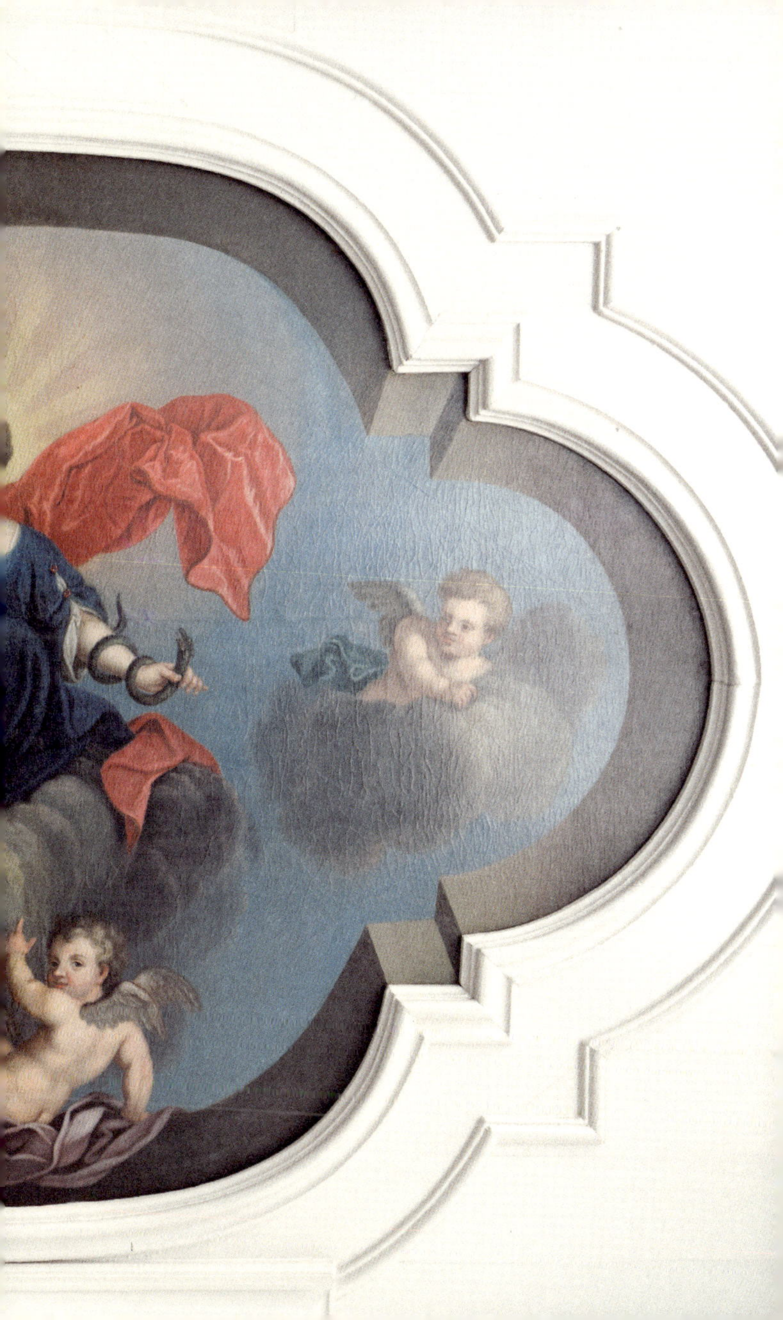

Keizersgracht 64 364

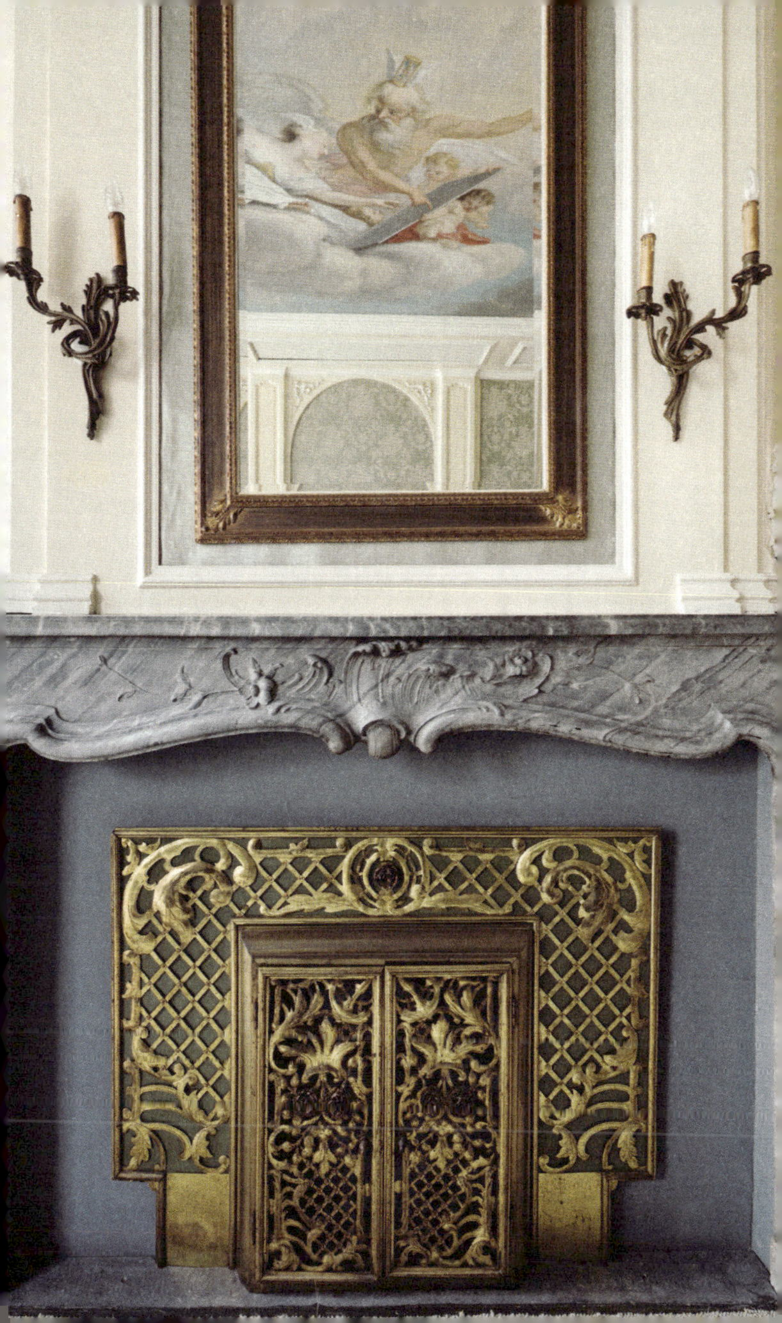

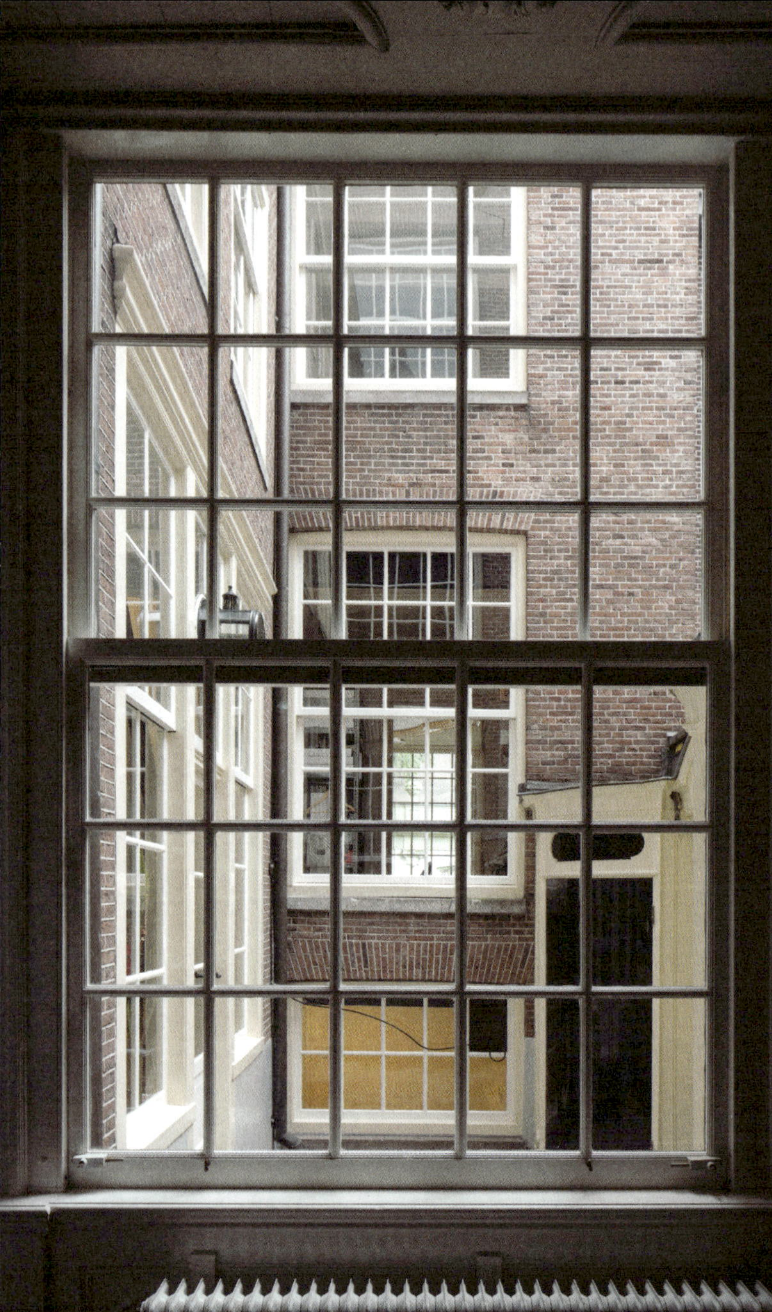

Interior

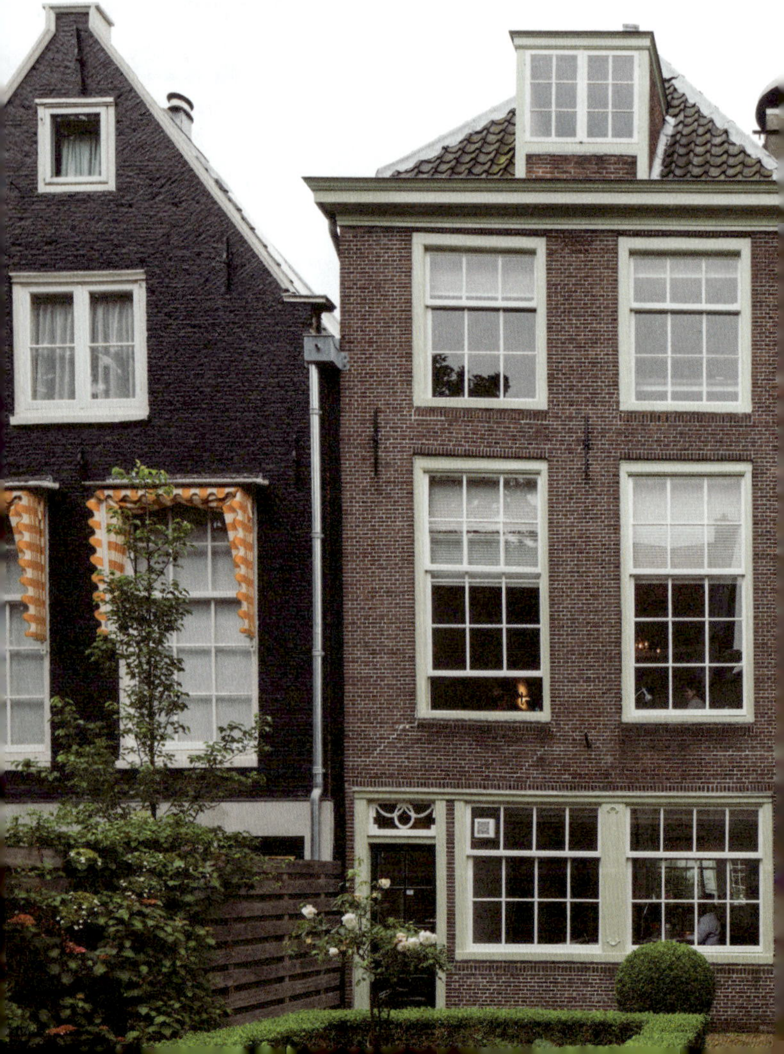

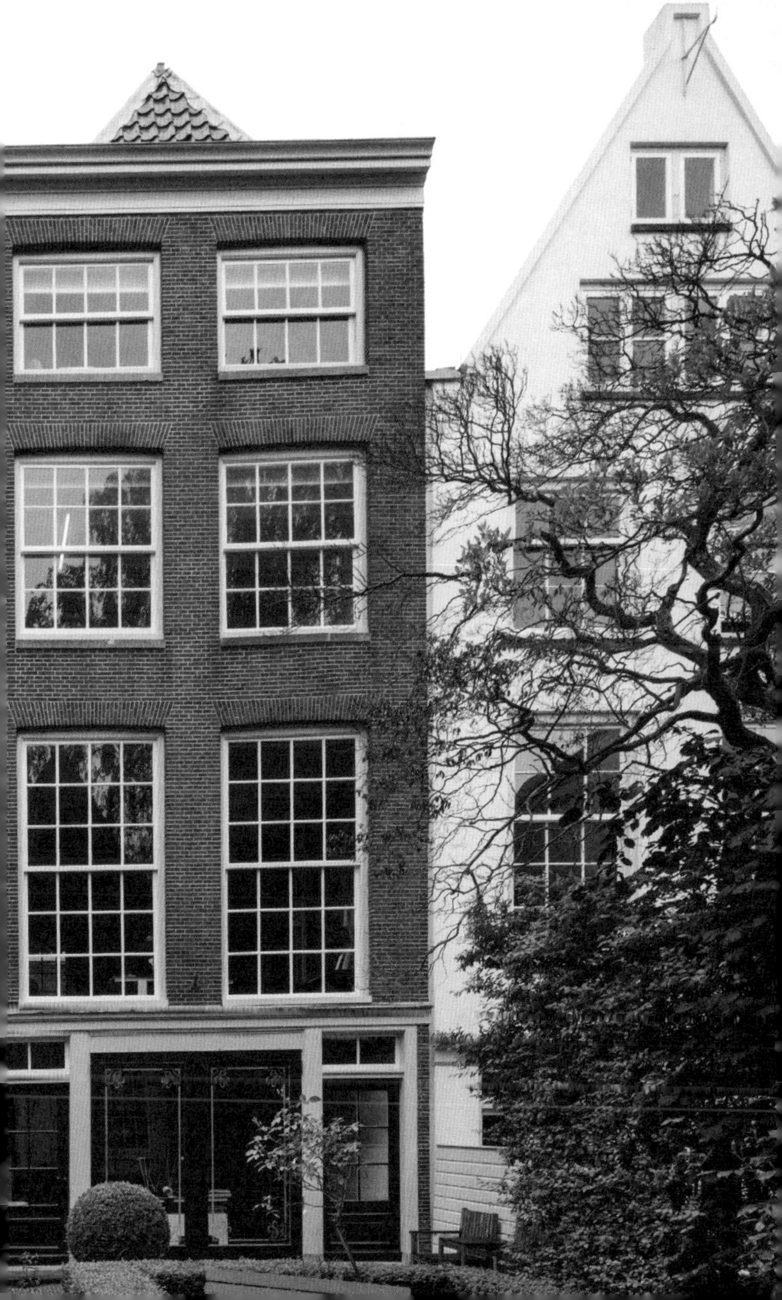

Garden houses

Garden houses have been a fixed element of canal houses since the second extension of the canal ring in the mid-17th century. In 1663, the law (local by-law) prescribed that a building of no more than 12 feet (3.4 metres) high and 15 feet deep (4.25 m) was allowed over the entire width of the property behind the canal house. The space between the main house and this garden building at the far end of the property was meant to be laid out as a garden and had to remain undeveloped. A number of the so-called keurblokken ('by-law blocks'), as the green spaces between the canal houses are still known, have remained reasonably intact, while less greenery has survived in others over the course of the years. In addition to interest in private gardens, the further construction of the canal ring also went hand in hand with the planting of long rows of trees along the street side of the canal. These were mainly lime tree at first, but more elm trees quickly followed, because they turned out to be good at withstanding urban life. The *Dutch elm* was grown in an urban tree nursery. Today, there are approximately 75,000 elms (40 types) in Amsterdam. A garden house was often given the same lavishly ornamented facade as the canal house (at the front and rear). The occupants therefore had a beautiful view of the garden and the grand facade decorated with ornaments at the far end of the property from the back room (the most important room of the house). Stories differ about how these garden houses were used in those days, from a place to keep chickens, a washhouse or a privy to a room for serving tea (comparable to the use of gazebos along the river Vecht, where city dwellers spent their summers on their country estates in the 18th century.) One of the most important design drawings of a garden and garden house in the 17th century that has been preserved is that of Philips Vingboons for Herengracht 412. It is considered to be the city's oldest example. Just like many buildings along the Amsterdam canals, the accompanying garden houses fell into disrepair in the 1960s and 1970s. At the end of the 20th century, the City of Amsterdam carried out an emergency repair by placing the most important garden houses on the municipal monument register, after the Cultural Heritage Agency of the Netherlands expressed no interest in doing so. Approximately 150 garden houses, primarily from the 18th century, were preserved. The closed ornamental gardens, which were originally laid out in a geometric pattern and decorated with vases and statues, have repeatedly been adapted to changing fashions over the course of time. Most canal gardens remain private. Today, you can get a good impression of what a keurblok is at a number of museums with gardens, such as Museum Van Loon, Huis Marseille and the Cromhouthuis.

Interior

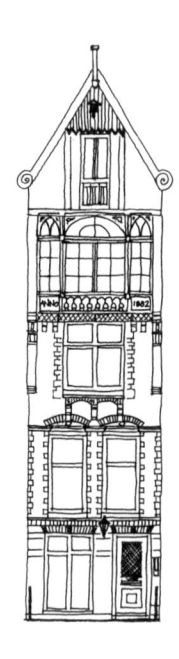

Reguliersgracht 63

Address
Reguliersgracht 63

Town
Amsterdam

Built
1882

Acquisition
1974

Restoration
2003

Restoration architect
Stadsherstel

Current use
House and office

Interior

This listed building is the most complete 19th century house in Amsterdam. Both the interior and the exterior of this five-storey canal house have been completely renovated. It was built in 1882 and fitted out with an executive house and showrooms for the carpentry, construction and real estate company Zeeger Deenik & Zoon. The firm had been located on the Reguliersgracht since 1819 and would celebrate its 150th-year anniversary there in 1963. The new house was for master carpenter Zeeger Deenik (1844 – 1906) and the richly decorated interior had to show the high level of craftsmanship. The wealth of workmanship was rediscovered under thick overpainting following extensive colour research by Rescura. It turned out that a rare and exceptionally undamaged 19th century interior lay hidden under all kinds of layers. After a three-year restoration by Stadsherstel, the building regained its showroom function: now as the example of Amsterdam, late-19th century building and interior decoration. The interior was completely restored to its original state. The showroom on the first floor, for example, where the woodwork, from floorboards, panelling, wall posts and ceiling joints to the fireplace, was painted as it used to be, namely in oak imitation. The panels of the wall posts are embellished with palmette stencils and accented with a leaf garland border and pilasters with beautifully carved festoons. The second floor also has a wealth of decoration. The mantelpiece, with its twisted pillars decorated with vines, immediately catches the eye. The initials of the owner Zeeger Deenik are incorporated into the

Reguliersgracht 63

chimney bar, together with the year that the interior was completed, 1883. The mirror on the mantelpiece is framed with pilasters with beautifully carved festoons. On the casing, there is the proverb: 'Effen is slecht treffen'(Can be difficult to please everyone). Other details include the wooden ceiling, divided into sections with woodcarvings, of the front room on the second floor, and the references to the tools of painters, sculptors, architects and craftsmen. The sliding doors to the back room have etched and gilded glass windows, which are decorated with the portraits of two prominent 17th century architects: Hendrick de Keyser and Jacob van Campen.

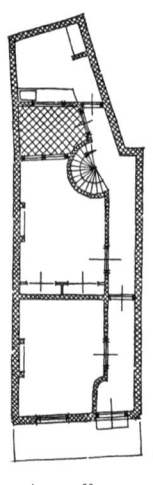

Lower floor 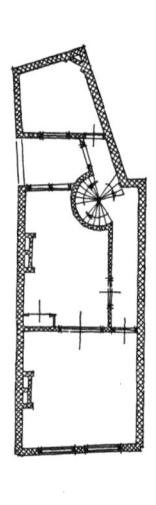   First floor 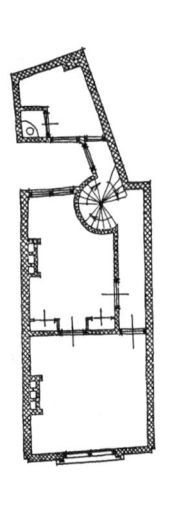   Second floor

Interior

Interior second floor before the start of the restoration

Urban development

Fourth extension

The Reguliersgracht is part of the fourth extension or urban expansion of Amsterdam. The activities began in 1658 and the canal was ready for development by the end of 1664. The canal, named after the Reguliersklooster (Reguliers Monastery) that would have stood at the spot where the Utrechtsestraat and Keizersgracht now cross each other, was not always popular. In 1901, the city government want to fill in part of the canal for the laying of a tram line. The Amstelodamum society and the writer Jan Ligthart came to its defence and ultimately thwarted the plans. The Reguliersgracht from the Herengracht is probably the most photographed cityscape in Amsterdam and a fixed attraction for the canal cruise boats, due to the many consecutive bridges. Famous occupants include the 17th century engraver and cartoonist Romeyn de Hooghe and the 18th century decorator and interior designer Daniel Marot.

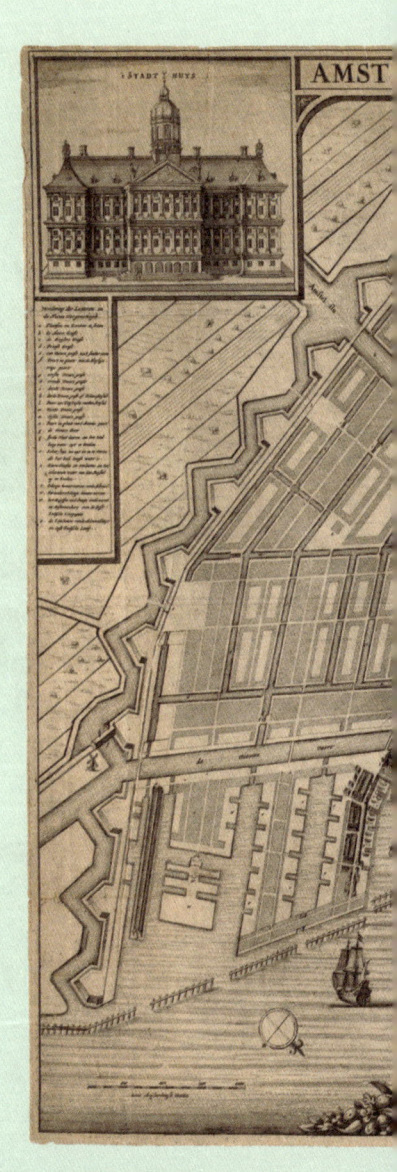

M. MET DE NIEUWE VERGROOTINGH.

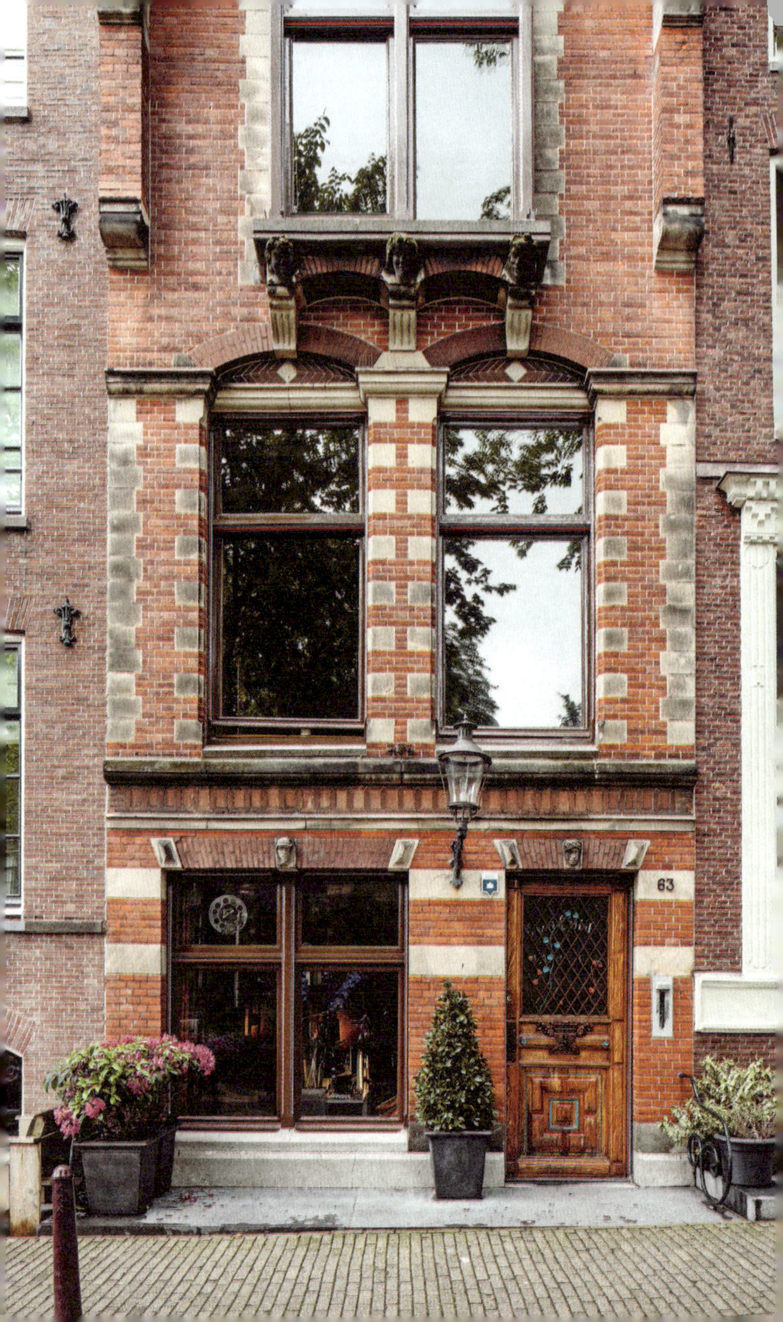
63

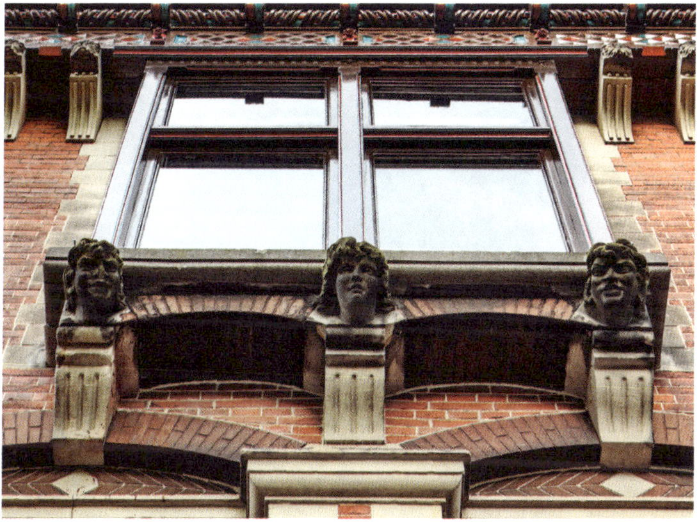

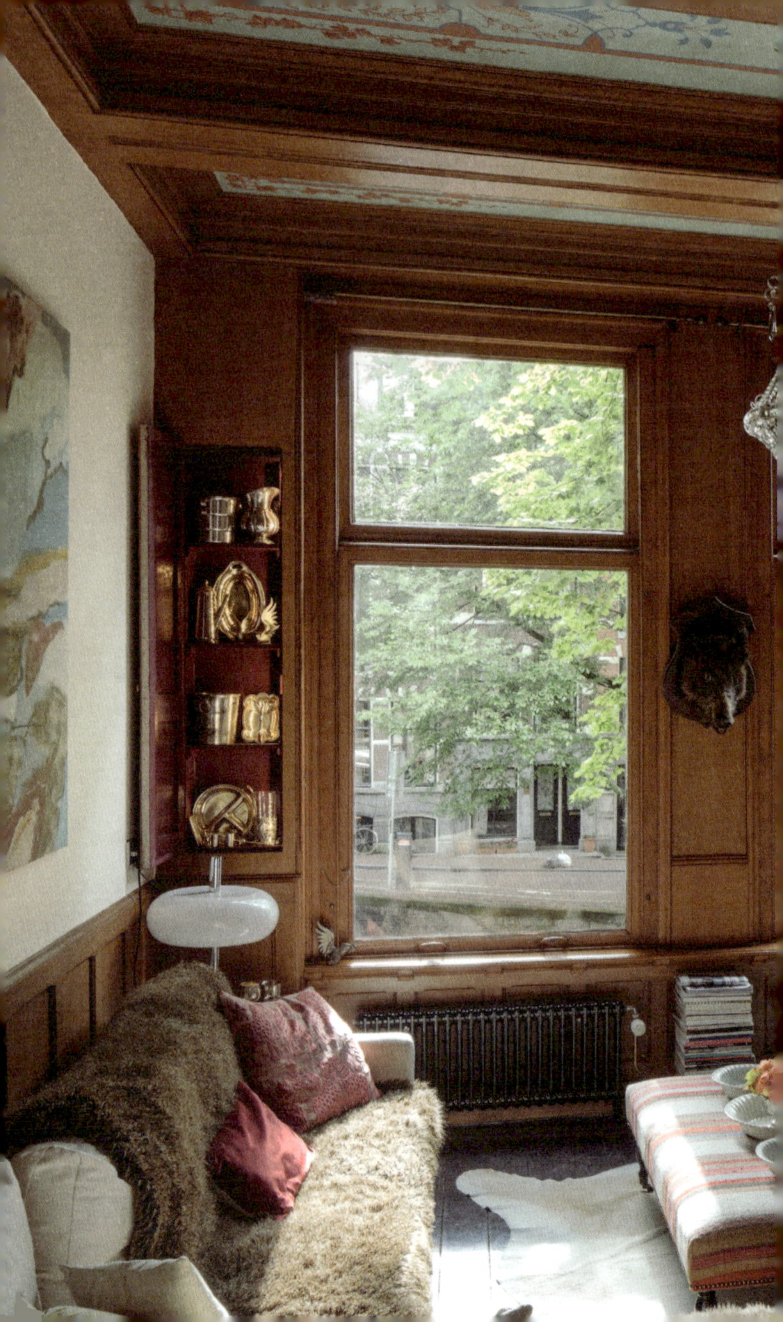

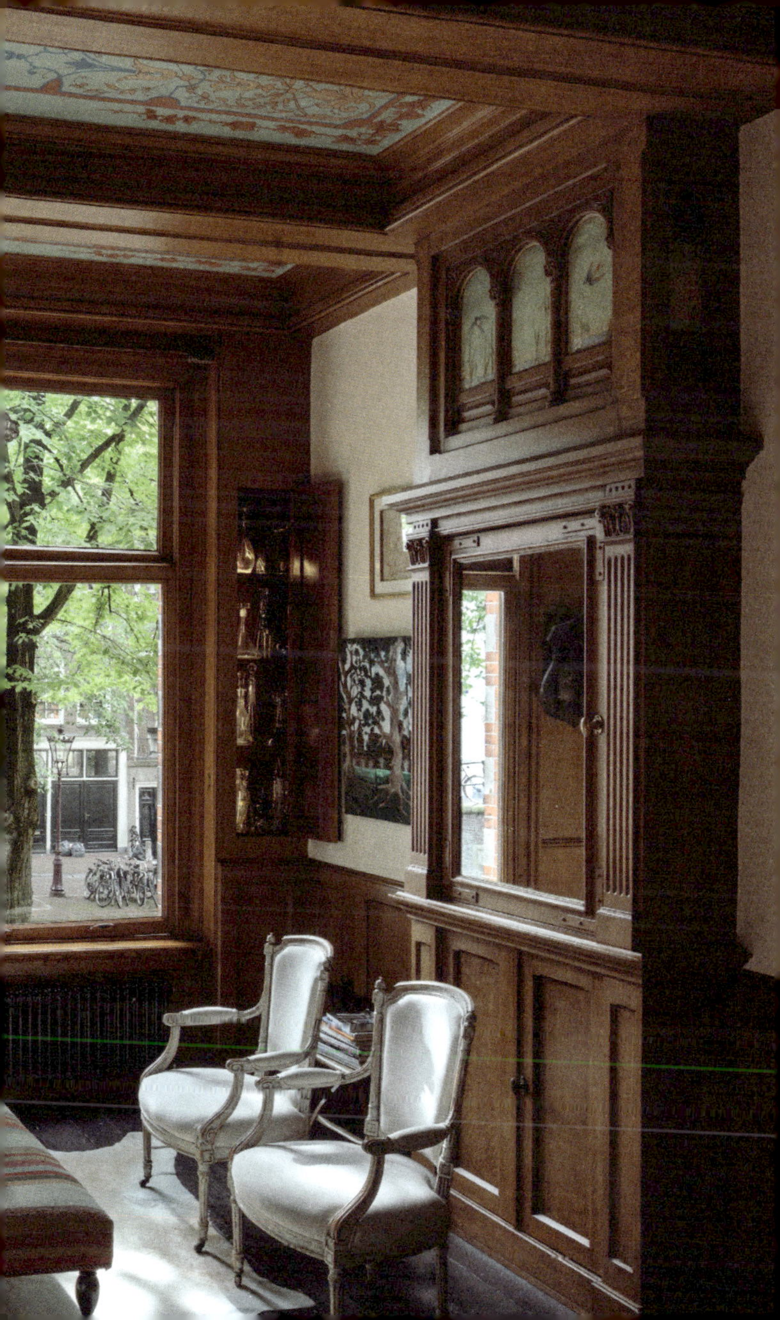

Reguliersgracht 63 382

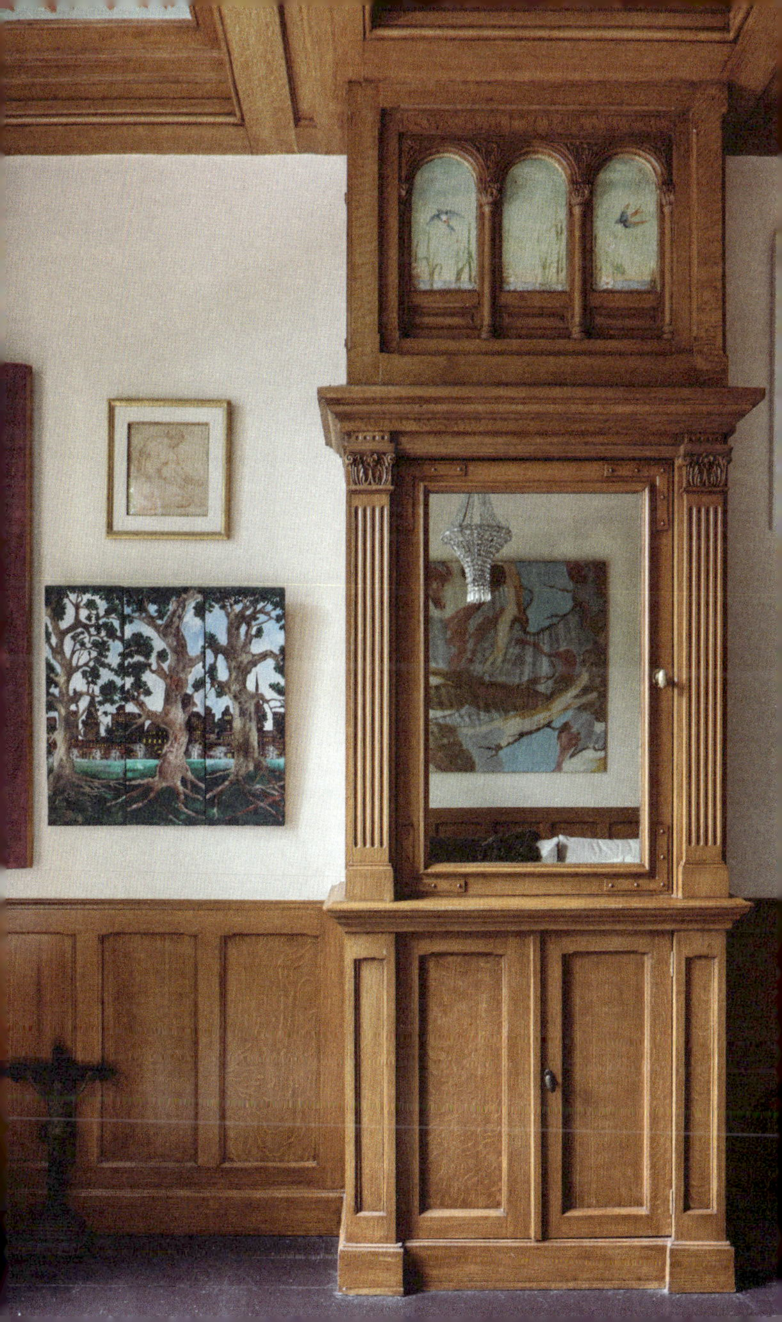

EFFEN IS SLECHT TREFFEN

Interior

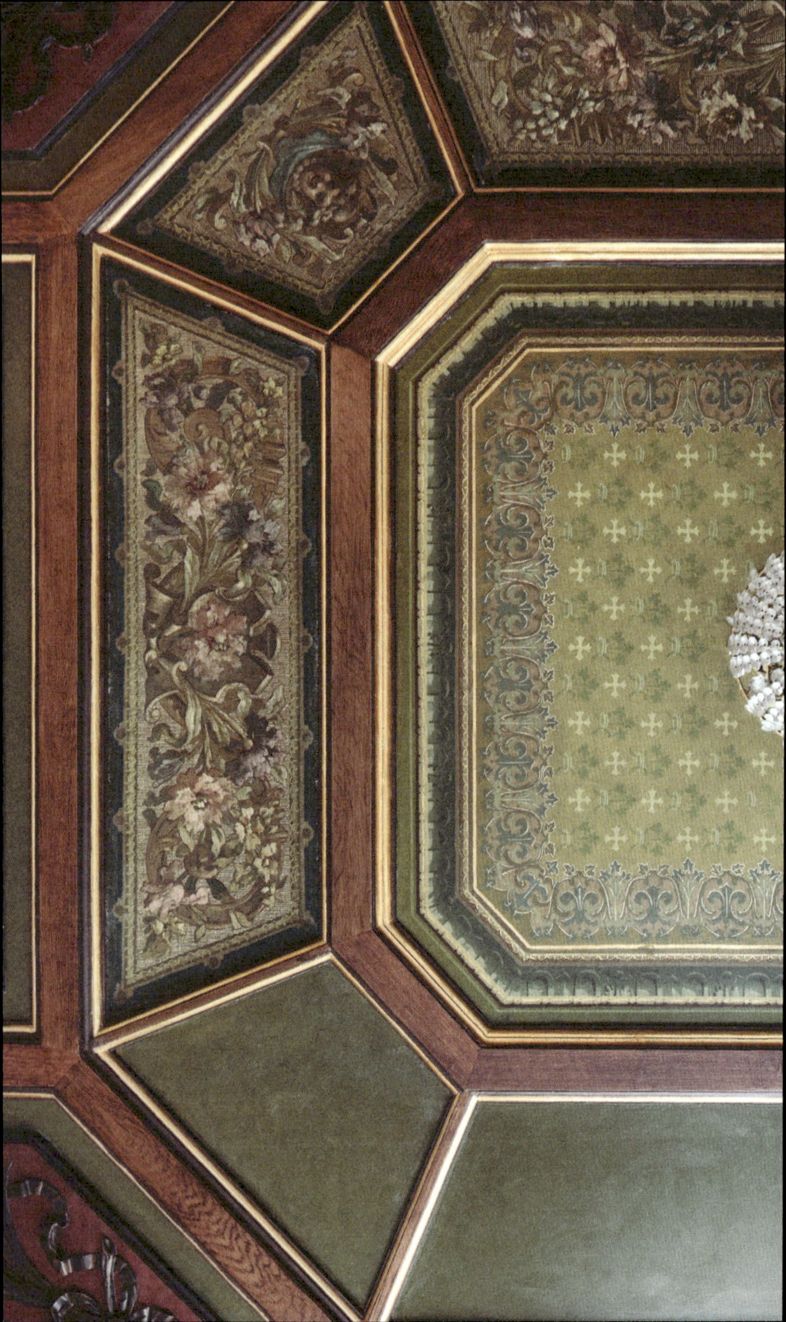

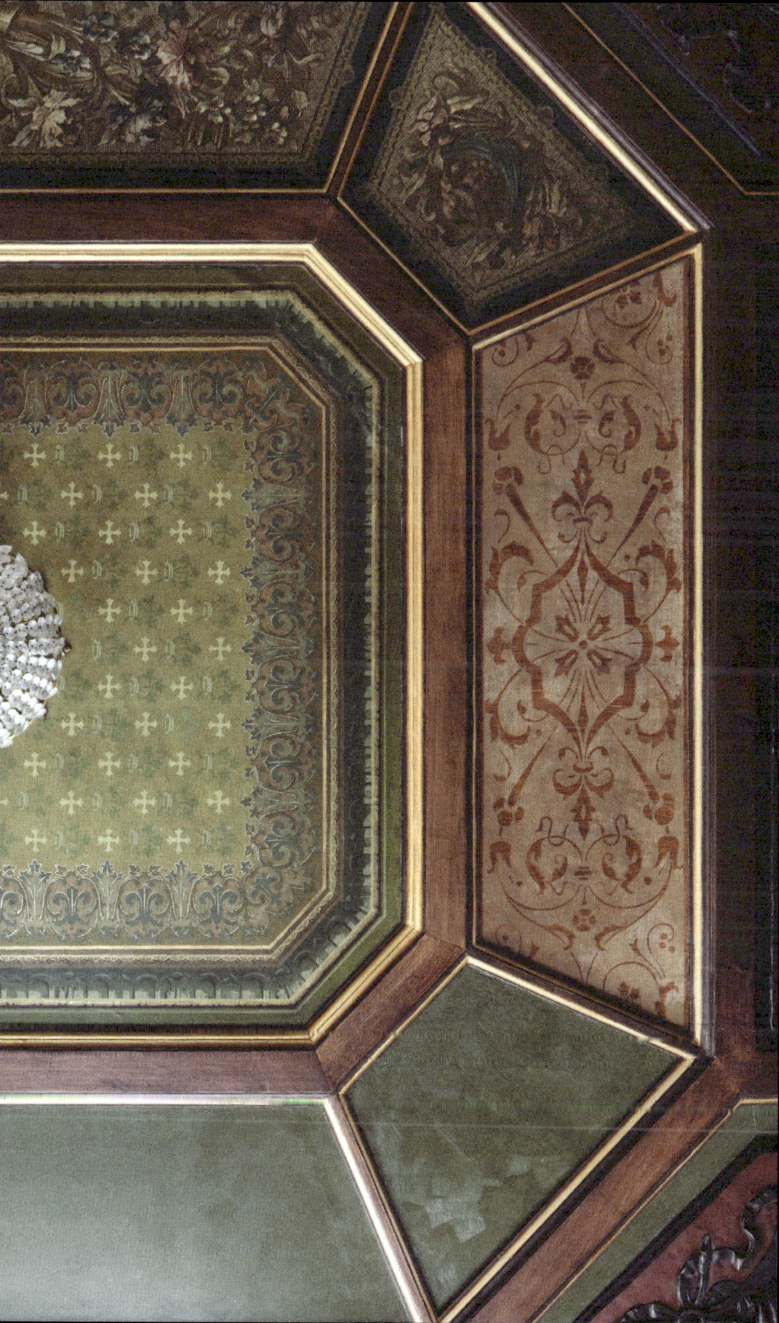

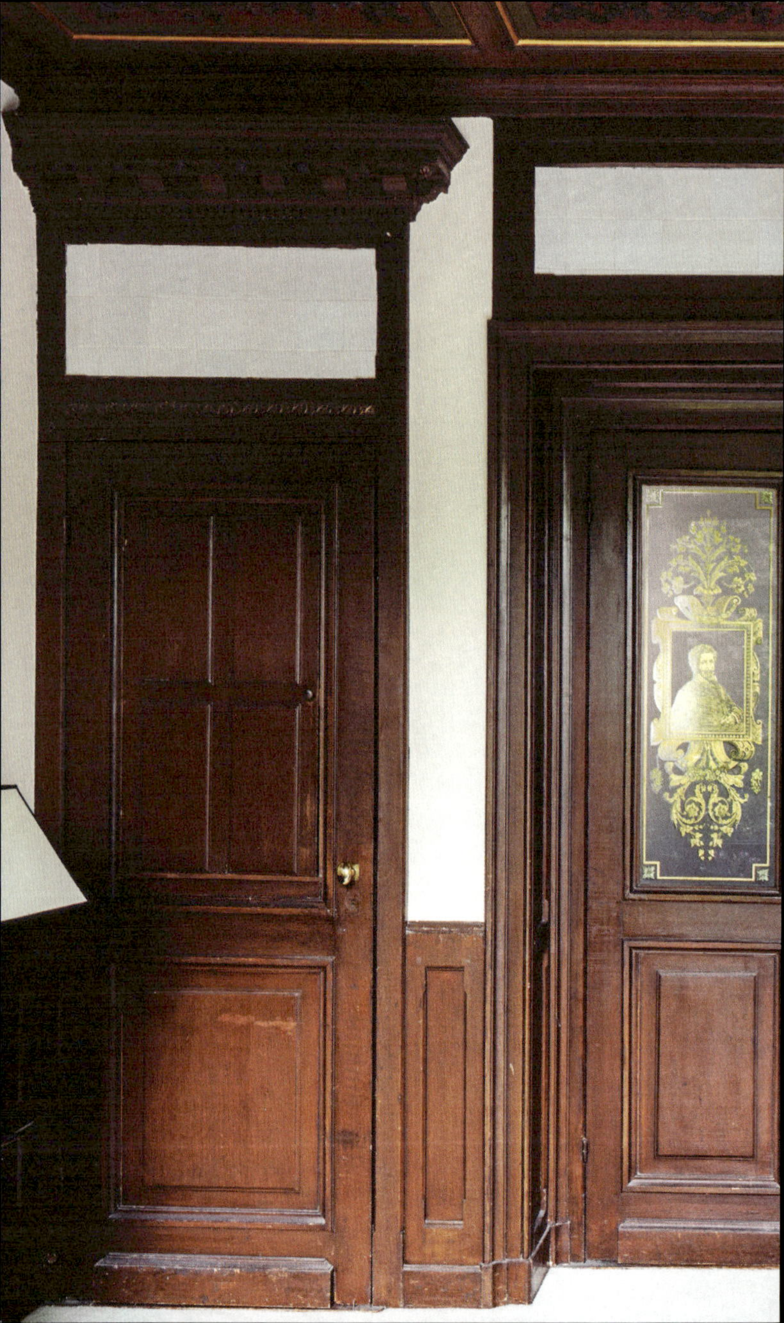

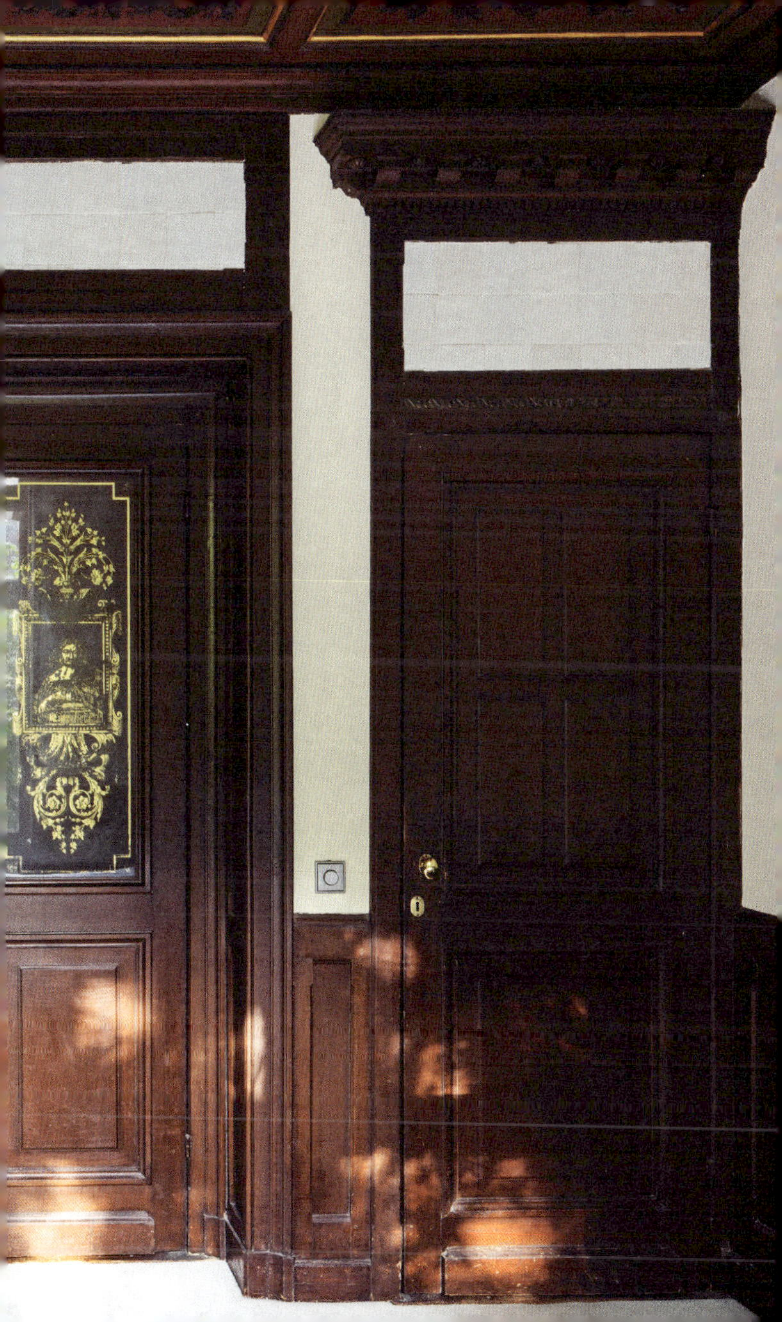

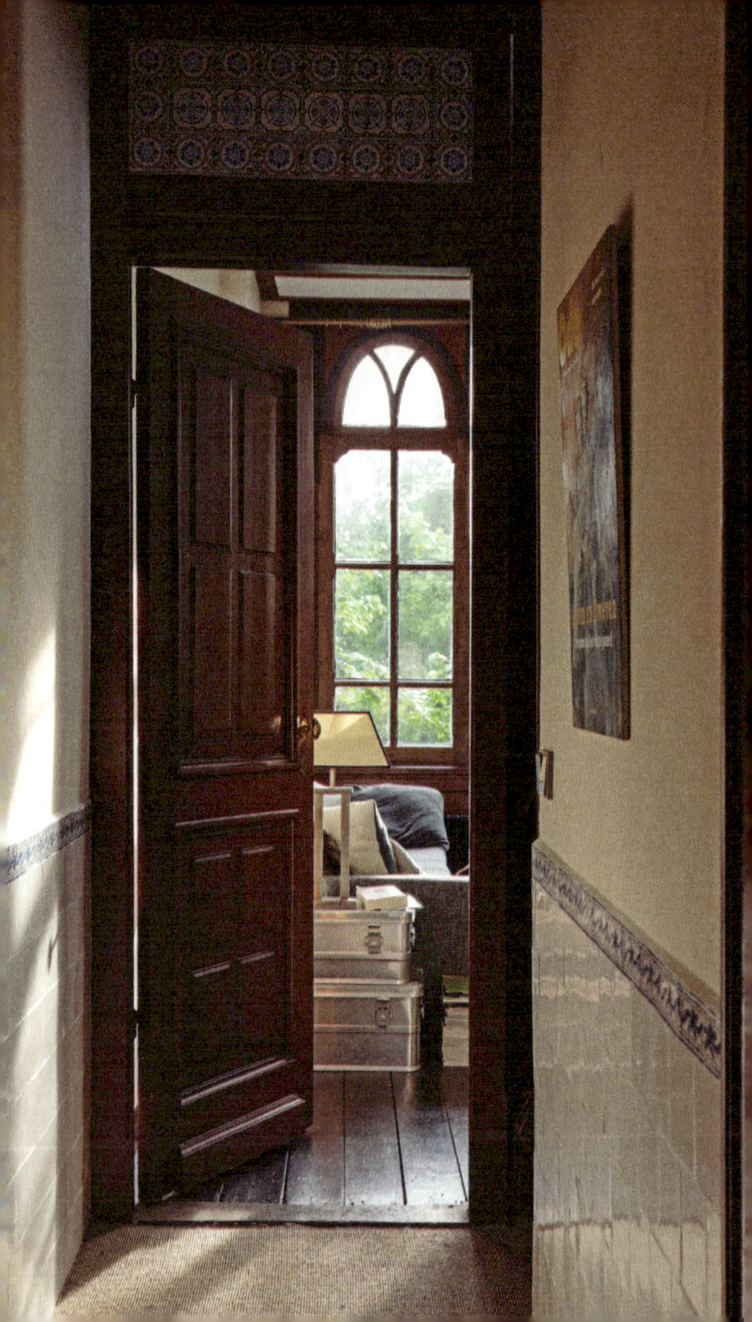

Interior

Reguliersgracht 63

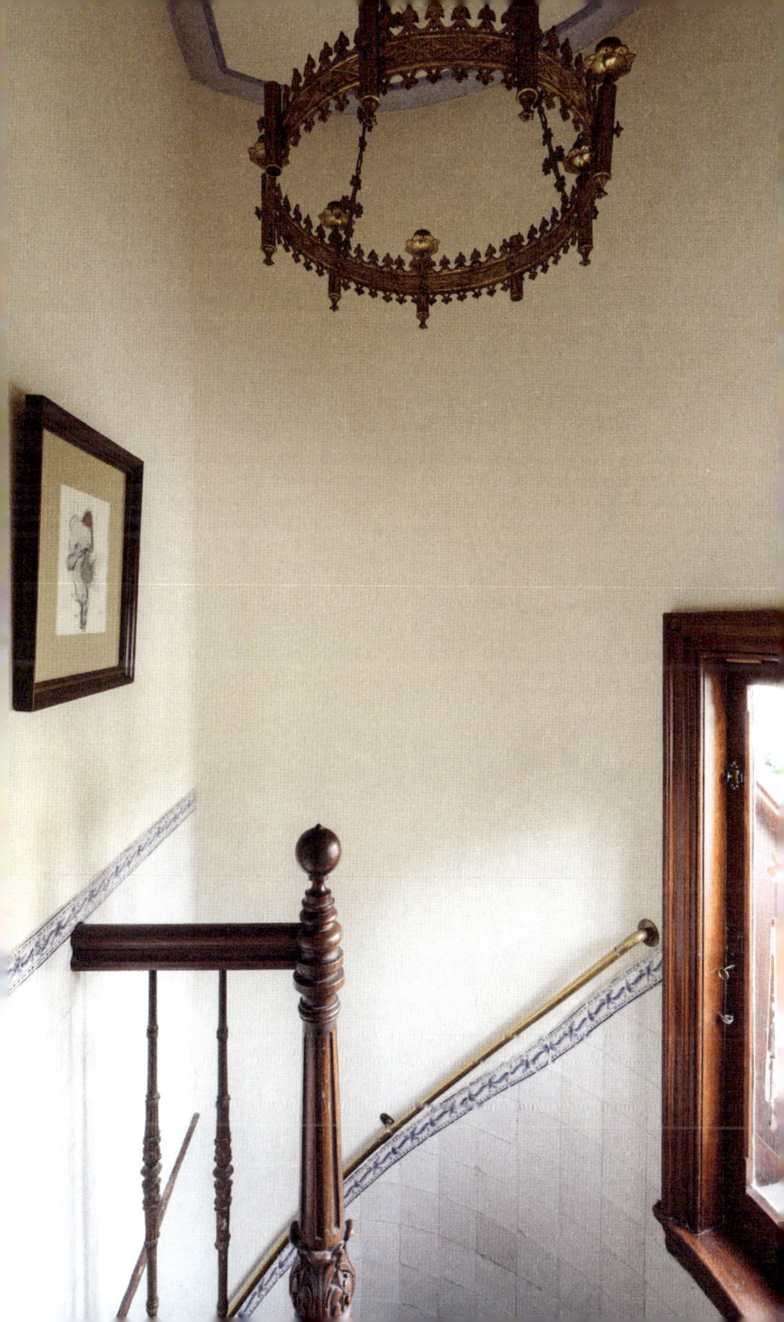

Architect Isaac Gosschalk

The influential architect Isaac Gosschalk (1838-1907) is the designer of this building. The design differs entirely from the completed building. It shows a cornice gable and a hip roof with an ornamental triangular gable end as finishing touch. However, the building has a gable end with a protruding bargeboard. The uppermost floor is executed like a wooden front with lots of glass. There is no basement, while on the ground floor there are two rooms that are not connected with each other, a front office and a rear office (or mangling room). He is also the architect of the Westergasfabriek and numerous Amsterdam buildings including the Heineken brewery. Architect of the members' club 'de Groote Club' on the Dam 1870/72, Reguliersgracht 57-59 (1879) and the Panorama building on the Plantage Middenlaan (1880), restaurant 'die Port van Cleve' on the Nieuwezijds Voorburgwal (1888), but also the train station of Groningen (1893). Three years before the building of Reguliersgracht 63, Gosschalk designed Reguliersgracht 57-59 for Deenik : a new workshop alias shop with a home above it. If you are standing on the canal, it is clear the same designer worked on this: both buildings have a lot of international and historical period features in the facade. In the case of number 63, that includes the timber construction of the bay window in English Queen Anne style on the third floor and the Dutch Renaissance. However, in terms of both facades Gosschalk references a medieval German atmosphere, which is characteristic of the historical interest of Gosschalk.

Portrait, 1886

De Groote Club, corner Kalverstraat / Paleisstraat (demolished 1913)

Interior

Panorama building Plantage Middenlaan (demolished 1935)

Brewery 'De Hooiberg' bought by Gerard Heineken in 1863 and replaced by new buildings on Stadhouderskade

Beverwijk presbytery

Address
Breestraat 101

Town
Beverwijk

Built
18th century

Acquisition
2011

Restoration
2012 – 2014

Restoration architect
Veldman Rietbroek Smit

Current use
Office

An extensive study preceded the restoration of the shell and the paintings in the period room of the former presbytery in Beverwijk. The initiative of Stadherstel through the purchase of this nationally listed building ties in with a long tradition. In the Golden Age, wealthy Amsterdam citizens bought plots in Beverwijk and the surrounding area in order to build town houses and country homes for personal use, mostly in the summer. The new inhabitants also brought prosperity to the agricultural Beverwijk. Researchers roughly indicated on a map of Daniel van Breen which buildings in the second half of the 17th century it would have concerned. The fact that not only the houses but also the complete plots were coloured in on the map is even more impressive. The merchant's house had already been in Amsterdam hands. (See page 398)

Beverwijk presbytery

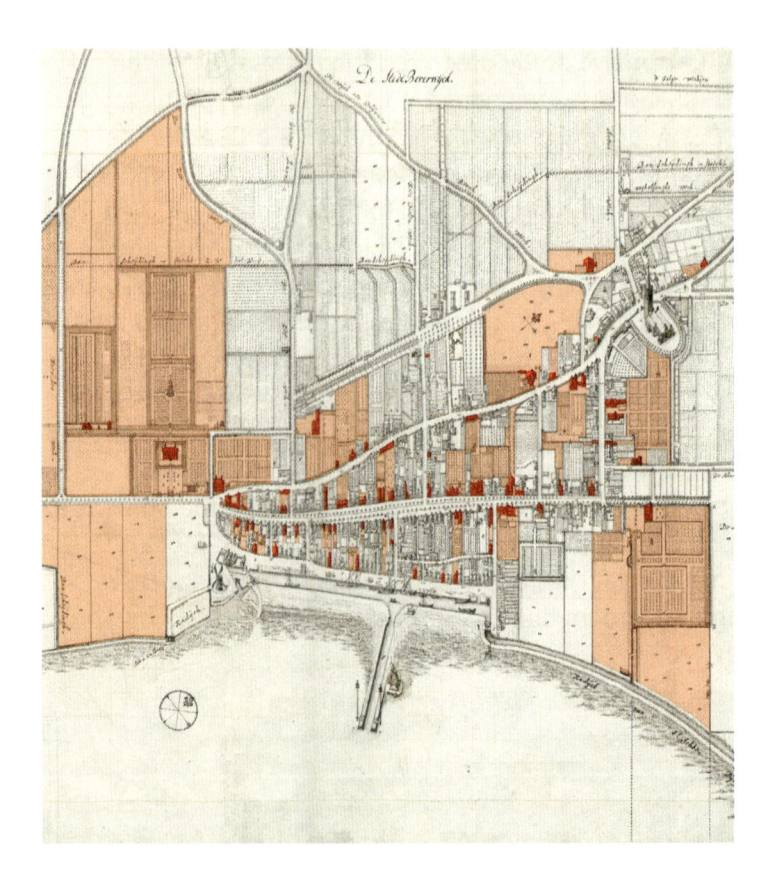

The presbytery in the centre of Beverwijk is on the corner of the Bloksteeg with the front facade on the Breestraat. Two rectangular building volumes connected behind each other are located behind the front facade. The first volume has two storeys and a hip roof. It is approximately 14 metres wide and nine metres deep. There is a space of nineteen by seven metres behind that of a storey with a hip roof. A composite structure was placed on three quarters of this with a truncated hip roof (special dormer). The roofs are covered with dark grey (braised) Roman roof tiles. The brick facades were constructed in cross bond, in which the brickwork has a weather-struck joint. Frames, windows, doors, gutters and ornaments are made of wood and painted in off-white or dark green. The plinth and weather bars are made of Belgian fossil. The front door is painted white. The biggest refurbishment during the use of the town house as presbytery is perhaps a change to the bay window on the rear facade at the same time as the construction of the church.

Interior

Front facade

Plan ground floor

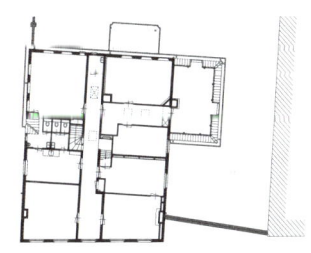

First floor

Beverwijk presbytery

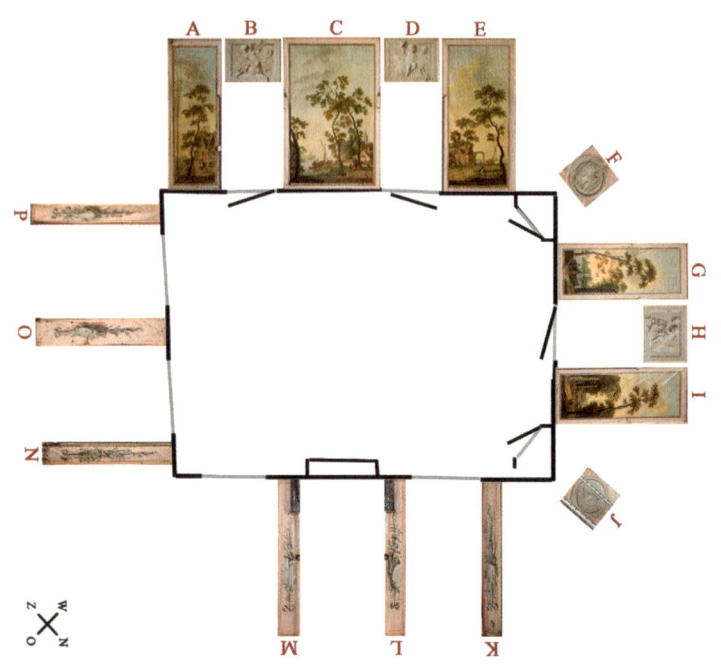

Schematic layout period room with position wall coverings

The 18th century period room

The architecture which we see now was created through the combination of numerous small buildings. In the 18th century, an Amsterdam merchant had a beautiful period room with wall paintings designed in his country home. The one in Beverwijk is considered unique, Stadsherstel put together an advisory committee of 20 members for its restoration. A team of specialists restored the works of Jacobus Luberti Augustini (Haarlem 1748 – 1822), who was trained by his father, who was also a landscape painter of large wall coverings. When you enter on the Breestraat, you see richly decorated stucco ceilings with a pattern of flowers and bows. Above all doors opening out onto the hall, there is a same kind of ornamentation in the form fruit, scales, music instruments, gardening tools and urns. This style is also utilised in the period room (the front room on the right-hand side). The corner sections of the cornices are even more richly decorated, with symbols of Law, Trade and Religion. The five large wall coverings, made around 1760, display idealised Dutch landscapes. Between and next to the windows, six small canvases, the *grisailles*, can be seen, each canvas with a different theme: Poetry and Painting, Music, Architecture, Sculpture and Science or Industrial.

Interior

401

Wall (southwest) after removing wall paintings

Sensitive edge of Landscape G

Landscape G before restoration

Grisaille M during removing surface dirt

Detail Landscape G during varnish removal

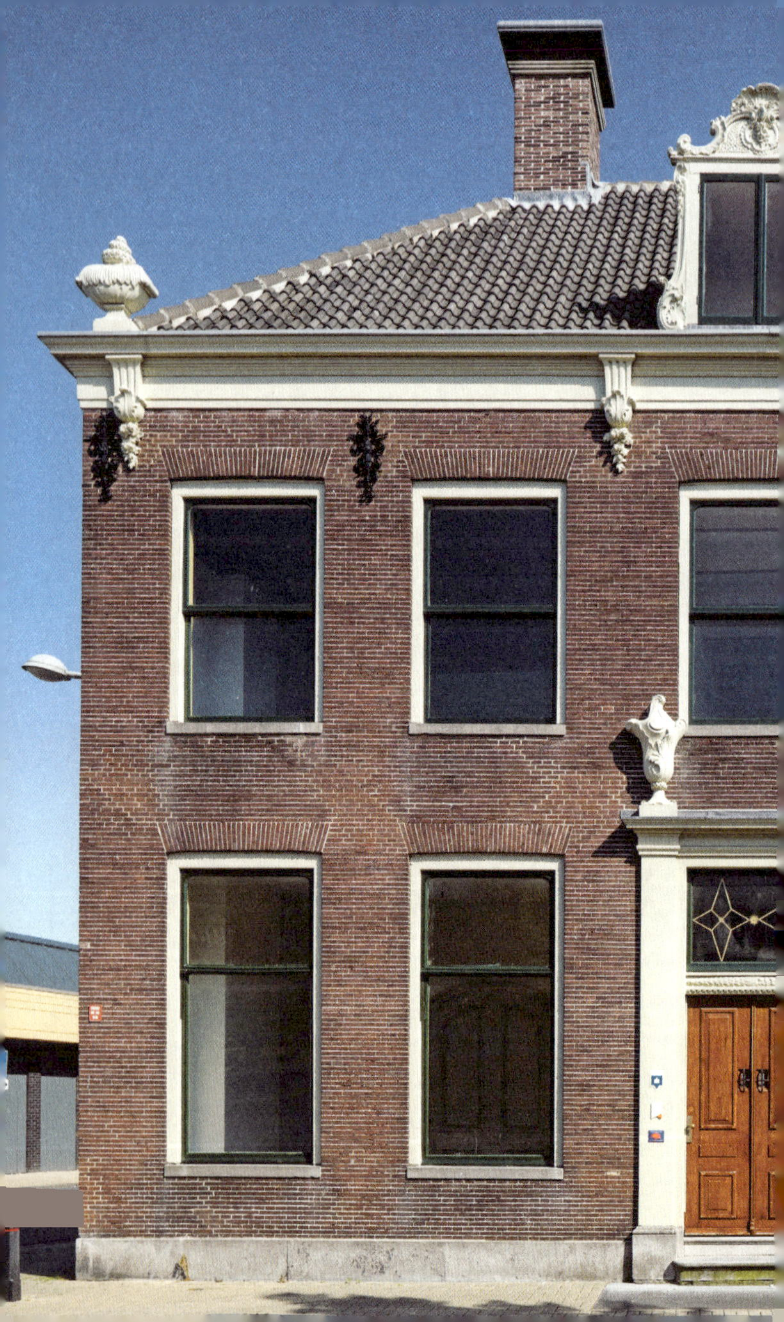

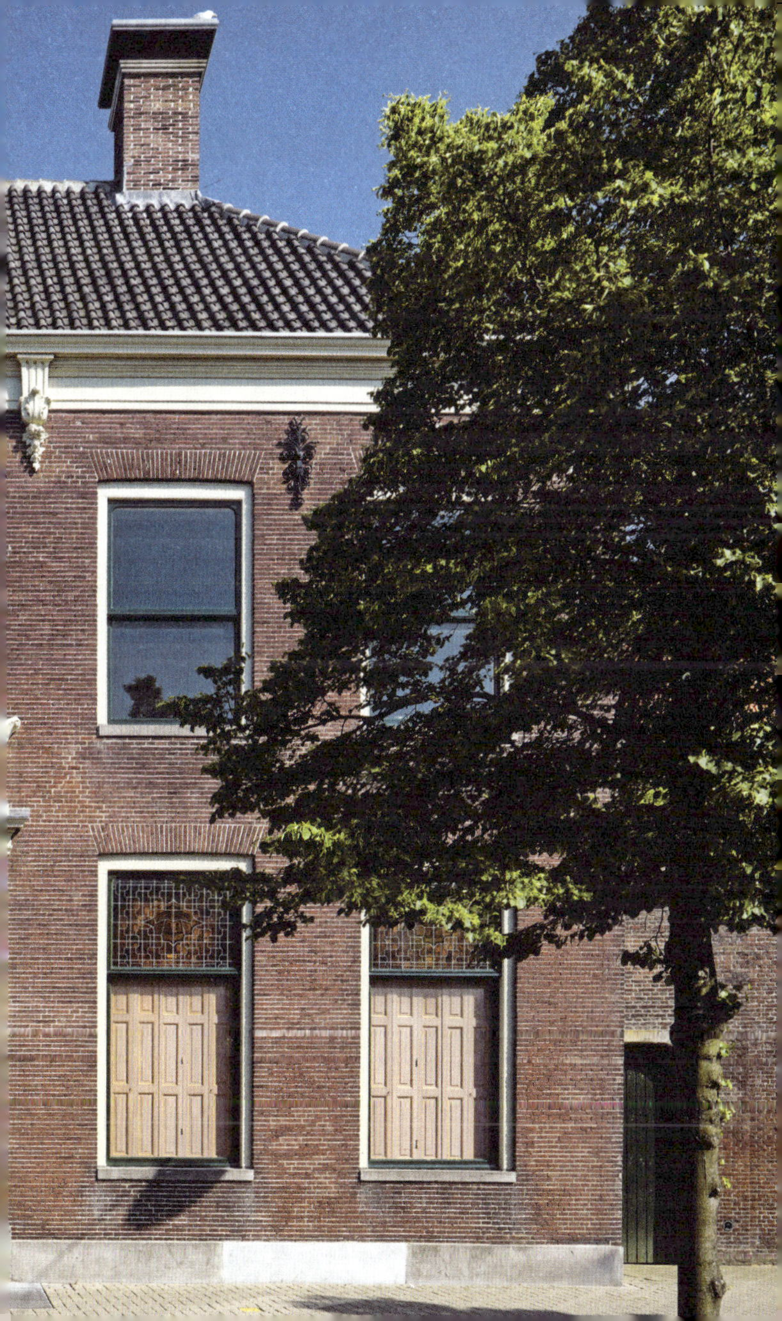

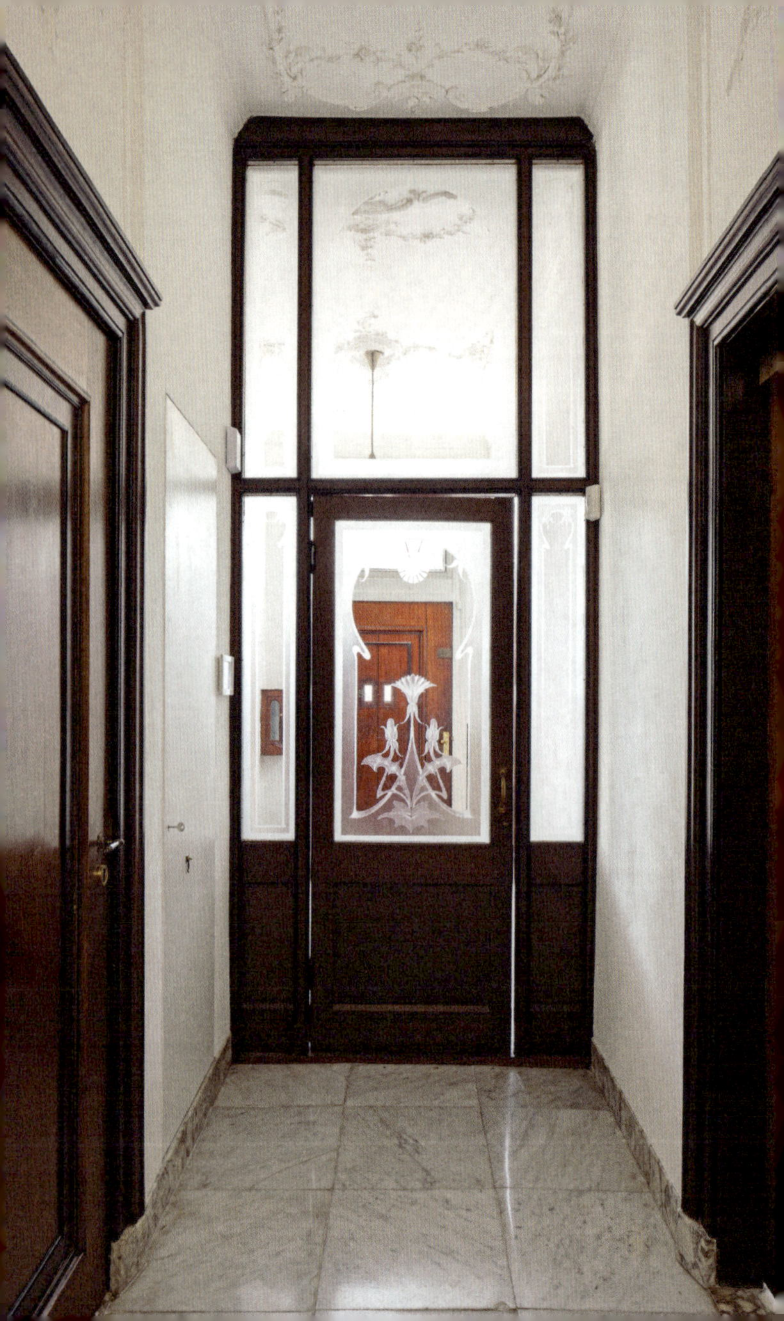

Interior

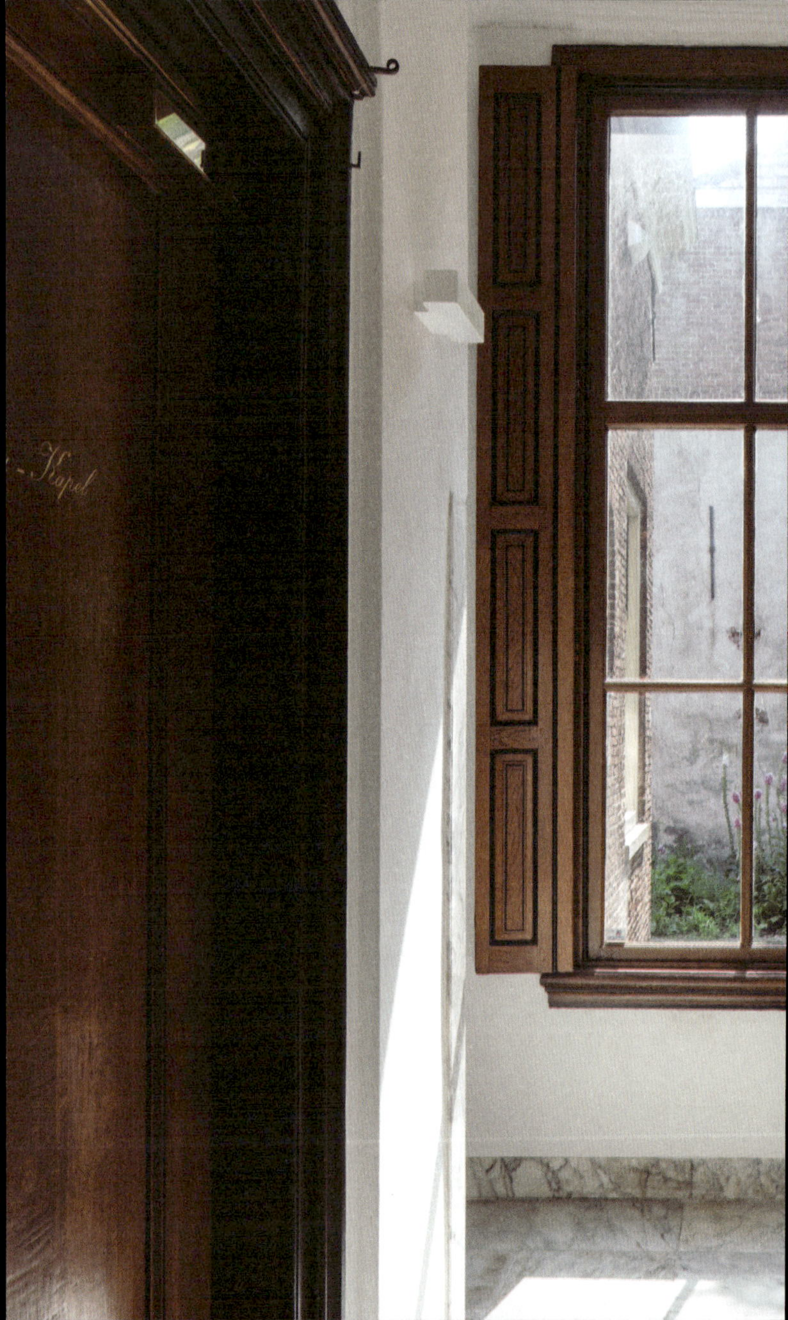
-Kapel

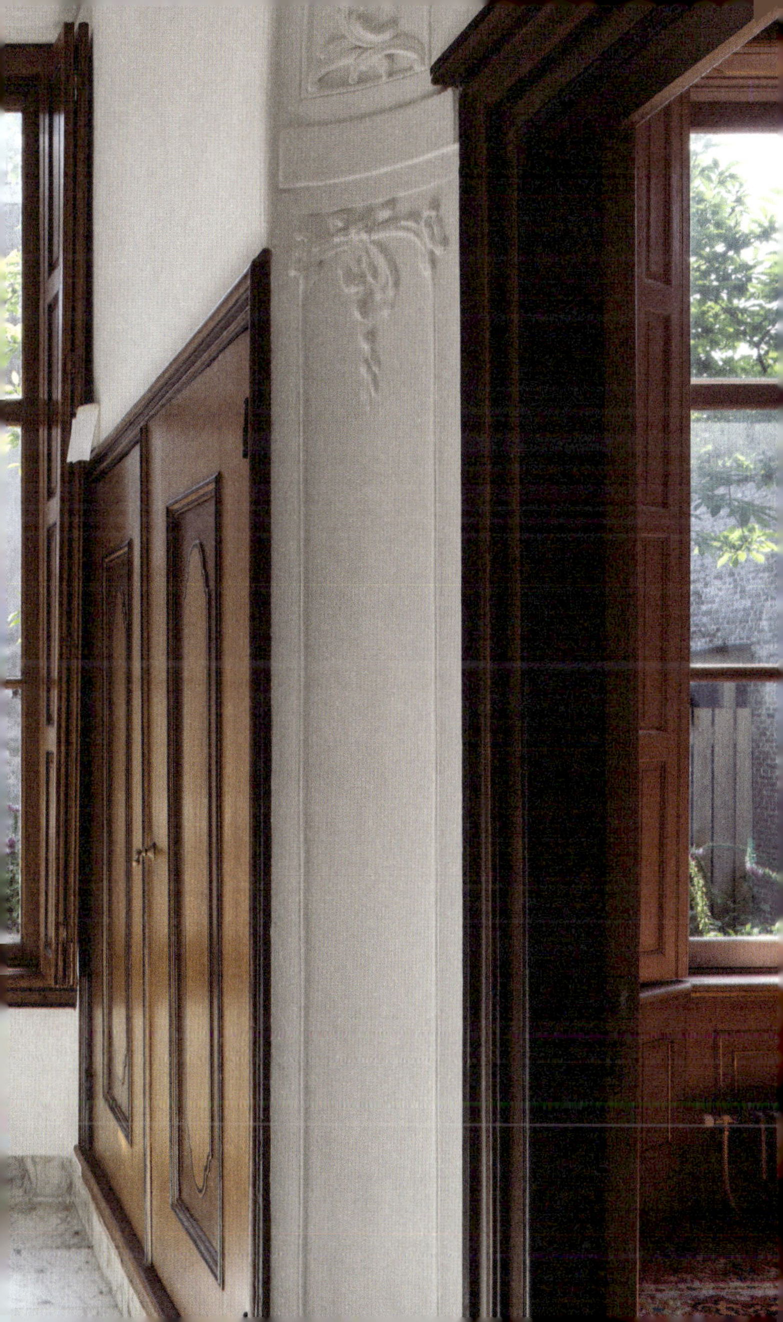

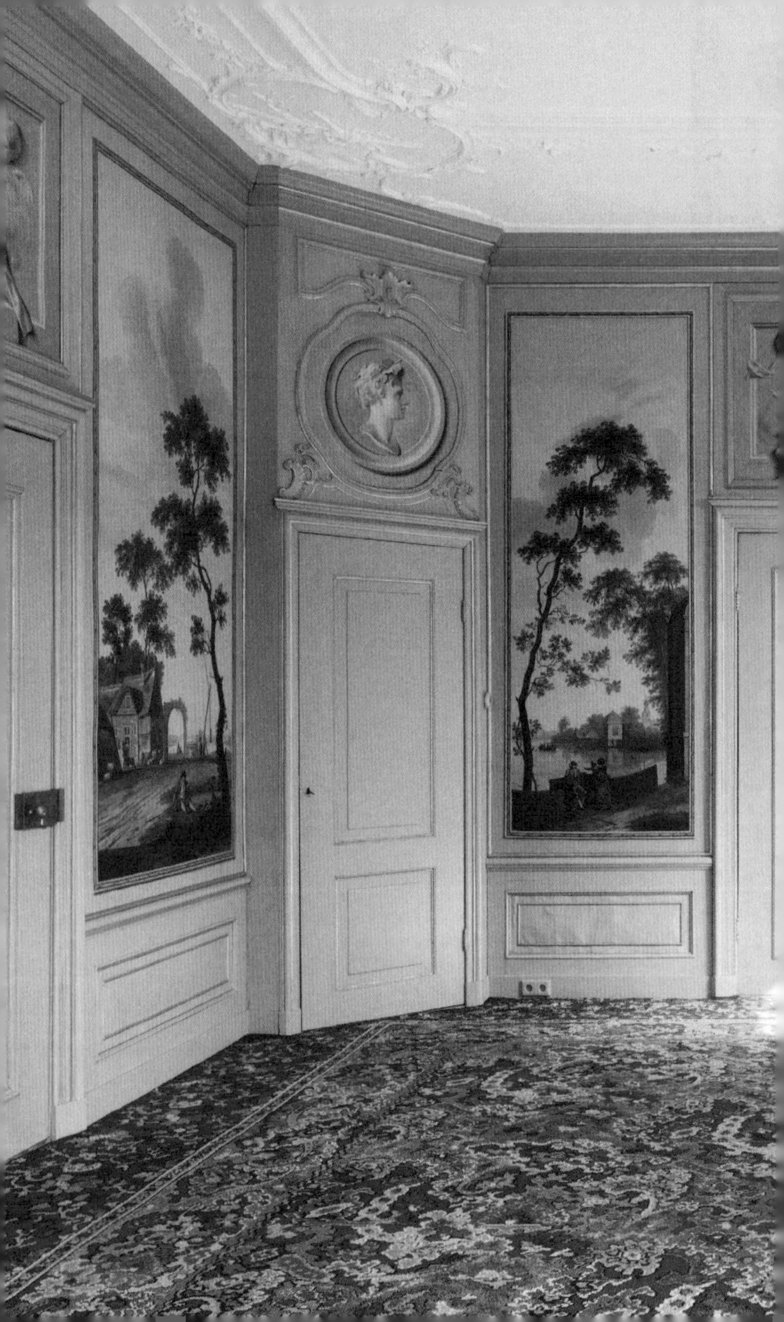

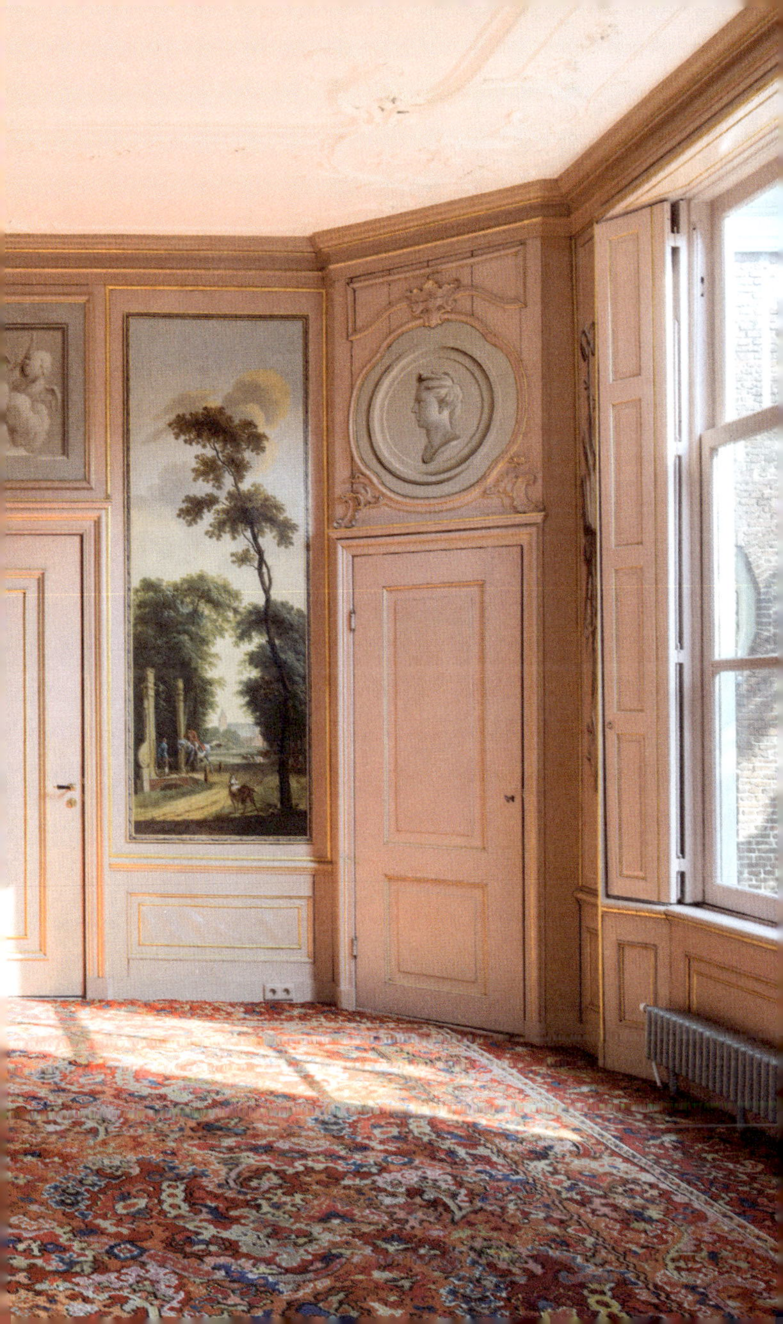

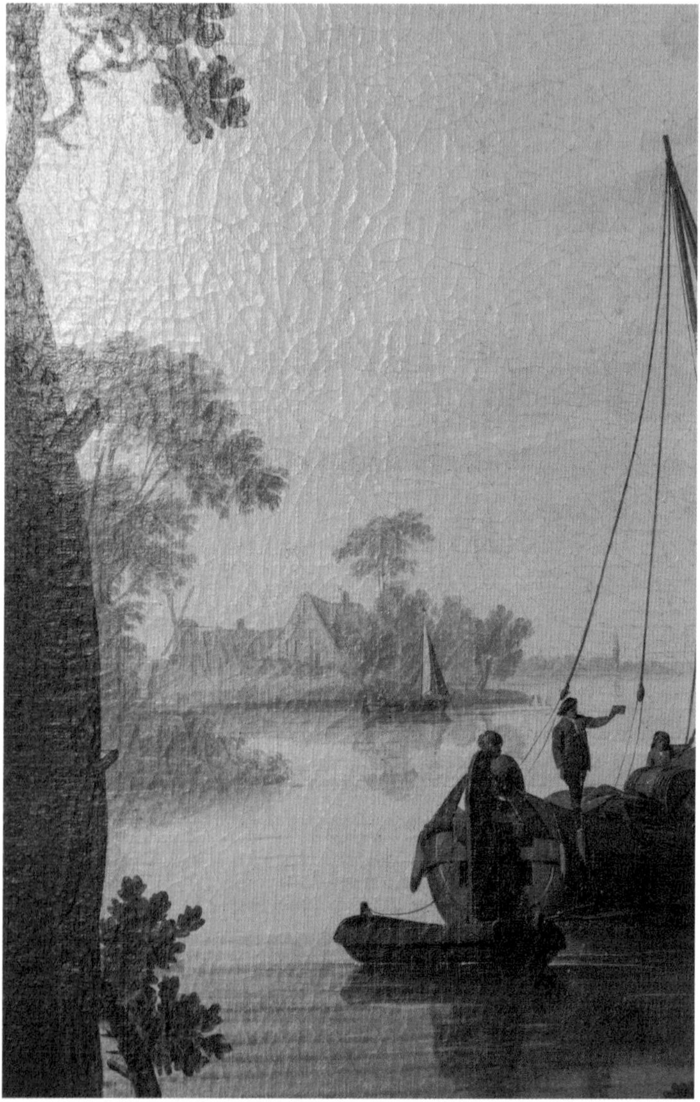

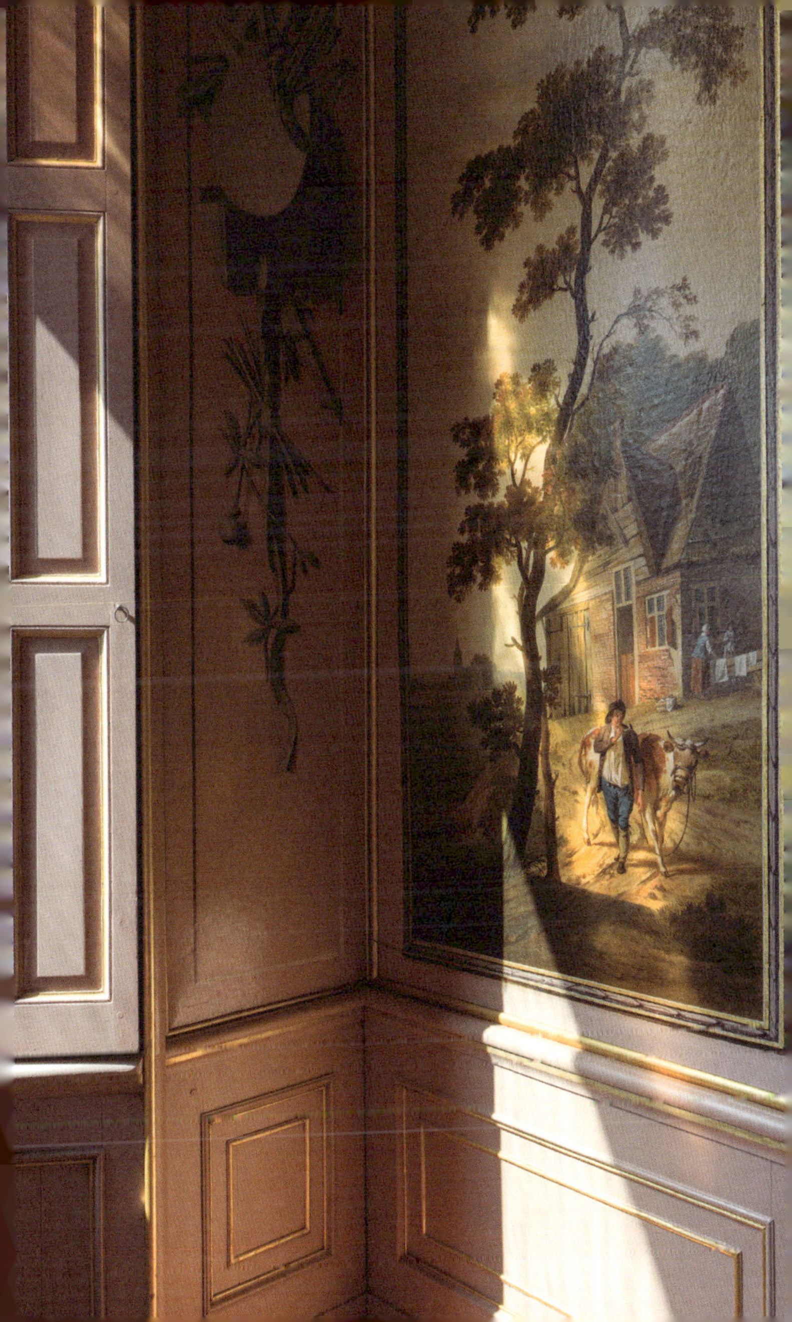

412

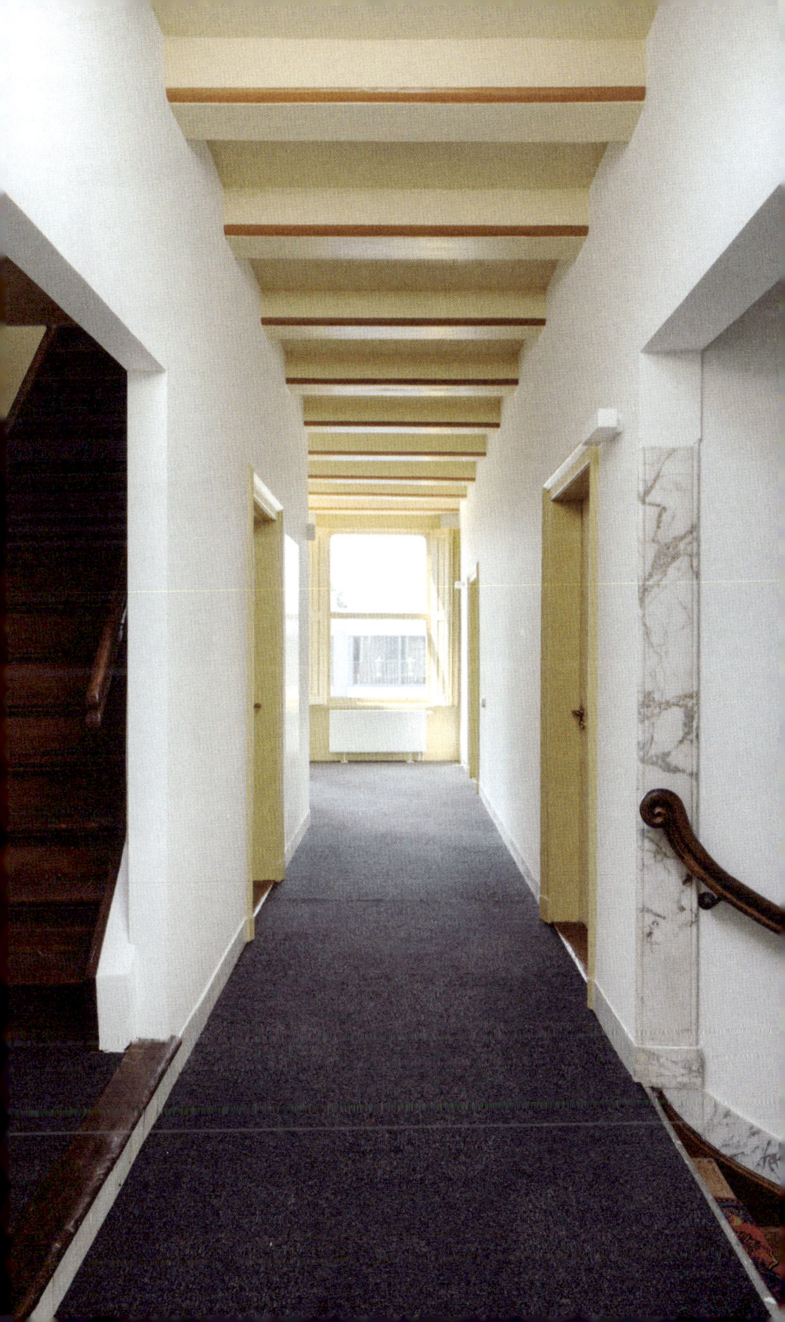

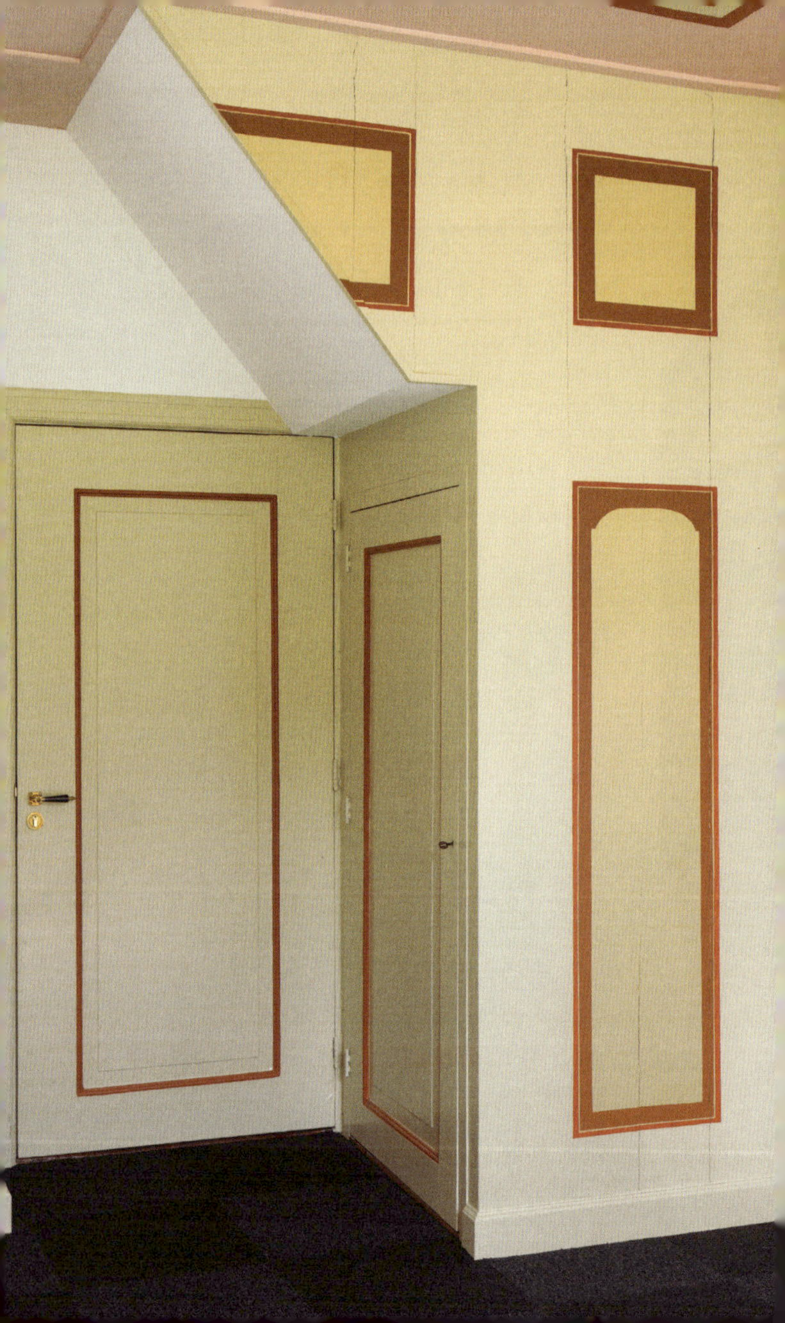

Interior

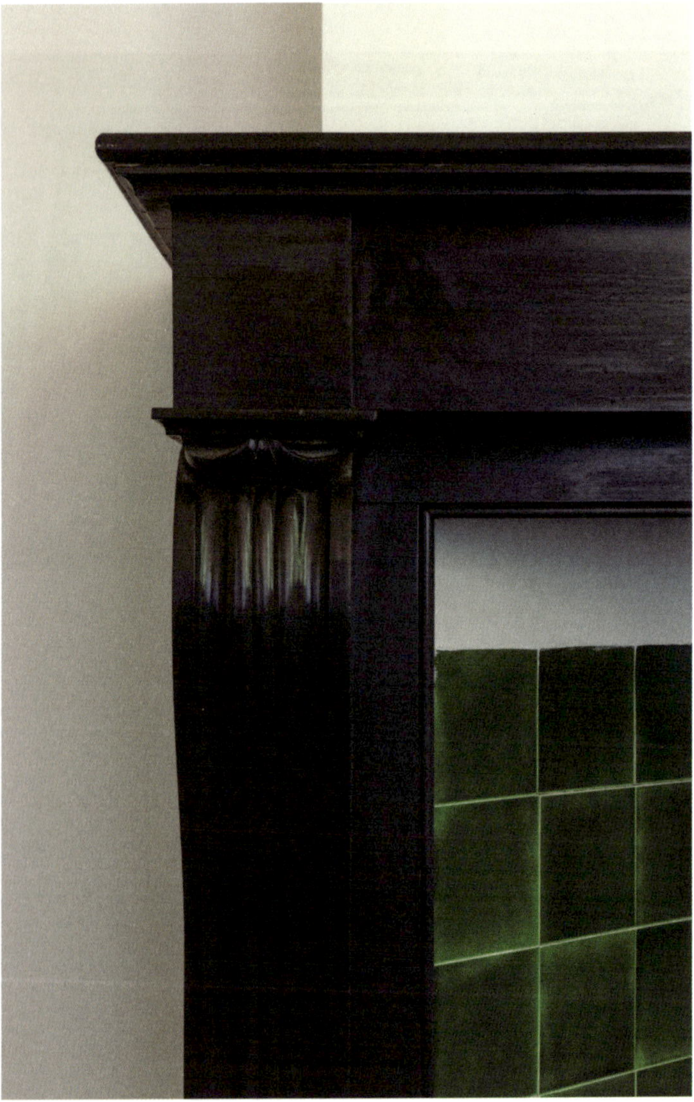

Reuse of gables

In July 2009, the 17th century nationally listed building Runstraat 4 (the 9 streets) was ready after a substantial restoration that lasted one and a half years. The building, purchased in 1988, underwent a true metamorphosis, to which the Association of Friends of Stadsherstel contributed with the financing of a new gable. It started with a packed front facade and a top that had disappeared. The remainder of the facade dated from the mid-18th century, while the front was from about 1800. The original bell gable can still be seen on a 1917 photo at the image collection of the municipal archives (Beeldbank Stadsarchief). During the restoration, however, a 'new' neck gable top was placed on the building, which came from the defunct listed building wharf next to the Uilenburger Synagogue. A clock with a suitable width could not be found. The specimen, which as appropriate in terms of architectural style and elevation, counteracts the later trivialisation of the facade. The relocation of the gables is somewhat controversial in the world of listed buildings. It would be falsification of history and affect the authenticity. However, Stadsherstel bases its views on the fact that gables used to be made in series in the studios of stonemasons. Builders could pick out an appropriate specimen on the spot for the house under construction. The tops are, therefore, actually interchangeable. The tops of demolished buildings were already being reused on other houses in the 17th and 18th century. The reuse of tops has also occurred many times in the last decades with the approval and even encouragement of, for example, Amsterdam Monuments and Archaeology. This form of urban restoration greatly enriches the cityscape. The Association of Friends of the Amsterdam Inner City is doing its utmost to have the historic gables of demolished buildings replaced. Thijs Kaas is the architect who worked out the plans for Runstraat 4 in detail and supervised the construction. The gable was restored and replaced by Snoep and Vermeer natural stone works.

Runstraat 4
Amsterdam

Neck gables

Amstel 87
Amsterdam

Amstel 95
Amsterdam

Bloemgracht 34
Amsterdam

Binnen Vissersstraat 23
Amsterdam

Geldersekade 78
Amsterdam

Herengracht 35
Amsterdam

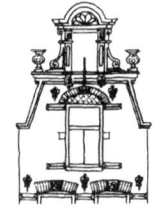

Herenstraat 36
Amsterdam

Hoogte Kadijk 12
Amsterdam

Hoogte Kadijk 76
Amsterdam

Kerkstraat 192-194-196-198
Amsterdam

Gables 419

Kerkstraat 396
Amsterdam

Lange Leidsedwarsstraat 31
Amsterdam

Langestraat 76
Amsterdam

Nieuwe Herengracht 219-221
Amsterdam

Nieuwe Nieuwstraat 27
Amsterdam

Nieuwe Prinsengracht 29
Amsterdam

Noorderdwarsstraat 7
Amsterdam

Oude Looierstraat 55
Amsterdam

Oudezijds Voorburgwal 1
Amsterdam

Prinsengracht 1A
Amsterdam

Roomolenstraat 11
Amsterdam

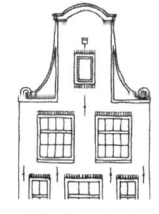

Vijzelgracht 39
Amsterdam

Bell-shaped gables

Amstel 316-318
Amsterdam

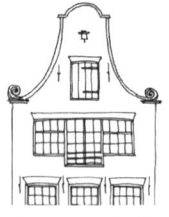

Brouwersgracht 62
Amsterdam

Eerste Laurierdwarsstraat 50
Amsterdam

Geldersekade 15
Amsterdam

Herenmarkt 9
Amsterdam

Kerkstraat 326
Amsterdam

Koestraat 20
Amsterdam

Kerkstraat 184-186-188
Amsterdam

Koestraat 22
Amsterdam

Lange Niezel 22
Amsterdam

Leliegracht 36
Amsterdam

Gables

Muiderstraat 24
Amsterdam

Nieuwe Herengracht 45
Amsterdam

Nieuwe Nieuwstraat 19
Amsterdam

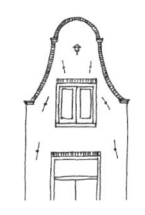

Noorderkerkstraat 2
Amsterdam

Oudezijds Voorburgwal 67
Amsterdam

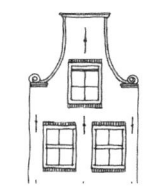

Prins Hendrikkade 87
Amsterdam

Prinsengracht 5
Amsterdam

Rusland 10-12
Amsterdam

Spinhuissteeg 12
Amsterdam

Spuistraat 61
Amsterdam

Spuistraat 255B
Amsterdam

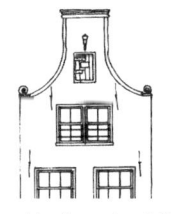

Utrechtsedwarsstraat 106
Amsterdam

Cornice fronts

Amstel 176
Amsterdam

Bergstraat 2-4
Amsterdam

Brouwersgracht 135
Amsterdam

Egelantiersgracht 53
Amsterdam

Haarlemmerdijk 55
Amsterdam

Herengracht 325
Amsterdam

Herenstraat 34
Amsterdam

Kalkmarkt 10
Amsterdam

Kerkstraat 323
Amsterdam

Nieuwe Herengracht 47
Amsterdam

Nieuwe Herengracht 49
Amsterdam

Gables

Nieuwe Herengracht 71
Amsterdam

Nieuwe Leliestraat 183
Amsterdam

Oudezijds Achterburgwal 199
Amsterdam

Oudezijds Voorburgwal 2
Amsterdam

Overtoom 371-373
Amsterdam

Prinsengracht 206
Amsterdam

Reguliersgracht 70
Amsterdam

Reguliersgracht 95
Amsterdam

Rusland 27
Amsterdam

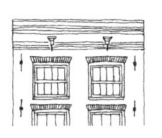

Singel 368
Amsterdam

Vinkenstraat 74
Amsterdam

Warmoesstraat 15
Amsterdam

Spout gables and stepped gables

Bethaniënstraat 14
Amsterdam

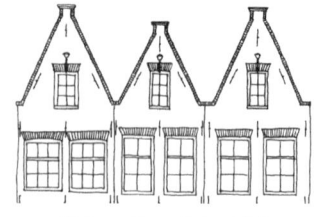

Dirk van Hasseltsteeg 2-6
Amsterdam

Oudezijds Kolk 1
Amsterdam

Leidsegracht 106
Amsterdam

Marnixstraat 291
Amsterdam

Pijlsteeg 35
Amsterdam

Tuinstraat 51-55
Amsterdam

Spuistraat 255B
Amsterdam

Korte Prinsengracht 5
Amsterdam

Lange Niezel 10
Amsterdam

Sint Annenstraat 12
Amsterdam

Relocation

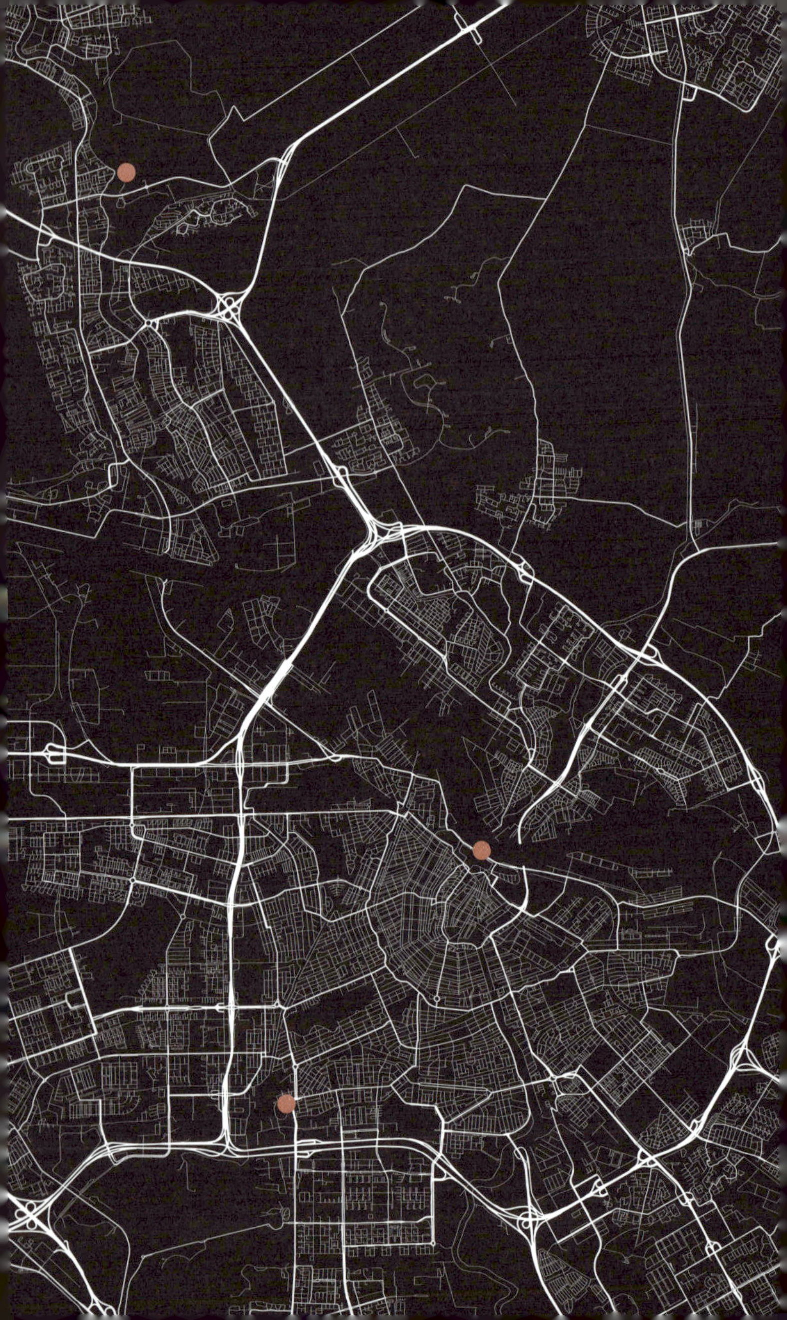

428	**De Kwakels 1**, Zaanse Schans
428	**Kalverringdijk 1**, Zaanse Schans
428	**Kalverringdijk 3**, Zaanse Schans
428	**Kalverringdijk 5**, Zaanse Schans
428	**Kalverringdijk 7**, Zaanse Schans
428	**Kalverringdijk 8**, Zaanse Schans
428	**Kalverringdijk 9**, Zaanse Schans
428	**Kalverringdijk 10**, Zaanse Schans
428	**Kalverringdijk 11**, Zaanse Schans
429	**Kalverringdijk 17**, Zaanse Schans
429	**Kalverringdijk 19**, Zaanse Schans
429	**Kalverringdijk 21**, Zaanse Schans
429	**Schansend 1**, Zaanse Schans
429	**Zeilenmakerspad 1**, Zaanse Schans
429	**Zeilenmakerspad 2**, Zaanse Schans
430	**Zeilenmakerspad 3**, Zaanse Schans
430	**Zeilenmakerspad 4**, Zaanse Schans
430	**Zonnewijzerspad 1 – 2**, Zaanse Schans
430	**Zonnewijzerspad 5**, Zaanse Schans
430	**Zonnewijzerspad 6**, Zaanse Schans
430	**Zonnewijzerspad 7**, Zaanse Schans
430	**Zonnewijzerspad 8**, Zaanse Schans
448	**Weaver's House**, Zaanse Schans
460	**Naco House**, Amsterdam
470	**Olympic post office**, Amsterdam

Zaanse Schans

428

De Kwakels 1
Zaanse Schans
2009

Kalverringdijk 1
Zaanse Schans
2009

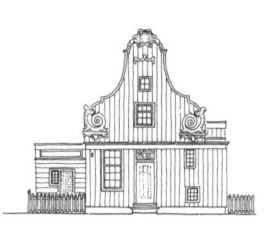

Kalverringdijk 3
Zaanse Schans
2009

Kalverringdijk 5
Zaanse Schans
2009

Kalverringdijk 7
Zaanse Schans
2009

Kalverringdijk 8
Zaanse Schans
2009

Kalverringdijk 9
Zaanse Schans
2009

Kalverringdijk 10
Zaanse Schans
2009

Kalverringdijk 11
Zaanse Schans
2009

Relocation

429

Kalverringdijk 17
Zaanse Schans
2009

Kalverringdijk 19
Zaanse Schans
2009

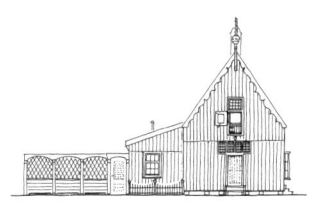

Kalverringdijk 21
Zaanse Schans
2009

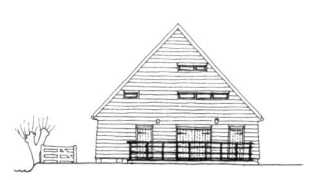

Schansend 1
Zaanse Schans
2009

Zeilenmakerspad 1
Zaanse Schans
2009

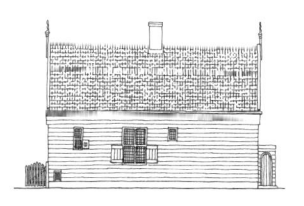

Zeilenmakerspad 2
Zaanse Schans
2009

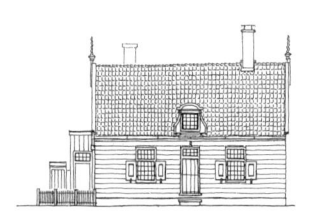

Zaanse Schans

Zeilenmakerspad 3
Zaanse Schans
2009

Zeilenmakerspad 4
Zaanse Schans
2009

Zonnewijzerspad 1-2
Zaanse Schans
2009

Zonnewijzerspad 5
Zaanse Schans
2009

Zonnewijzerspad 6
Zaanse Schans
2009

Zonnewijzerspad 7
Zaanse Schans
2009

Zonnewijzerspad 8
Zaanse Schans
2009

The reason for establishing Stadsherstel Zaanstreek was the acquisition of 23 monumental houses on the Zaanse Schans at the end of 2009. The area of activity of the new organisation, a collaboration between the local housing association Parteon and Stadsherstel, includes the preservation of historic heritage in the municipality of Zaanstad. The Zaanse Schans, a neighbourhood in this municipality to the north-west of Amsterdam, is a fine example of a historic village, although it did not yet exist 70 years ago. It is situated on the east bank of the river Zaan in the peat landscape of the Kalverpolder. The village has developed into one of the most well-known Dutch tourist attractions with millions of visitors each year. It is not a museum formally, but in light of the current aim and intention to preserve the historic heritage, it does come close to a museum experience. The houses and shops can, however, be rented normally. The Zaanse Schans is a purpose-designed architectural structure, a reconstruction of a local ribbon village that would have existed in the 17th and 18th century.

Relocation

The neighbourhood has not, therefore, undergone a centuries-old historical development. The heritage here is made up of original restored houses, workshops and mills that were, for the most part, moved to this spot between 1961 and 1974, supplemented by a number of replicas. The buildings or building sections have also been transported since that time by boat and lorry or flatbed trailers to a location where they have been given a new, second life. For example, Zonnewijzerspad 1 – 2 was brought to the Schans in its entirety by lorry. Kalveringdijk 17 – 19 arrived by boat. The historic buildings hindered urban developments at their original location and they now have the status of nationally listed building or municipal monument in their new setting due to their high architectural-historical value. The same applies to the mills. Only the substructures of the dye mill De Kat (originally an oil mill), as well as the oil mill De Bonte Hen and the mill De Os, are still located on their original land. In the village one can find, among other things, the Museum of the Dutch Clock, Bakery Museum De Gecroonde Duyvekater and a replica of the first grocery store of the Dutch supermarket chain Albert Heijn (founded in Zaandam). The fact that relocation remains topical is proven, among other things, by the plans for the establishment of the Mill Museum from Koog aan de Zaan and the reconstruction of a weaver's house from Assendelft.

Relocation

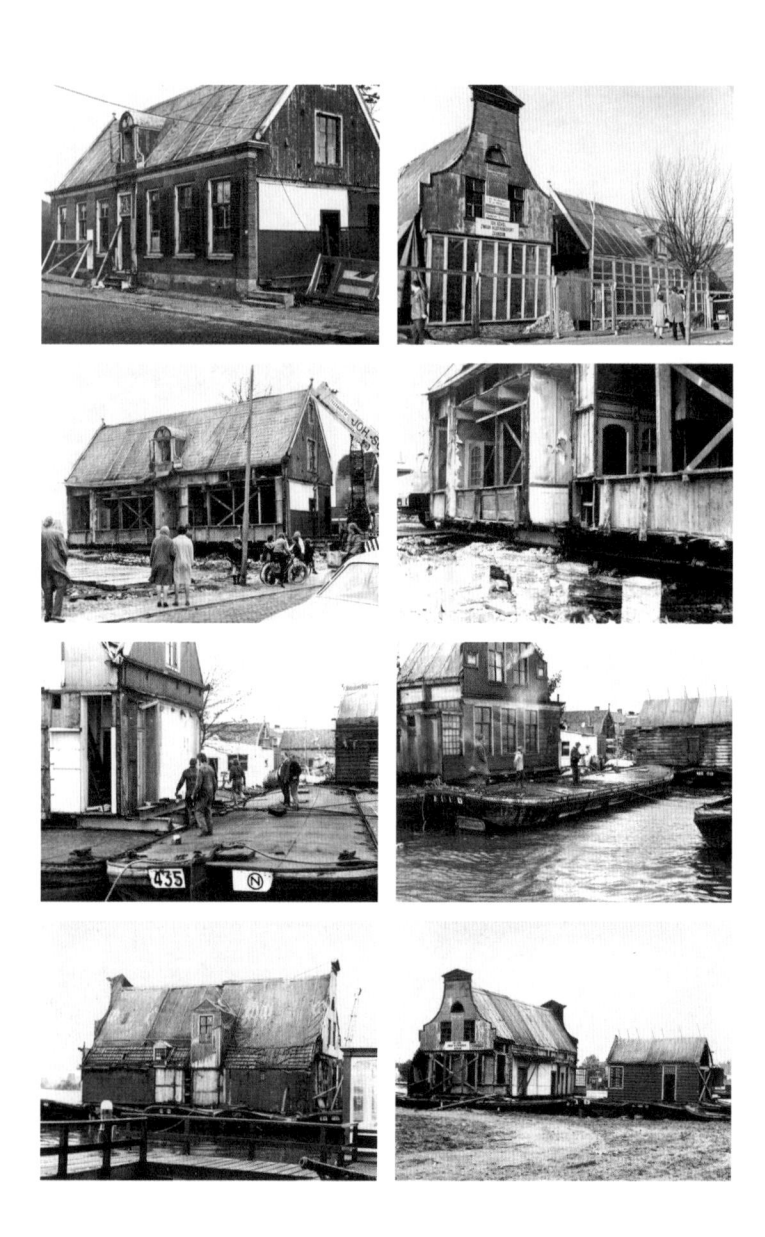

Zaanse Schans

'T KOOPMANSHUYS D'MOL A° 1795

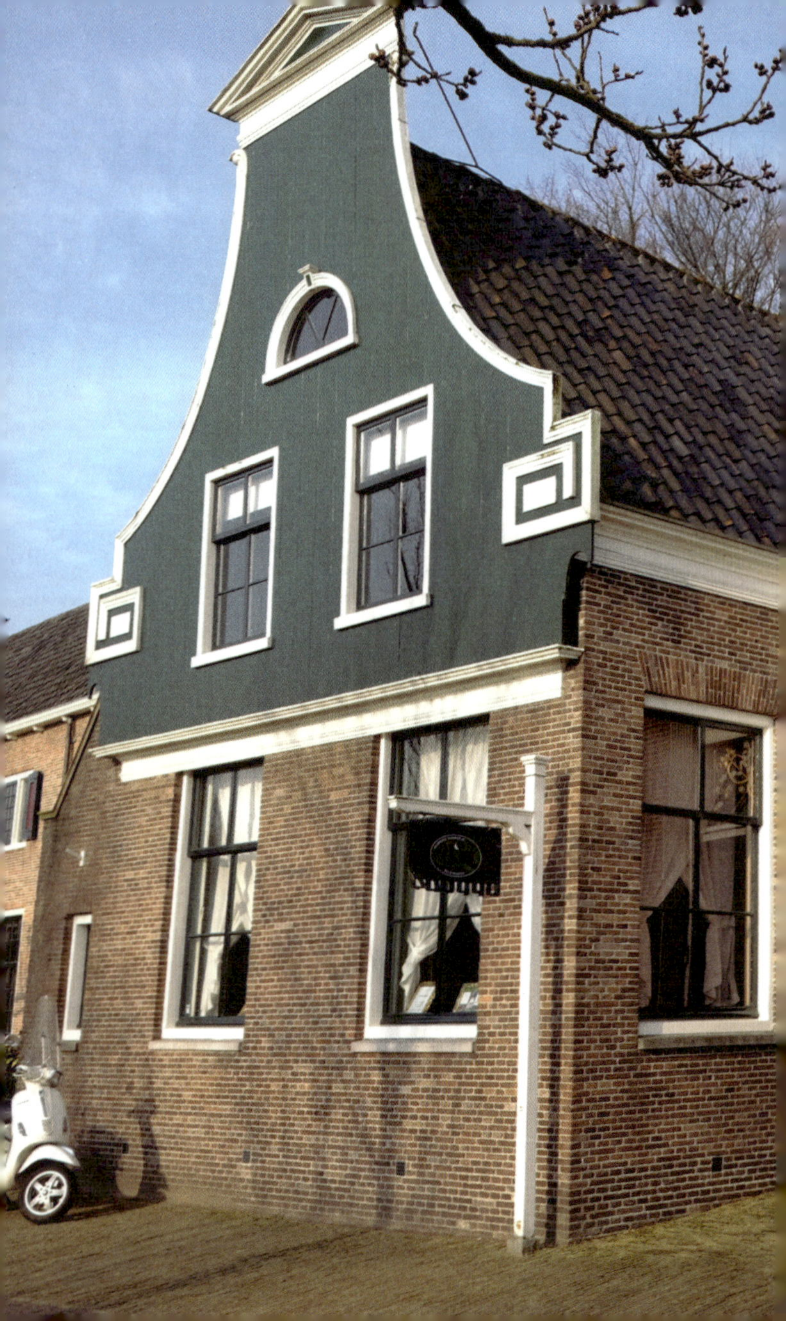

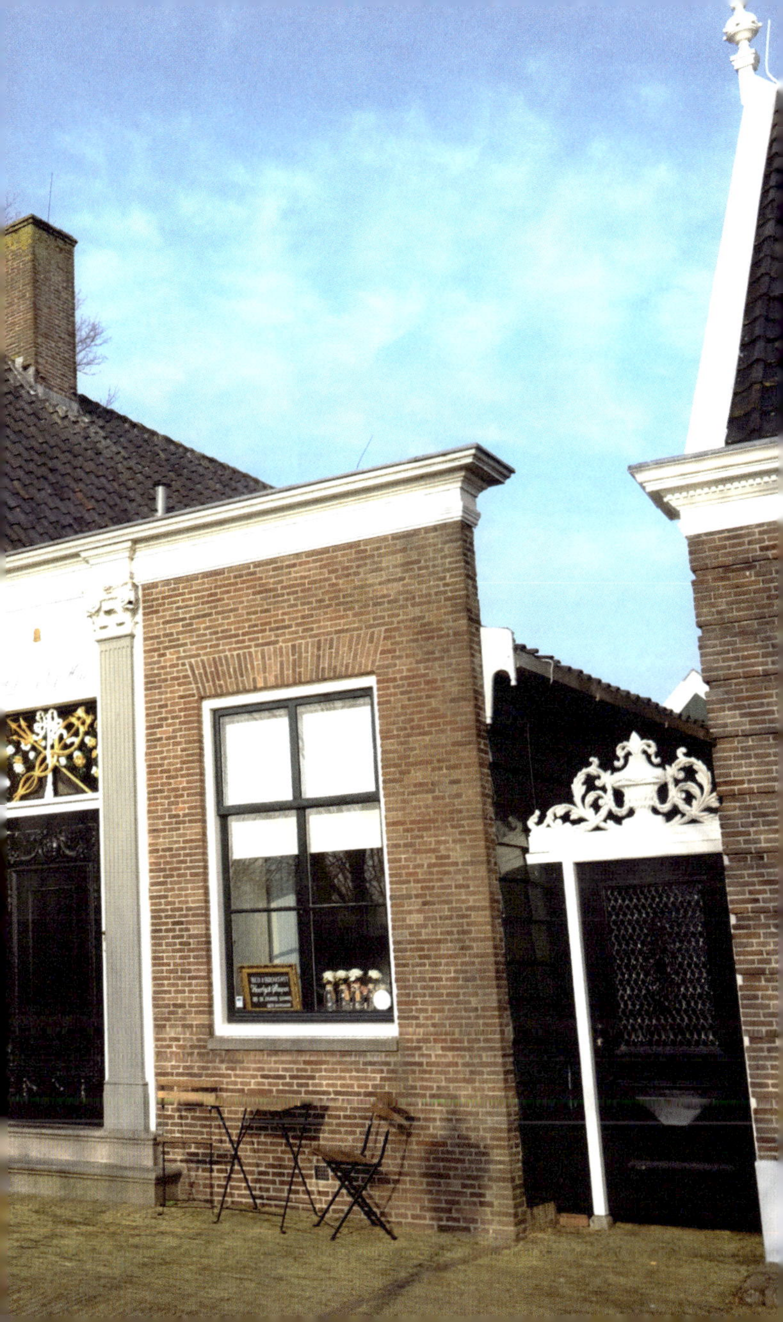

Zaanse Schans

438

Relocation 439

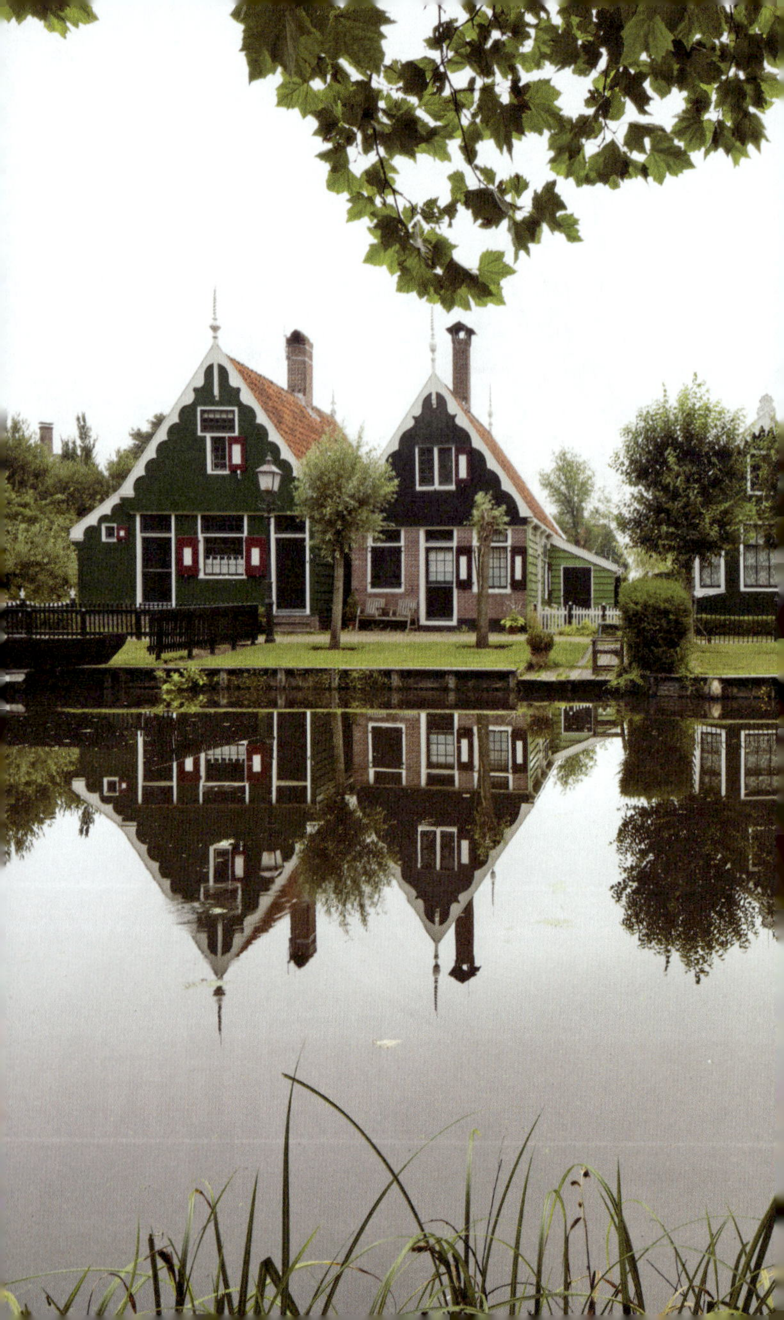

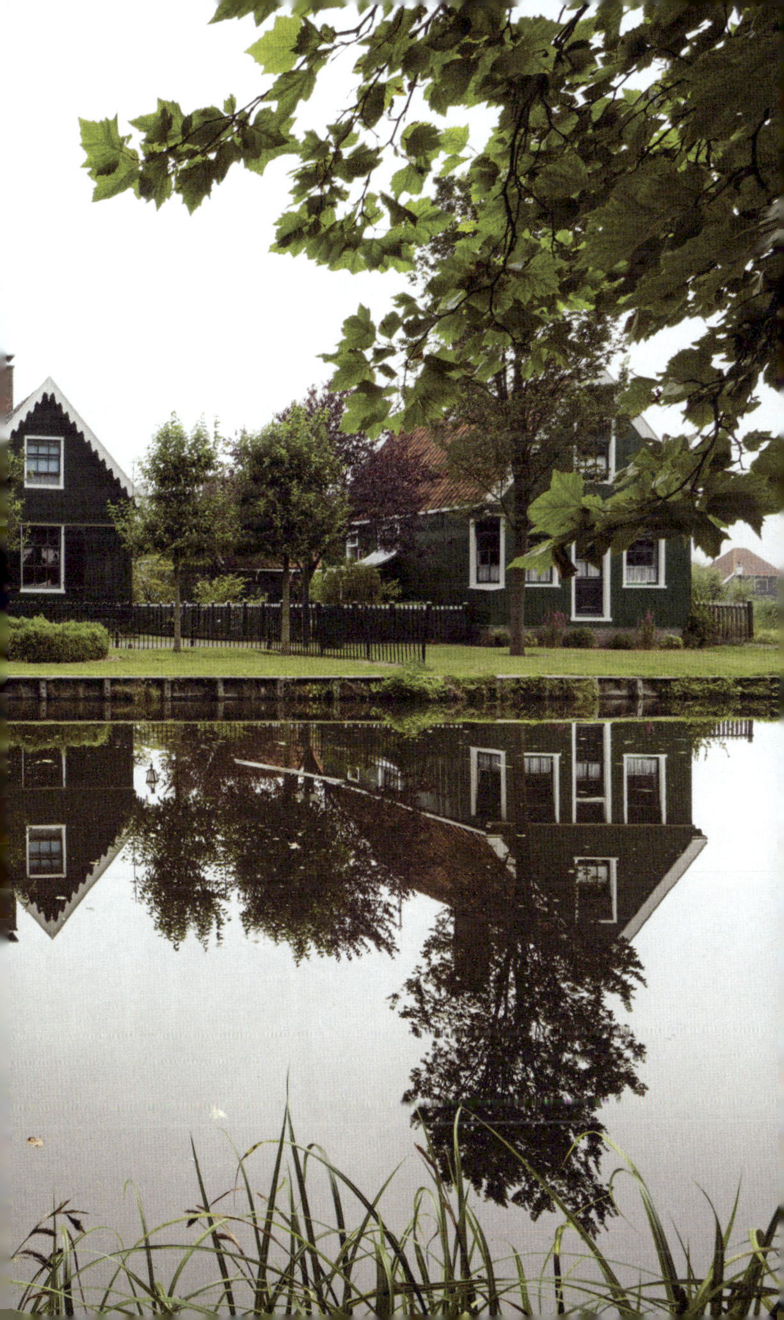

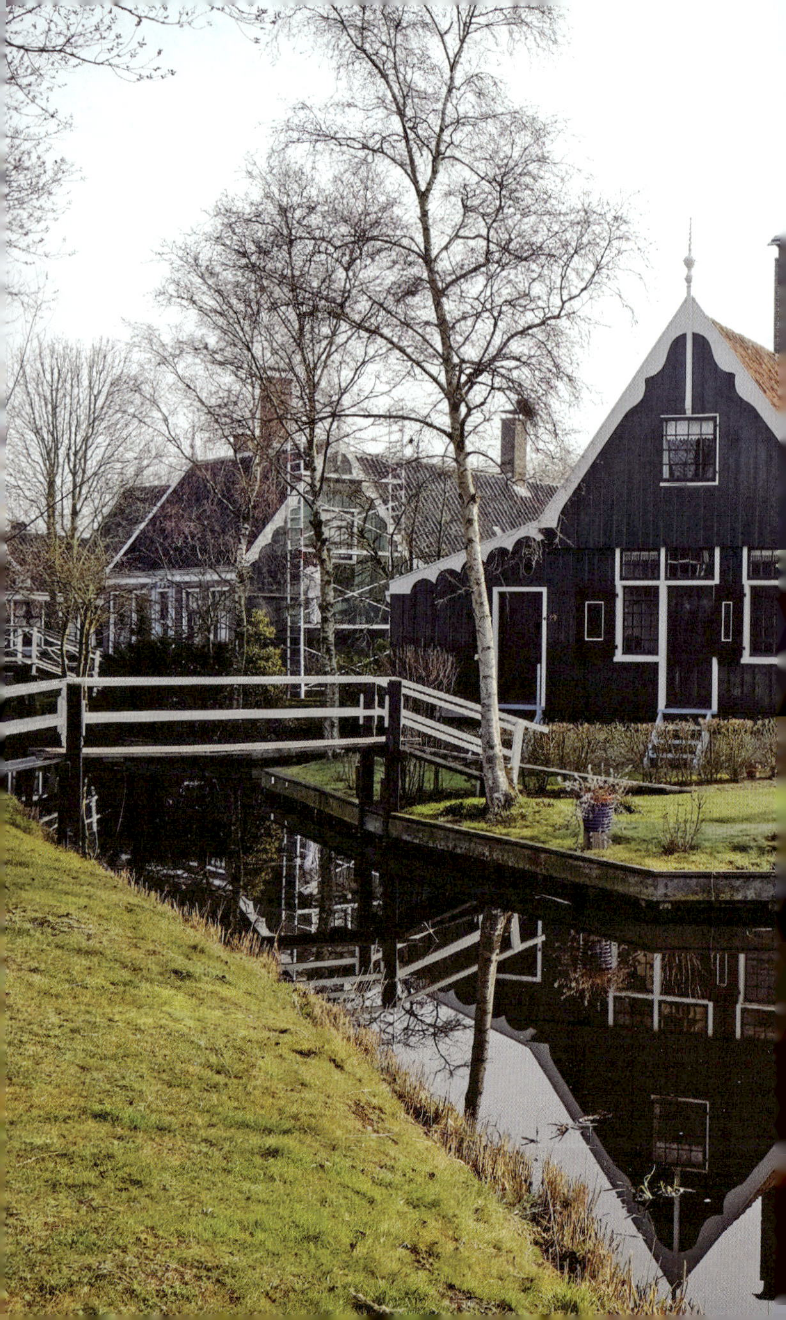

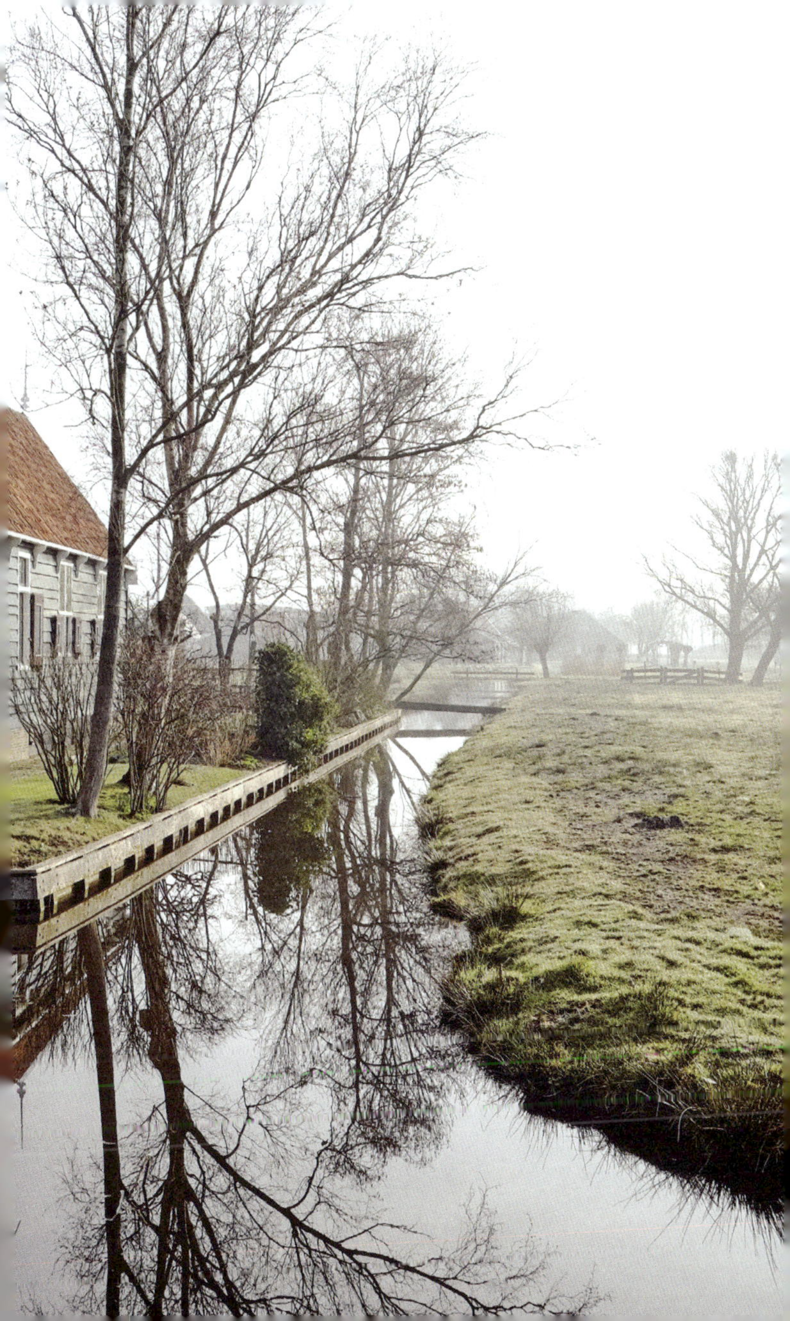

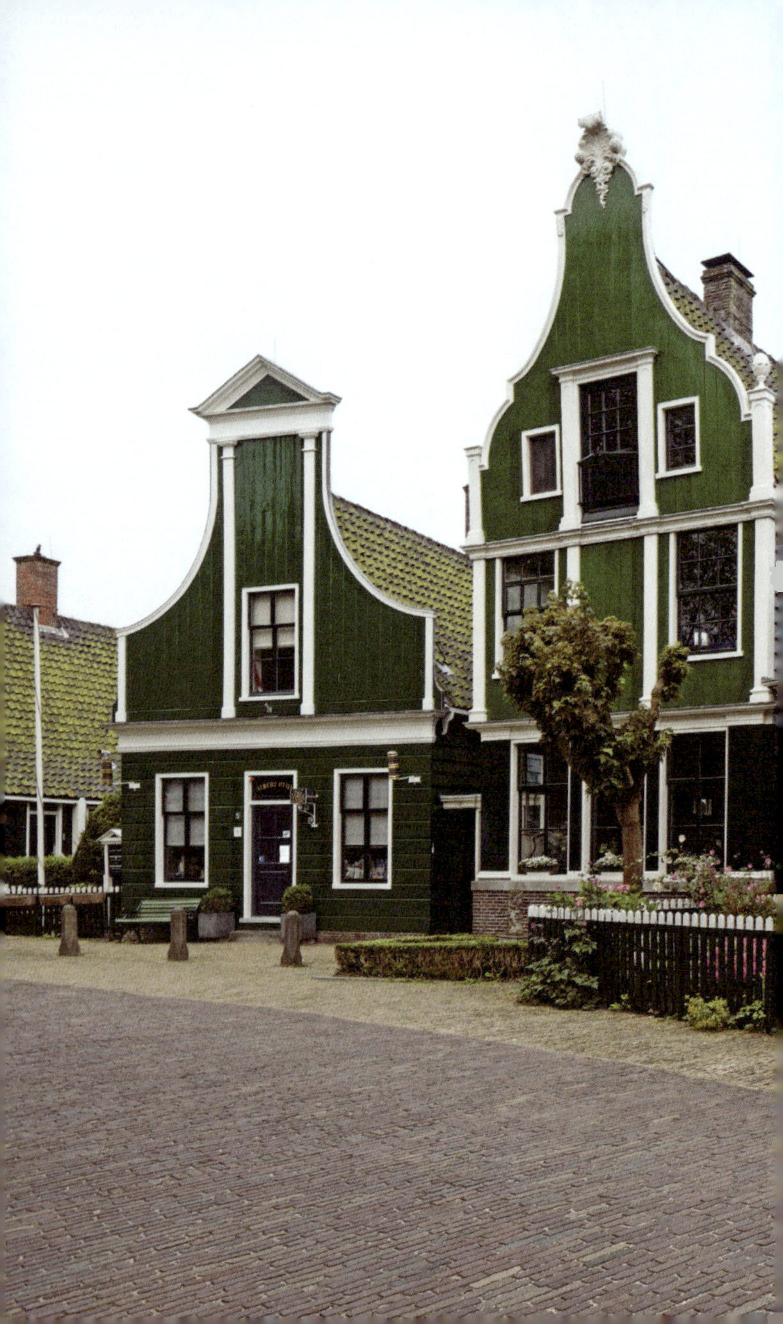

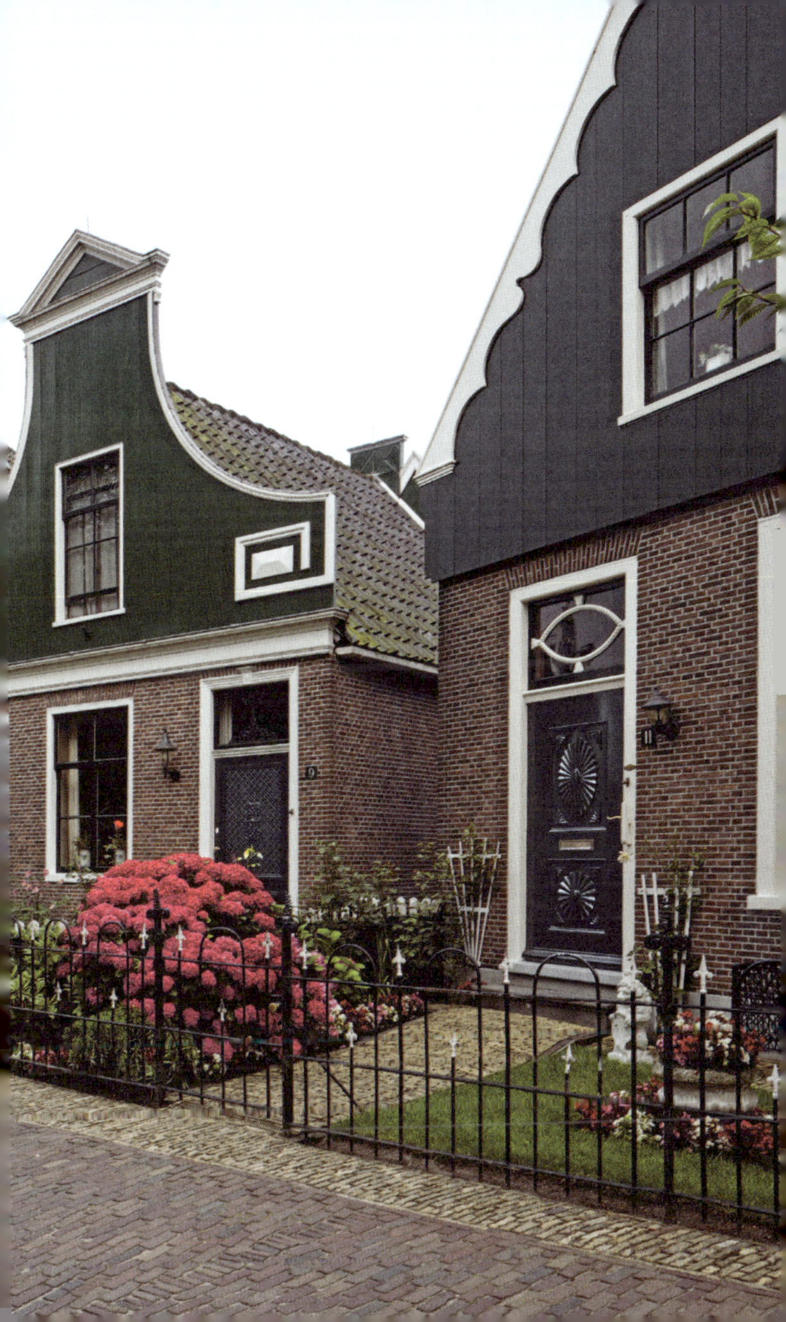

Timber construction

The timber frame is the most important structural element in both the wooden house, also in a partially petrified form, and the lignified brick house. Most wooden trusses have a timber corbel between the knee brace and the beam, on which the ornamentation was concentrated. A truss structure, the (timber) frame of the house or the farmhouse support the roof and the upper floors. The exterior walls are often not load-bearing. There was a brisk timber industry in North Holland. The light material was very useful on a waterlogged soil with poor bearing capacity.

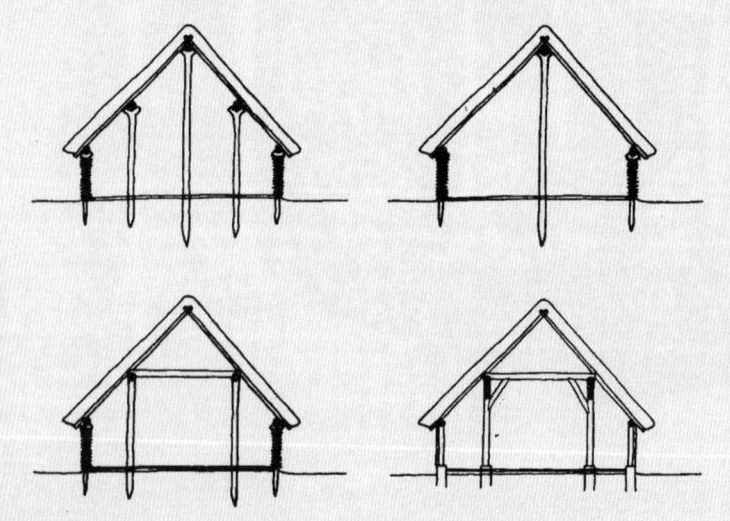

Load-bearing structures clockwise: the oldest form, a reinforced form, a three-nave aisled house with a truss and a longitudinal beam.

Relocation

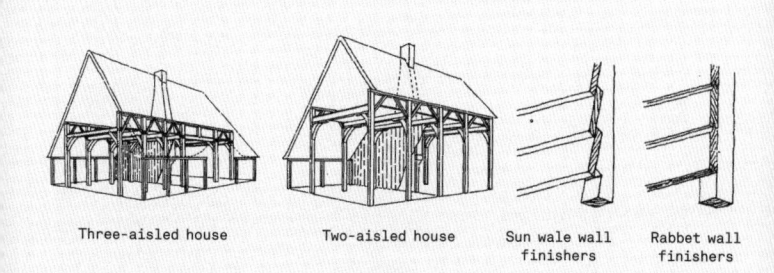

Three-aisled house

Two-aisled house

Sun wale wall finishers

Rabbet wall finishers

Garret floor bridging common joint kidsbars

Attic floor with V-side cut sections

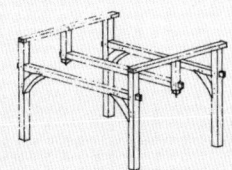

Anchor beam construction

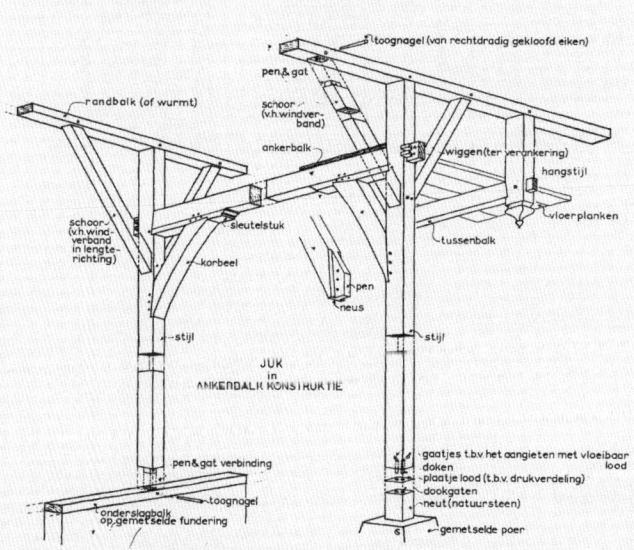

Scheme of timber frame construction

- toognagel (van rechtdradig gekloofd eiken)
- randbalk (of wurmt)
- pen & gat
- schoor (v.h. windverband)
- ankerbalk
- wiggen (ter verankering)
- hangstijl
- schoor (v.h. windverband in lengterichting)
- sleutelstuk
- vloerplanken
- korbeel
- tussenbalk
- pen
- neus
- stijl
- stijl

JUK in ANKERBALK KONSTRUKTIE

- pen & gat verbinding
- onderslagbalk op gemetselde fundering
- toognagel
- gaatjes t.b.v. het aangieten met vloeibaar lood
- doken
- plaatje lood (t.b.v. drukverdeling)
- dookgaten
- neut (natuursteen)
- gemetselde poer

Weaver's House

448

Address	Acquisition	Restoration architect
Zeilenmakerspad 8	**2001**	**Hooyschuur Architecten**

Town	Restoration	Current use
Zaanse Schans	**2015**	**Weaver's museum**

In 2011, a 17th century weaver's house in Assendelft was surveyed, documented, examined in a building-historical manner and taken apart with the idea being to give it a spot at the Zaanse Schans. Unfortunately, it had to be removed from its original location due to urban developments and Stadsherstel purchased it. The house was built between 1722 and 1730 on the Dorpstraat 861 – 863 and it functioned as a home weaving mill until the beginning of the 20th century, making canvas and mill sailcloth among other things. It is a semi-detached house built out of wood from pine trusses, with a room at the rear in which five looms were set up. The building is therefore characteristic of the weaving industry from Assendelft and Krommenie, which once flourished thanks to hundreds of home weavers. The facade demonstrates the plainness that is so characteristic of the 18th century architecture from the region. Before the reconstruction began in 2015, the monumental components were stored for a period until there was a feasible plan. It is not just the craftsmanship of weaving that was shown in the weaver's house. The reconstruction turned out provide extremely usable information for the further knowledge development of the regional timber construction.

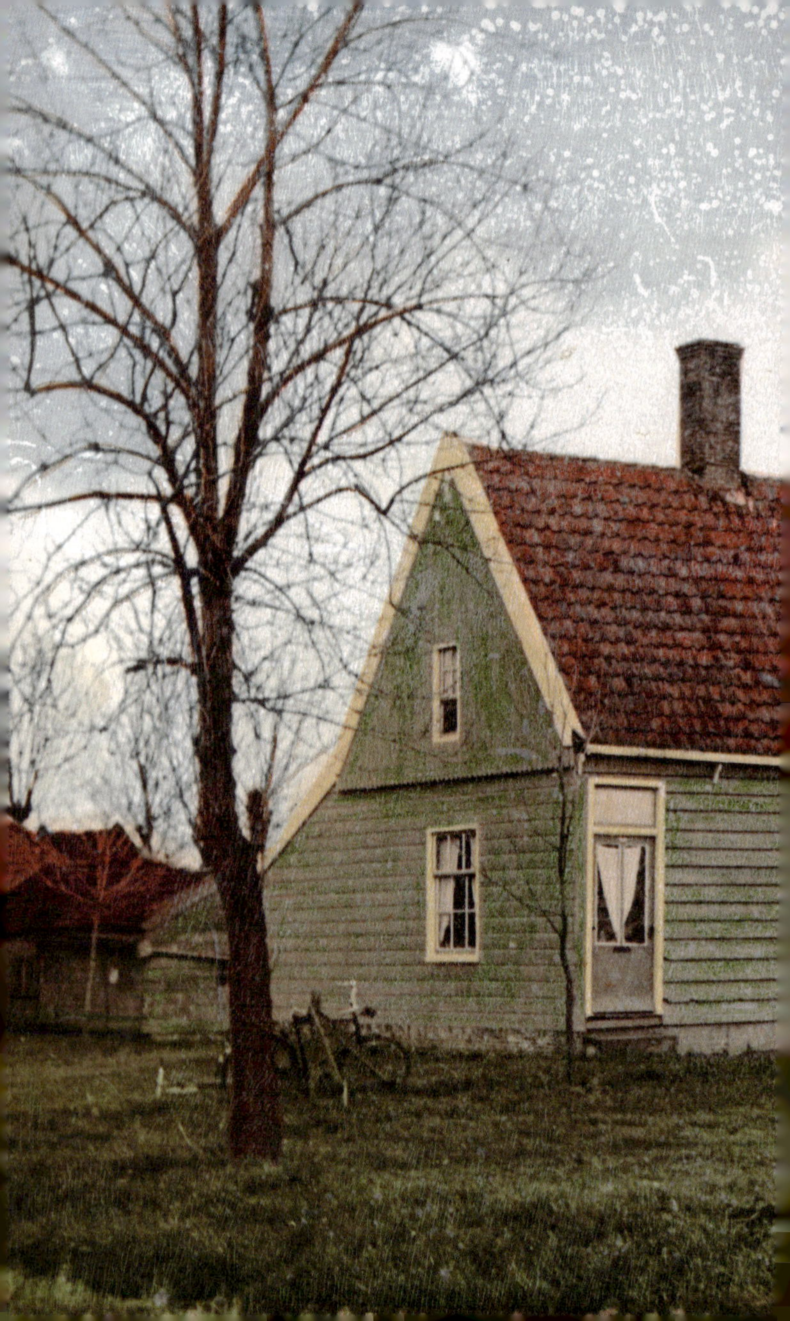

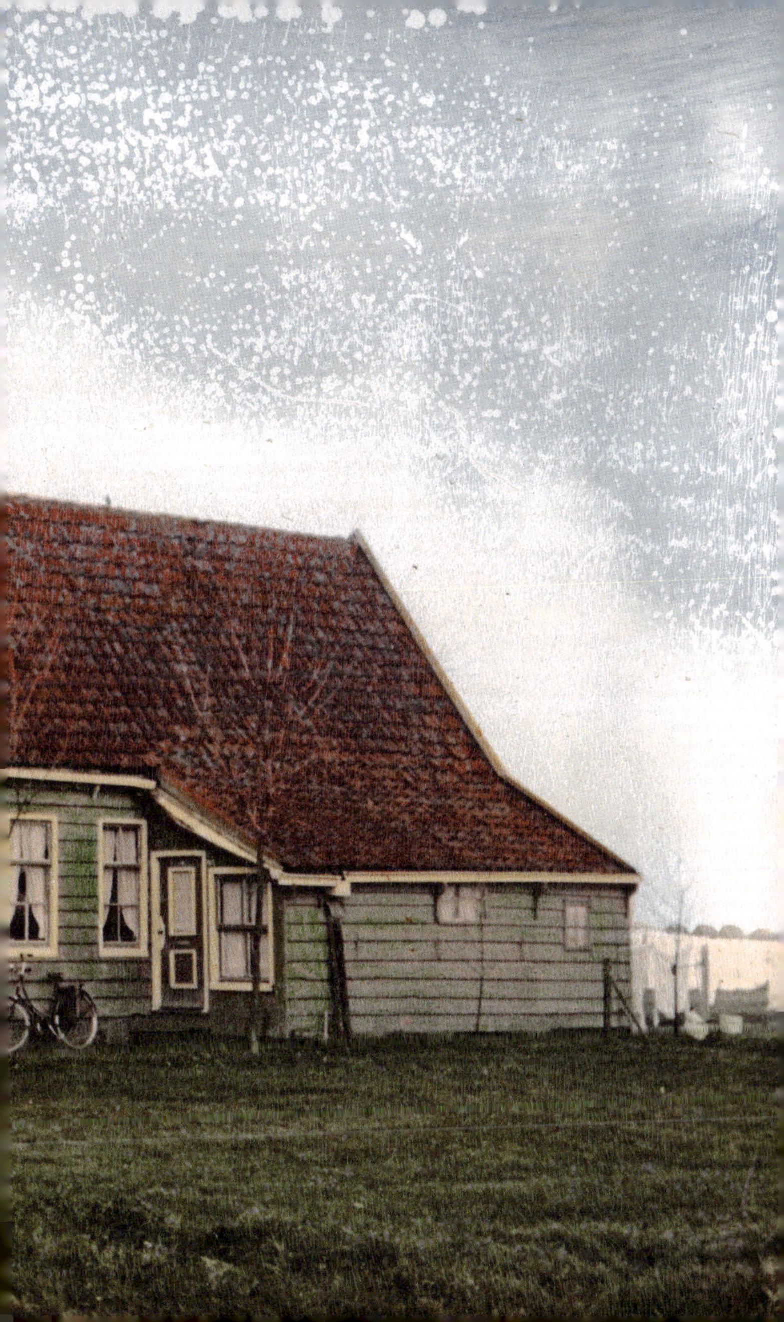

Weaver's House

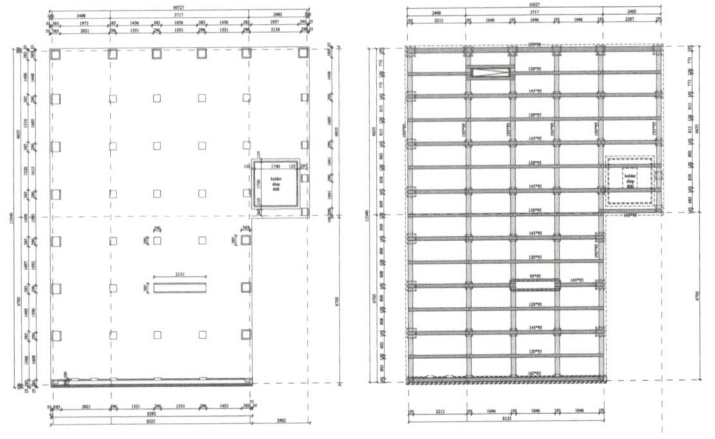

452

Lower level, builders estimate drawing foundation (left) and supporting structure

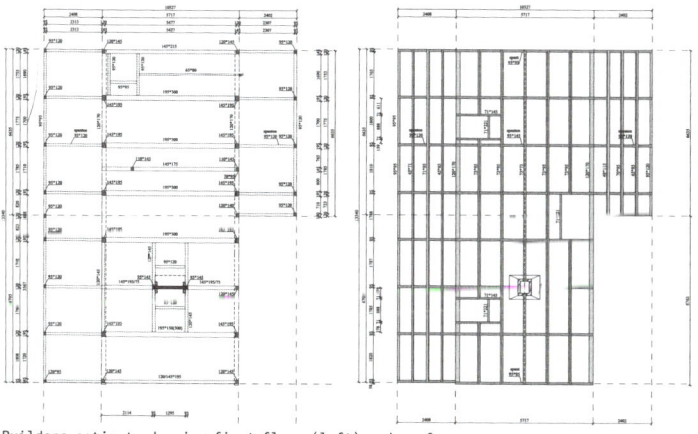

Relocation

Builders estimate drawing first floor (left) and roof

Weaver's House

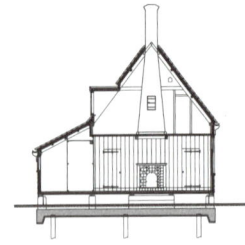

Cross-section living area

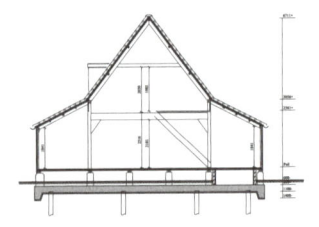

Cross-section working area

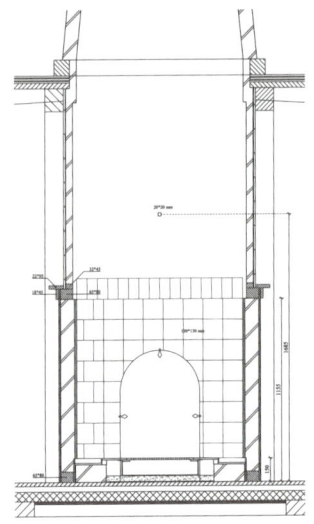

Drawing fireplace

Relocation

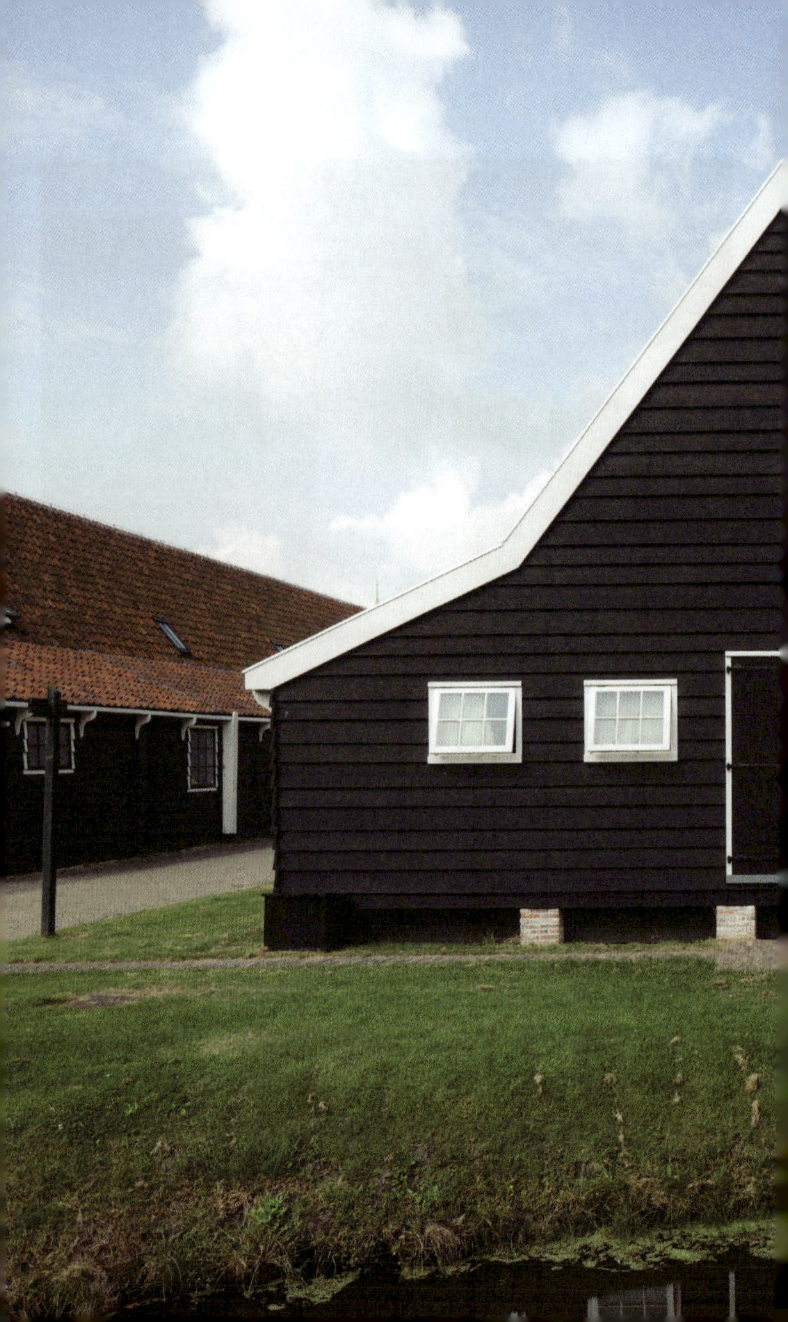

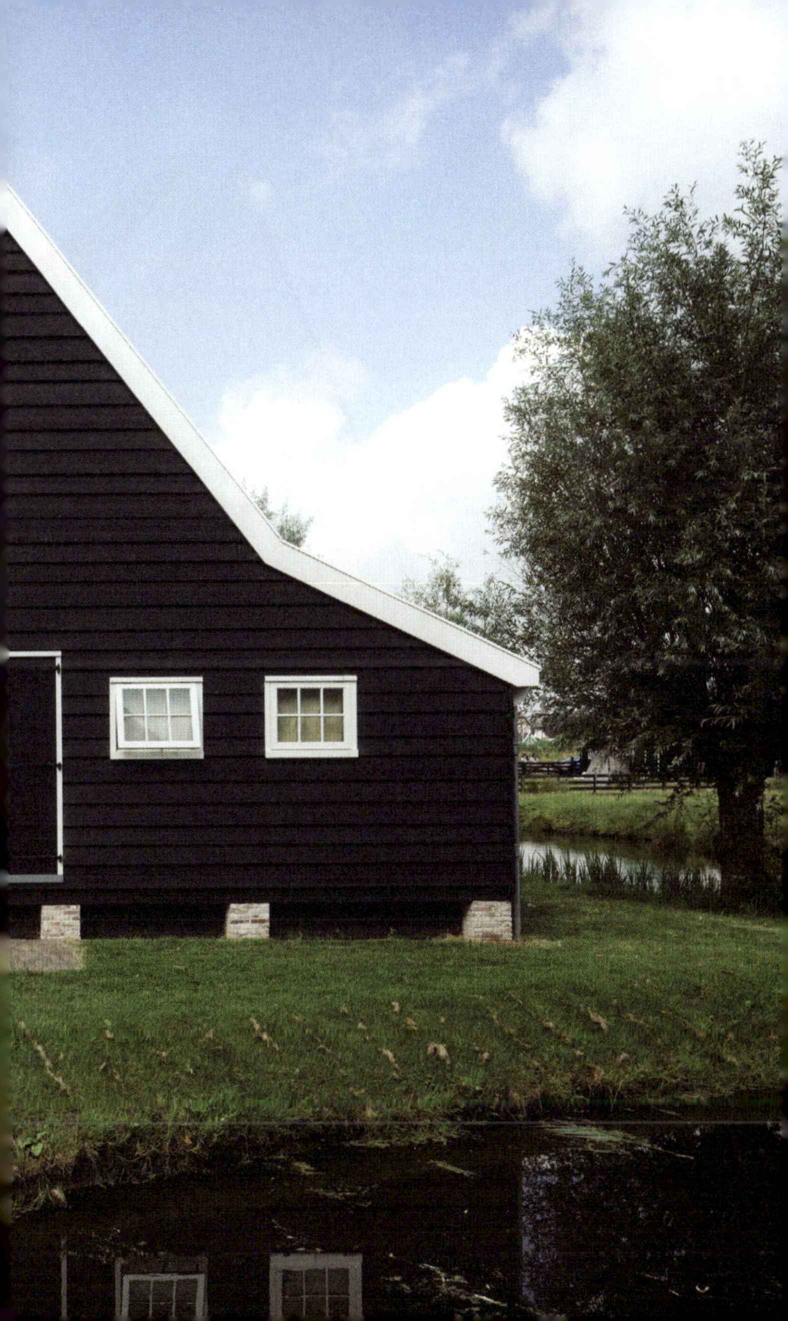

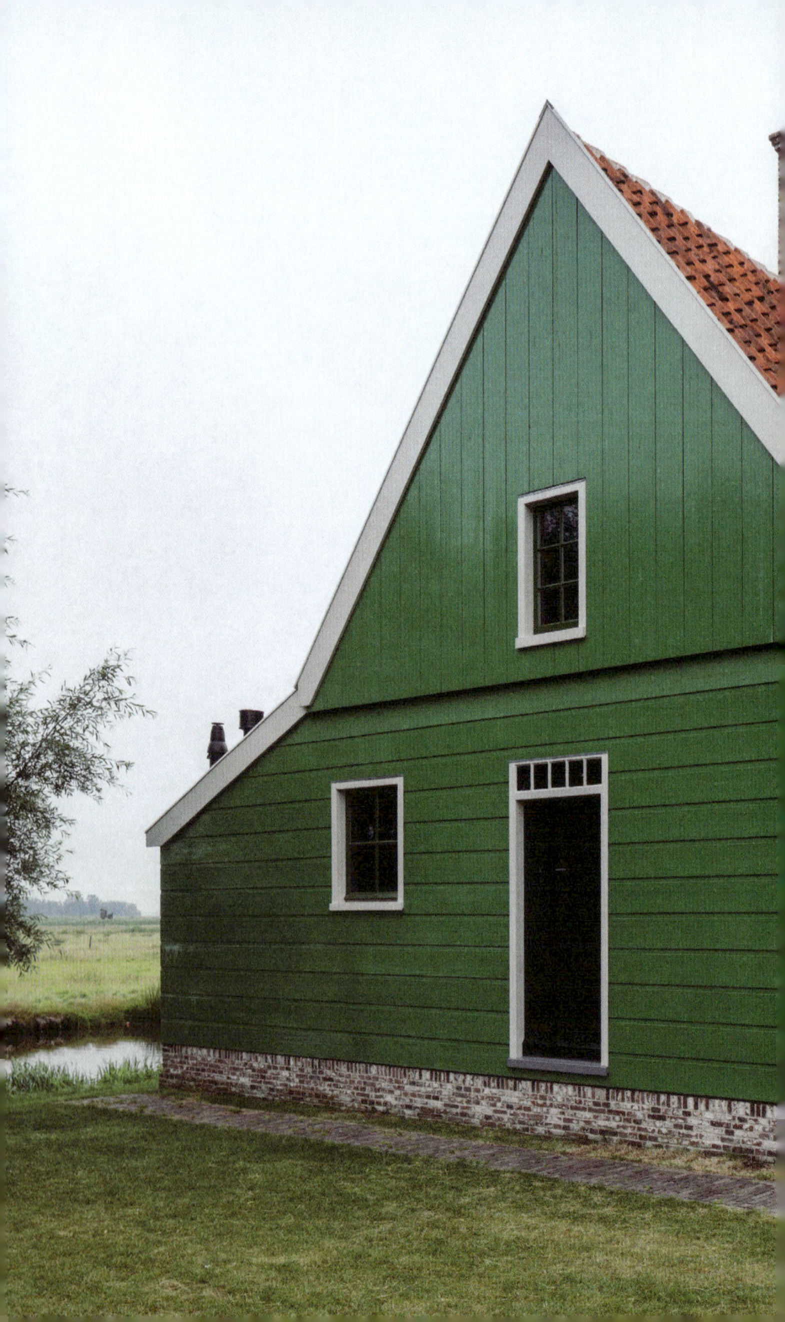

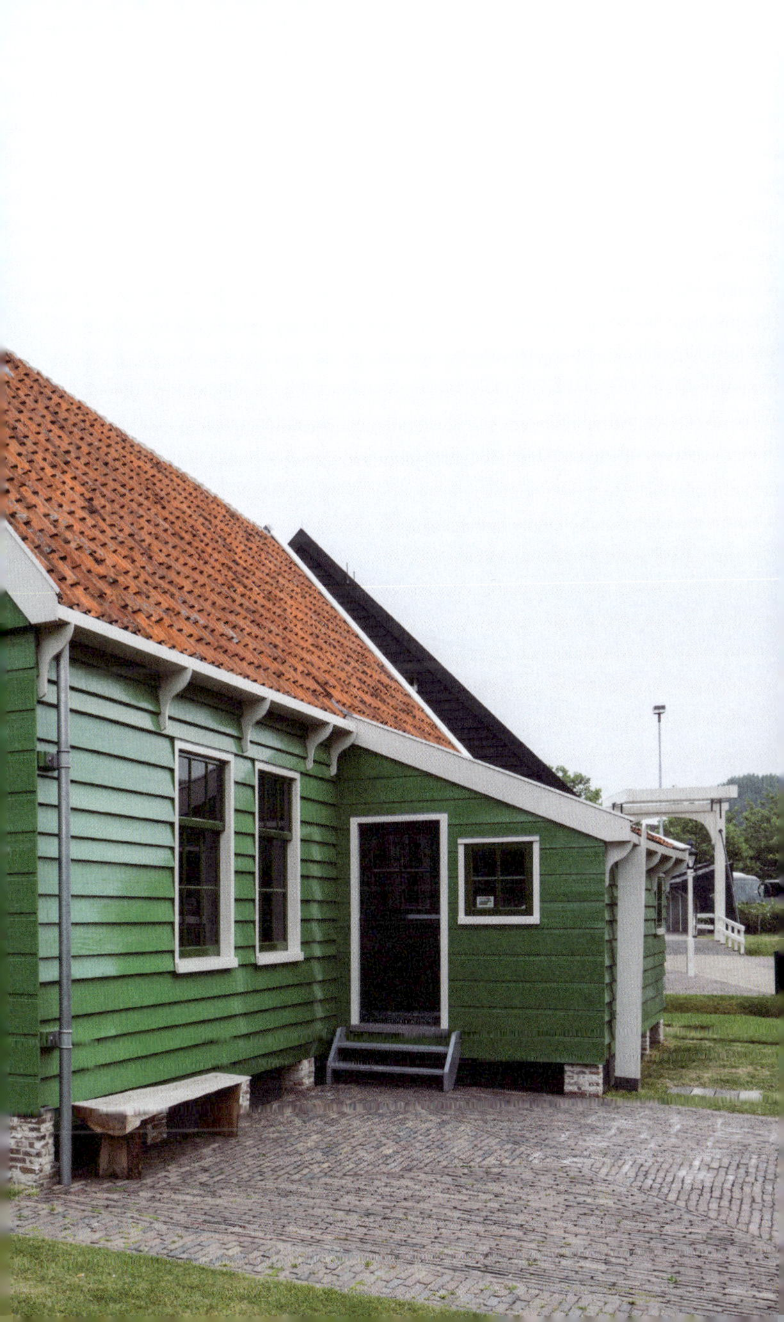

Naco House

460

Address **De Ruyterkade 84, steiger 7**	Built **1919**	Restoration architect **Kentie en Partners Architecten B.V.**
Town **Amsterdam**	Acquisition **2016**	Current use **In storage**
	Restoration **2017**	

The unusual Naco House (NACO-huisje) was located on pier number 7 on the river facing side of Amsterdam Central Station between 1919 and 2004. The Amsterdam School listed building had to make way for the large-scale refurbishment of the train station and the construction of the Noord/Zuidlijn (North/South line) of the Amsterdam metro. In 2004, the building, packed entirely in a steel frame, was placed on a pontoon and transported with a tugboat to the Isaac Baarthaven in Zaandam, where it is now waiting to be put back and restored.

Naco House

The Scheepvaartkantoor (Shipping Office) was built in 1919 based on the design of the architect Guillaume (G.F.) la Croix (1877 – 1923), commissioned by the shipping agency J.G. Koppe's Scheepsagentuur N.V. The nickname comes from the last user, the shipping department of the Noordhollandsche AutoCar Onderneming (North Holland Coach Company, NACO), which had its office from 1960. The wooden building on poles, also known as the Minangkabause house, has a rectangular floor plan with a half-open ground floor, an upper floor and a saddle roof. It references the architecture of the former

Dutch East Indies, with a facade sloping forward and an ascending roof. There is a roof plane on the waterfront. The roof plane sloping forward is also given extra emphasis by means of a long flag pole. On the land side, the office is decorated with flaming saw motifs that stick out on the right sides, as well as narrow corbels under the connected window. The roof boarding parts, which are placed in a V-shape on either side of a vertical post and applied further horizontally, are attached to steel battens.

J.G.KOPPES SCHE

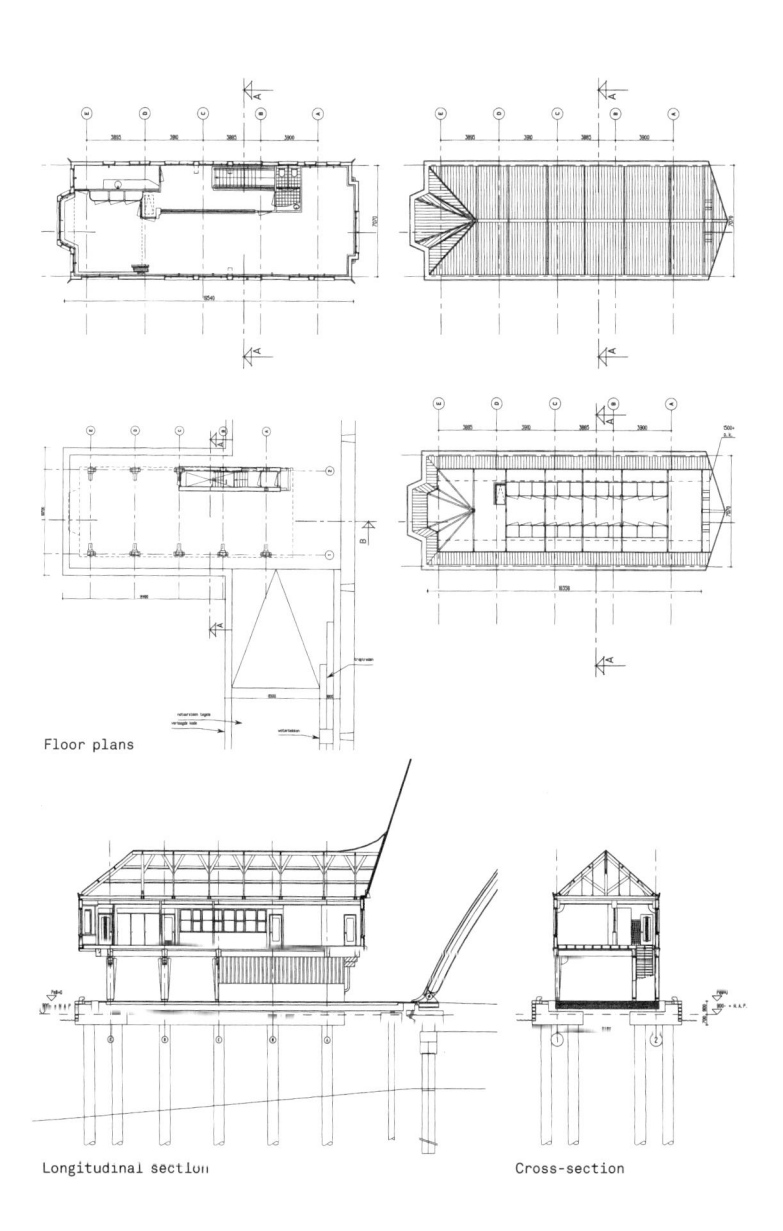

Relocation

Floor plans

Longitudinal section

Cross-section

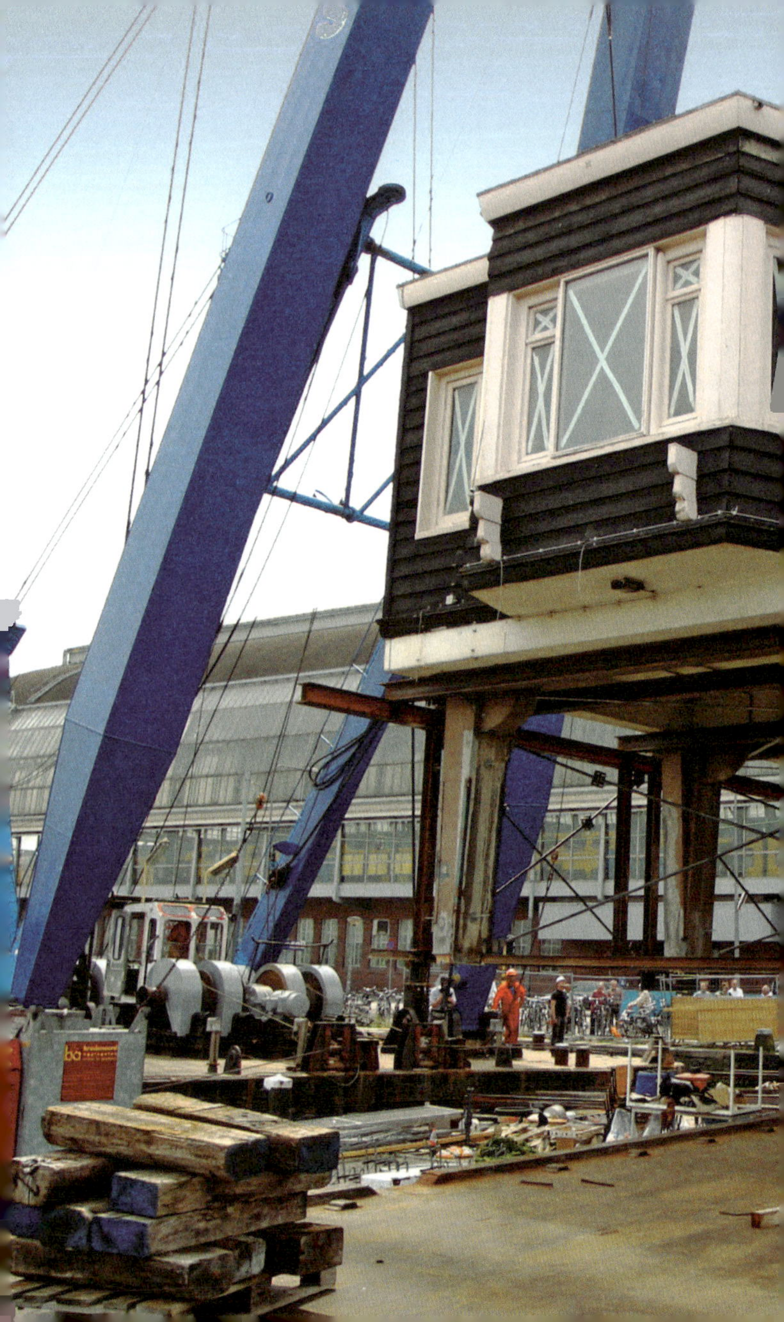

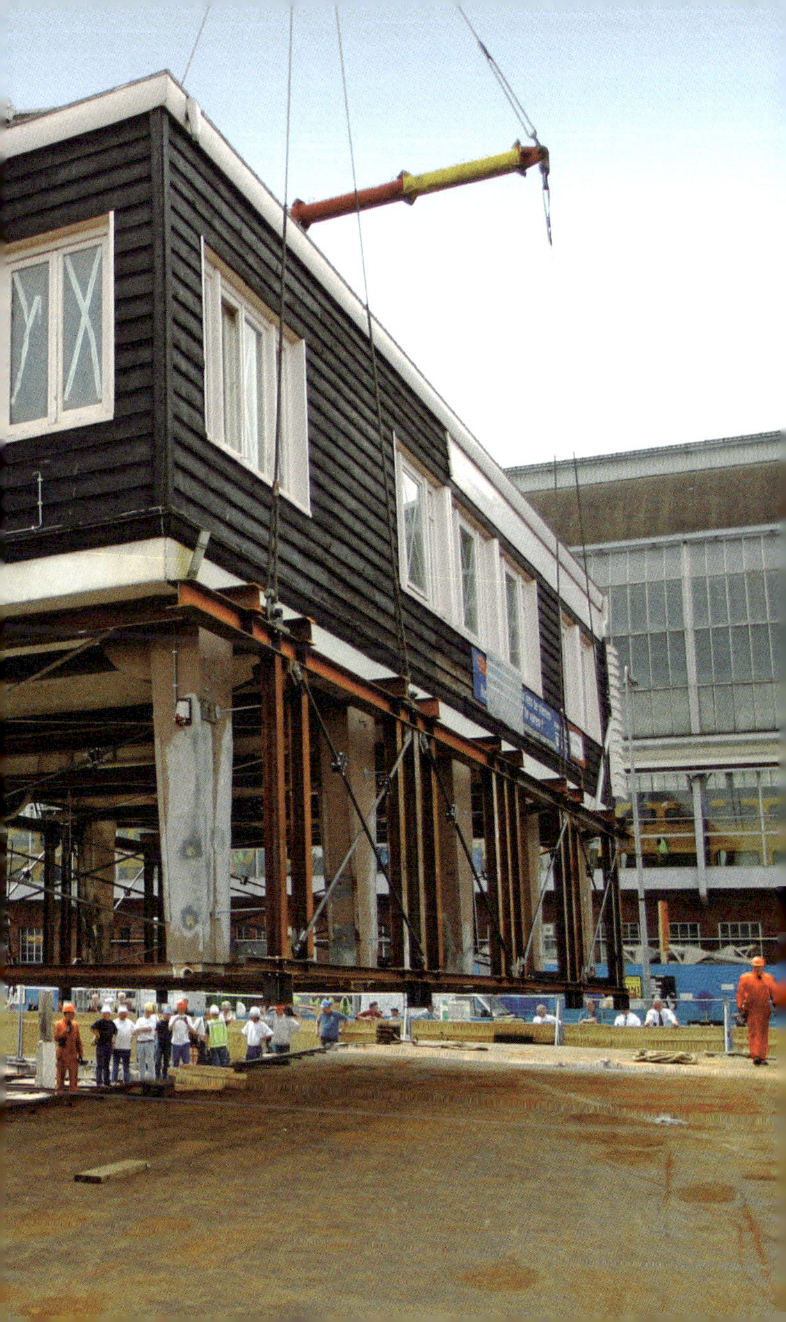

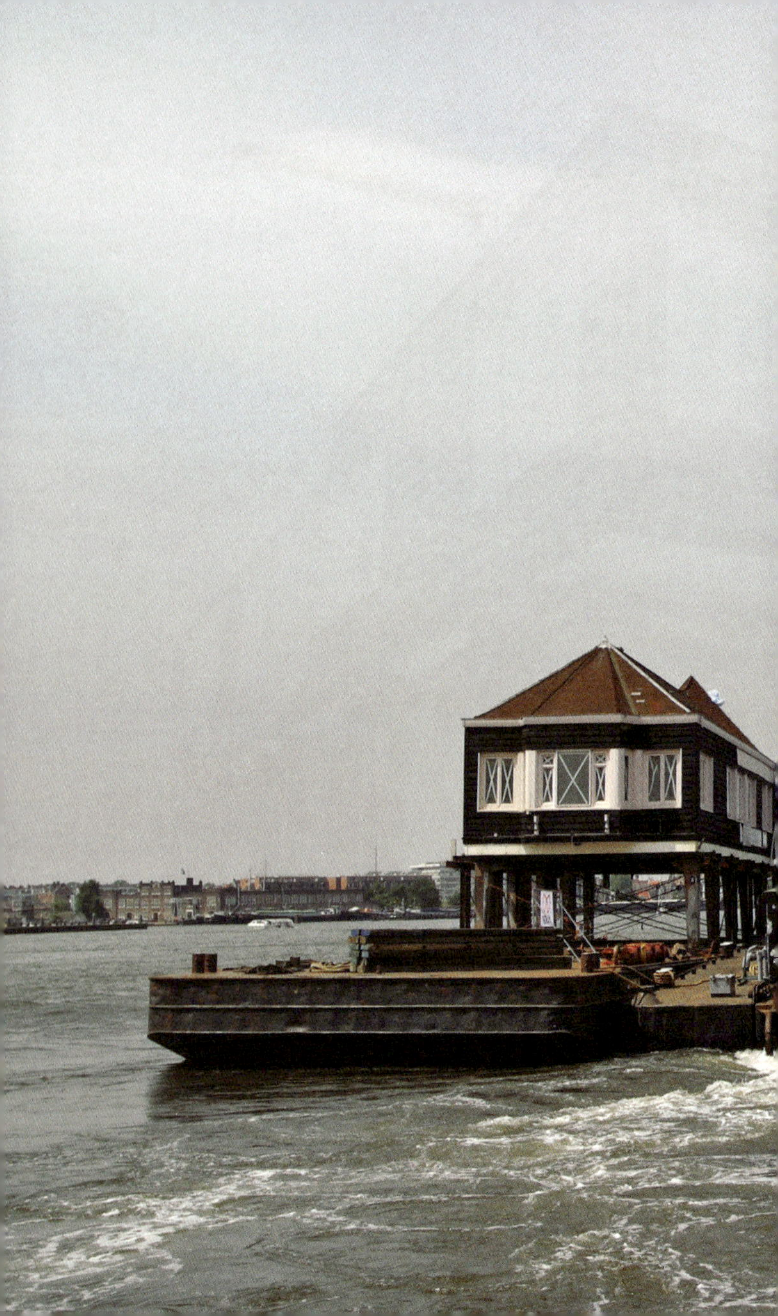

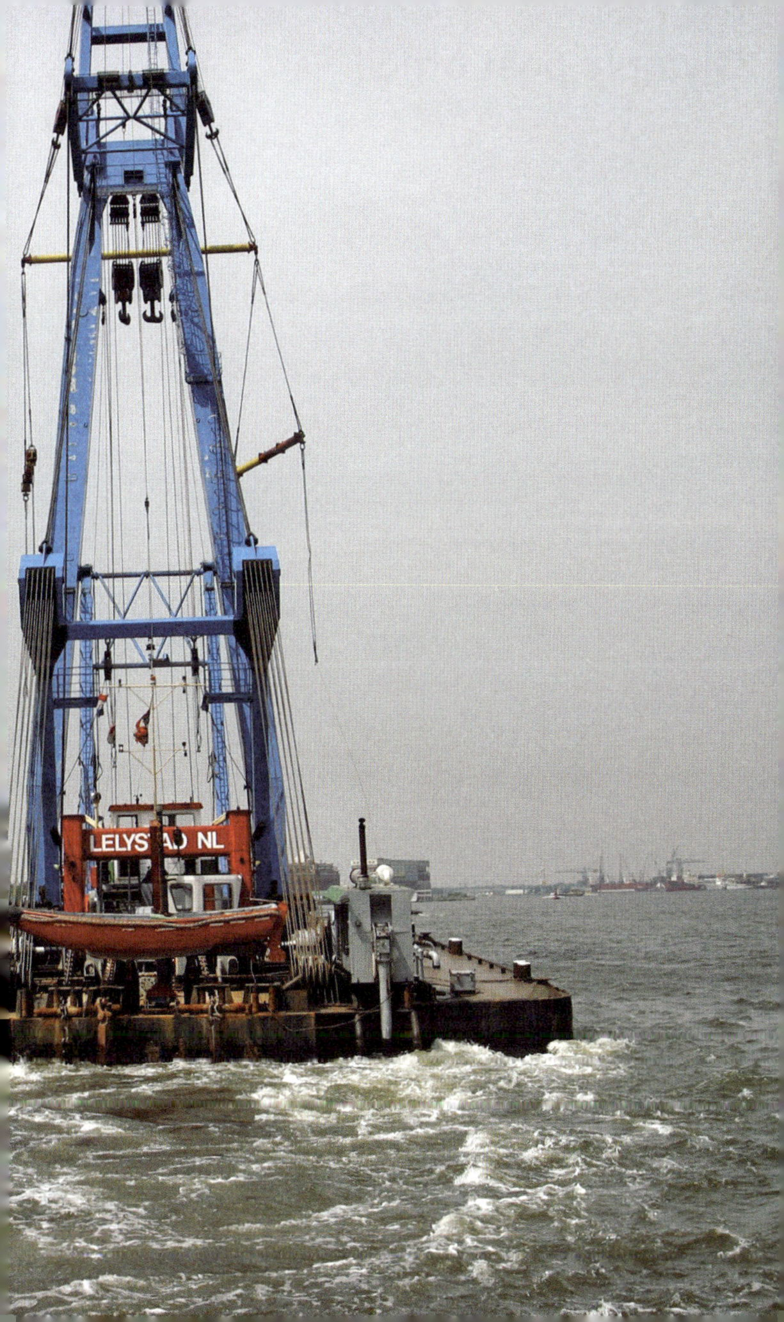
LELYSTAD NL

Olympic post office

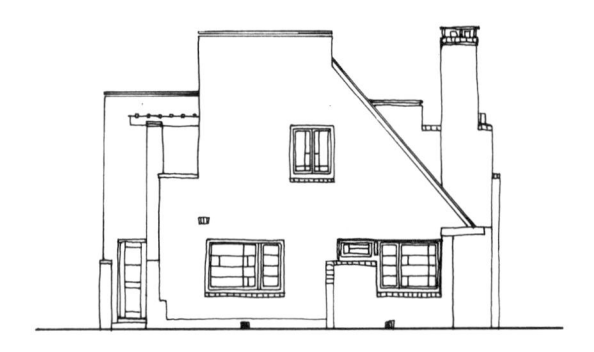

Address **Stadionplein 18**	Built **1928**	Restoration architect **CASA Architecten**
Town **Amsterdam**	Acquisition **2006**	Current use **Cultural space**
	Restoration **2007**	

The post office was designed by the architect Jan Wils as one of the ancillary buildings for the Summer Games of 1928 next to the Olympic Stadium. All ancillary buildings were demolished after the games except for the post office and a staff accommodation. The advanced plans to demolish it at a later date were prevented in the late-20th century by moving it forty metres. The sport complex is by far the most famous work of Wils. Between the wars, it was considered representative of the modern architecture with a distinctive syntax, and was inspired by the architecture of the Amsterdam School, in addition to the work of Frank Lloyd Wright and De Stijl group of Piet Mondriaan and Theo van Doesburg (of which he was a member). His buildings are both elegant yet economical in shape as a result of the emphasis on horizontal and vertical lines, as well as lively and organic. The ladder-type window that was used here, with the typical subdivision of glazing bars, is characteristic of the period.

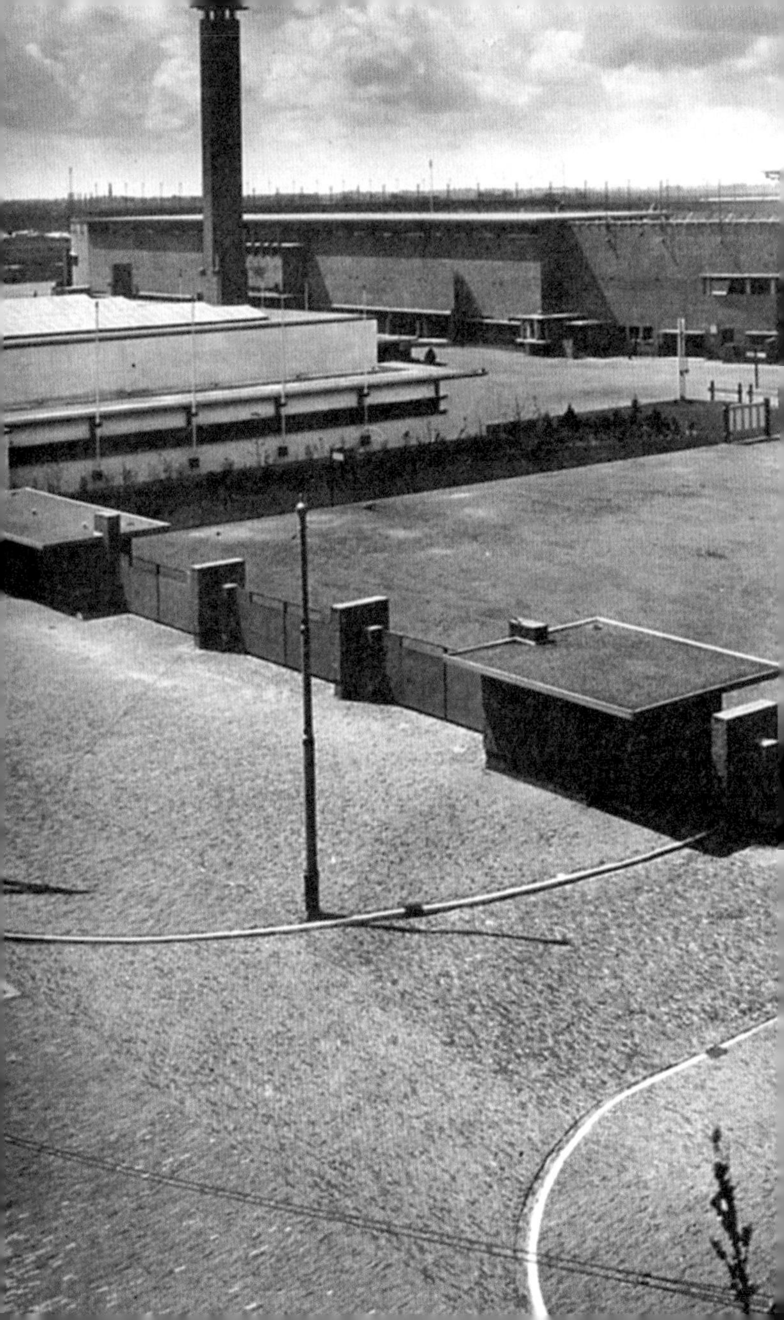

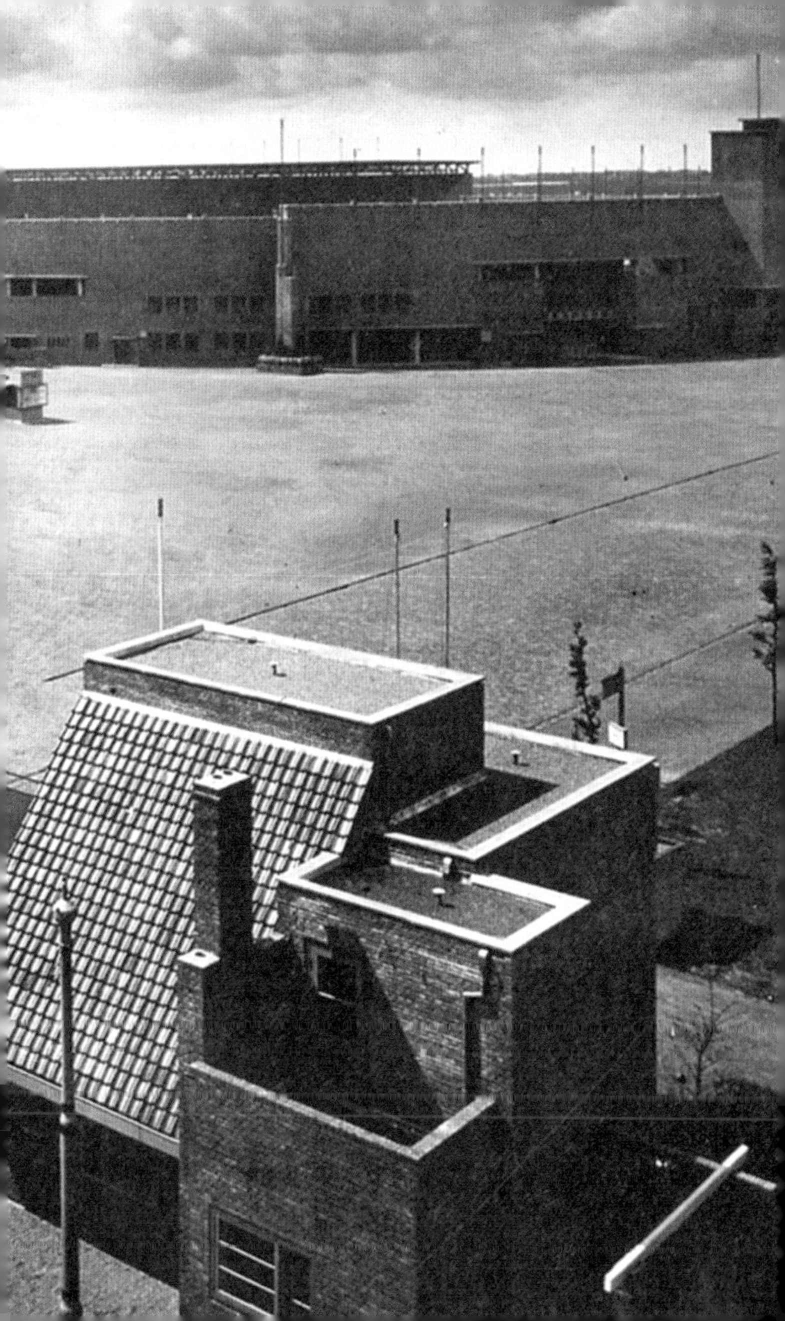

Olympic post office

After Stadsherstel started to take care of the threatened historic building, a complicated technical operation was executed in a relatively short space of time of 10 weeks. Based on the principle of the 'lift and shift method', the house was moved from 50 metres to a distance of 9 metres away from the Citroën garage (1929 – 1931), which was also designed by Jan Wils. The building was separated from its foundations, fitted with a steel corset and placed on a steel frame. The steel corset was subsequently lifted up gently and shifted on rails to the concrete floor of the new spot. The restoration could begin a few years later, after it became clear that it could remain at the current location. The driving of foundation piles into openings in the concrete floor was the first operation in the restoration process. On the basis of detailed building historical research into the original details and colours, they proceeded to hack out the pointing and clean the facades. The brickwork was originally applied as a raked joint and later flush, due to moisture problems. The layout of the nationally listed building was changed to a limited extent and is now optimally usable for meetings and exhibitions.

Relocation 475

Olympic post office

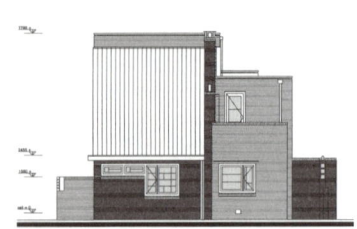

476

Views front, back and side wall

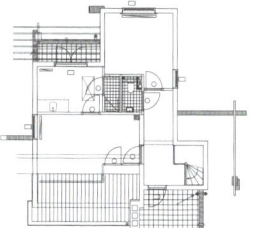

Relocation

First floor

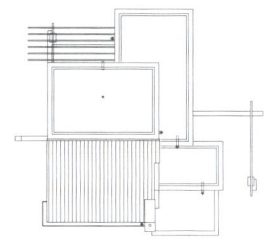

Attic

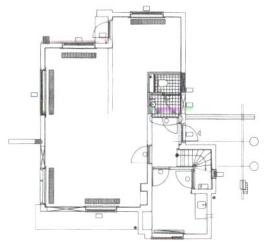

Plan, lower floor

Cross-section

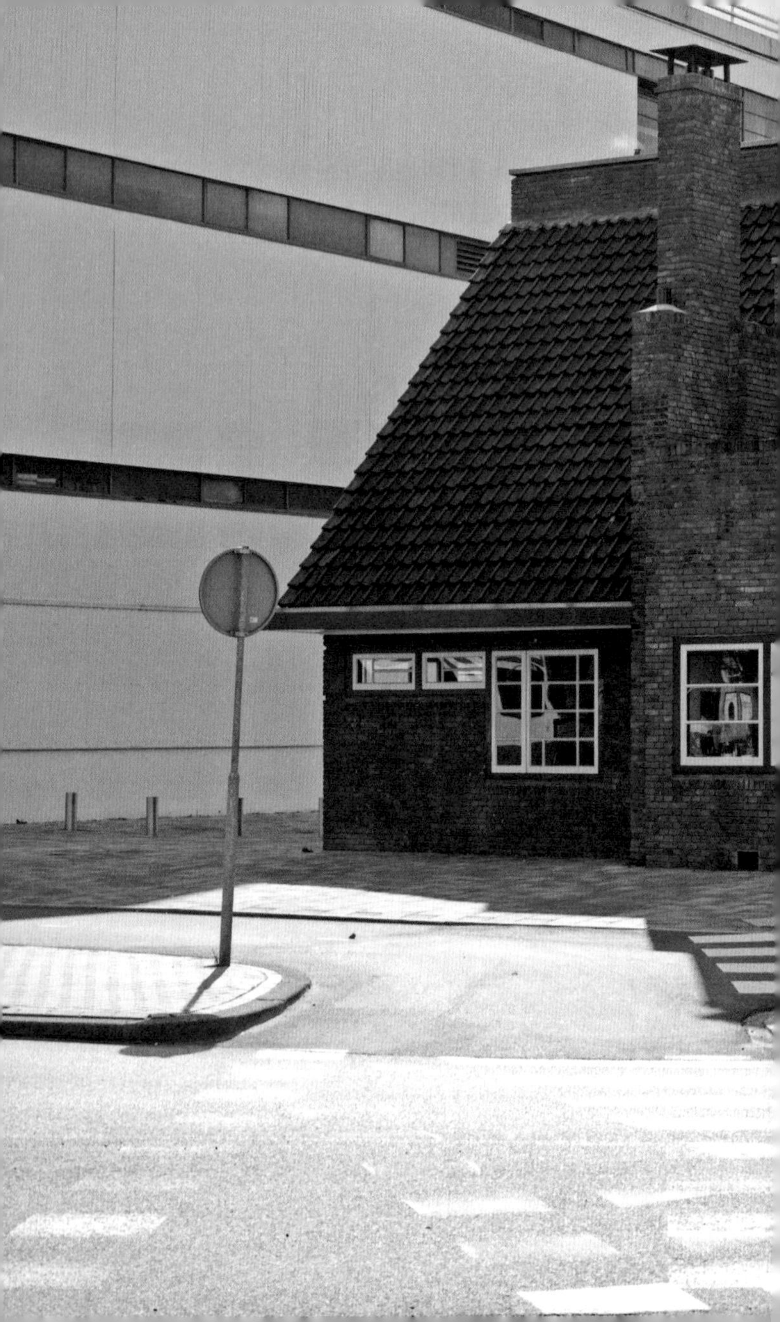

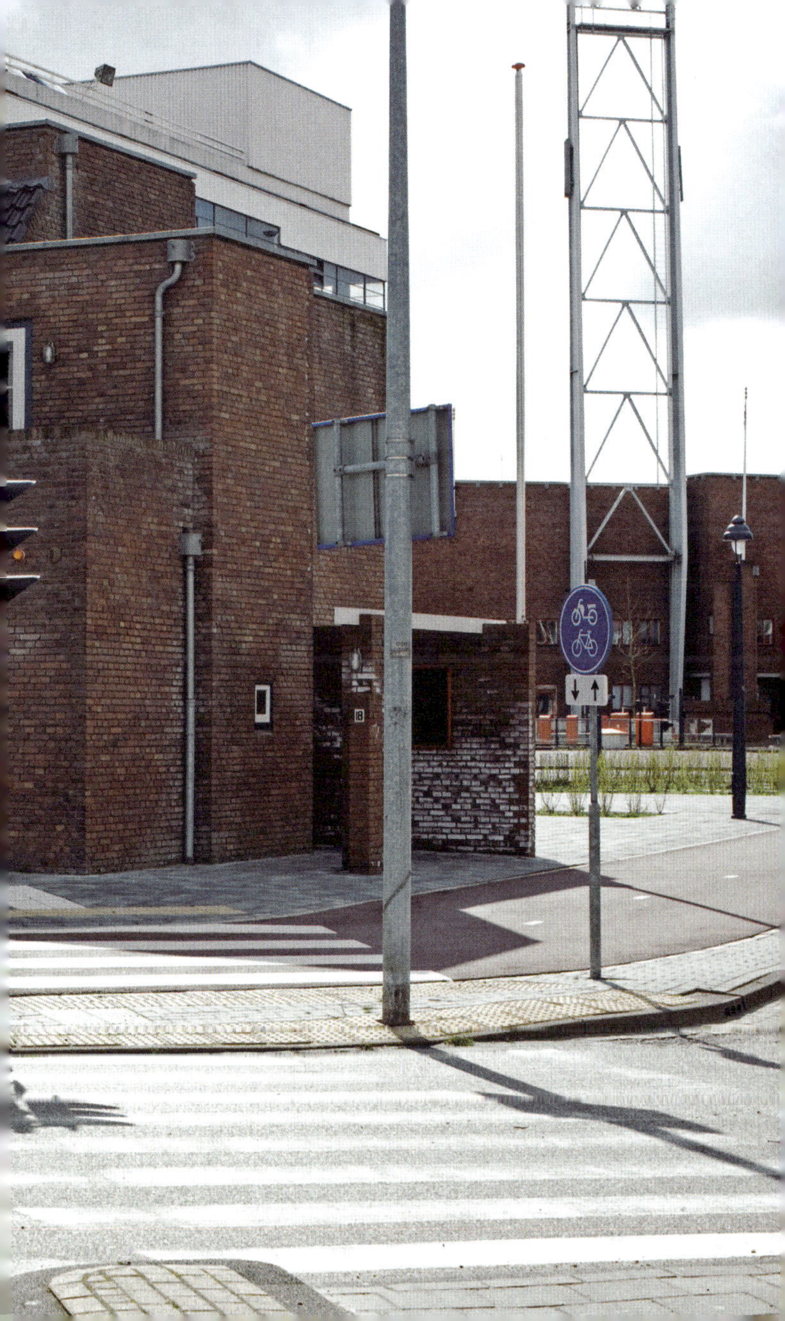
18

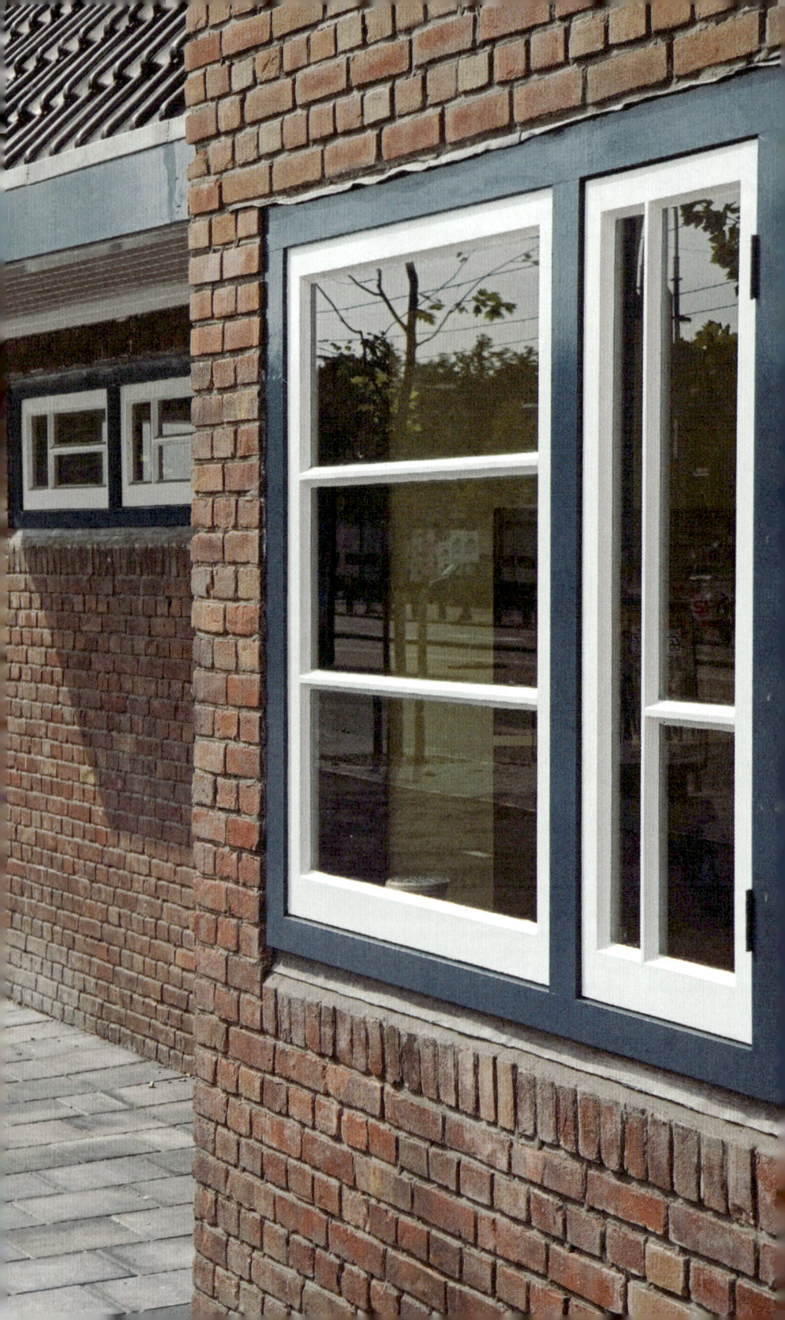

Colour in Amsterdam

In the early years of Stadsherstel, the colour palette was limited to very dark canal green (grachtengroen), a mixture of ochre with white (Bentheim yellow), the colour that was based on Bentheim sandstone, and white. The canal green sometimes had a more bluish version, after Bremen green (Bremergroen) fell into disuse around 1830 due to discolouration and the toxicity of the paint, but that was all. In general, the canal green was used for doors and windows without glazing bars, T-windows (T-ramen) and Empire style windows (Empire ramen). Small windows were mostly white. One saw Bentheim sandstone used for the ornaments on the facades and gables. Because the sandstone was porous and discoloured, and in order to obtain a waterproof surface, it was given an extra painted layer in the same colour. Apart from that, the colour also appeared on frames and fronts.

The choice of the colours mostly depended on a historical colour research with a kleurentrapje, a type of colour chart where the paint is made visible layer for layer in boxes alongside each other. Archive material helped further in tracing the colour schemes. Should the past have been completely erased, then one looked at the neighbouring buildings or a colour that suited the brick or the thickness of the timber for the frames best. At present, Stadsherstel determines the colours in consultation with the architect and requests permission from Monuments & Archaeology Department City of Amsterdam.

Colour

As a result of changing views on restoration, a little more freedom is created. In the past, it was customary to reconstruct entire buildings, or to restore elements to a particular character of an era. In this view on restoration, an original colour palette was chosen. In the current view on perception, there is a desire to ensure the historical interventions in a building remain visible and new elements and different colours remain visible preferably. In general, Stadsherstel adheres to the colours that were used over the course of centuries, sometimes with an exception, such as the building Dirk van Hasseltsteeg 4. The very narrow, dark and plain alleyway was in need of some cheer, which is why an orange combined with a heavier Bentheimer was chosen in this instance. In the Oudezijds Armsteeg, the municipality deemed plastered white facades to be desirable. They were clad with white and blue tiles, different from what the municipality prescribed. However, it turned out that the concept, a nod to the miniature houses of KLM, was well-suited to this run-down part of the city centre at that time.

Oiled facades

In the past, facades were oiled in order to give them a uniform colour and to make them water-repellent. Firstly, the colour was predominantly red, matching the Leiden bricks. Later in the 18th century, a darker type of brick came on the market and the coat of paint became brown and sometimes black. If buildings are oiled, Stadsherstel often brings back the same colour oil. It also happens that a facade is painted white with the wrong paint, as a result of which moisture can no longer migrate out of the brick. In most cases, the coat of paint disappears then when restoring the facades and the original appearance re-emerges. In most cases, the coat of paint disappears during a restoration of the facades and the original appearance re-emerges, as with the building Oudezijds Achterburgwal 164.

Colour 483

Oiled facades Roestraat 5 and 7

Colour 484

Period room Breestraat Beverwijk

Colour in the interior

Similar views are customary for the paintwork of the interior. In the case of new interiors as a contemporary addition to the existing historic buildings, the choice of colours is much greater. In the case of special interiors, the colour is often determined on the basis of historical colour research, as was done with the unique period rooms in de Breestraat 101 in Beverwijk, where an extensive committee of specialists advised on the colours to be used.

Colour

Interior Weaver's House, Zaanse Schans

Colour 487

Colour 488

Gilded floral painting of Oak and Acanthus on panel door, Reguliersgracht 63

Industrial

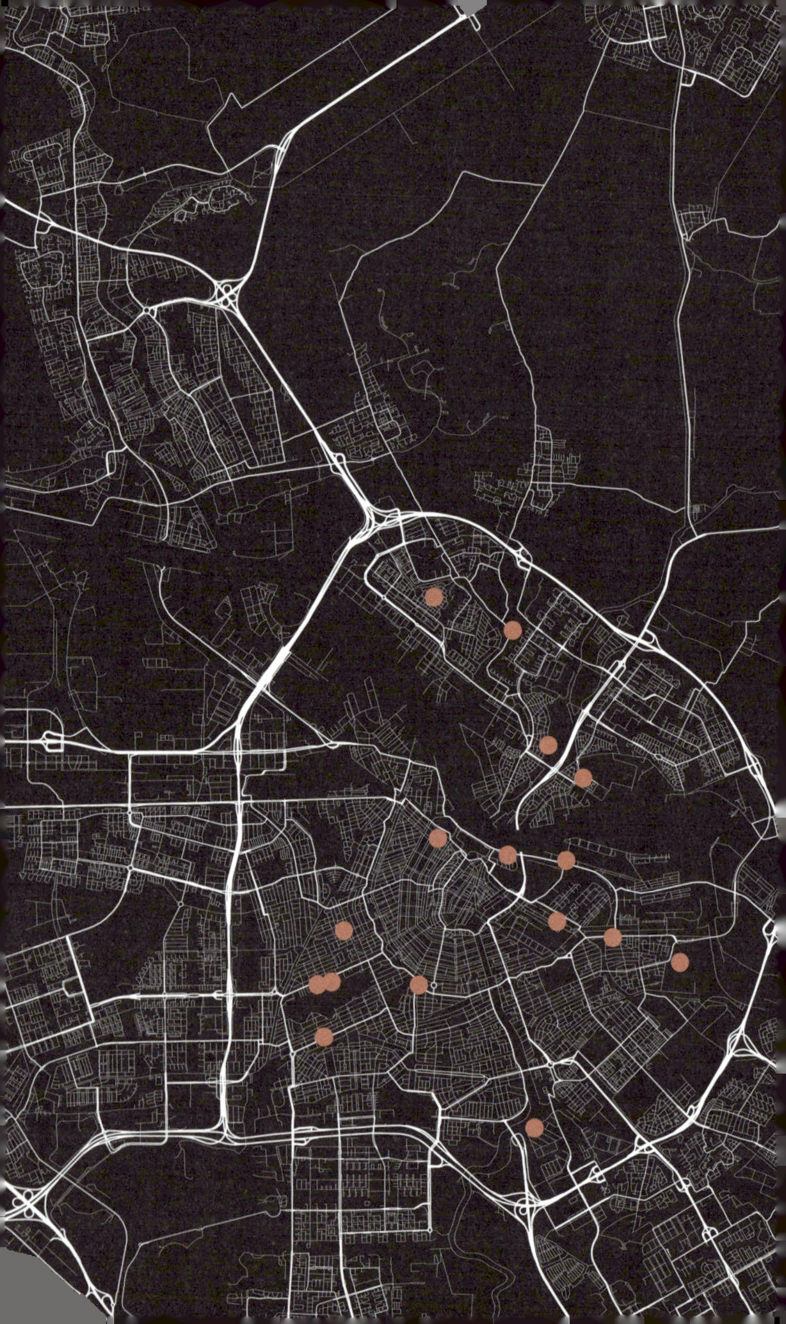

494	**School of Dik Trom**, Oosthuizen
494	**Zonnehuis**, Amsterdam
494	**Bucking Kadoelen**, Amsterdam
494	**Nursery Johanna Margaretha**, Amsterdam
494	**Zamenhofstraat 28A**, Amsterdam
494	**West-Indisch Huis**, Amsterdam
495	**Horse tram depot**, Amsterdam
495	**Manure stables**, Amsterdam
495	**Privaathuisjes**, Amsterdam
495	**Rioolgemaal F**, Amsterdam
495	**Zuider Gasworks**, Amsterdam
495	**Gemaal Zeeburg**, Amsterdam
495	**Flevo bucking**, Amsterdam
496	**Fire station Oud Nico**, Amsterdam
510	**Pakhuis de Zwijger**, Amsterdam
530	**Kromhout wharf**, Amsterdam
544	**De Hallen**, Amsterdam

The 'European Route of Industrial Heritage' (ERIH) a tourist network currently contains, 19 regional routes providing information about the history of landscape and industry. One of the routes, the Hollandroute, takes you past a number of examples around the North Sea Canal, among which the Zaanoevers – including the Zaanse Schans – the NDSM wharf and the Cruquius steam pumping station. The location illustrates the diversity of the industrial history. Everything that stems from the daily work of people, such as factory buildings, bridges, locks, mills and also the material traces of the industrial society forms part of this communal culture. Textile, industry and war, accommodation and architecture and energy are the most common themes. For example, the Heineken Brewery building, the NDSM wharf, the Schip (the Amsterdam School residential complex) and the Westergasfabriek (now part of a city park) have been earmarked. After the opening of the North Sea Canal in 1876 and the continuing mechanisation, the industry in the region expanded enormously. The food industry on the river De Zaan developed into what was referred to as the Voorraadkast van Nederland (Pantry of the Netherlands). Rice-husking plants, bread and rusk factories, canning factories and chocolate factories formed important economic pillars of the region. Other important industrial sectors were

Lightship no. 6 'Haaks'

the shipbuilding industry (NDSM), the machine industry (Stork-Werkspoor) and the diamond industry. Stadsherstel contributed to the repurposing of a warehouse, a wharf and a former tram terminal. Also a start was made on the renovation of a building on the Hembrugterrein close to Zaandam (see Landscape).

Former tram depot

Industrial

School of Dik Trom
Etersheim 8, Oosthuizen
2012

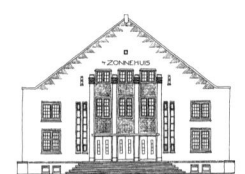

Zonnehuis
Zonneplein 29-30-30A, Amsterdam
2005

Bucking Kadoelen
Landsmeerderdijk 213,
Amsterdam
2014

Nursery Johanna Margaretha
Wingerdweg 98, Amsterdam
2011

Zamenhofstraat 28A
Amsterdam
2008

West-Indisch Huis
Herenmarkt 91-99, Amsterdam
1977

Industrial

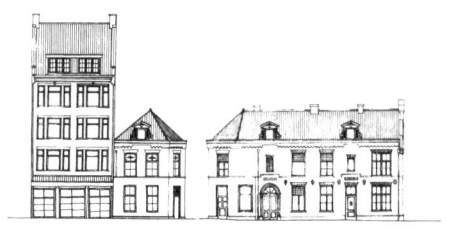

Horse tram depot
Overtoom 373, Amsterdam
2004

Manure stables
Vondelpark 6B-6C,
Amsterdam
2005

Privaathuisjes
Valeriusplein 7-8, Amsterdam
2014

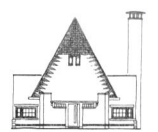

Rioolgemaal F
Ruysdaelkade 2-4,
Amsterdam
1996/2000

Zuider Gasworks
Korte Ouderkerkerdijk 45,
Amsterdam
2014

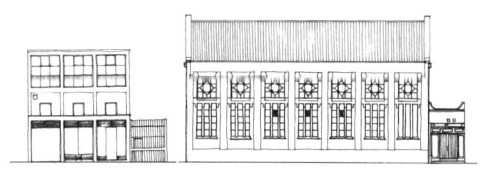

Gemaal Zeeburg
Zeeburgerdijk 50-54, Amsterdam
1991

Flevo bucking
Flevopark 13, Amsterdam
2010

Oud Nico fire station

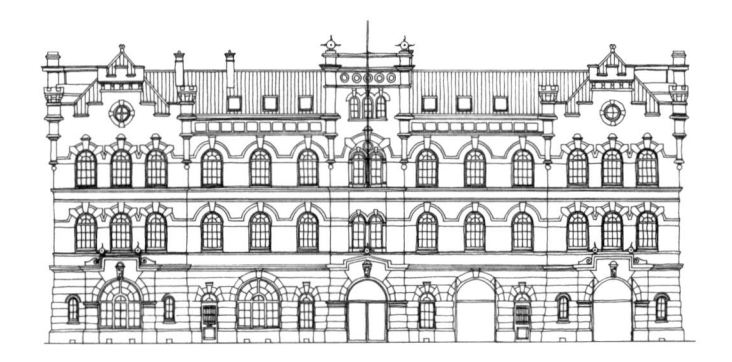

Address
De Ruijterkade 144-147-149-150

Town
Amsterdam

Built
1890 – 1899

Acquisition
2006

Restoration
2011

Restoration architect
CASA architecten

Current use
Studios, offices and residential space

Five years after being purchased, the building was restored by CASA architects in 2011. After the departure of the fire service in 1973, it was put into use as a studio space with homes. The restoration was focused on improving the indoor climate, a change in the layout and the expansion of the floor space for new functions. The basic principle of the restoration was that the homes and studios on the floors would be maintained for the users at that time. The ground floor and the forge had to be transformed into an office and workspace for companies in the creative sector. An extension with extra floor space was necessary for a break-even operation.

Oud Nico fire station

Fire station decorated with 50th anniversary of the Amsterdam fire service, 1924

The fire station 'N' on De Ruijterkade 144, 146-150, alongside the river IJ, between the Muziekgebouw and Amsterdam Central Station, was built by the architects B. de Greef and W. Springer from the Public Works Department in 1890. It has been a nationally listed building since 2001 with cultural historical, architectural and typological value, as one of the first fire stations following the establishment of the professional fire service in 1874. Numerous fire stations were built in a short space of time spread throughout the city. All fire stations were given a type designation with a code letter. There was a need at this location with the expansion of the dockland area alongside the IJ. It was built using multi-coloured brick and designed in an eclectic style with motifs borrowed from the Renaissance and the Middle Ages, and references to castle buildings. The decorated keystones above the large round arch openings on the ground floor are fitted with the attributes of the fireman and a salamander as the symbol of fire. Behind the main entrance on the rear side of the building, there is a 'corridor' placed at right angles and a centrally located stairwell with a double staircase as access to the other floors.

Industrial

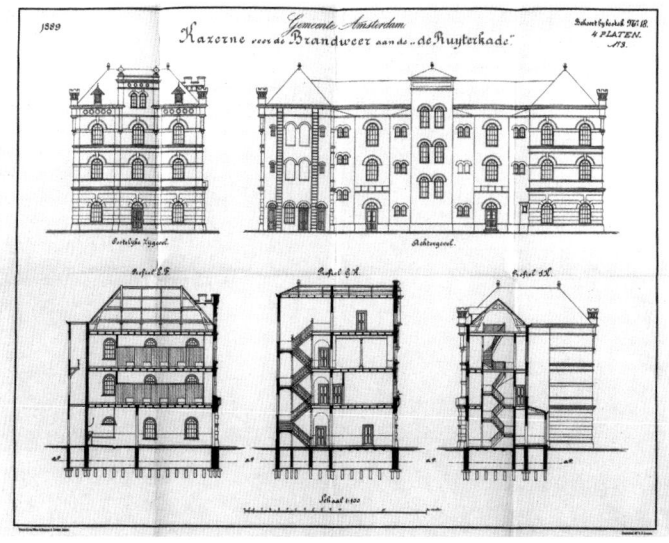

Blueprint, 1889

The workspaces, the coach house with stables and the signal room were originally located to the right on the ground floor. The sleeping quarters for 44 firemen were situated above the coach house. The hose tower and climbing tower are still clearly recognisable at the rear. The waiting room and the canteen in the left part of the building used to serve as a common room for the crew. The canteen proprietor lived next to the kitchen. The division fire officer and the chief fireman had their office and home on the 1st and 2nd floor. In 1905, the fire station was expanded with a freestanding forge, three years later once again with extra sleeping quarters at the rear, and in 1911 with a storage space for tools, which was connected with the main building by a brick wall and an archway. After replacing horsepower with steam power, various rooms were once again converted. The sliding poles by the main staircase and the right staircase date from that time. The working area, which included part of the centre, the Eastern Harbour District and Amsterdam North, ensured there was a rich history of fires. The renowned steam fire boat 'Jason' was located in front of the door of Nico for almost its entire career from 1904 to 1963.

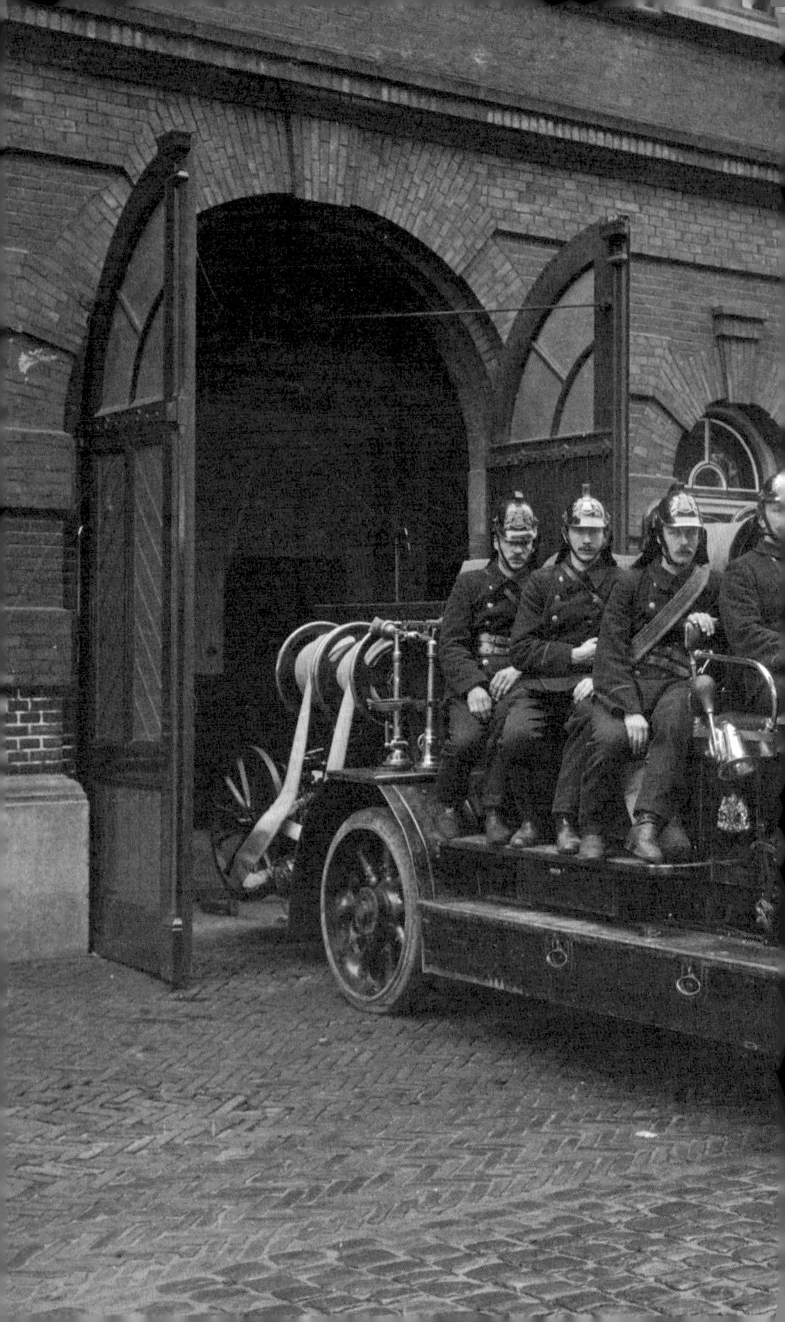

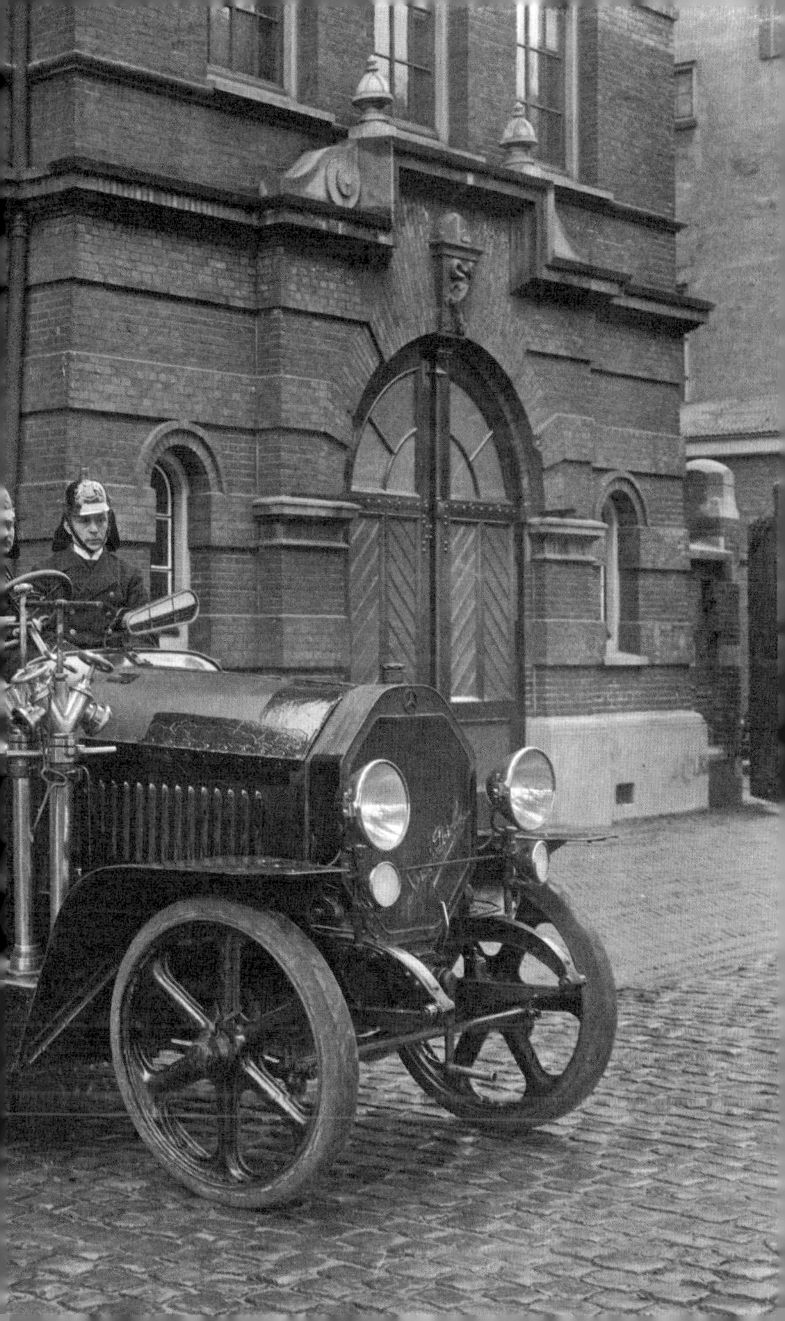

Architect Bastiaan de Greef

Bastiaan de Greef (1818-1899), son of the 'architect of the royal palaces' Jan de Greef, was born in Paleis Noordeinde, which was being refurbished at the time by his father. After the appointment of his father as city architect of Amsterdam in 1820, the family took up residence at the Timmertuin. In 1856, the stadsfabrieksambt (public works), which as an organisation had not changed much since the 16th century, became the new Dienst der Stads Publieke Werken (City Public Works Department). The supervisory director was replaced by an alderman and the technical management was entrusted with a city architect, a city engineer and a director. Jan de Greef became city architect like his son later. In 1890, Bastiaan de Greef retired after a term of office of 56 years. His successor was A.W. Weissman. The fire station on the IJ followed an earlier design by him, the Weesperplein fire station (1873). In 1875, he was responsible for the design of the Binnengasthuis and he built the Blauwbrug, once again in collaboration with Willem Springer, in 1883.

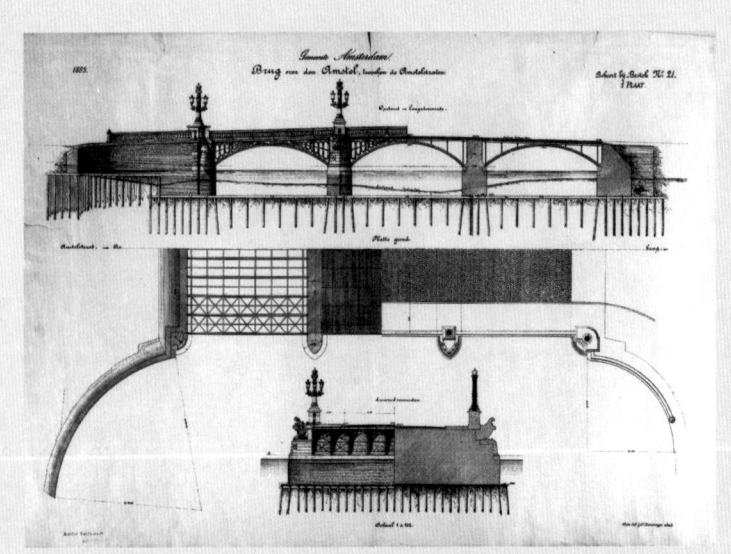

Drawing Blauwbrug

Industrial

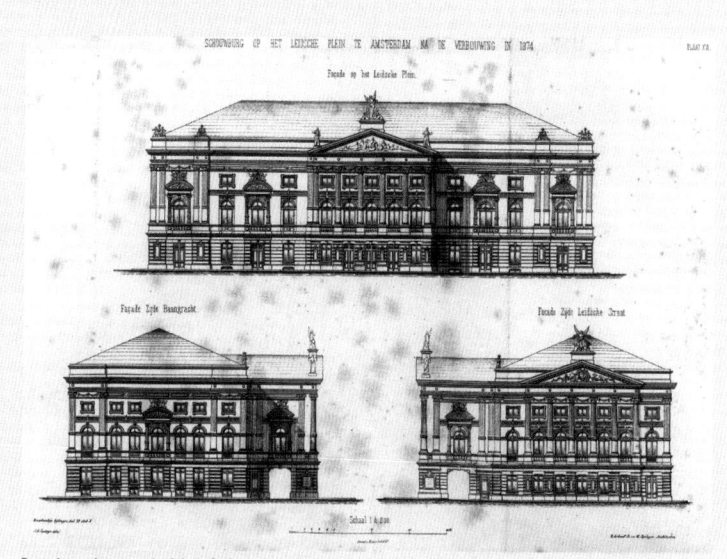

503

Drawing theatre Leidseplein

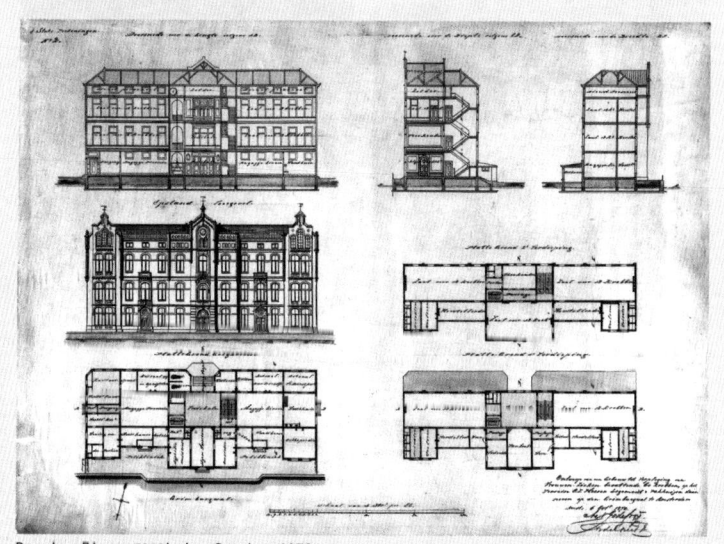

Drawing Binnengasthuis, October 1870

Oud Nico fire station

Restoration

During the refurbishment, massive blocks of new buildings from the Oosterdok project and the extension plans of the Eastern Harbour District emerged in the direct vicinity of Oud Nico. The character of a freestanding fortress had to be maintained in the design for the restoration. Following research into alternatives, the necessary extension was placed at the rear between the main stairwell and the side ressault. This was an elaboration on previous extensions from right after the building work. For the sake of the architectural clarity, a choice was made to design these modest extensions as abstract volumes. The volumes, just like the mezzanine floors, were kept separate from the existing monumental brickwork facades. Perforated aluminium wall cladding lends the exterior the desired anonymous character and also forms the fixed sun blinds on the southern-facing facades. There was a lot of rising damp and salts in the walls, both inside and outside. In order to improve the indoor climate, all units were fitted with air-conditioning systems with heat recovery. The original layout always remained the guideline for the restoration and transformation. The ground floor can currently be split into a maximum of 8 separate business units.

Oud Nico fire station

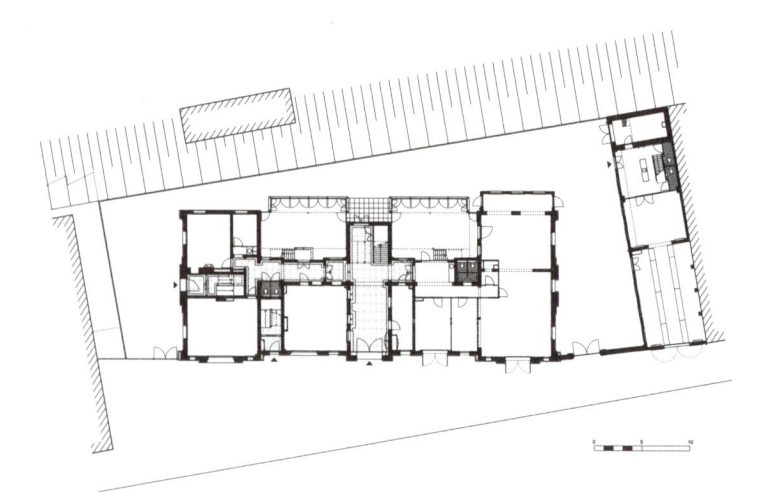

506

Ground plan of the transformation

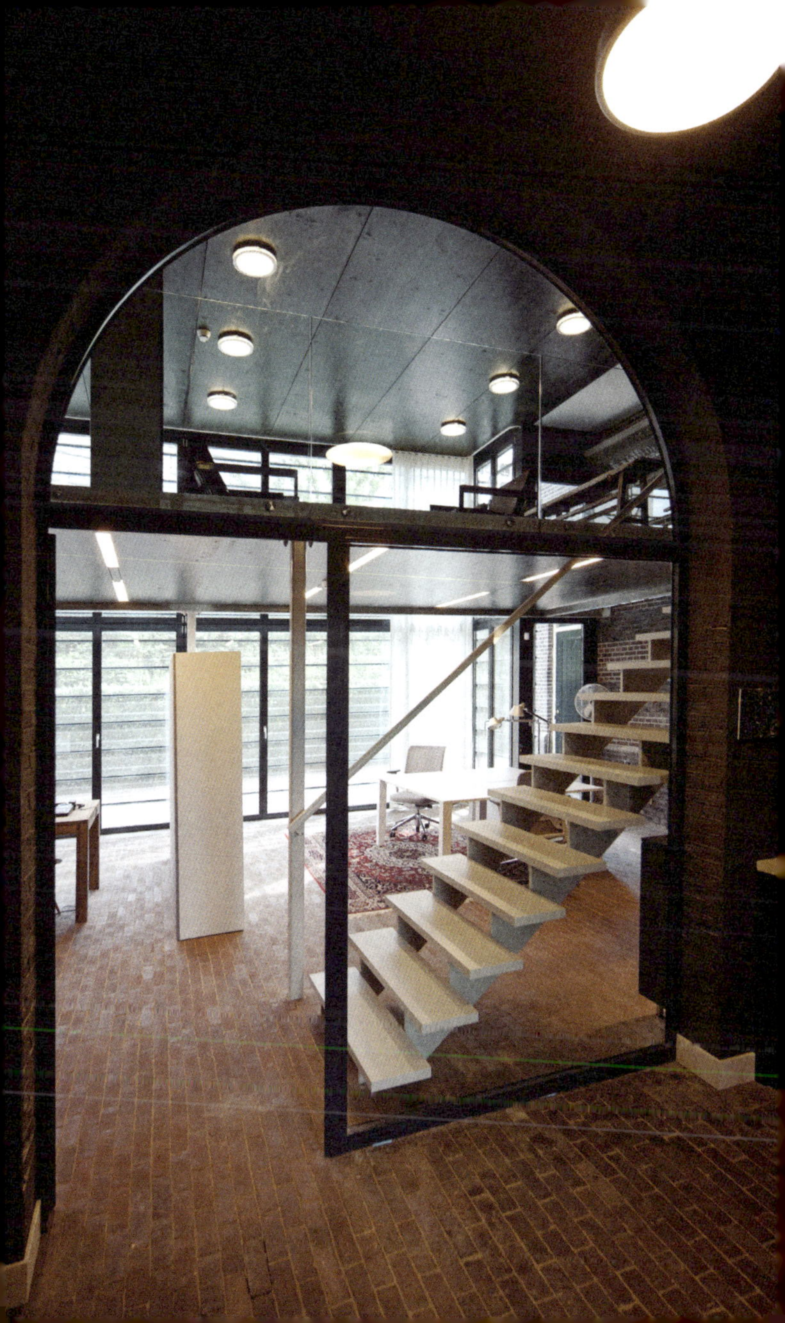

DE RUIJTERKADE
Centrum

150

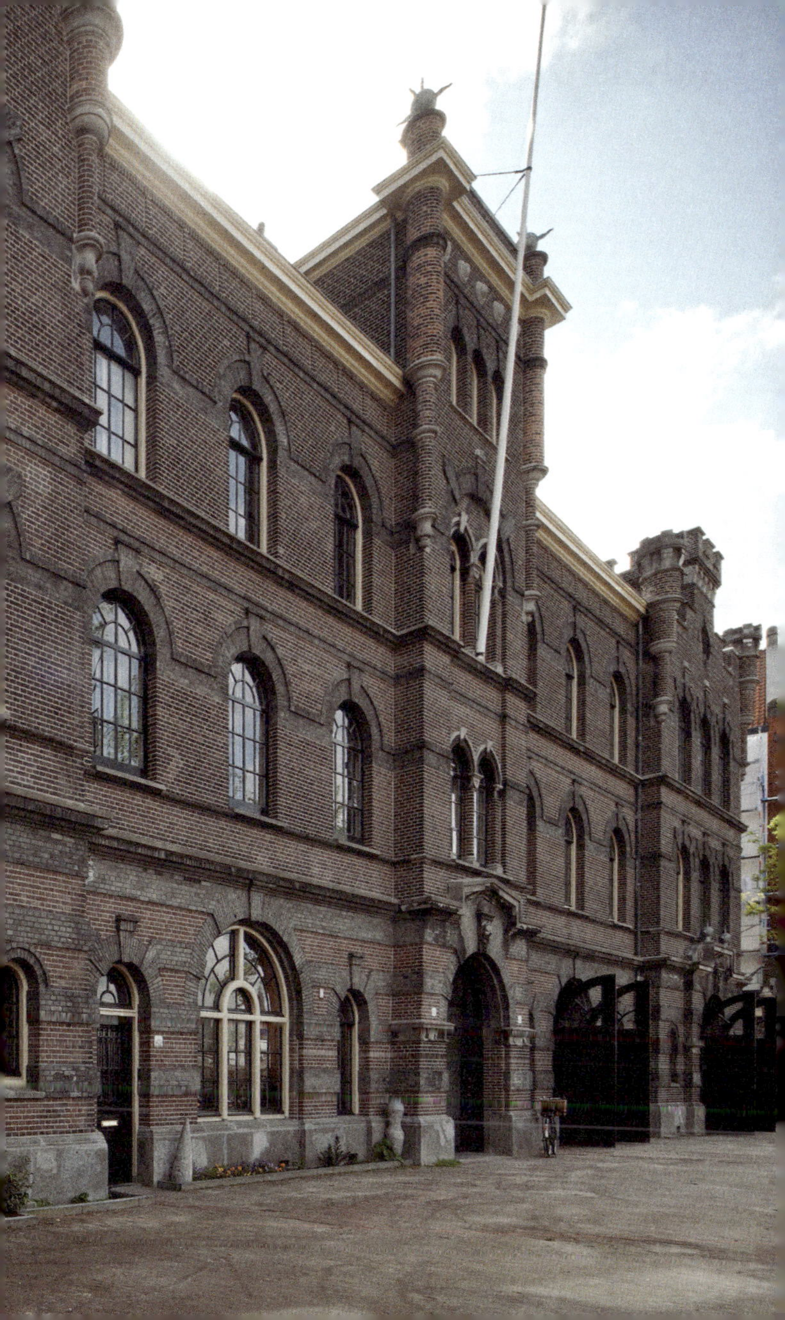

Pakhuis De Zwijger

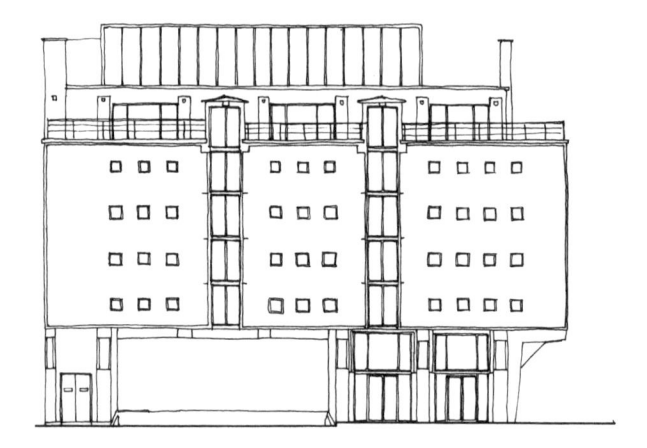

510

Address	Built	Restoration architect
Piet Heinkade 179-181	**1933 – 1934**	**André van Stigt**

Town	Acquisition	Current use
Amsterdam	**2005**	**Transformed to a location for the creative industry, studios, offices, cafe and restaurant**

Restoration
2006

De Zwijger is the only part of the series of warehouses on the Oostelijke Handelskade (Eastern Trade Wharf) that has preserved its original silhouette during the large-scale housing developments on the IJ river at the end of the 20th century, partly due to the fact that this is the only remaining Amsterdam warehouse constructed in concrete from the period between the wars. In the 1980s, the building became vacant and it turned to be one of the most important pop rehearsal spaces of the city - and an underground hotspot with concerts and parties. With the demolition of Vrieshuis Amerika, several squatters were given the opportunity by the municipality to continue part of the activities in De Zwijger, albeit on a more commercial basis. They established the De Zwijger foundation. At the same time, the municipal council decided to build the connecting bridge with the Java-eiland (one of the new residential areas in the harbour) through the former warehouse, instead of demolishing it. However, after the completion of the bridge, the Housing Department of the municipality stated that the warehouse had become dilapidated and could collapse due to the pile-driving from the surrounding new building projects. The Municipal Executive issued a demolition permit for it. The Cuypersgenootschap, an association that strives to preserve built heritage from the 19th and 20th century, immediately requested nationally listed building status and this was granted in 2001, so that demolition was cancelled. Nothing has been heard since about the alleged dilapidation. In the meantime, a plan was developed and worked out for a 'Warehouse for the creative industry', a breeding ground and workshop, and a meeting place for media artists, cultural entrepreneurs and producers. A location with radio and TV studios, a media lab and a cinema, editing rooms, offices, a large hall and catering establishments. A place for professionals and public, with creation and presentation under one roof. With programming of documentary film, music, theatre, debate, radio and TV, installations, exhibitions and festivals. The foundation come into contact with the architectural firm J. van Stigt in the autumn of 2003, which had already given many listed buildings a new lease of life, such as the Entrepotdok and the Oranje Nassaukazerne. André van Stigt, who had previously refurbished the Vondelkerk, Posthoornkerk and Majellakerk for the Amsterdams Monumenten Fonds (Amsterdam Monument Fund, AMF), asked if the AMF – currently part of Stadsherstel Amsterdam N.V. – was prepared to acquire the former warehouse, and work out the plans further together with the foundation and the architectural firm. Stadsherstel researched the feasibility of the project and in September 2004, the municipal council approved the necessary subsidies, so that the restoration could begin in April of the following year.

Industrial

Pakhuis De Zwijger

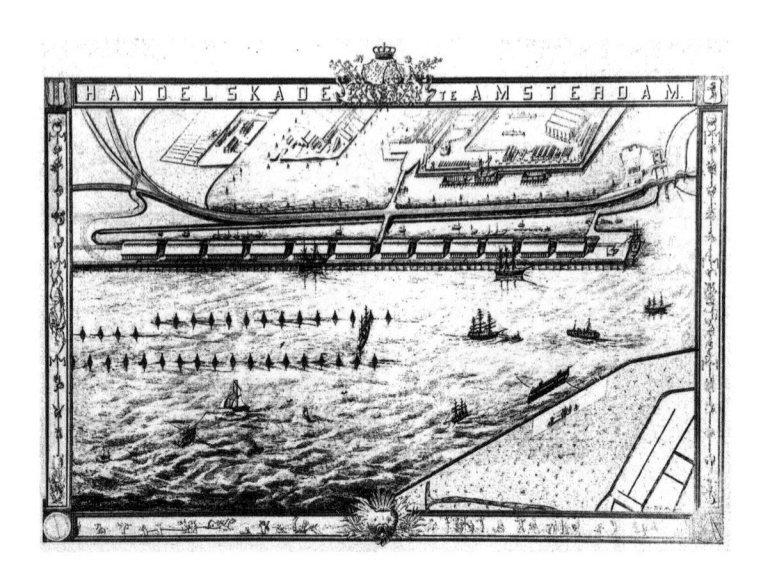

Urban development

Following the official opening of the North Sea Canal on 1 November 1876, large ships gained access once again to the old port of Amsterdam. A number of years before that, the municipal council had decided, under pressure from the government, to agree to the construction of a train station (Amsterdam Central Station) in the open waterfront. At the time, the city still tried to unite the interests of shipping industry and railways, but the constant raising and lowering of the bridges caused great delay.

The construction of the Oostelijke Handelskade with an inner harbour offered a solution. An additional advantage of the new, modern wharf was the better exploitation opportunity of the (expensive) steam ships. These could only be made profitable by having them travel around as much as possible. In the past, sailing ships could sometimes lie still in the harbour for months. It had to be possible to load and unload the steam ships as quickly as possible with modern cranes and there was no room for this in the old port. In 1879,

Industrial

400 metres (of the planned 2,000) of the wharf was ready for exploitation. Following some initial problems, the first warehouse was opened in 1884. It was built by the public limited company N.V. Handelskade, based on a design by W. van Lookeren Campagne and E. Confeld von Felbert. The 200-metre-long building consisted of three parts: Asia, Europe and Africa. Amsterdam thus obtained the first modern warehouse situated next to deep water and railway. The Blaauwhoedenveem trading company – which had taken over N.V. Handelskade in 1888 and thus become owner of the Asia, Europe and Africa warehouses – had a second warehouse constructed in 1893 – 1895. The 100-metre-long building consisted of two parts, America and Australia, and was designed by H. Moen and G. van Arkel. In the same year as the completion of America and Australia, the Handelskade was finished and expanded, in stages, to almost 2,200 metres.

Pakhuis De Zwijger

Building

Pakhuis De Zwijger on the Oostelijke Handelskade was built in the years 1933 – 34, based on a design by J. de Bie Leuveling Tjeenk in cooperation with structural engineer K. Bakker. The commissioning party was Blauwhoedenveem-Vriesseveem, which had concentrated its Amsterdam activities along the IJ river following a cost-cutting merger. At the same time, the warehouses Europe and Africa were tackled. Europe had already been expanded in 1920 with offices and staff houses, and was thoroughly refurbished by Tjeenk and Bakker in 1935. Africa was replaced following a fire in 1913 by a completely new warehouse based on a design by A.J. Joling, one of the earliest examples of mushroom slabs in the Netherlands. The reinforcement of the facade entirely constructed in concrete lay too close on the surface, however, and would therefore rust. Tjeenk and Bakker made a new facade. Following several thorough refurbishments once again in 1963 and 1971, listed building status could not ultimately be granted to Europe anymore and the building was ready for demolition in 1999. Africa was, in the meantime, a nationally listed building, among other things due to the unique floors. Just like the Africa warehouse, De Zwijger was constructed in reinforced concrete. In order to prevent problems like with Africa and to improve the insulation, the concrete frontages were clad with half-brick walls. De Zwijger was used as a refrigerated warehouse for the temporary storage of perishable products.

Industrial

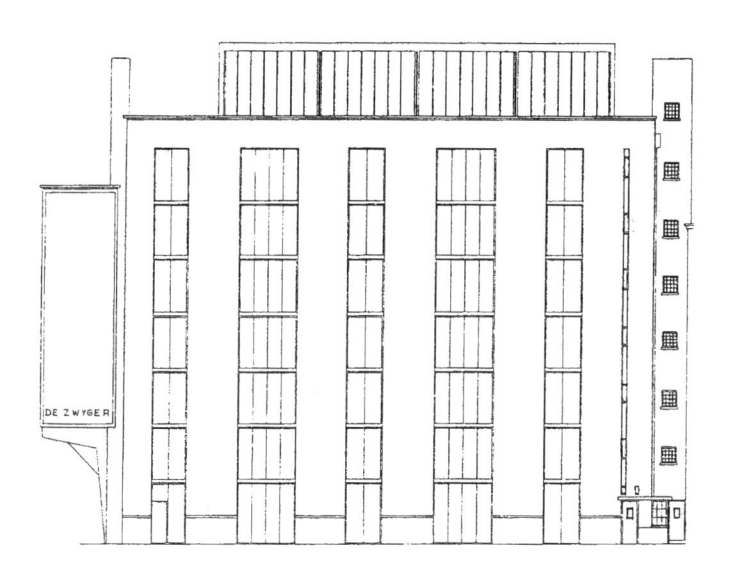

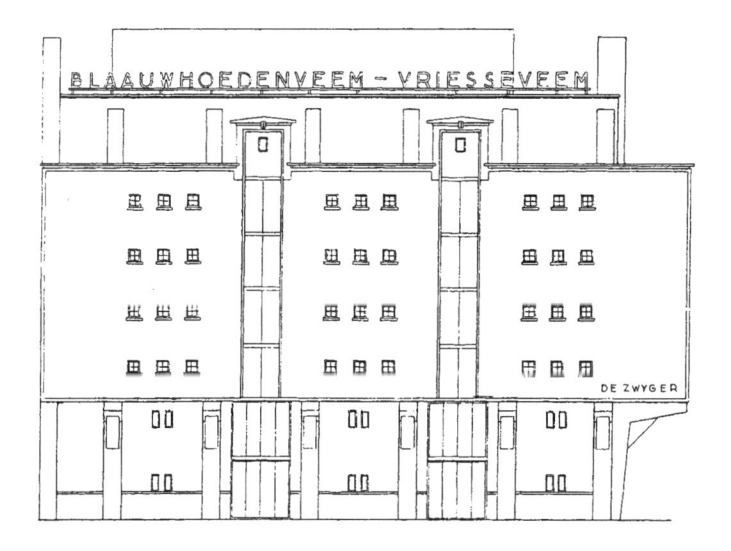

EXPEDITEURS

DE ZVYGER

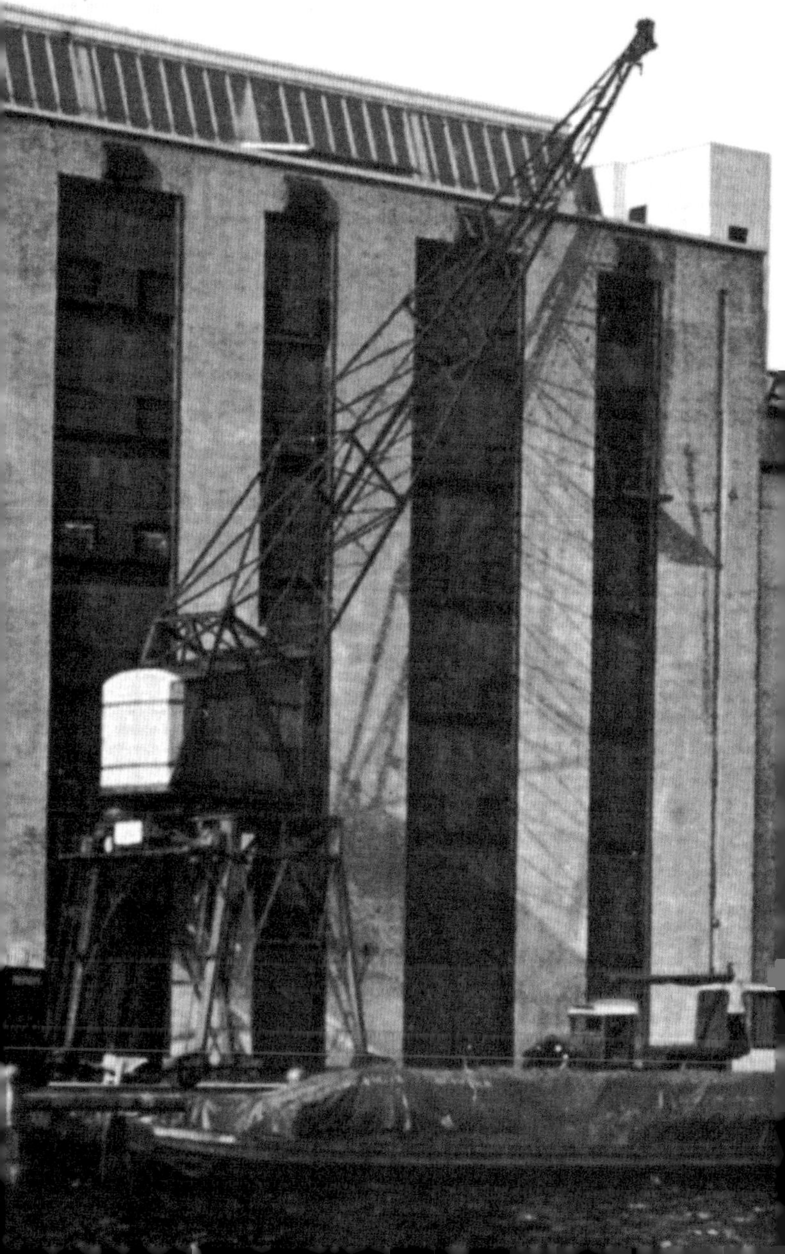

Pakhuis De Zwijger

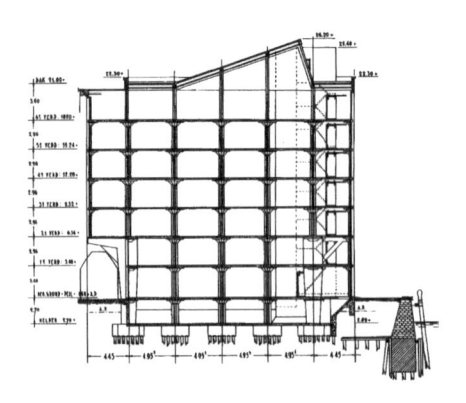

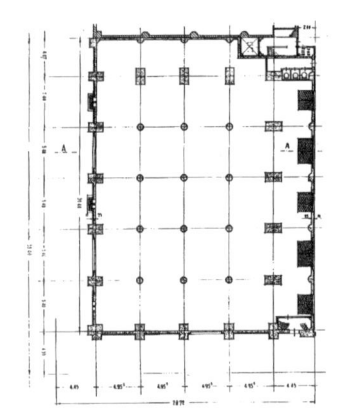

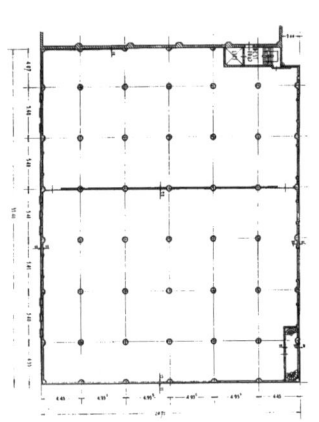

Restoration plan, sections and plans

The former refrigerated warehouse is a beautiful example of the close cooperation between the disciplines of the structural and civil engineer. The building has seven stories and a cellar. The floors are made up of undivided rectangular spaces for the refrigerated storage of large quantities of goods. The concrete load-bearing structure consists of mushroom columns and corbels, the latter supporting substantial corbelling on the southern and eastern side, and situated indoors on the northern and western side. The facades were clad with an insulating brick layer and fitted with a well-considered facade

Industrial

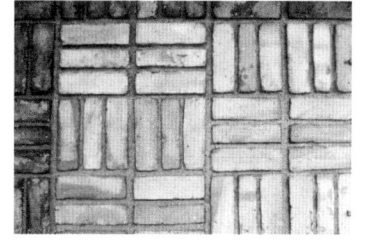

Construction work about 1920

composition (with windows, loading doors and hoisting gear) and meticulous detailing. The recessed top floor has a sawtooth roof with windows on the northern side for the purpose of sample lofts. De Zwijger is one of the most important examples of the few remaining utilitarian buildings in the harbour from an architectural-historical, structural and typological standpoint. De Zwijger is one of the most important industrial buildings in Amsterdam and has international allure, according to the Amsterdam monument experts.

Architect

Architect Jan de Bie Leuveling Tjeenk

Jan de Bie Leuveling Tjeenk (1885–1940) was an important figure in Dutch architecture in his time, among other things for his work for the Jaarbeurs in Utrecht and his own house Villa Troostwijk on the Museumplein in Amsterdam, which shows the influence of American architect Frank Lloyd Wright. He also designed a small block of flats, completed in 1937, and located on the Paulus Potterstraat behind his own villa and next to the current Van Gogh museum. In 1936, he was commissioned for the refurbishment of Paleis Soestdijk (the house of Queen Juliana at that time).

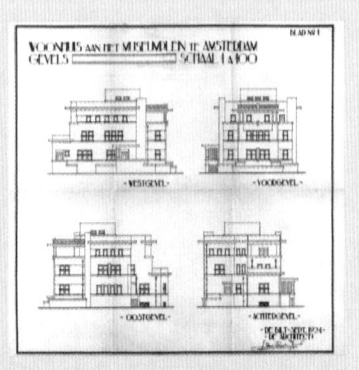

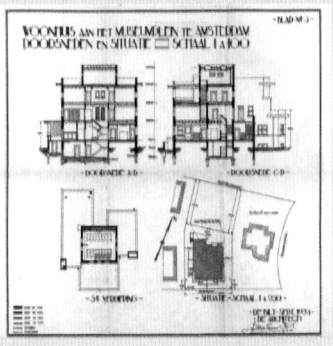

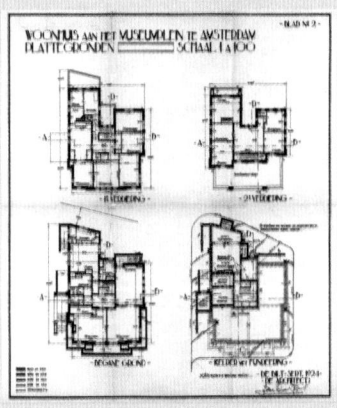

Industrial 523

Villa Troostwijk about 1929

Pakhuis De Zwijger

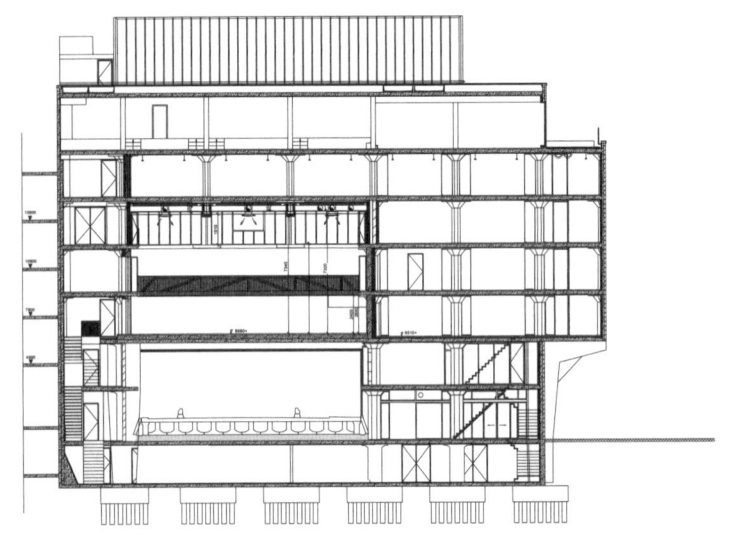

Section final design

Section interior design

Industrial

525

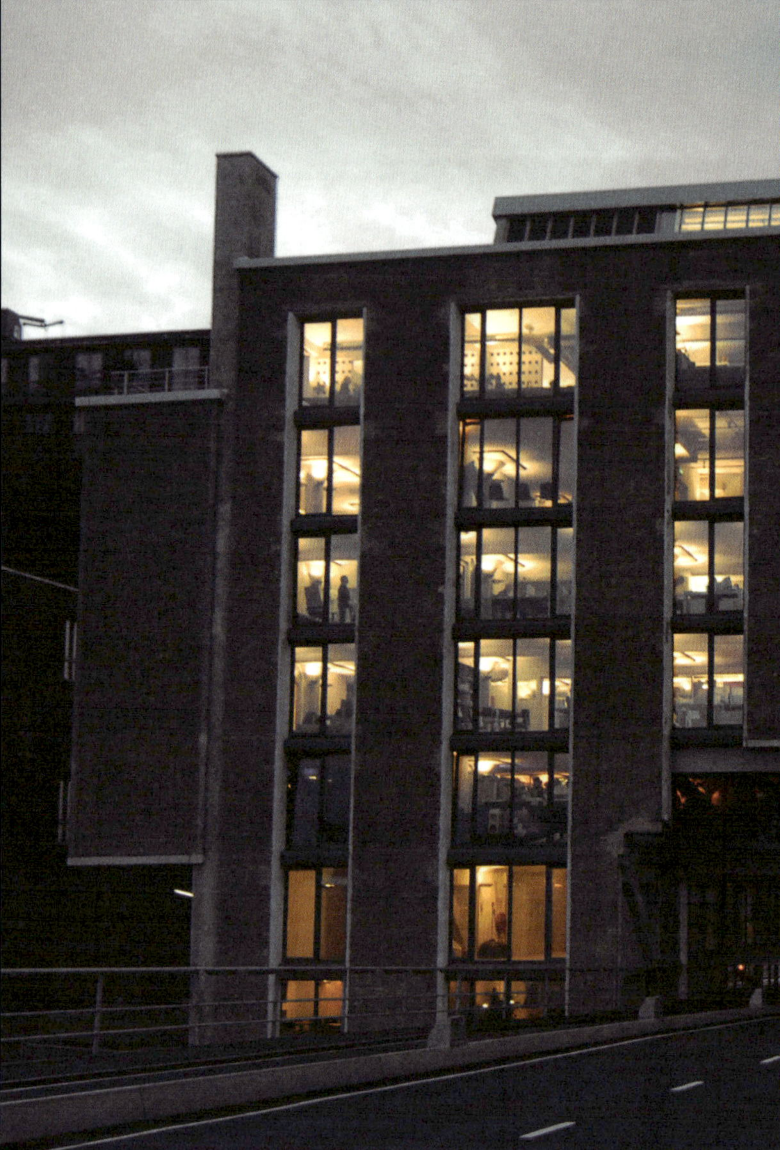

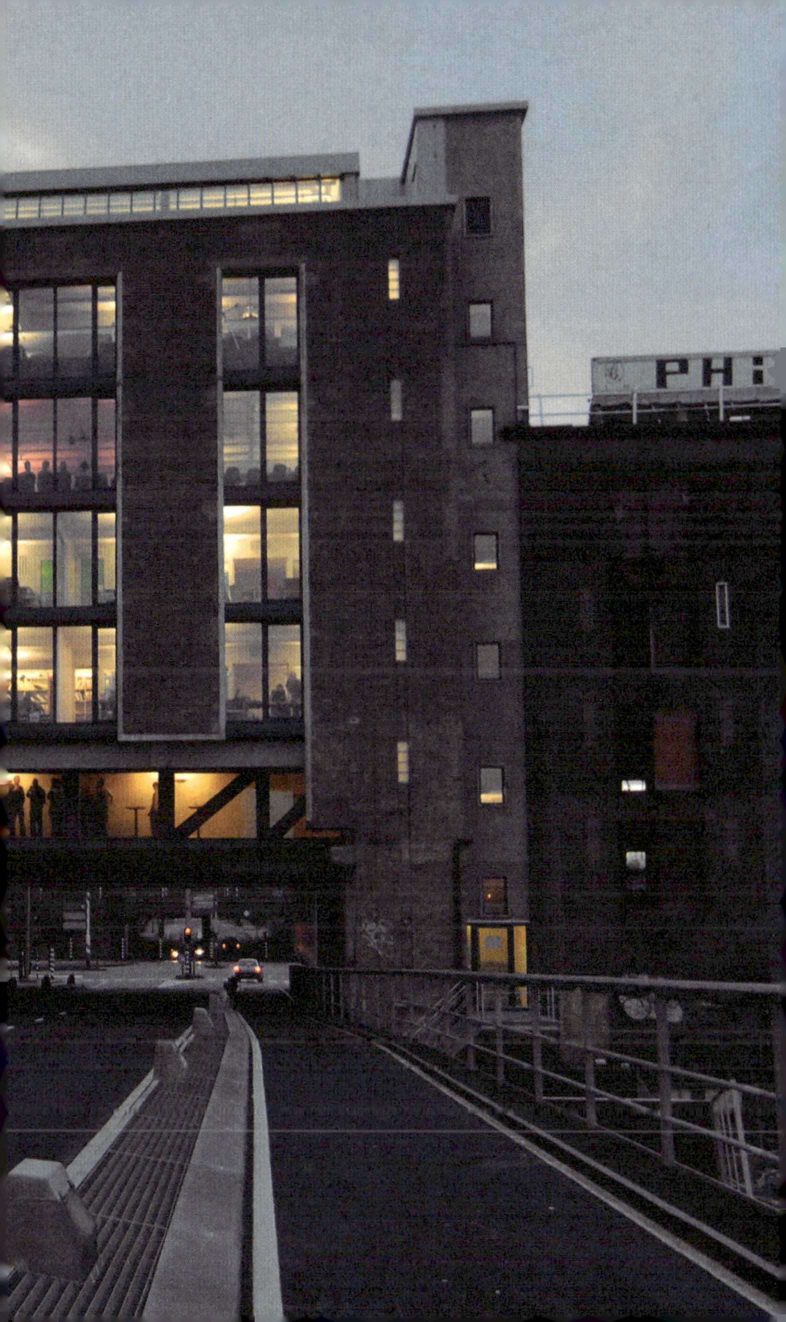
PH

AFRIKA

PAKHUIS DE ZWIJGER
DE ZWYGER
THE FUTURE OF EVERYDAY LIVING
21

Kromhout wharf

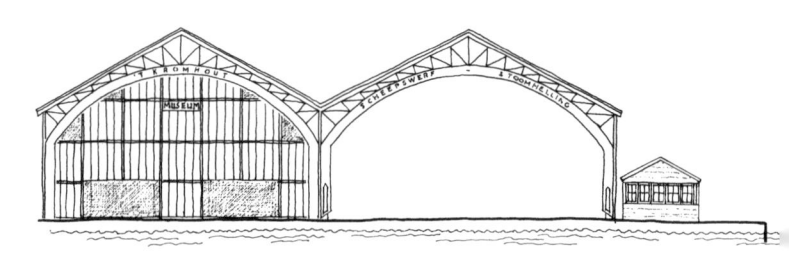

530

Address
**Hoogte Kadijk 147 ·
Kruithuisstraat 17-25**

Town
Amsterdam

Establishment shipyard
1757

Construction of main roof
1888, second roof 1899

Acquisition
1998

Restoration
2003

Restoration architect
**Duinker Van der
Torre samenwerkende
architecten B.V.**

Current use
**6 commercial spaces
and museum**

In 1998, the Kromhoutcomplex on the Hoogte Kadijk 147 / Kruithuisstraat 17 – 25 was acquired by Stadsherstel. In 2003, work began on the restoration of the wharf, which was constructed in 1757. The building is currently being used as a commercial space and as a museum with its own room hire. The large roof originates from 1888, a second version followed in 1899. As a result of the restoration, part of the Amsterdam maritime history was revived. A place where the nostalgic smell of diesel from droning Kromhout engines forms a lasting memory. In 1967, the ship-related activities ended, in the same way as many places within the city boundaries. In 1975, the wharf was saved from demolition. The Westkap is partly in use again as a shipyard, surrounded by old ships. The Oosthal is partly decorated with the collection of the Kromhout museum and tells the historical story of this area as shipyard quarter and the story of the Kromhout firm in particular. Numerous wharfs were established on the Nieuwe Vaart in the 19th century.

Kromhout wharf

About 1902

European industrial heritage

Werf 't Kromhout (Kromhout wharf) was created in the mid-18th century alongside a historic Amsterdam sea dyke, now the Hoogte Kadijk. The wharf owes its name to Doede Janzn. Kromhout, whose wife bought a site where two anchor smiths previously plied their trade. The shipyard, now the museum and tourist attraction Werf 't Kromhout, developed into a modern and successful example of shipbuilding. The roots for the legendary Kromhout engines were planted here from the previous turn of the century. The complex was recently included in the Hollandroute, one of the regional routes of the European Route of Industrial Heritage. England, the Netherlands and Germany form the basis of the organisation for the preservation of the industrial heritage and provide information about the local history of the landscape and industry on the basis of regional routes. The route which 't Kromhout shipyard forms part of takes you past the North Sea Canal, the Zaanoevers, the Zaanse Schans, the NDSM wharf and the Cruquius steam pumping station.

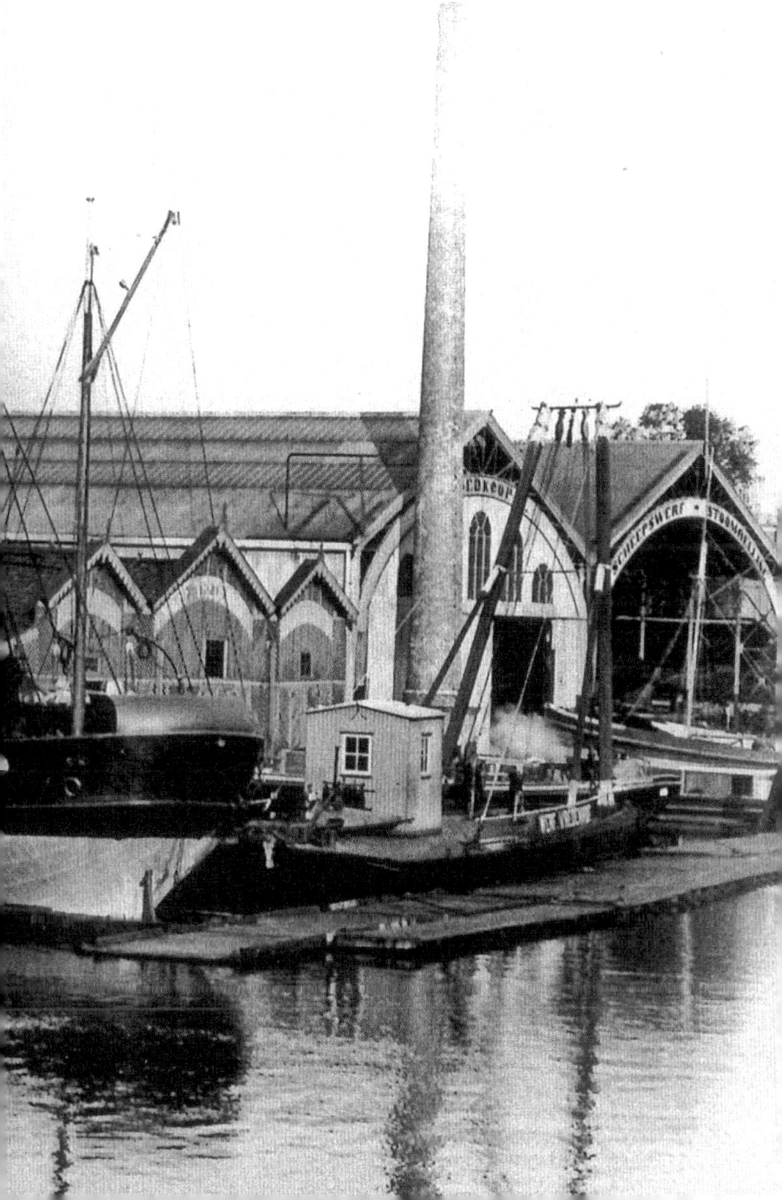

Kromhout wharf

The Kromhout Motoren Fabriek (Kromhout Engine Factory), builder of lorries, coaches and ship engines

In 1867, the wharf was bought by Daniël Goedkoop, a member of a family from the eastern part of the Netherlands that was occupied with all kinds of activities on and alongside the water. For example, they operated a towing service with steam boats on the relatively new North Holland Canal. The company quickly transferred to building iron ships. In 1887, the wharf was covered with a roof, the riveted trusses of which came from a hall of the World Fair. The electric lighting was fitted later. The machine manufacturing and boiler construction were also later additions. The first steam boiler was delivered in 1900. After several years, the company succeeded in bringing a reliable four-stroke petrol engine on the market. In 1908, the engine departments moved from Kromhout to a new factory on the Ketelstraat in Amsterdam North, bordering the river IJ.

Industrial

A few years later the company successfully produced a new two-stroke engine design, the 35 hp R.O. Kromhout engine. R.O. stood for Ruwe Olie (Crude Oil) and that meant that the engine could run on many different fuels (from petrol to gas oil). One of their next designs was the high-pressure engine from 1926. Kromhout looked for new, related activities and in 1932 a licensing contract was entered into with the company Gardner from Manchester, England for the construction of high-speed four-stroke diesel engines, suitable for cars, ships and stationary use. The Kromhout-Gardner engines were used, among other things, in coaches, lorries and tractors, first of all in buses of the Amsterdam transport company.

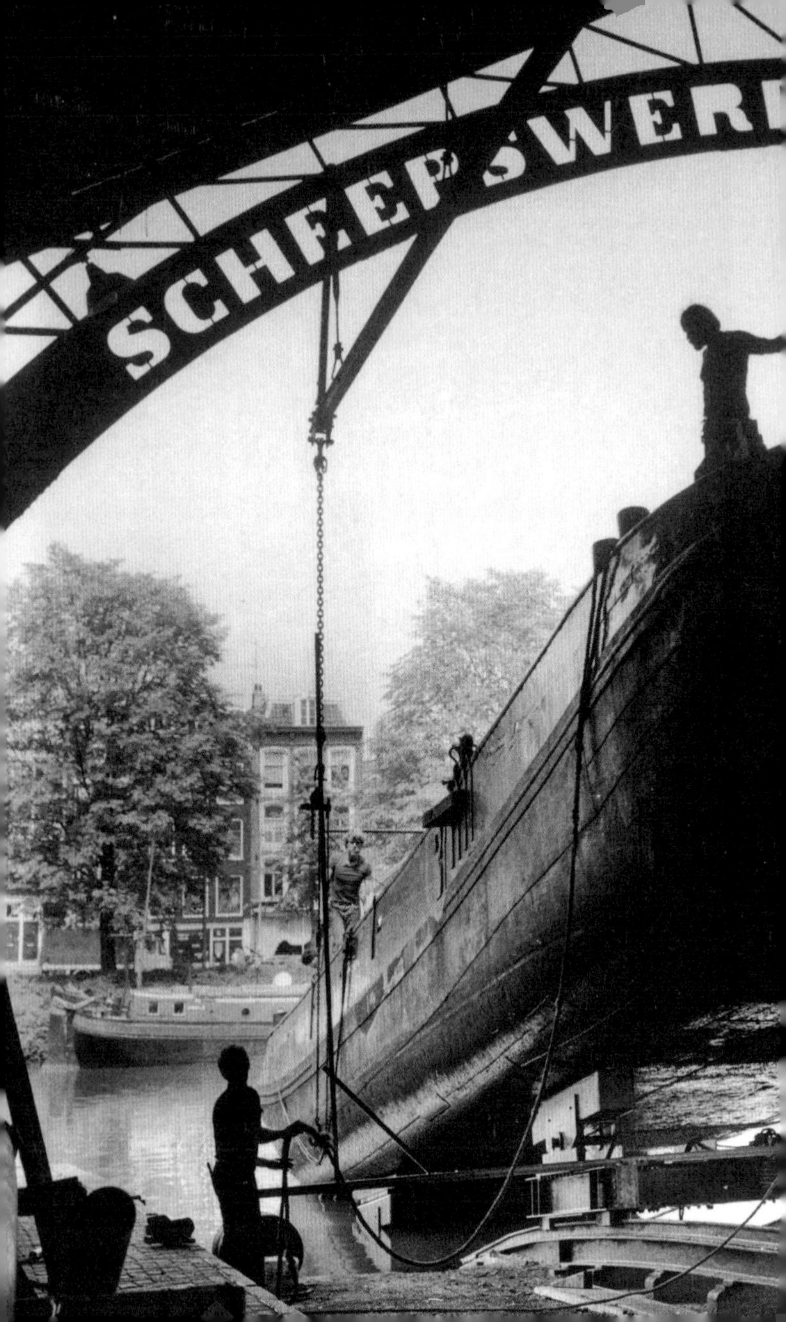
SCHEEPSWER

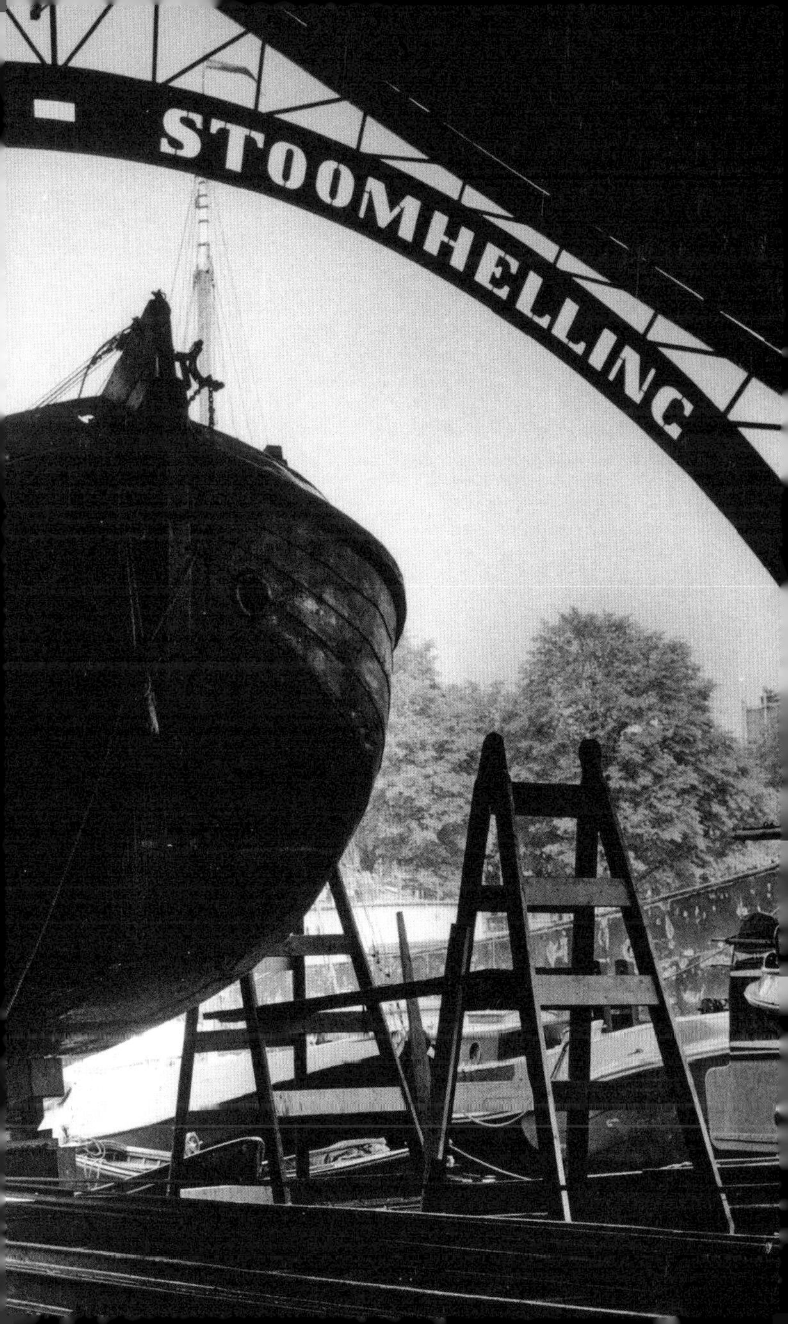
STOOMHELLING

Kromhout wharf

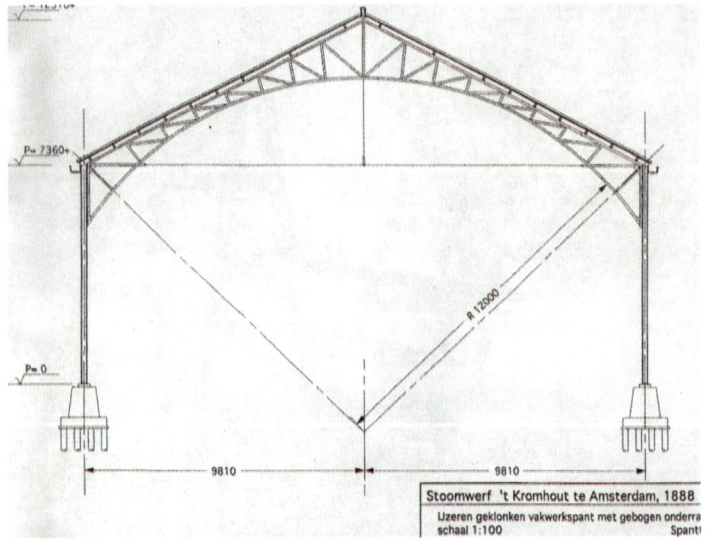

Stoomwerf 't Kromhout te Amsterdam, 1888
IJzeren geklonken vakwerkspant met gebogen onderra
schaal 1:100

Industrial

Kromhout wharf

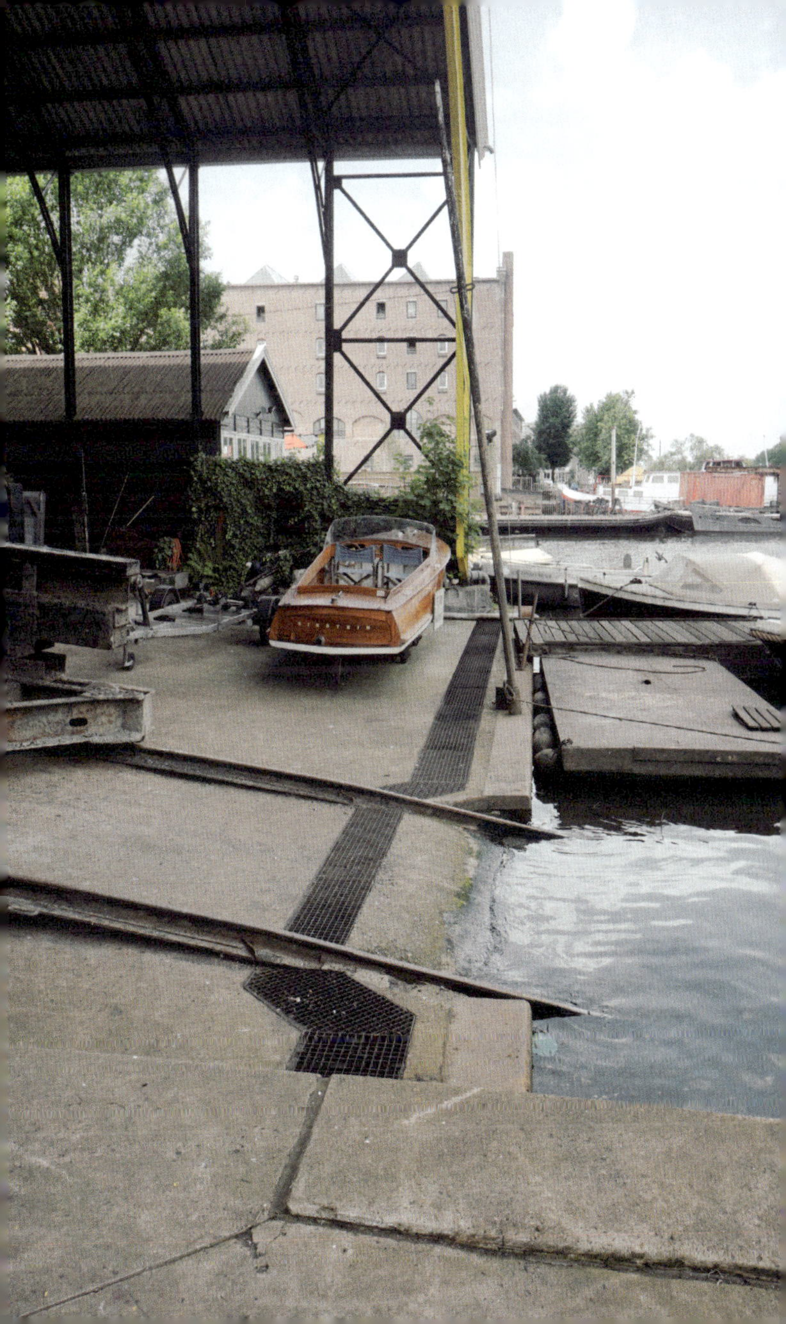

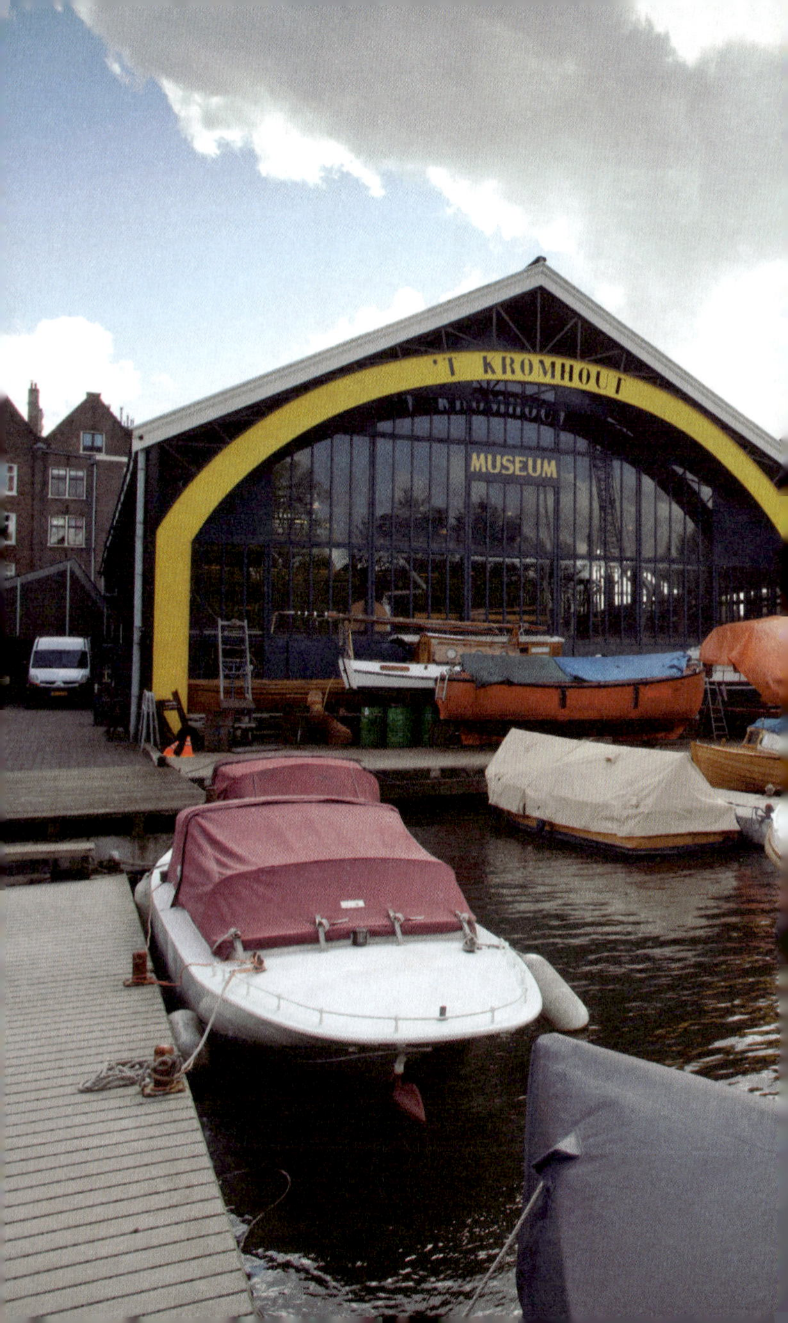
'T KROMHOUT
MUSEUM

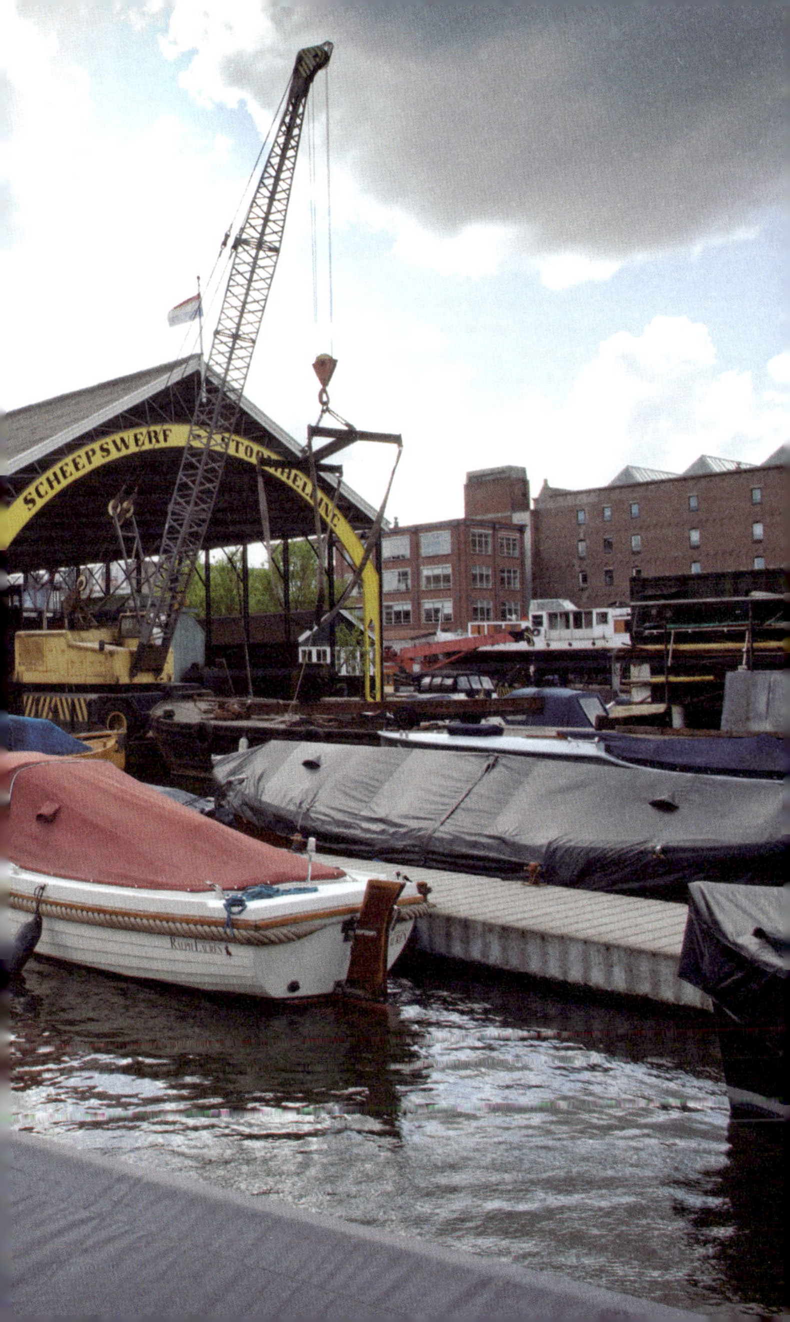
SCHEEPSWERF

De Hallen

Address
Hannie Dankbaarpassage 1-19, Bilderdijkkade 60-62, Tollensstraat 61

Town
Amsterdam

Built
1906

Acquisition
2013

Restoration
2014

Restoration architect
André van Stigt

Current use
Shops and 6 short stay apartments

The Tollenstraat tram depot in Oud West, built in 1907, fell into disuse in the 1990s. The large area between the Kinkerstraat and Ten Kate market, the 'working class' part of the Kinkerbuurt neighbourhood, and the more beautiful buildings on the Bellamyplein and Bilderdijkkade were partly neglected. After years of deliberation, the plan of architect André van Stigt and the Tram Remise Ontwikkelingsmaatschappij (Tram Depot Development Company, TROM) to redevelop the remains of the depot buildings was given the green light in 2011. A plan that would preserve as much of the listed building as possible and accommodate a number of diverse functions, or at least that was the assignment of the city district. In addition, Hall 17, which runs from Tollensstraat 61 to Bilderdijkkade 62, also had to be included. That was not the case up until then and this placed a little too much burden on TROM. Stadsherstel took responsibility for this part.

De Hallen

Horsetram shortly before electrification, to Nassauplein 1916

Horses had been stabled in the south wing of Hall 17 for some time. The hay was on the first floor. The first horse tram had ridden through the city since 1875. The electrification of the tram network proceeded so quickly, however, that Hall 17 changed function and became, among other things, a warehouse and distribution point for the work clothing. Between the wars, the facade of the south wing made way for a parking area for the cars that were necessary for the maintenance of the overhead wires. Two staff houses were located at the head of the Tollenstraat, with the ground floor house extended into Hall 17. At the other end, on the Bilderdijkkade, there was the director's office with an internal staircase to the director's house on the first floor. This house had its own internal staircase to the attic, as a result of which a double staircase was created. The driver lived on the second floor.

Industrial

Tram depot

De Hallen

Hall 17 before restoration

Staircase at the time of the reconstruction

Industrial 549

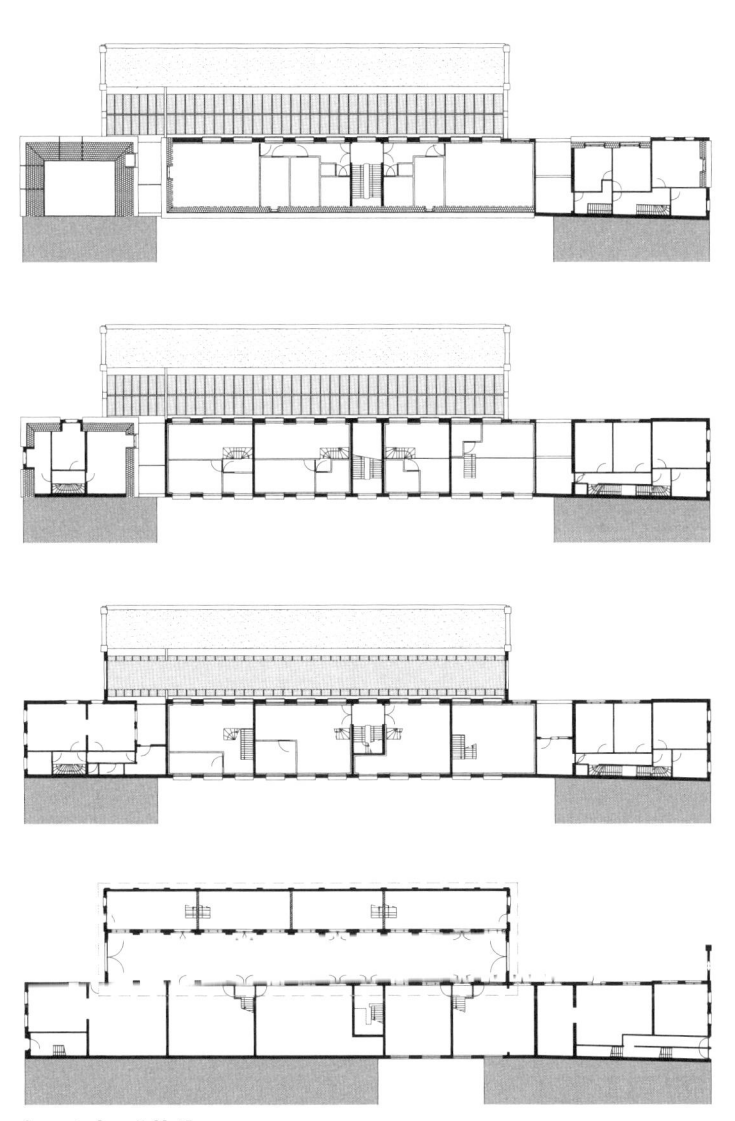

Current plans Hall 17

De Hallen

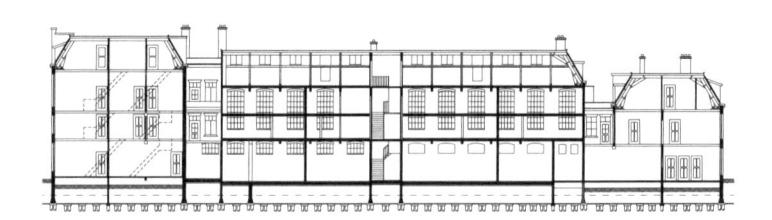

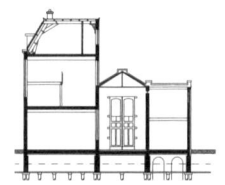

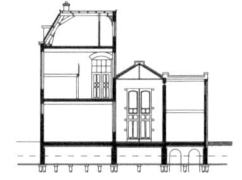

550

Front view and longitudinal sections Hall 17

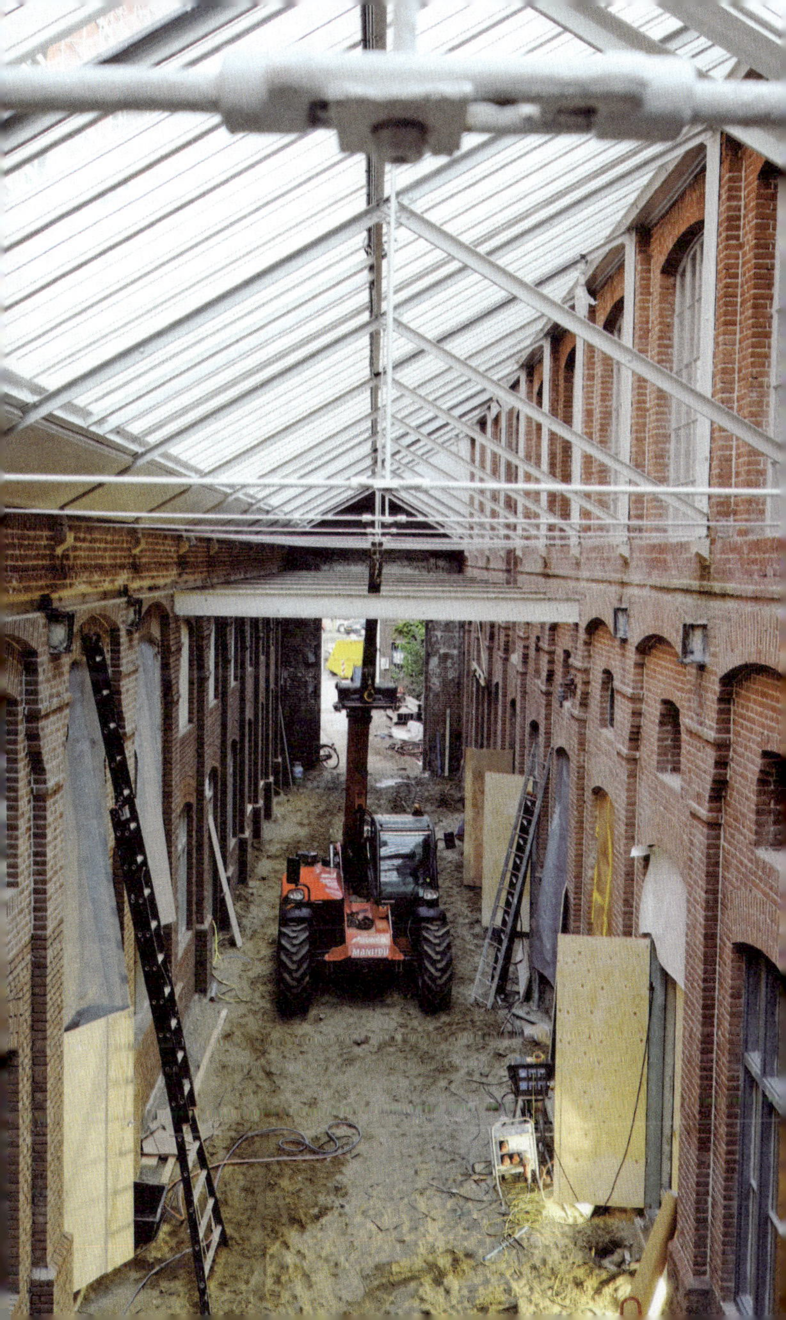

Architect

J. van Stigt architects

The building projects of the Amsterdam architectural firm of André van Stigt are usually connected with the reuse of existing (listed) buildings. This often concerns sober and efficient restorations with solutions that are focused on obtaining harmony between old and new. Through meticulous and contemporary detailing, a connection is sought with the existing architecture and the listed buildings are only interfered with on functional grounds (of use). The refurbishments of the Entrepotdok, the Oranje Nassaukazerne, the Graansilos, Pakhuis de Zwijger, several Cuypers churches and the Olympic Stadium, all in Amsterdam, show affinity with the historical context, the details and adaptations on a large and small scale. In particular, finding new uses for buildings so that they once again become a living part of the city and the surroundings forms an important part of the refurbishment process.

Amsterdam Lyceum

Industrial

Oranje-Nassaukazerne

Entrepotdok

De Hallen

The development of the former tram depot into De Hallen area demonstrates pre-eminently that restoration of built heritage can lead to powerful economic development. This applies across the world for all these types of restorations and repurposing projects, but De Hallen also shows that to get the process to that stage can take a very long time (almost 20 years in Amsterdam West). And that is also often the case elsewhere. Some power of persuasion is required to get across the advantages and people often think in terms of costs, instead of revenues. De Hallen is a new meeting place in the city outside the centre and provides space for all kinds of (artisan) training programmes and has given an enormous boost to the neighbourhood, to such an extent that there are complaints about too much commotion. The composition of the neighbourhood itself is changing. Richer people are coming to live there, a development that currently applies to the whole of Amsterdam.

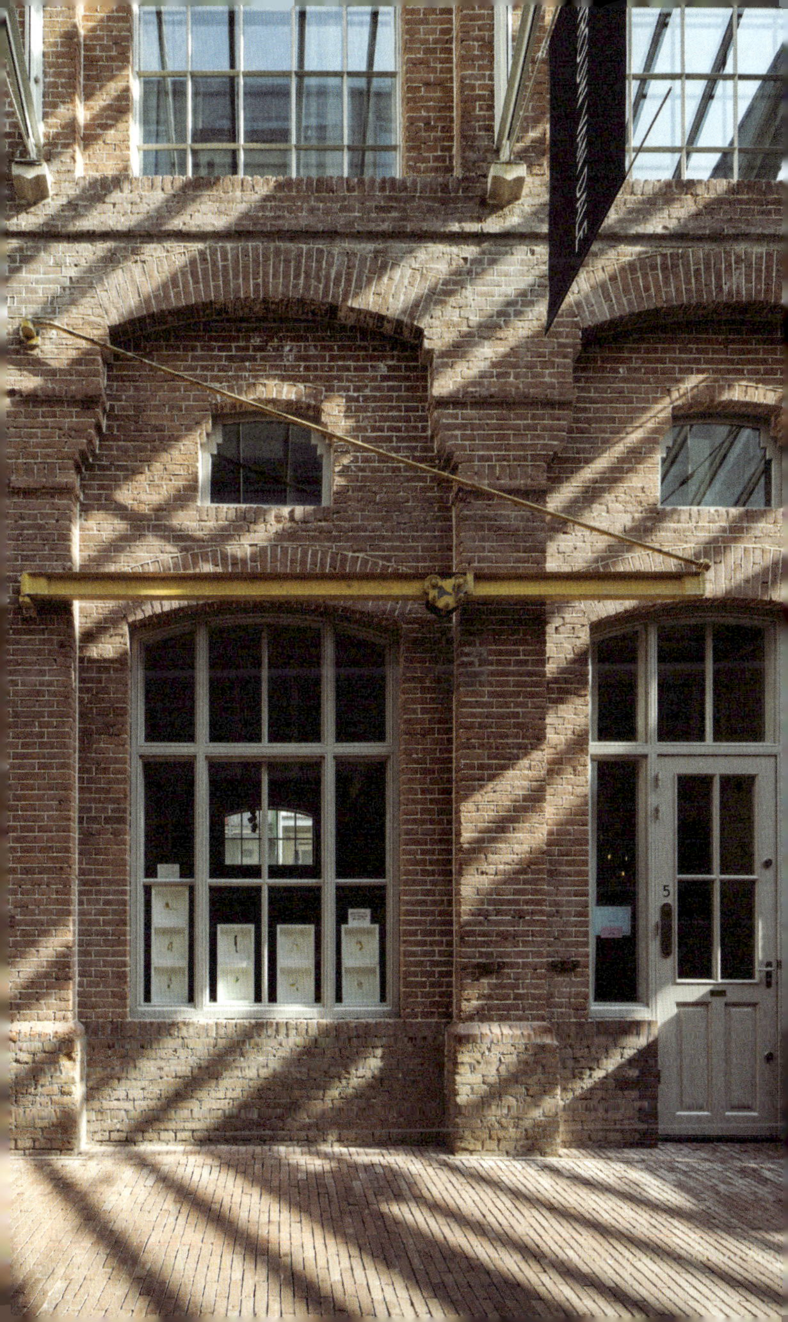
5

Passages

In the renovated Hall 17, where the demolished facade on the north side was reconstructed, shops and studios were located below and there were short-stay houses and apartments on the floors above. Hall 17 is a relatively small section and a modest but essential contribution to De Hallen. It forms part of the passage that runs from Bilderdijkkade to the Ten Katestraat and is usually open to the public. An important axis for pedestrians has thus been added to the neighbourhood, which also contributes to the revitalisation of this part of Amsterdam West, in addition to all the facilities added. The part of the passage that runs through Hall 17 is now called the 'little passage'. The 'big passage' is obviously located in the former tram depot. A place has therefore been created in Amsterdam that is reminiscent of the hey-day of the passages in Paris from the end of the 18th century until the mid-19th century. This city still had 150 of these in 1870, a number of beautiful examples of which have been restored to their former glory. They were initially made from brick and wood and had simple windows. The passages later became lighter in construction and they also provided more light due to the large amount of glass set in cast iron. They were very popular, because the inhabitants of Paris did not have to walk through the noisy streets. They could stroll here through dry, clean and artfully decorated spaces with beautiful shops and good light. It was to the advantage of the shop owners that they could display their goods in large shop windows. At the time, the passages were built in busy districts with theatres, restaurants and cafés that were frequented by writers and other artists.

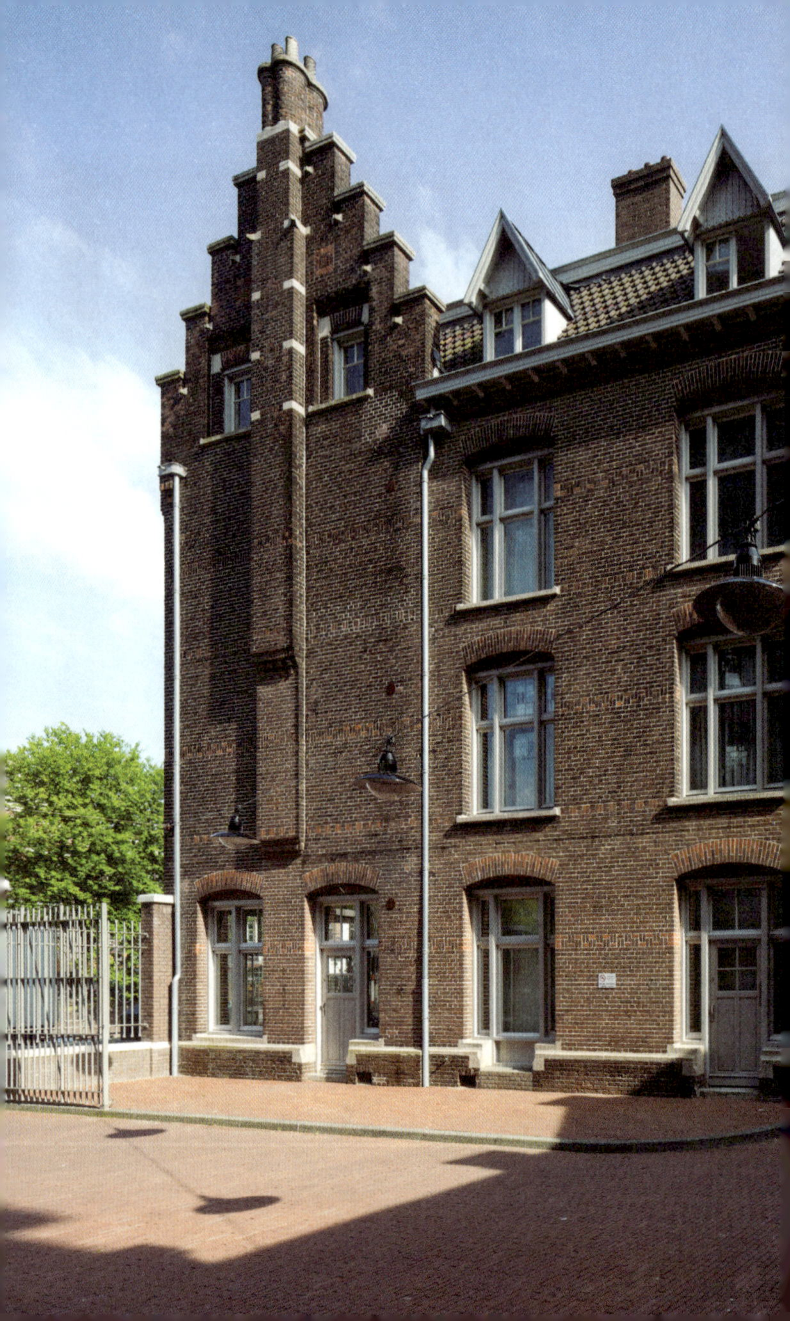

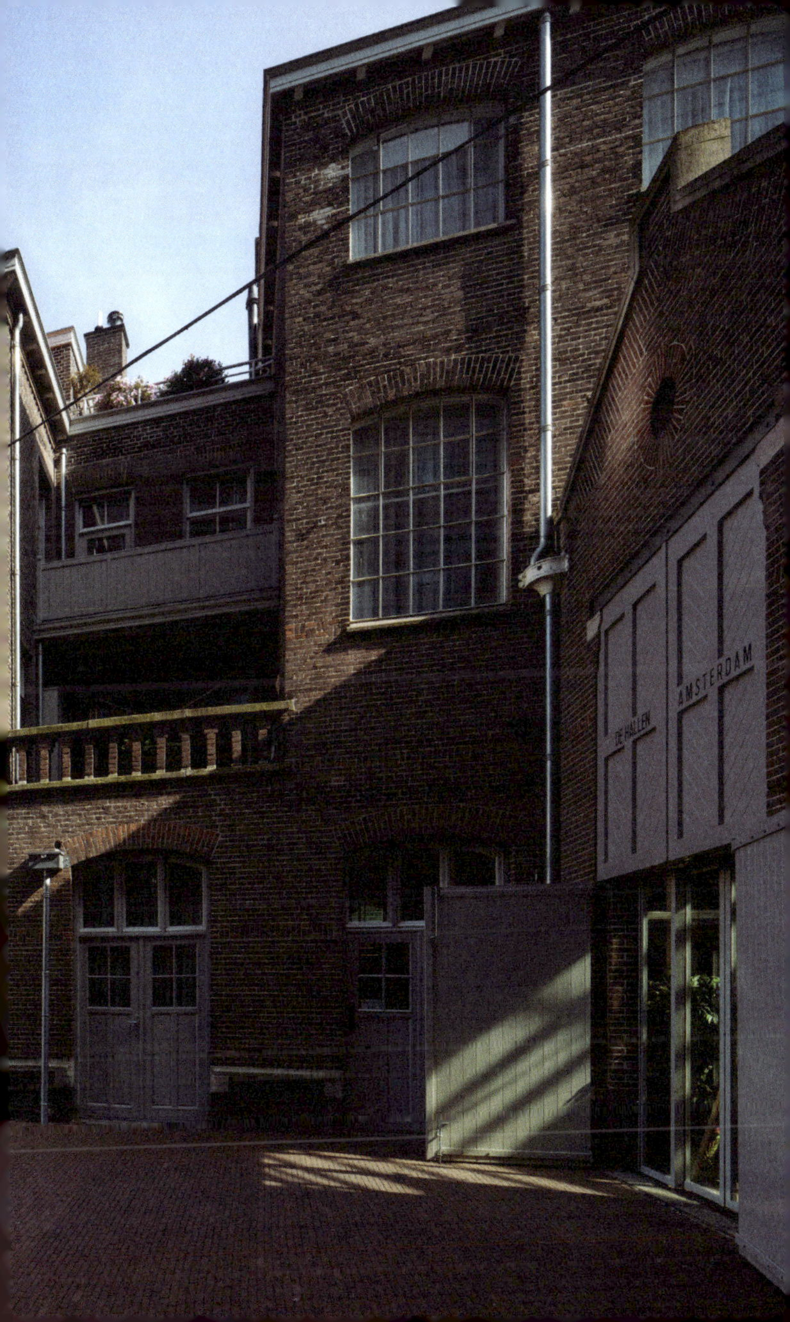
DE HALLEN
AMSTERDAM

De Hallen

New gable stones in Amsterdam

There are an estimated 1,600 gable stones in Amsterdam. The first gable stones appeared in the second half of the 16th century and were used as a 'gable sign' up until the 18th century.[1] The gable stones hewn from natural stone are often colourfully painted and have a connection with the profession of the original occupier of the building. The slab with an inscription and emblematic scene in relief decorates the front or side facade of a building. The gable stones lent the building a unique, recognisable identity, before the arrival of house numbers. Around 1967, the young sculptor Hans 't Mannetje began restoration work in the municipal warehouse of building fragments, pieces of sculpture work, gable stones and stucco fragments that came from demolished buildings. The aim of the Association of Friends of Amsterdam Gable Stones, which was established in 1991, is: 'The preservation, in the widest sense of the word, of gable stones, especially in Amsterdam. The return of old gable stones, which had been stored in museum basements, to public streets. Stimulating the production of modern gable stones'. It is important that the phenomenon of the gable stone is no longer exclusively, or chiefly, seen as a closed chapter in the cultural history, but as a genre of applied sculpture which, following a slump since 1800, has sprung into life once again today and is practised with imagination, creativity and craftsmanship.

Gable stones

In 1991, Stadsherstel had a gable stone made by Wim Vermeer set into the shop house on the Keizersgracht and the corner of Leliegracht as a tribute to the great expert on the Amsterdam house and employee at the Amsterdam Monuments & Archaeology (1953-1989), Henk Zantkuijl. The stone consists of a relief with an hourglass and the text monument en zorg (monument and care).

Gable stones

Gable stones

564

In 1981, Stadsherstel received a gable stone for its 25th anniversary from the Municipal Executive. The restoration works on the Blaeu Erf were in full swing at that time and the stone was given a spot at the Nieuwezijds Voorburgwal 97, corner of Sint Nicolaasstraat. It depicts a ring with 25 gilded keys with the years 1956 and 1981 and the number 25 in the top left.

Gable stones

The gable stone in the Geurt Brinkgreve house on the corner of the Bloedstraat and the Oudezijds Achterburgwal 69 is a gift for its 65th anniversary for its efforts within the historic building community. The figure (a standing man with a raincoat) made by Hans 't Mannetje in 1982 includes the text restauro (I restore).

Gable stones

The old name for the Nieuwmarkt neighbourhood is 'De Lastage'. The gable stone in the building on the Rechtboomssloot 42 is a reminder of the boarded-up block of houses in this neighbourhood prior to the construction of the metro in the 1970s. The protests ultimately led to the restoration of old street patterns.

Gable stones

Gable stones

To mark his 25th anniversary as employee at the architectural firm H. Rappange, J. van Druten received a gable stone with a T-square, the text tekenaar (draughtsman) and 1982, and his insignia, from his colleagues. The stone by 't Mannetje is in the building Reestraat 7. Van Druten was a draughtsman for many facades of buildings within the canal ring. In 1957, Joop was employed as second draughtsman for the architect H.F. Rappange sr., who had taken over his firm from Jan de Meijer. As the saying went: 'If van Druten has surveyed a building it can safely burn down; on the basis of his drawings you can rebuild it precisely'.

Abroad

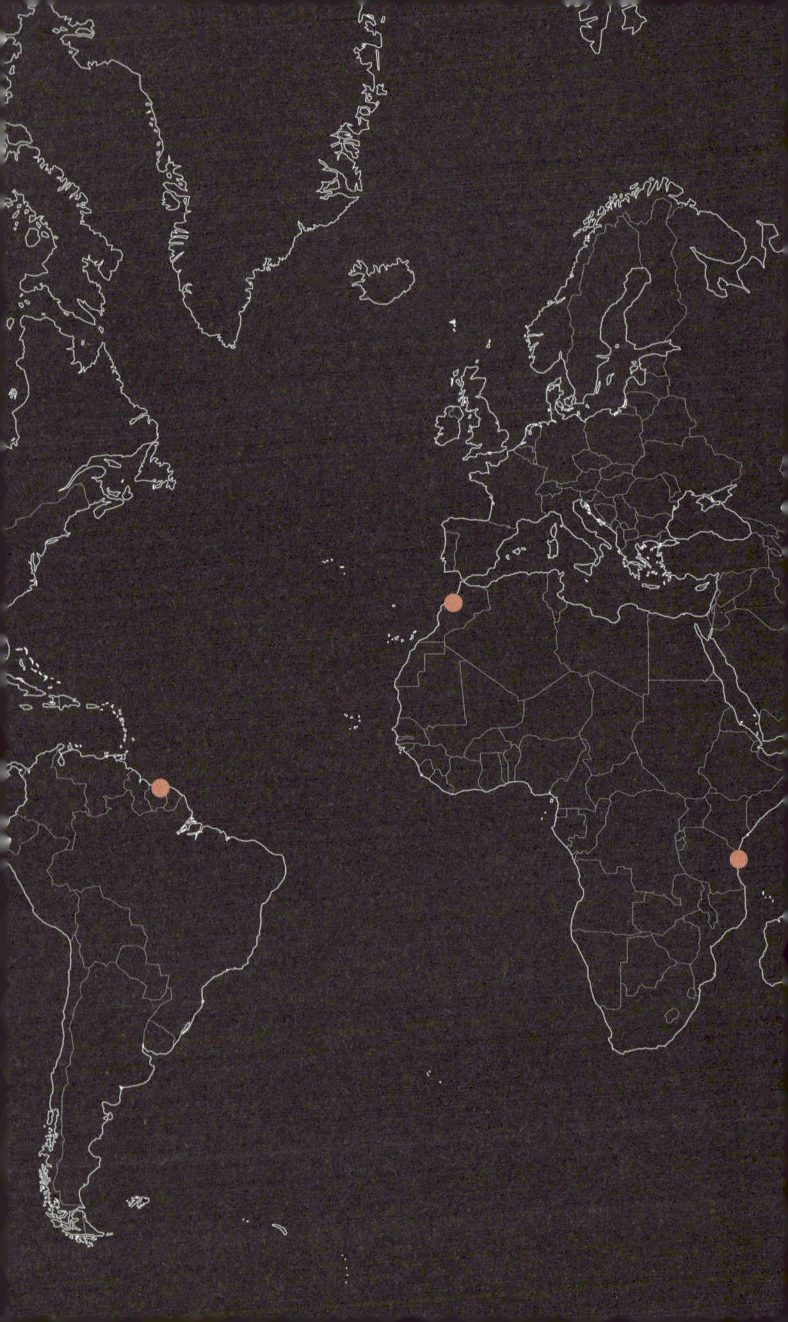

572 **Casablanca**
580 **Zanzibar**
586 **Suriname**

Casablanca

Dutch Culture, which provides a practical framework for international cultural exchange on behalf of the central government, calls in Stadsherstel with some regularity, for example in Brazil and Indonesia. This was how, for example, involvement in several repurposing projects in the Moroccan city of Casablanca arose, a culture that Amsterdam has close ties with due to the origin of a large group of residents. The cooperation between Amsterdam and Casablanca ties in with the international objectives of the Department of Social Development (Dienst Maatschappelijke Ontwikkeling, DMO). It focuses on countries of origin, such as Morocco, Turkey, Ghana, the Netherlands Antilles and Aruba, as well as a number of specifically chosen cities. Building networks and providing access to information is an important component, in addition to financing. The Stadsherstel model forms part of the research, in cooperation with the local historic buildings organisation Casamémoire, which focuses on modern architecture from 1920 – 1960, and a local architectural firm, into the possible repurposing of a modernist cathedral. On the outskirts of the city centre of the Moroccan city that has approximately seven million inhabitants, one can find Les Anciens Abattoirs de Casa (1920). The vacant complex, a former abattoir, is situated in an area with a relatively large amount of open space and will be transformed for future use by cultural entrepreneurs. Youth, culture and talent development are the key concepts in the plan of action. The temporary use of the unrestored building should lead to a basis of support for the plans among

Abroad 573

Gateway to the former abbatoir

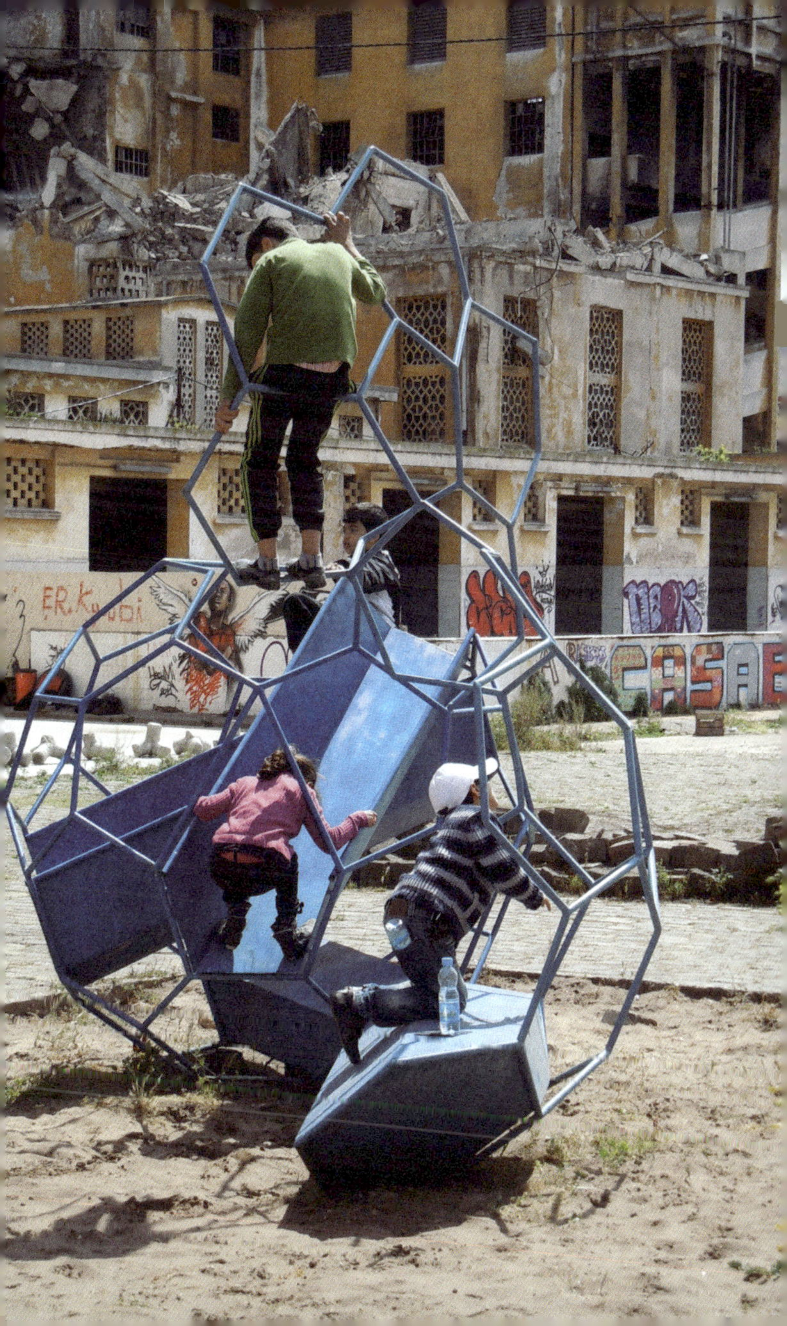
CASAB

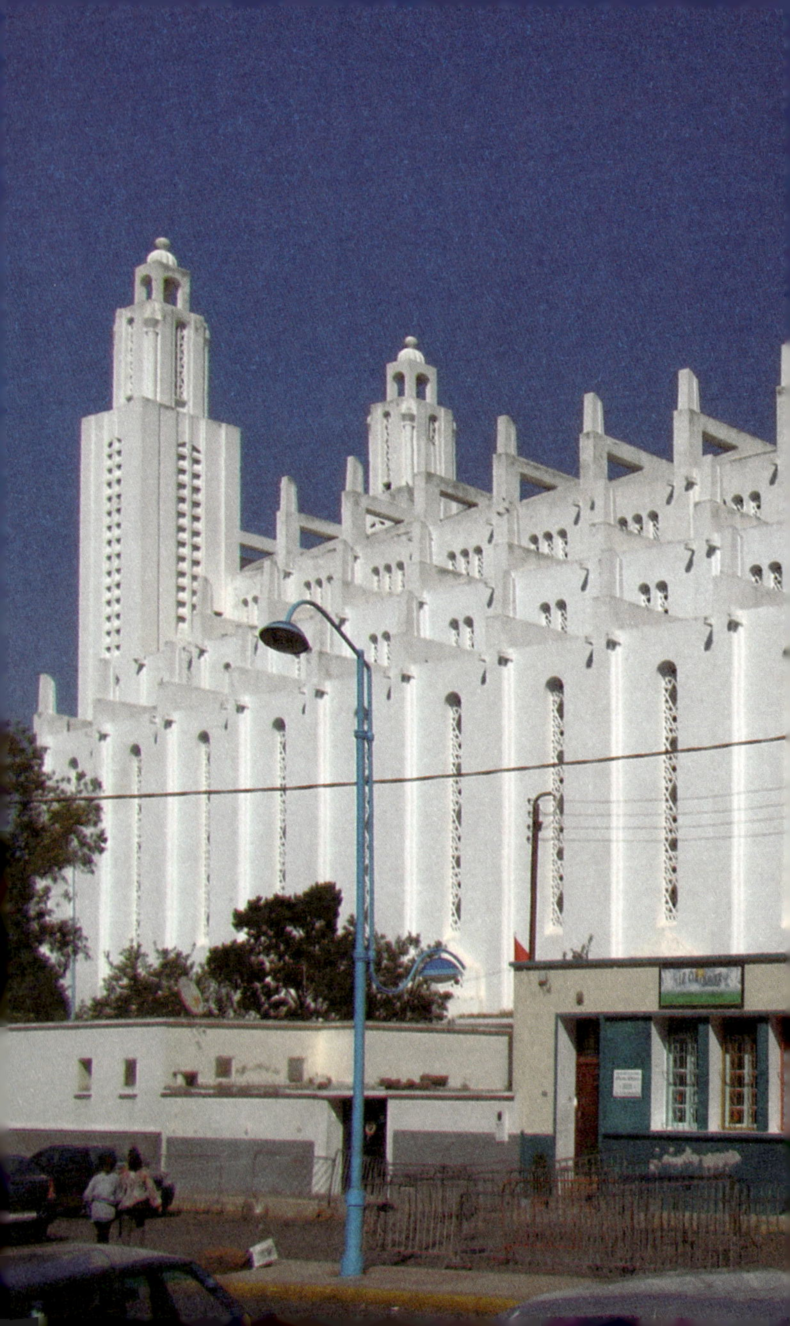

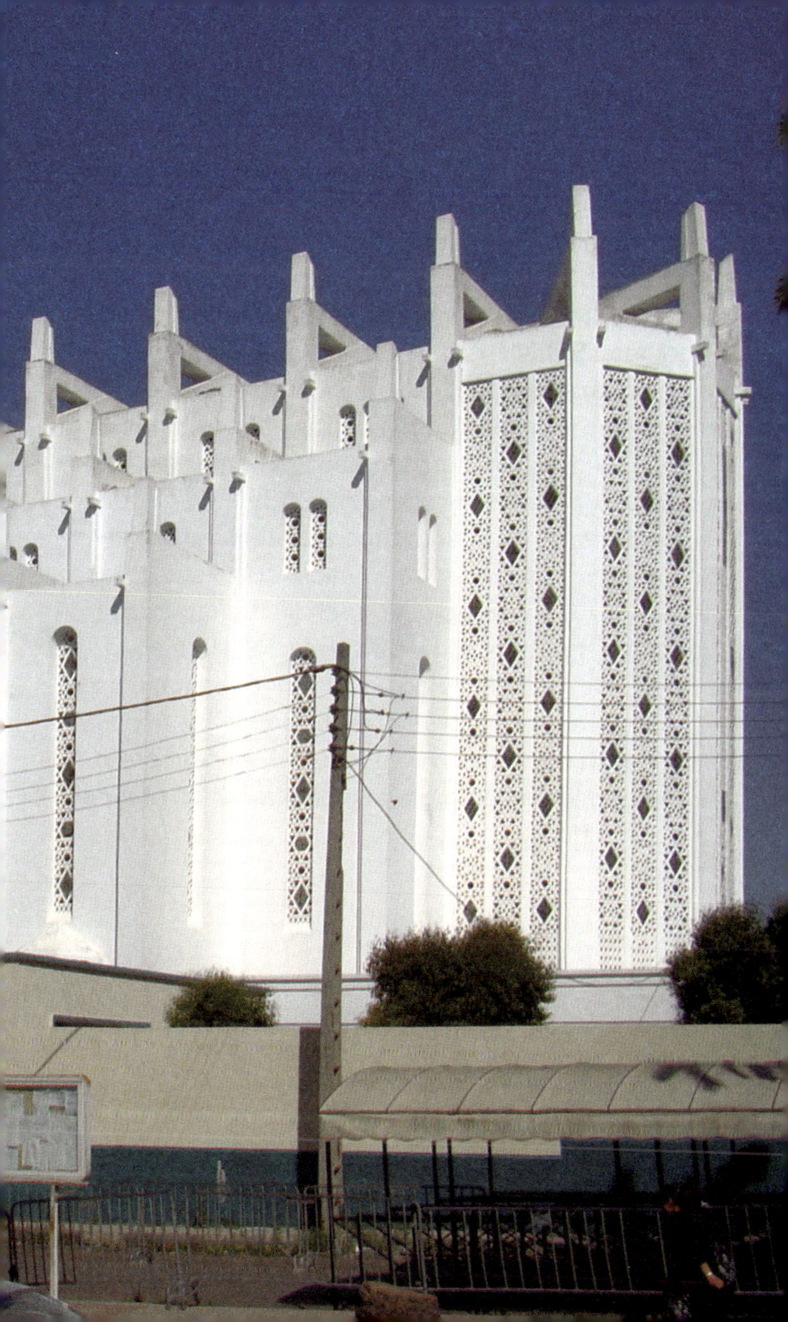

all parties concerned, including potential investors. For example, the designLAB of the Gerrit Rietveld Academy built a playground for children on the grounds together with local artists in just three weeks. The play area has, in the meantime, become a meeting place for mothers. Stadsherstel is increasingly developing into an organisation that executes complex projects and also exchanges knowledge in cooperation with local, provincial and national governments. In order to steer the complex process of redesignation in the right direction, a start was made under the architectural supervision of a project leader from Stadsherstel specialised in the more complex projects, such as the repurposing of industrial heritage. How do you tackle such a restoration further? How do you arrange the finances? With private money, public funds or both? It is up to the authorities at each location to follow this up, in order to transform the recommendations in all kinds of areas into a concrete business plan.

Abroad

Zanzibar

A few years ago, Stadsherstel cooperated in the organisation of the international symposium Urban Heritage Inc., about the effect of the Amsterdam organisation and what could be contributed to initiatives outside Europe. The visit of foreign professionals to the city and the participation of students was the start of further international cooperation. Muhammad Juma, director of the Ministry of Spatial Planning in Zanzibar (Tanzania), also participated in the symposium. Zanzibar also has Unesco world heritage sites, namely Stone Town, which was established by sultans from Oman who sailed past the East African coast in the 19th century. Juma turned out to be very interested in the model of Stadsherstel. Six months later, a group of specialists from Tanzania renewed acquaintance with the monuments policy in Amsterdam. The working visit was also an opportunity to meet Dutch members of African Architecture Matters (AAm), who supervise a number of projects in East Africa and possess a good network there. Following contact with the Tanzanian business community in order to set up a Stadsherstel Zanzibar (Zanzibar Urban Restoration Company) in Stone Town, Hifadhi Zanzibar became a reality in 2015, which only has shareholders who are active locally. An inventory was made of buildings that are eligible for purchase. An Amsterdam business model, based on a share capital with a modest dividend, rent and no purchase, and good structural maintenance of the building, also form the basis here. The district Ng'ambo, which literally means 'The Other Side', is separated from Stone Town by a creek that has now been

Abroad

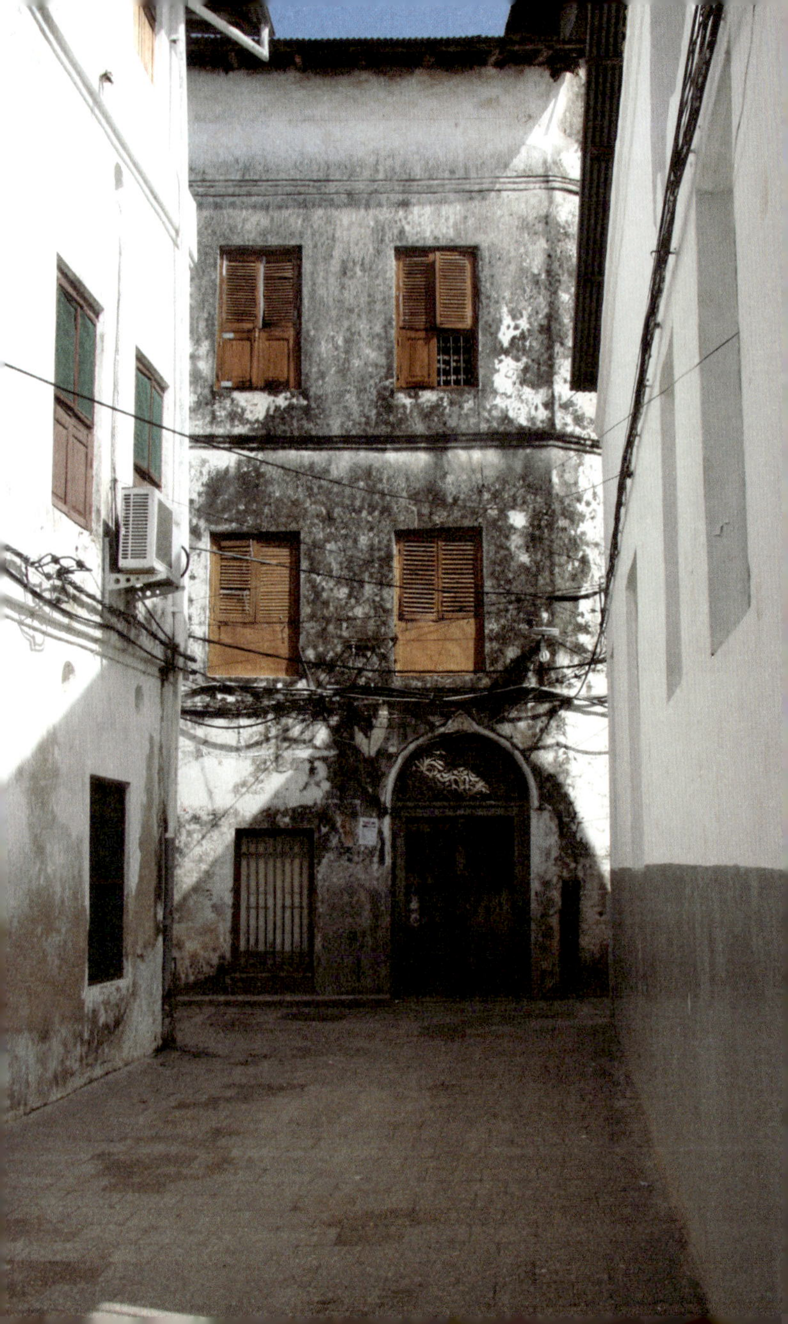

Abroad

drained. Stone Town can be compared to the canal ring in Amsterdam and Ng'ambo can be compared to a more folksy Jordaan district or the 19th century De Pijp district. It is a poor 'Swahili' district, where enormous 1970s flats (Michenzani Blocks) from the time of Tanzanian Socialism are located at important crossroads, which have landed like Eastern European meteorites in the close-knit urban fabric. The history and practice of urban renewal in the Jordaan and De Pijp is relevant in this respect and with the assistance of funds via the Ministry of Foreign Affairs and the Netherlands Enterprise Agency (Rijksdienst voor Ondernemend Nederland, RVO) a more intensive cooperation has arisen between the local government, the City of Amsterdam and Hifadhi.

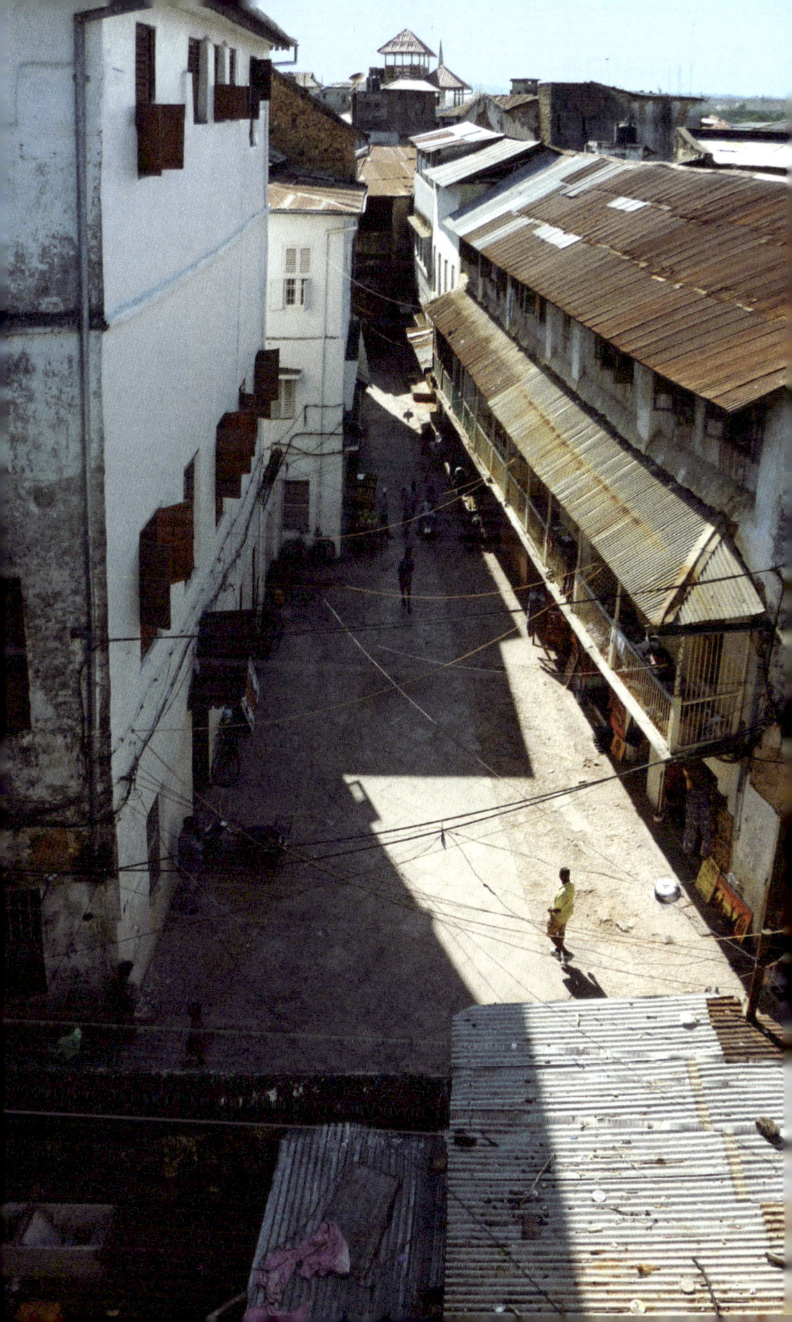

Suriname

In almost all cases of cooperation with parties abroad, the question arises how it is possible for a private company to restore and maintain built heritage without structural financial help from the government. Given the fact that Stadsherstel advised already before that time, internationalisation only truly started with the Suriname Built Heritage Foundation (Stichting Gebouwd Erfgoed Suriname, SGES) in 2006. The historic heart of Paramaribo, the capital of the former Dutch colony, has been on the Unesco world heritage list since 2001. In the same year, both countries also started establishing a shared cultural heritage, in the interest of preserving the material and immaterial memories of the past. The preservation of historic buildings is one of the areas of cooperation. Many of the protected buildings in Paramaribo are in a poor state of repair. The population has largely moved to the outskirts of the town, which is similar to what happened in Amsterdam between 1960 and 1980. The government in Suriname is also not planning to spend a lot of energy and resources on repairing and preserving built heritage. Private owners generally prefer to let their wooden buildings fall into disrepair rather than refurbish them, since the plot is worth more without instead of with a historic wooden house. The analogy with Amsterdam in the 1960s was the initial reason for setting up a similar company in Suriname. The idea of gradually buying up, restoring and renting out buildings with Surinamese and foreign shareholders appealed enormously. There has been regular contact with SGES since 2008 and there are

Abroad

usually two working visits per year. Although the most important Surinamese banks and insurance companies indicated their willingness to become shareholders in April 2010, it still took a long time to actually set up thepublic limited company that enabled cooperation with the government. There was once again a striking analogy with Stadsherstel as it was also set up by bankers, who in the meantime are looking at the bigger picture. They are satisfied with a moderate return and see the greater benefit of a revitalised Amsterdam. Stadsherstel is the platform where financial, profit-making institutions are organised around a social purpose. That is the reason why it is increasingly asked to come and explain how the organisation works, precisely in areas where governments are unable to preserve their built history. Ultimately, the Paramaribo Urban Restoration Foundation (Stichting Stadsherstel Paramaribo) was set up in 2011 in order to purchase the first building on the Julianastraat 56. The owner wanted to sell and there were sufficient funds available, but the legal vehicle was lacking. In 2014, the public limited company Suriname Urban Restoration (Stadsherstel Suriname NV) became completely independent, separate from the Surinamese government, with three other buildings that were purchased and restored. A fifth building is currently in the pipeline. Stadsherstel Amsterdam was also introduced to the successful network in Suriname that had been brought together by the City of Amsterdam over the years.

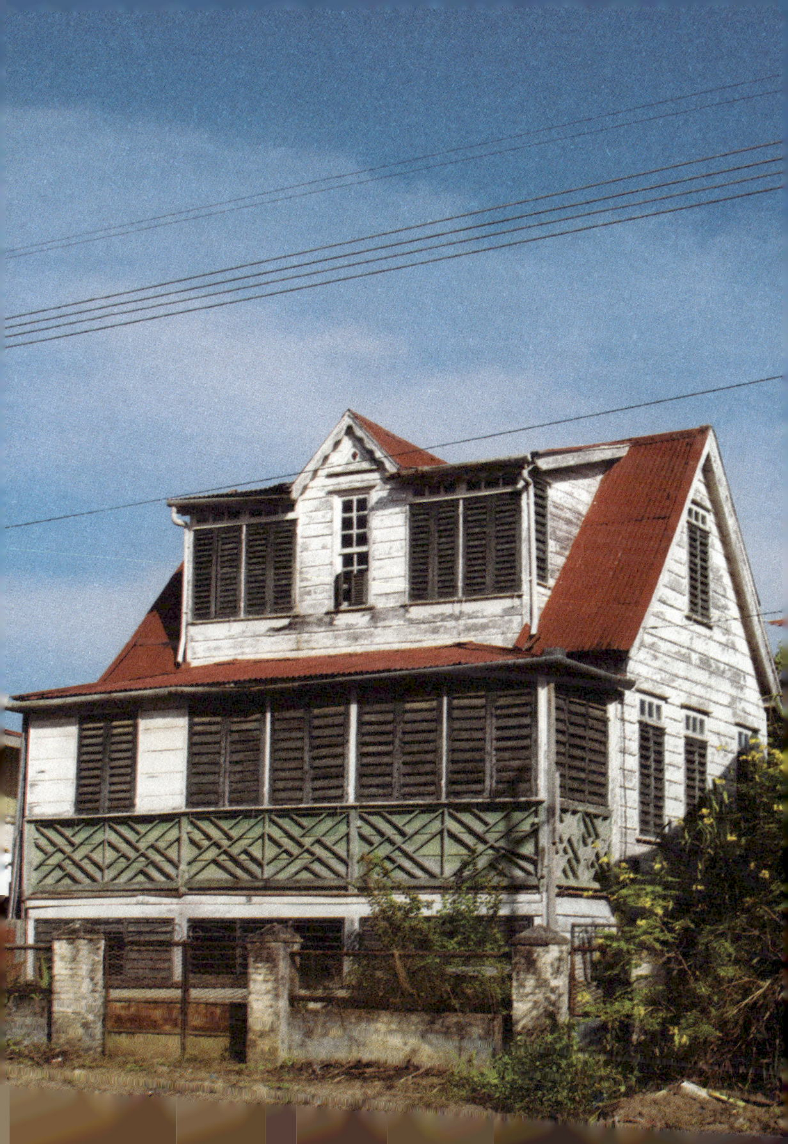

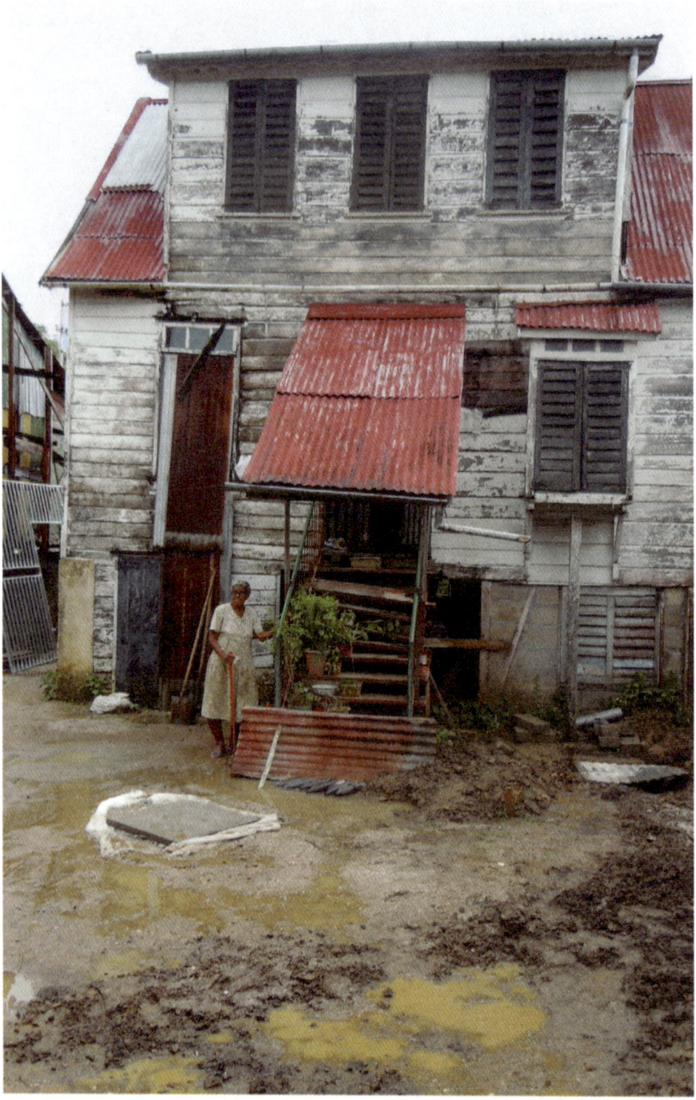

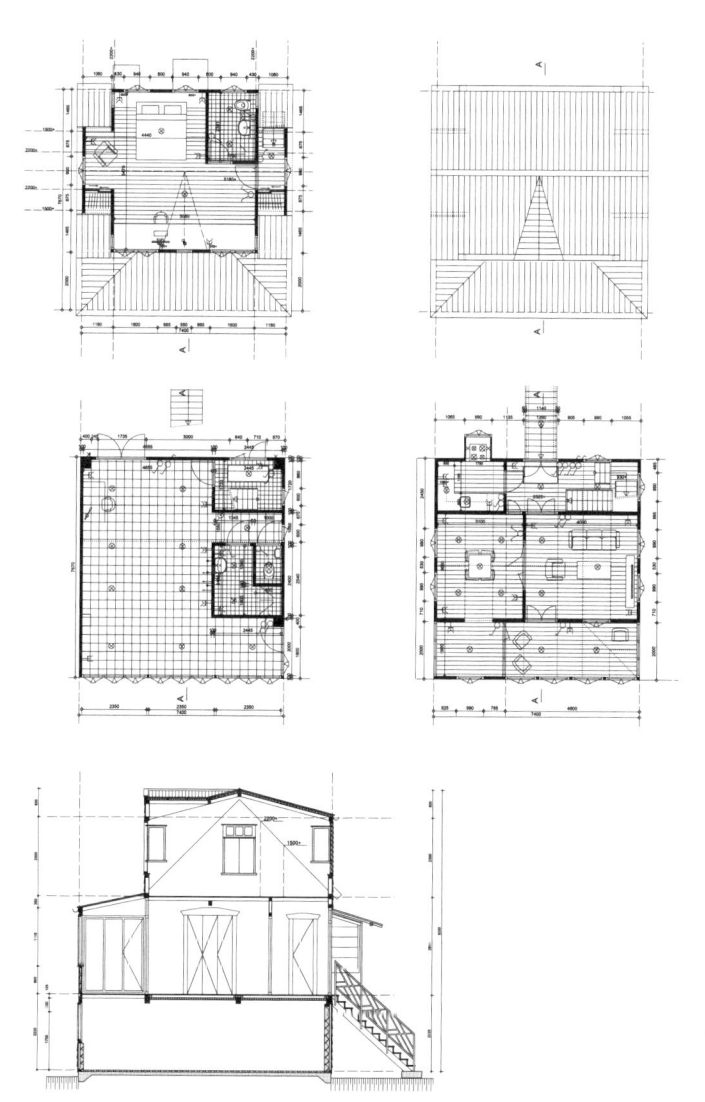

Floor plans of the restored house, basement,
first and second floor and roof

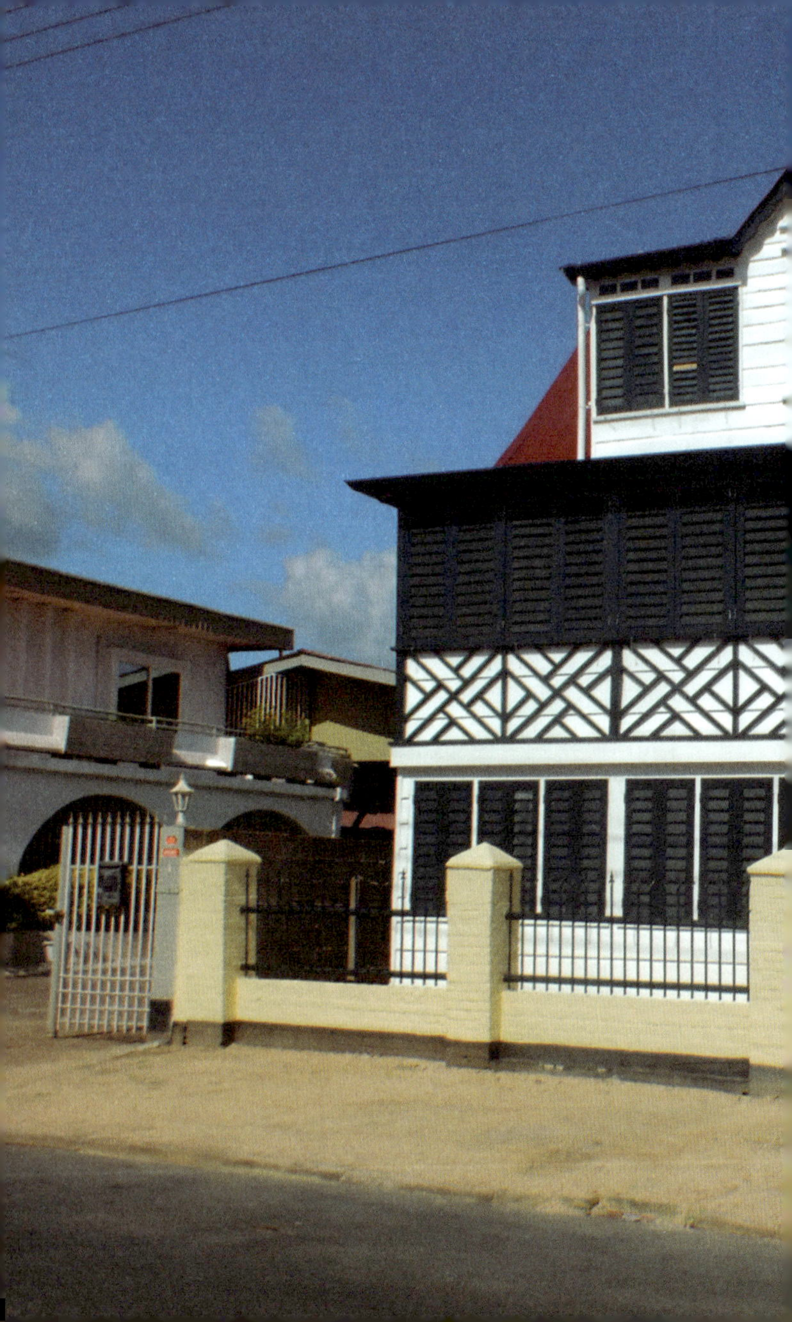

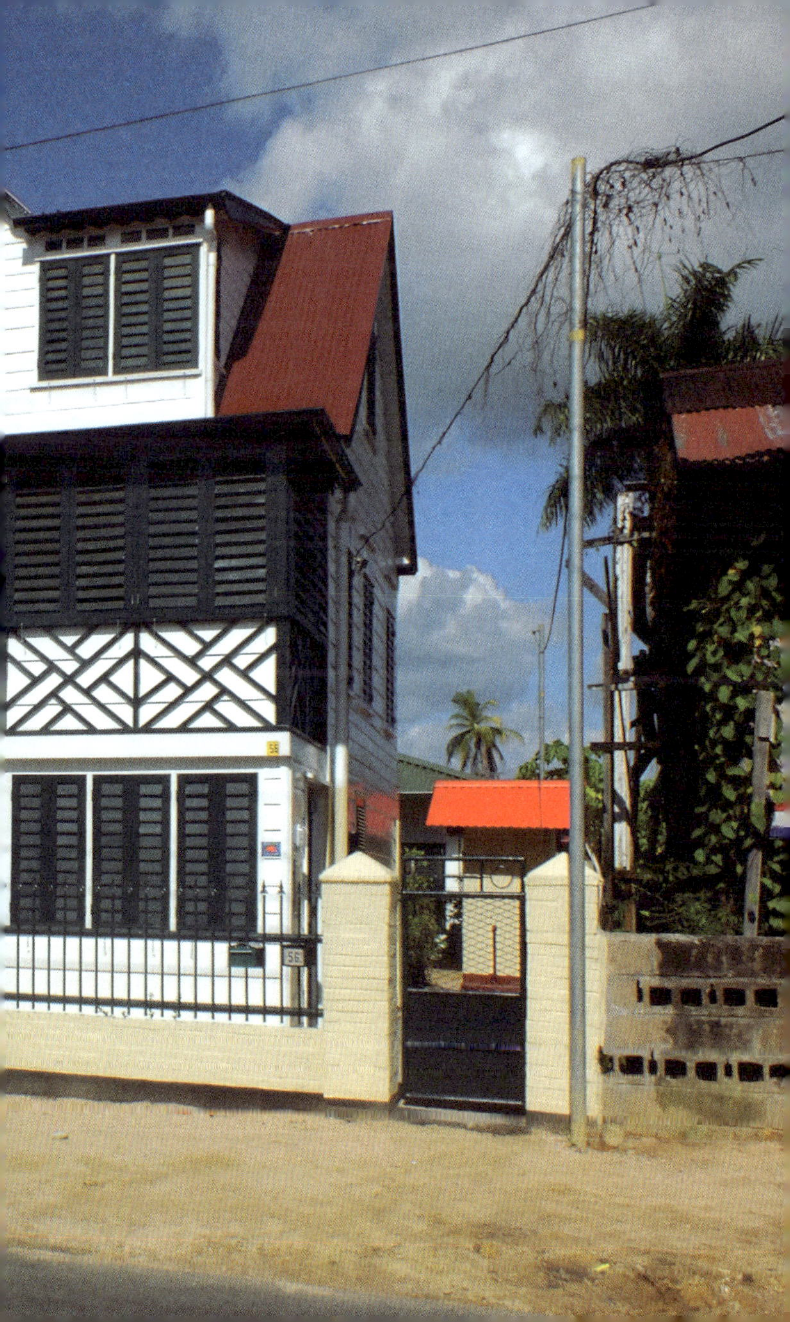
56
56

A side effect of that was a further intensification of the cooperation between Stadsherstel and the City of Amsterdam. The involvement of the general public, an important subject within the so-called twinning project, established by the Dutch Ministry of Foreign Trade and Development Cooperation, provides subsidies that enable Stadsherstel, the Suriname Built Heritage Foundation and Suriname Urban Restoration to work intensively on raising awareness about the Surinamese built heritage. For example, work is being carried out on setting up an Association of Friends of Urban Restoration in Suriname (Vereniging Vrienden van Stadsherstel Suriname) and on recruiting members, securing financial support, arranging excursions to historic buildings and heritage education. Another activity is the organisation of work training programmes for young builders in Suriname. That requires apprentice trainers, who are not only good at carpentry, but can also communicate their experience of all kinds of details concerning timber construction, which they often recognise, in turn, from traditional Surinamese architecture. Two experienced Surinamese general foremen were introduced to organisations in Amsterdam that specialise in educating apprentice trainers in the building sector. The restoration of a neglected shop at the corner of the Zwartenhovenbrugstraat and the Hoogestraat, in an area where almost all historic architecture has been demolished, is an example of a work training programme.

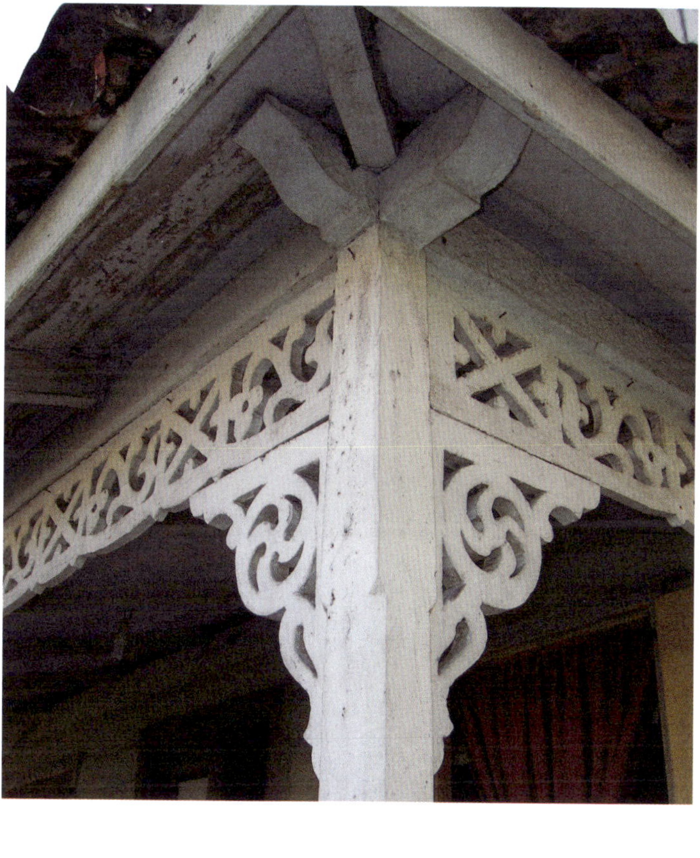

Suriname

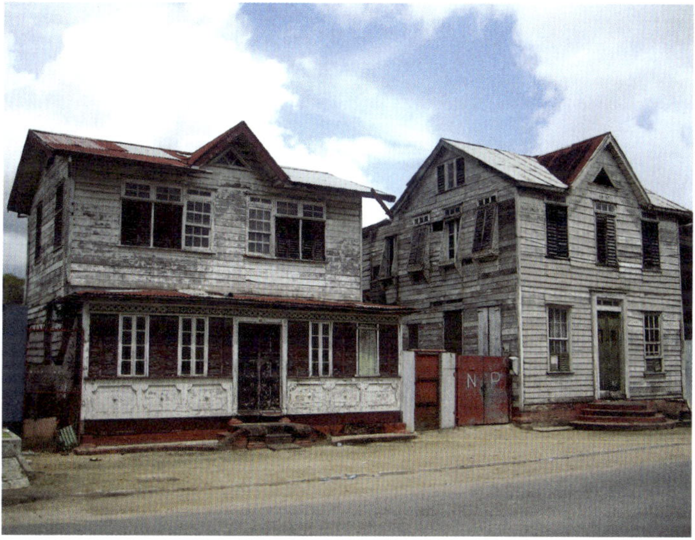
N P

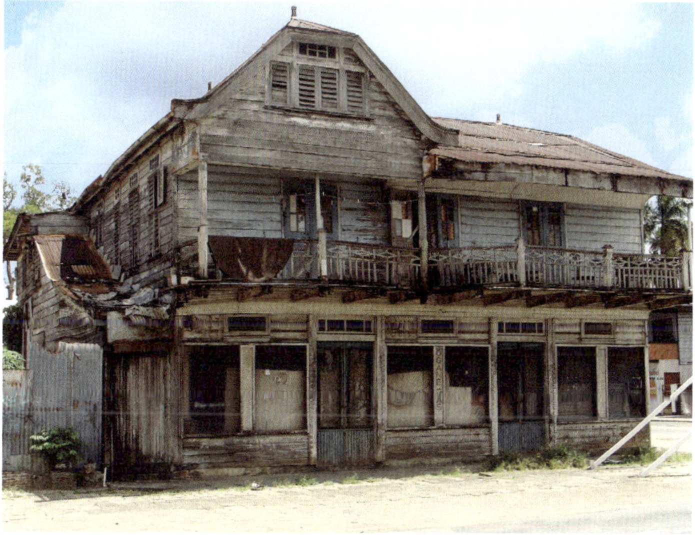

Finding Stories

Outside of the Netherlands, more importance is often attached to the stories or history that belong to a building or district than to the bricks. Who built it with accompanying family ties, the traditions (anthropology), history and 'stories' appeal at least as much to the imagination when appreciating the heritage.
The story is also important for the improvement of a district like Ng'ambo, where the chance of success increases by considering all kinds of values and by calling on the help of the residents present. In order to further develop this immaterial heritage, a delegation from Zanzibar visited the Amsterdam urban renewal at the beginning of 2016 and their stay ended with the seminar 'Finding Stories'. In collaboration with Dutch specialists, the research into the 'stories' in Ng'ambo can be continued. The Dutch monument organisations will learn afresh from a relatively unknown phenomenon. You can see another example of 'finding stories' at the house on the Julianastraat 56 in Paramaribo. This historic building was built by the father of the current occupant at the beginning of the 20th century. The house is representative of the typical Surinamese, and more generally, Caribbean way of building with wood. The stories about the origins of the street and who has lived there, the knowledge about the history of the creation of the district even play a role in property rights, which are slightly more complicated compared to Dutch standards. Old plantations in Suriname can, for example, have thousands of owners. Of course, that is not laid down in writing, thus it requires good and ample investigation. A documentation centre and archive was recently opened there, where information about Surinamese history, much of it originating from the Netherlands, is stored.

Abroad

Paul Morel in Suriname

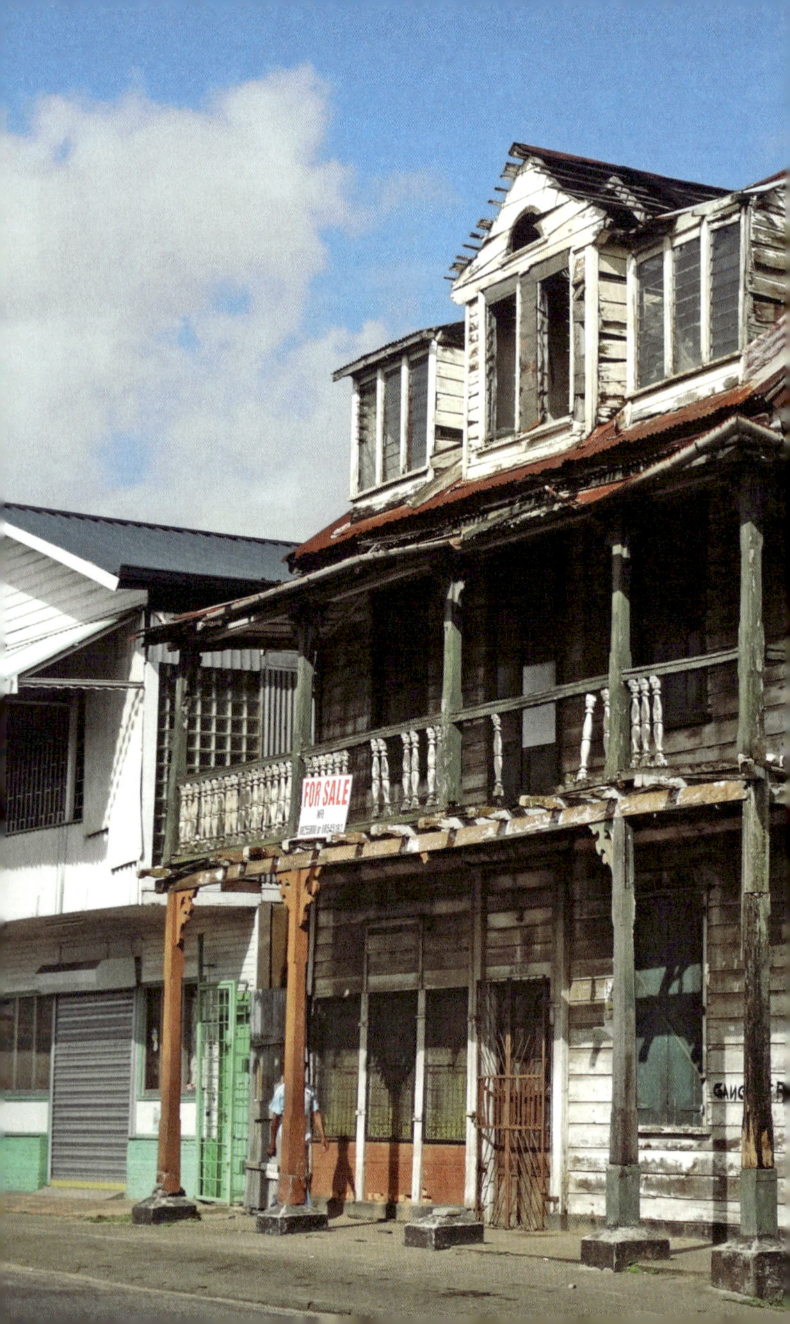
FOR SALE

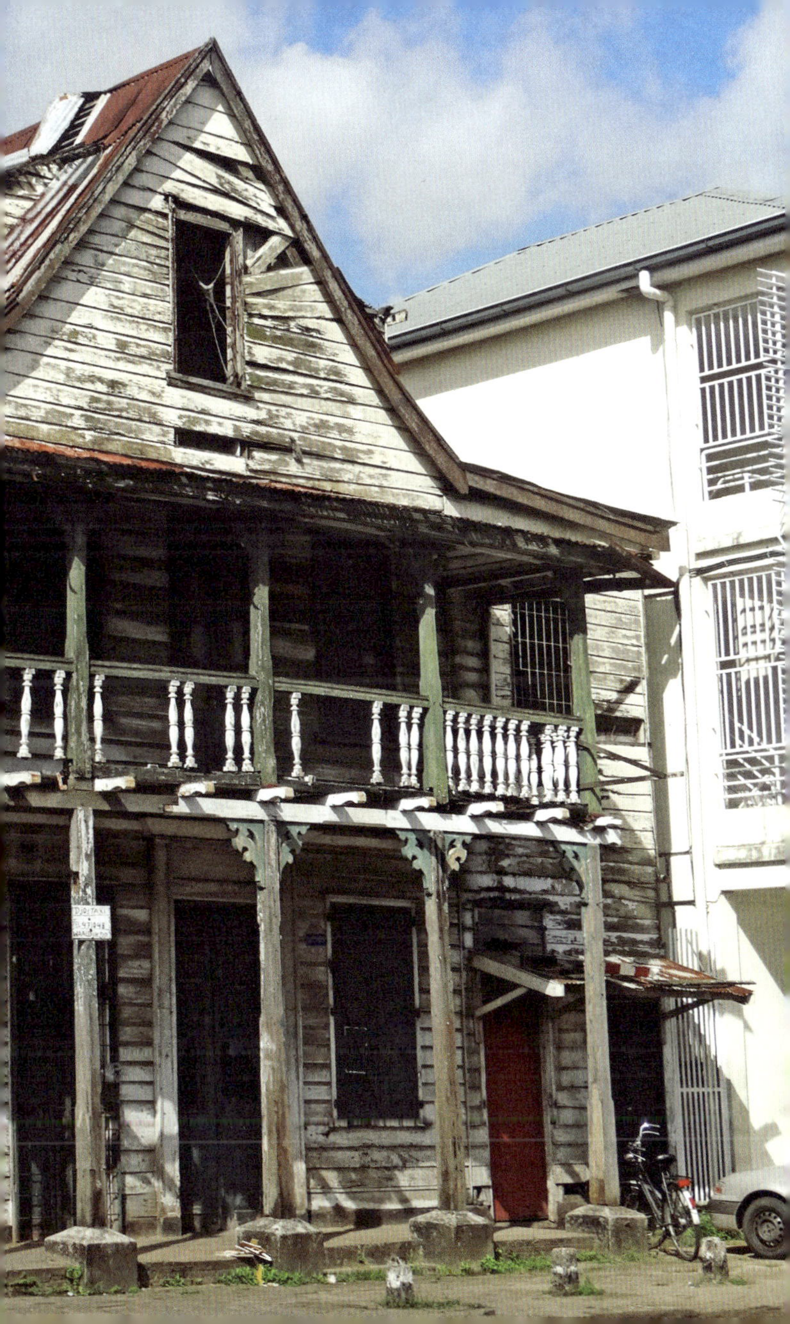

Suriname

Zwartenhovenbrugstraat 116

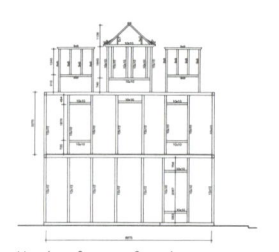

Wooden frames facade

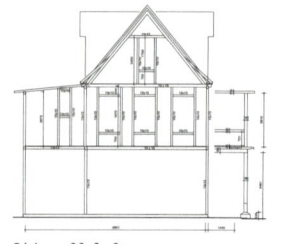

Side wall left

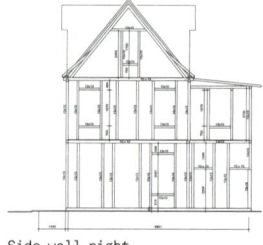

Side wall right

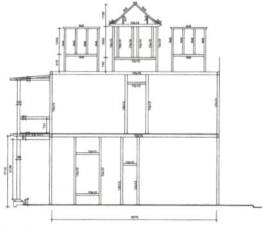

Back

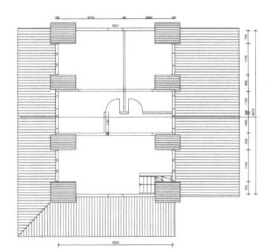

Abroad

Second floor

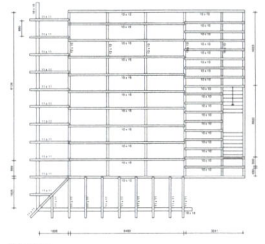

Beams

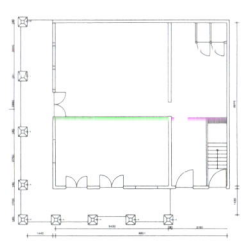

Ground floor

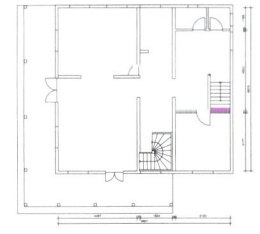

First floor

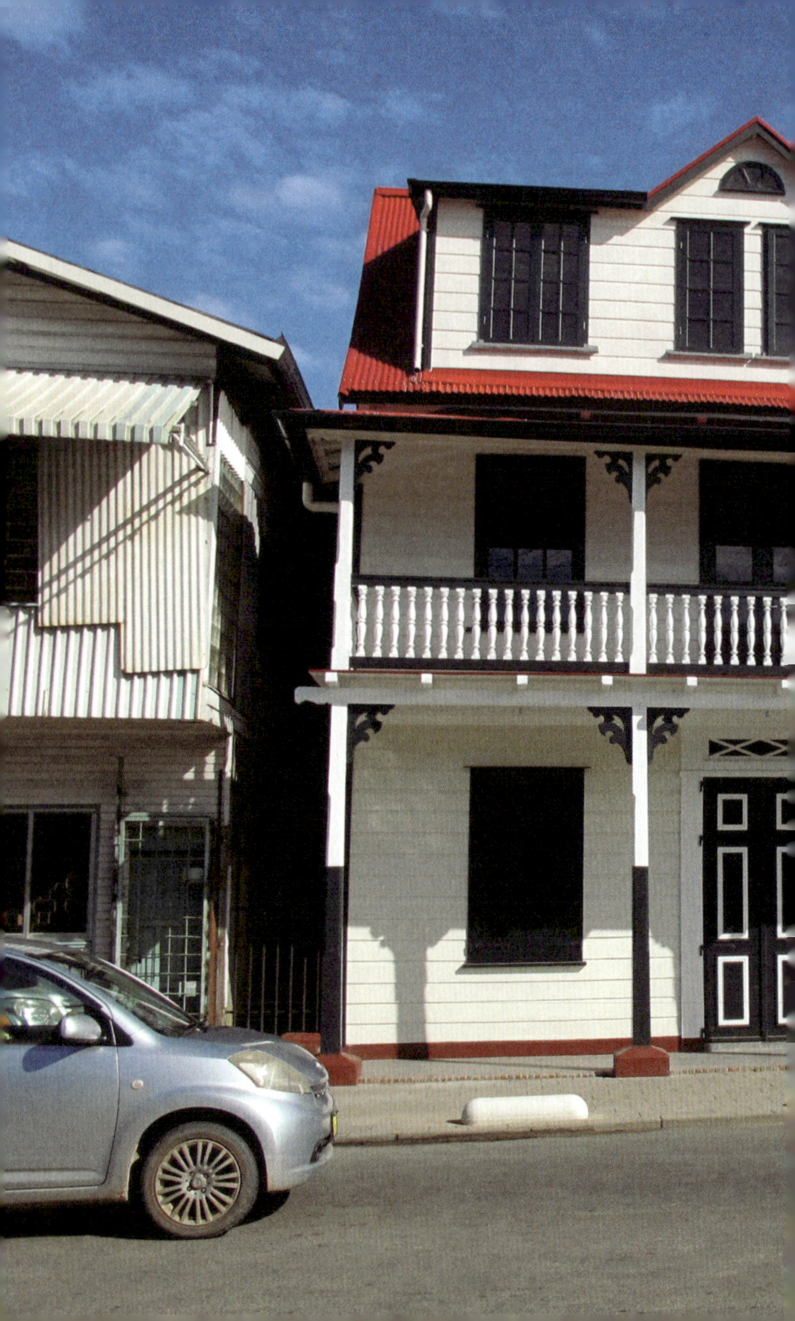

Note of translator Mark Speer

*Herstel

The Dutch noun 'herstel' and the verb 'herstellen' are ambiguous terms with multiple meanings, connotations and values (see, e.g., section above entitled 'Name'). The English 'restoration' comes close, but does not quite cover all of these subtleties.

One connotation is 'repair', as in to repair, rectify or correct something that is wrong.

Another connotation is to 'restore' or 'rehabilitate', in the sense of returning something to the state or situation that it was in previously.

Another connotation of 'herstel' is health-related: 'recovery', 'recuperation', 'restoration', 'convalescence', which can of course also be applied to physical objects, such as a city centre.

And yet another connotation is 'compensation', i.e. to redress a grievance or repair and compensate damage. In the context of the problem of the city centre of Amsterdam, 'herstel' can therefore refer to much more than merely the 'physical restoration' of its buildings.

The main difference between 'herstel' and 'restore', is that the English word 'restore' is almost inevitably used as a modifier, and that often determines which connotation is being used. For example, in English you would say 'he was restored to good health', whereas in Dutch it would suffice to say 'he is *hersteld*'. And because of this difference, the Dutch word 'herstel' leaves much more open to interpretation than the English 'restore'.

The author and translator have therefore chosen to leave the word 'herstel' in Dutch in the text and let the reader interpret which connotations apply at his or her discretion.

Credits

Images

Sonia Mangiapane
pp. 182–183, 234–240, 254–255, 267, 282–287, 289, 294–295, 299, 308–309, 314–315, 330, 332–333, 338–344, 348–349, 353–369, 371, 378–393, 402–416, 440–441, 444–445, 454–459, 483–484, 486–488, 554–555, 558–560, 562–568

Amsterdam Archives
pp. 12, 23, 99, 144–145, 153, 158–159, 186–187, 206, 226–227, 280–281, 376–377, 394–395, 466–467, 502–503, 522, 533, 546, 472

Thanks to the photographers
**Aart Jan van Mossel,
Ernest Annyas,
Sjors van Dam**

Drawings

Buildings
**Jan Bernt Knijtijzer,
Kees Kerkhoven,
Marina Oleynik**

The other drawings are derived from the project architects and the book *Bouwen in Amsterdam. Het Woonhuis in de Stad* by Henk Zantkuijl.

Maps
Haller Brun

Texts

For the project texts is quoted from written sources by Onno Boers, Geurt Brinkgreve, Guido Hoogewoud, Gustav Leonhardt, Juliet Oldenburger, Vincent van Rossem, Walther Schoonenberg and Henk Zantkuijl in the journals of the Cuypersgenootschap, Friends of the Amsterdam Inner City, Association of Friends of Amsterdam Gable Stones, Monuments & Archeology, and the archives of Zaanstad, Amsterdam and the Friends of Stadsherstel.

Colophon

Essay
Fred Feddes
Photography
Sonia Mangiapane
Idea and composition
Gaston Bekkers

Design
Haller Brun
Sonja Haller, Pascal Brun

Stadsherstel
Stella van Heezik, Onno Meerstadt and Paul Morel

Translation essay
Mark Speer
Translation project texts
Richard Glass
Production
Harmen Kraai

Lithography
Mariska Bijl
Printing
Wilco Art Books, Amersfoort

Paper
100 g Munken Kristall Rough 1.4 and 80 g Biotop
Fonts
Plantin, Theinhardt and Akkurat Mono

International distribution
Idea Books, Amsterdam
www.ideabooks.nl

ISBN 978 94614 005 74 (Dutch)
ISBN 978 94614 005 81 (English)

© 2016
Architectura & Natura
Stichting August Kemme Fonds
Leliegracht 22
1015 DG Amsterdam
www.architectura.nl

All rights reserved. No part of this publication may be reproduced, stored in a retrieval system, or transmitted in any form or by any means, electronic, mechanical, photocopying, recording or otherwise, without the prior written permission of the publisher.

Despite the fact that the publisher has done his utmost to find all copyright holders of the illustrations, for rights owners please contact in writing A&NP, info@architectura.nl.

This publication is sponsored by:
Creative Industries Fund NL
Prins Bernard Cultuurfonds
Provincie Noord-Holland
Dutch Culture
P.W. Janssen's Friesche Stichting
Stadsherstel